Chapterwise DPP *for* JEE Advanced

CHEMISTRY

Collection of 560+ MCQs based on NCERT

Improves your Score by at least 20%

26 Chapters based on NCERT

Scoring Grid	DAILY PRACTICE PROBLEM DPP CHAPTERWISE CC06 - CHEMISTRY			
	Total Questions	20	Total Marks	74
	Attempted		Correct	
	Incorrect		Net Score	
	Cut-off Score	24	Qualifying Score	35
	Success Gap = Net Score – Qualifying Score			
	Net Score = (Correct × 4) – (Incorrect × 1)			

• **Corporate Office** : 45, 2nd Floor, Maharishi Dayanand Marg, Corner Market,
Malviya Nagar, New Delhi-110017
Tel. : 011-49842349 / 49842350

Typeset by Disha DTP Team

Printed at : Repro Knowledgecast Limited, Thane

DISHA PUBLICATION

For further information about books from DISHA,
Log on to www.dishapublication.com or email to info@dishapublication.com

Disha's Bestseller for
JEE Advanced

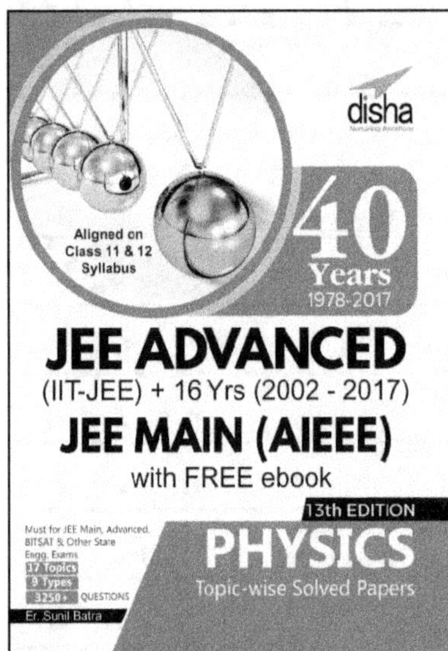

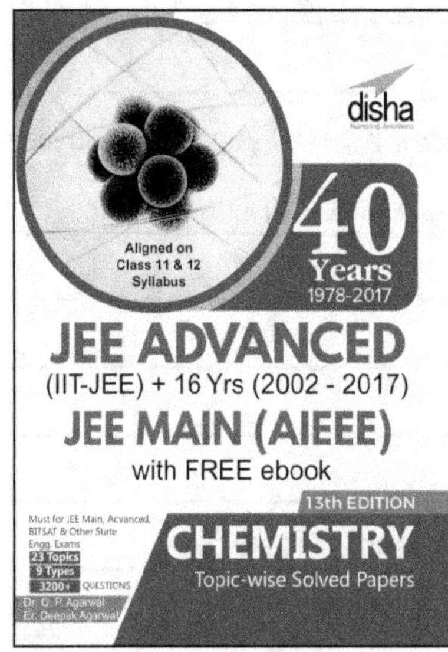

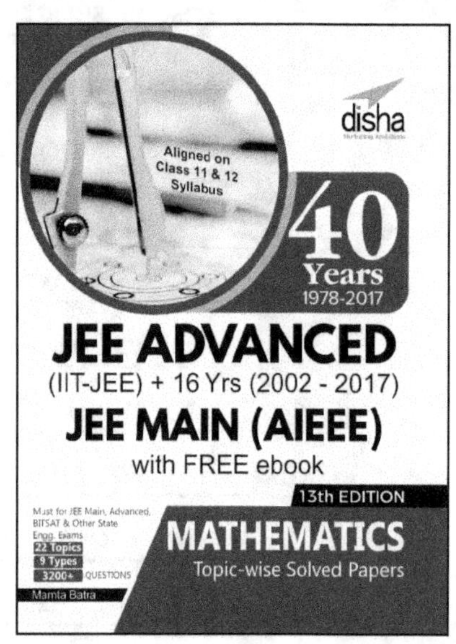

Date : [ ]   Start Time : [ ]   End Time : [ ]

CHEMISTRY $\boxed{CC01}$

SYLLABUS : Some Basic Concepts of Chemistry

Max. Marks : 74   **Time : 60 min.**

GENERAL INSTRUCTIONS

- The Daily Practice Problem Sheet contains 20 Questions divided into 5 sections.
  Section I has **5** MCQs with ONLY 1 Correct Option, **3** marks for each correct answer and **−1** for each incorrect answer.
  Section II has **4** MCQs with ONE or MORE THAN ONE Correct options.
  For each question, marks will be awarded in one of the following categories:
  Full marks: **+4** If only the bubble(s) corresponding to all the correct option(s) is (are) darkened.
  Partial marks: **+1** For darkening a bubble corresponding to each correct option provided NO INCORRECT option is darkened.
  Zero marks: If none of the bubbles is darkened.
  Negative marks: **−2** In all other cases.
  Section III has **5** Single Digit Integer Answer Type Questions, **3** marks for each Correct Answer and 0 marks in all other cases.
  Section IV has Comprehension/Matching Cum-Comprehension Type Questions having **5** MCQs with ONLY ONE correct option, **3** marks for each Correct Answer and 0 marks in all other cases.
  Section V has **1** Matching Type Questions, **2** mark for the correct matching of each row and 0 marks in all other cases.
- You have to evaluate your Response Grids yourself with the help of Solutions.

Section I - Straight Objective Type

This section contains 5 multiple choice questions. Each question has 4 choices (a), (b), (c) and (d), out of which **ONLY ONE** is correct.

1. If 0.20g chloride of a certain metal, when dissolved in water and treated with excess of $AgNO_3$, yields 0.50g of AgCl, the equivalent mass of the metal is (Ag = 108, Cl = 35.5)
   (a) 21.90   (b) 20.04
   (c) 40.08   (d) 43.80

2. In what ratio the amounts of H_2SO_4 and H_3PO_4 react with the same amount of NaOH to form normal salts?
   (a) 1 : 1   (b) 3 : 2
   (c) 2 : 3   (d) 1 : 3

3. Blue vitriol ($CuSO_4 \cdot 5H_2O$) is often added to swimming pools to kill algae. It is prepared by the reaction between copper metal and hot sulphuric acid to give $CuSO_4$ (aq) and SO_2 (g). If one mole of copper is reacted with one mole of sulphuric acid, then the molecules of SO_2 (g) obtained will be
   (a) 3.0×10^{23} (b) 6.023×10^{23}
   (c) 3.0×10^{24} (d) $64 \times 6.023 \times 10^{23}$

RESPONSE GRID	1. ⓐⓑⓒⓓ	2. ⓐⓑⓒⓓ	3. ⓐⓑⓒⓓ

Space for Rough Work

4. The maximum number of molecules are present in

(a) 15 L of H_2 gas at STP (b) 5 L of N_2 gas at STP

(c) 0.5 g of H_2 gas (d) 10 g of O_2 gas

5. An organic compound whose empirical and molecular formula are same, contains 20% carbon, 6.7% hydrogen, 46.7% nitrogen and the rest oxygen. On heating it yields ammonia, leaving a solid residue. The solid residue gives a violet colour with dilute solution of alkaline copper sulphate. The organic compound is

(a) NH_2COONH_4 (b) $HCOONH_4$

(c) NH_2NHCHO (d) NH_2CONH_2

Section II - Multiple Correct Answer Type

This section contains 4 multiple correct answer(s) type questions. Each question has 4 choices (a), (b), (c) and (d), out of which **ONE OR MORE** is/are correct.

6. 0.2 mol of Na_3PO_4 and 0.5 mol of $Ba(NO_3)_2$ are mixed in 1L of solution. Which of the following is/ are correct about this system?

(a) 0.2 mol of barium phosphate precipitate is obtained

(b) 0.1 mol of barium phosphate precipitate is obtained.

(c) Molarity of Ba^{2+} ions in the resulting solution is 0.2

(d) Molarities of Na^+ and NO_3^- ions are 0.6 and 1.0 respectively.

7. 100 mL mixture of CO and CO_2 is mixed with 30 mL of oxygen and sparked in a eudiometer tube. The residual gas after treatment with aqueous KOH has a volume of 10 mL which remains unchanged when treated with alkaline pyrogallol. If all the volumes are under the same conditions, point out the correct option(s).

(a) The volume of CO that reacts, is 60 mL.

(b) The volume of CO that remains unreacted, is 10 mL.

(c) The volume of O_2 that remains unreacted, is 10 mL.

(d) The volume of CO_2 that gets absorbed by aqueous KOH, is 90 mL.

8. Which of the following statements are correct for a solution of H_2O_2 having a strength of 17 g/litre ?

(a) The volume strength of H_2O_2 solution is 5.6 at 1 atmosphere pressure and 273 K temperature.

(b) The molarity of given H_2O_2 solution is 0.5 M

(c) 1 mL of the given H_2O_2 solution will give out 2.8 mL of O_2 at 2 atmosphere pressure and 273 K temperature

(d) The normality of given H_2O_2 solution is 2N.

9. 10 mL of a gaseous hydrocarbon is exploded with 200 mL of oxygen. The gaseous product was then allowed to cool and attain room temperature and pressure, the volume was then found to be 180 mL. This mixture of gases was then passed through KOH solution followed by anhydrous $CaCl_2$. The resulting gas measured 100 mL. The hydrocarbon is

(a) C_4H_8 (b) C_8H_6

(c) C_8H_8 (d) C_4H_6

Section III - Integer Type

This section contains 5 questions. The answer to each of the questions is a single digit integer ranging from 0 to 9.

10. A 20 cm^3 mixture of CO, CH_4 and He gases was exploded by an electric discharge at room temperature with excess oxygen. The volume contraction was found to be 13.0 cm^3. A further contraction of 14.0 cm^3 occurred when the residual gas was treated with KOH solution. Find out the value of x if the composition of CH_4 in the mixture in terms of volume percentage is 5x.

11. A mixture of HCOOH and $H_2C_2O_4$ is heated with concentrated H_2SO_4. The gas produced is collected and on treating with KOH solution, the volume of gas decreases by one-sixth. Calculate the molar ratio of the two acids (HCOOH : $H_2C_2O_4$) in the original mixture.

<table>
<tr><td rowspan="2">RESPONSE
GRID</td><td>4. ⓐⓑⓒⓓ</td><td>5. ⓐⓑⓒⓓ</td><td>6. ⓐⓑⓒⓓ</td><td>7. ⓐⓑⓒⓓ</td><td>8. ⓐⓑⓒⓓ</td></tr>
<tr><td>9. ⓐⓑⓒⓓ</td><td colspan="2">10. ⓪①②③④⑤⑥⑦⑧⑨</td><td colspan="2">11. ⓪①②③④⑤⑥⑦⑧⑨</td></tr>
</table>

12. 2.68×10^{-3} moles of a solution containing an ion A^{n+} require 1.61×10^{-3} moles of MnO_4^- for the oxidation of A^{n+} to AO_3^- in acid medium. What is the value of n?

13. A 1.0 g sample of Fe_2O_3 solid of 55.2% purity is dissolved in acid and reduced by heating the solution with zinc dust. The resultant solution is cooled and made upto 100.0 mL. An aliquot of 25.0 mL of this solution requires 17.0 mL of 0.0167 M solution of an oxidant for titration. Calculate the number of electrons taken up by the oxidant in the reaction of the above titration.

14. Silver (atomic weight = 108 g mol^{-1}) has a density of 10.5 g cm^{-3}. The number of silver atoms on a surface of area 10^{-12} m^2 can be expressed in scientific notation as $y \times 10^x$. The value of x is :

Section IV - Comprehension Type

Directions (Qs. 15-19) : Based upon the given paragraphs, 5 multiple choice questions have to be answered. Each question has 4 choices (a), (b), (c) and (d), out of which **ONLY ONE** is correct.

PARAGRAPH-1

Some reactions are given in Column I and their n-factor and strength is given in Column II & III respectively.

Column I		Column II		Column III
(I) 9.8% H_2SO_4 by weight (d = 1.8 g mL^{-1})	(i)	n-factor = 3	(P)	3.6 N
(II) 9.8% H_3PO_4 by weight (density = 1.2 g mL^{-1})	(ii)	n-factor = 1	(Q)	1.2 M
(III) 1.8 N_A molecules of HCl in 500 mL	(iii)	n-factor = 2	(R)	1.8 equiv.
(IV) 250 mL of 4 N NaOH + 250 mL of 1.6 M $Ca(OH)_2$	(iv)	n-factor = 4	(S)	1.10 m

15. For 9.8% H_2SO_4 given in column I, the only correct combination is

  (a) (I) (iv) (P)   (b) (I) (ii) (Q)

  (c) (I) (iii) (S)   (d) (I) (i) (R)

16. For 1.8 N_A molecules of HCl given in column I, the only correct combination is

  (a) (III) (i) (P)   (b) (III) (ii) (R)

  (c) (III) (iii) (Q)   (d) (III) (ii) (S)

17. For 9.8% H_3PO_4 given in column I, the only correct combination is

  (a) (II) (i) (Q)   (b) (II) (iii) (S)

  (c) (II) (ii) (P)   (d) (II) (i) (R)

PARAGRAPH-2

From a mixture which makes up crude oil, a particular hydrocarbon ingredient (that is one containing hdyrogen and carbon atoms only) has been isolated. 10 g of this liquid are burned in excess of oxygen and the products are 31.4 g of carbon dioxide and 12.4 g of water.

18. The ratio of C : H in the substance i.e., the products) formed:

  (a) 1 : 1   (b) 1 : 2

  (c) 2 : 1   (d) 4 : 1

19. If we burn an equimolar mixture of the above hydrocarbon and oxygen in a closed vessel, then after the reaction the gaseous mixture present in the vessel will consist of

  (a) CO_2 and H_2O

  (b) CO_2, H_2O and O_2

  (c) CO_2, H_2O and hydrocarbon

  (d) CO_2, H_2O, hydrocarbon and oxygen

Space for Rough Work

Section V - Matrix-Match Type

This section contains 1 questions. It contains statements given in two columns, which have to be matched. Statements in column I are labelled as A, B, C and D whereas statements in column II are labelled as p, q, r and s. The answers to these questions have to be appropriately bubbled as illustrated in the following example. If the correct matches are A-p, A-r, B-p, B-s, C-r, C-s and D-q, then the correctly bubbled matrix will look like the following:

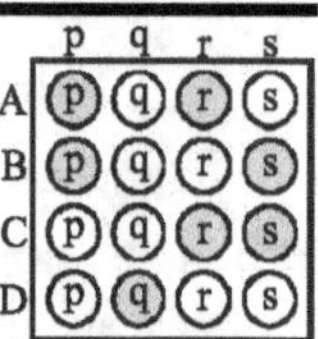

20.

	Column I		Column II
(A)	1.5 mole of $CO_2(g)$	p.	33600 ml at STP
(B)	3.0 g of H_2	q.	Total number of atoms $= 4.5 \times N_A$
(C)	1.5 mole of $O_3(g)$	r.	Weighs 72 g
(D)	1 mole of oxygen	s.	Weighs 32 g

RESPONSE GRID   20. A - ⓟⓠⓡⓢ; B - ⓟⓠⓡⓢ; C - ⓟⓠⓡⓢ; D - ⓟⓠⓡⓢ

DAILY PRACTICE PROBLEM DPP CHAPTERWISE 1 - CHEMISTRY			
Total Questions	20	Total Marks	74
Attempted		Correct	
Incorrect		Net Score	
Cut-off Score	26	Qualifying Score	38
Success Gap = Net Score − Qualifying Score			
Net Score = (Correct × 4) − (Incorrect × 1)			

DPP - Daily Practice Problems

Chapter-wise Sheets

Date :   Start Time :   End Time :

CHEMISTRY $\boxed{\text{CC02}}$

SYLLABUS : Structure of Atom

Max. Marks : 74   **Time : 60 min.**

GENERAL INSTRUCTIONS

- The Daily Practice Problem Sheet contains 20 Questions divided into 5 sections.
  Section I has **5** MCQs with ONLY 1 Correct Option, **3** marks for each correct answer and **−1** for each incorrect answer.
  Section II has **4** MCQs with ONE or MORE THAN ONE Correct options.
  For each question, marks will be awarded in one of the following categories:
  Full marks: **+4** If only the bubble(s) corresponding to all the correct option(s) is (are) darkened.
  Partial marks: **+1** For darkening a bubble corresponding to each correct option provided NO INCORRECT option is darkened.
  Zero marks: If none of the bubbles is darkened.
  Negative marks: **−2** In all other cases.
  Section III has **5** Single Digit Integer Answer Type Questions, **3** marks for each Correct Answer and 0 marks in all other cases.
  Section IV has Comprehension/Matching Cum-Comprehension Type Questions having **5** MCQs with ONLY ONE correct option, **3** marks for each Correct Answer and 0 marks in all other cases.
  Section V has **1** Matching Type Questions, **2** mark for the correct matching of each row and 0 marks in all other cases.
- You have to evaluate your Response Grids yourself with the help of Solutions.

Section I - Straight Objective Type

This section contains 5 multiple choice questions. Each question has 4 choices (a), (b), (c) and (d), out of which **ONLY ONE** is correct.

1. If the kinetic energy of an electron is increased four times, the wavelength of the de-Broglie wave associated with it would become

  (a) one fourth   (b) half
  (c) four times   (d) two times

2. An electron, e_1 is moving in the fifth stationary state, and another electron e_2 is moving in the fourth stationary state.

The radius of orbit of electron, e_1 is five times the radius of orbit of electron, e_2 calculate the ratio of velocity of electron e_1 (v_1) to the velocity of electron e_2 (v_2).

  (a) $5:1$ (b) $4:1$ (c) $1:5$ (d) $1:4$

3. If the shortest wavelength of the spectral line of H-atom in the Lyman series is X, then the longest wavelength of the line in Balmer series of Li^{2+} is

  (a) $9x$ (b) $\dfrac{x}{9}$ (c) $\dfrac{5x}{4}$ (d) $\dfrac{4x}{5}$

RESPONSE GRID   **1.** ⓐⓑⓒⓓ   **2.** ⓐⓑⓒⓓ   **3.** ⓐⓑⓒⓓ

Space for Rough Work

4. If we apply potential difference so that an electron is accelerated continuously in a vacuum tube such that a decrease of 10% occurs in its de-Broglie wave length. In such a case the change observed in kinetic energy of electron will be approximately

(a) a decrease of 11%   (b) an increase of 11.1%

(c) an increase of 10%   (d) an increase of 23.4%

5. The ratio of the frequency corresponding to the third line in Lyman series of hydrogen atomic spectrum to that of the first line in Balmer series of Li^{2+} spectrum is

(a) $\dfrac{4}{5}$ (b) $\dfrac{5}{4}$ (c) $\dfrac{4}{3}$ (d) $\dfrac{3}{4}$

Section II - Multiple Correct Answer Type

This section contains 4 multiple correct answer(s) type questions. Each question has 4 choices (a), (b), (c) and (d), out of which ONE OR MORE is/are correct.

6. The energy of an electron in the first Bohr orbit of H-atom is -13.6 eV. Then, which of the following statement(s) is/are correct for He^+?

(a) The energy of electron in second Bohr orbit is -13.6 eV

(b) The kinetic energy of electron in the first orbit is 54.46 eV

(c) The kinetic energy of electron in the second orbit is 13.6 eV

(d) The speed of electron in the second orbit is $2.19 \times 10^6 \, ms^{-1}$

7. Identify the elements of lowest atomic numbers which have the characteristics listed as below

A. Eleven p electrons

B. one electron with $m_l = 2$

C. Two electrons with $n = 3, l = 2$

(a) Cl, Ti, Sc   (b) Cl, Sc, Ti

(c) Cl, V, Cr   (d) Cl, Ti, V

8. If the wave number of 1st line of Balmer series of H-atom is 'x' then

(a) wave number of 1st line of lyman series of He^+ ion will be $\dfrac{108x}{5}$

(b) wave number of 1st line of lyman series of He^+ ion will be $\dfrac{36x}{5}$

(c) the wave length of 2nd line of lyman series of H-atom is $\dfrac{5}{32x}$

(d) the wave length of 2nd line of lyman series of H-atom is $\dfrac{32x}{5}$

9. According to Bohr's theory

(a) when a required amount of energy is supplied to an electron in an atom it jumps from lower orbit to higher orbit and remains there

(b) when a required amount of energy is supplied to an electron in an atom it jumps from lower orbit to higher orbit and remains there for very short interval of time and returns back to lower orbit, radiating energy

(c) the angular momentum of an electron is proportional to its quantum number, n

(d) the angular momentum of an electron is independent of its quantum number, n

Section III - Integer Type

This section contains 5 questions. The answer to each of the questions is a single digit integer ranging from 0 to 9.

10. Suppose velocity of an α–particle travelling towards the nucleus of a copper atom so as to arrive at a distance 10^{-13} metre from the nucleus of the copper atom is given by $x \times 10^y$. Then what will be the value of y?

11. An electron has a speed of 30,000 cm sec^{-1} accurate upto 0.001%. What is the uncertainty in locating it's position.

12. If the energies of two radiations of wavelength 800 nm and 400 nm are E_1 and E_2 respectively. Then calculate the value of E_2/E_1.

13. The work function (ϕ) of some metals is listed below. The number of metals which will show photoelectric effect when light of 300 nm wavelength falls on the metal is

Metal	Li	Na	k	Mg	Cu	Ag	Fe	Pt	W
ϕ (eV)	2.4	2.3	2.2	3.7	4.8	4.3	4.7	6.3	4.75

14. In an atom how many orbital(s) will have the quantum numbers; $n = 3, l = 2$ and $m_l = +2$?

Section IV - Comprehension Type

Directions (Qs. 15-19) : Based upon the given paragraphs, 5 multiple choice questions have to be answered. Each question has 4 choices (a), (b), (c) and (d), out of which **ONLY ONE** is correct.

PARAGRAPH-1

Directions (Qs. 15-17): By appropriately matching the information given in the three columns of the following table, give the answer of the questions that follows.

Bohr's theory successfully explains the hydrogen spectrum. It also explains the spectrum of some other one-electron system (H-like system) such as He^+, Li^{2+}, Be^{3+} etc. With the help of Bohr's theory we find out, Radius of the orbit in which the electron is revolving around the nucleus, Energy of electron in an orbits, velocity and wavelength.

Column I		Column II		Column III
(I) Radius	(i)	$\dfrac{2\pi Ze^2}{nh}$	(P)	$-\dfrac{Z^2}{n^2}\times 313.6$
(II) Velocity	(ii)	$\dfrac{n^2 h^2}{4\pi^2 mZe^2}$	(Q)	$R\times Z^2\left[\dfrac{1}{n_1^2}-\dfrac{1}{n_2^2}\right]$
(III) Energy	(iii)	$\dfrac{2\pi^2 me^4}{ch^2}$	(R)	$\left(\dfrac{Ze^2}{rm}\right)^{1/2}$
(IV) Wavelength	(iv)	$-\dfrac{2\pi^2\, mZ^2 e^4}{n^2\, h^2}$	(S)	$\dfrac{n^2}{Z}\times 0.0529$

15. The only correct combination of formula for the radius give in column I is
(a) (I)(ii)(P)   (b) (I)(iii)(R)
(c) (I)(ii)(S)   (d) (I)(iv)(Q)

16. The only correct combination of formula for the velocity given in column I is
(a) (II)(iii)(P)   (b) (II)(i)(R)
(c) (II)(ii)(S)   (d) (II)(iv)(Q)

17. The only correct combination of formula for the energy given in column I is
(a) (III)(i)(Q)   (b) (III)(ii)(R)
(c) (III)(iv)(S)   (d) (III)(iv)(P)

PARAGRAPH-2

Radial wave function depends on n and l but not on m. Thus each of the three p-orbitals have the same radial form. The wave functions may have positive or negative regions but their radial probability distributions (figure below) show the following features.

- Radial distributions may have several peaks, the number being equal to $(n-1)$.
- The outermost peak is by far the largest, showing where the electron is most likely to be found. The distance of this peak from the nucleus is a measure of the radius of the orbital and is roughly proportional to n^2 (although it slightly depends on l also)

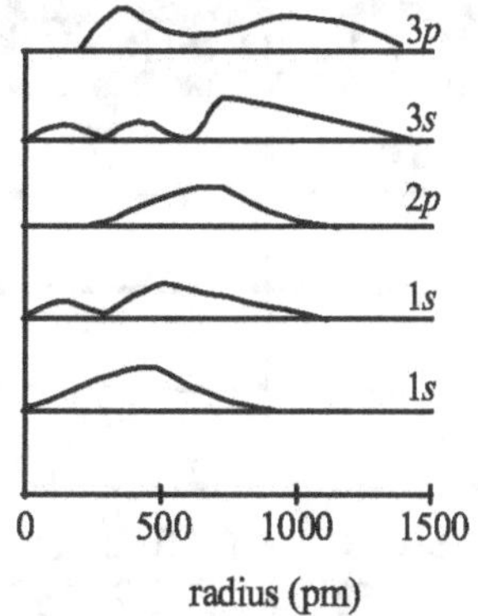

Space for Rough Work

Radial distributions determine the energy of an electron in an atom. The subsidiary maxima at smaller distances are not significant in hydrogen, but are useful in understanding the energies in many electron atoms.

The energies of atomic orbitals in hydrogen atom are given by the

formula $E_n = -\dfrac{R}{n^2}$

This shows that the energy depends only on the principal quantum number, n.

All orbitals with finite n represent bound electrons with lower energy. Energies of individual atoms or molecules are expressed in **electron volts** (eV) equal to about 1.602×10^{-19} J.

For many electron atoms

The orbital sizes and energies depend on the atomic number 'Z'

Average radius of an orbital $\approx \dfrac{n^2 a_0}{Z}$

Where a_0 = Bohr's radius (59 pm)

i.e., radius of $1s$ orbital of hydrogen atom

Also $E_n = -\dfrac{Z^2 R}{n^2}$

18. If the subsidiary quantum number of a sub-energy level is 4, the maximum and minimum values of the spin multiplicities are given by

  (a)   4,–4   (b)   9,1   (c)   10,1   (d)   10,2

19. The number of d-electrons in Fe^{2+} is **not** equal to that of

  (a) d-electrons in Iron

  (b) p-electrons in Neon

  (c) p-electrons in Chlorine

  (d) s-electrons in Magnesium

Section V - Matrix-Match Type

This section contains 1 questions. It contains statements given in two columns, which have to be matched. Statements in column I are labelled as A, B, C and D whereas statements in column II are labelled as p, q, r and s. The answers to these questions have to be appropriately bubbled as illustrated in the following example. If the correct matches are A-p, A-r, B-p, B-s, C-r, C-s and D-q, then the correctly bubbled matrix will look like the following:

20. If the shortest wavelength of spectral line of H-atom in Lyman series is x, then match the following for Li^{2+}

Column I		Column II
(A) Shortest wavelength in Lyman series	p.	$\dfrac{4x}{5}$
(B) Longest wavelength in Lyman series	q.	$\dfrac{4x}{9}$
(C) Shortest wavelength in Balmer series	r.	$\dfrac{x}{9}$
(D) Longest wavelength in Balmer series	s.	$\dfrac{4x}{27}$

RESPONSE GRID	
18. ⓐⓑⓒⓓ **19.** ⓐⓑⓒⓓ	
20. A - ⓟⓠⓡⓢ; B - ⓟⓠⓡⓢ; C - ⓟⓠⓡⓢ; D - ⓟⓠⓡⓢ	

DAILY PRACTICE PROBLEM DPP CHAPTERWISE 2 - CHEMISTRY

Total Questions	20	Total Marks	74
Attempted		Correct	
Incorrect		Net Score	
Cut-off Score	26	Qualifying Score	38
Success Gap = Net Score – Qualifying Score			
Net Score = (Correct × 4) – (Incorrect × 1)			

DPP - Daily Practice Problems

Chapter-wise Sheets

Date :   Start Time :   End Time :

CHEMISTRY $\boxed{\text{CC03}}$

SYLLABUS : Classification of Elements and Periodicity in Properties

Max. Marks : 74   **Time : 60 min.**

GENERAL INSTRUCTIONS

- The Daily Practice Problem Sheet contains 20 Questions divided into 5 sections.

Section I has **6** MCQs with ONLY 1 Correct Option, **3** marks for each correct answer and **−1** for each incorrect answer.

Section II has **4** MCQs with ONE or MORE THAN ONE Correct options.

For each question, marks will be awarded in one of the following categories:

Full marks: **+4** If only the bubble(s) corresponding to all the correct option(s) is (are) darkened.

Partial marks: **+1** For darkening a bubble corresponding to each correct option provided NO INCORRECT option is darkened.

Zero marks: If none of the bubbles is darkened.

Negative marks: **−2** In all other cases.

Section III has **4** Single Digit Integer Answer Type Questions, **3** marks for each Correct Answer and 0 marks in all other cases.

Section IV has Comprehension/Matching Cum-Comprehension Type Questions having 4 MCQs with ONLY ONE correct option, **3** marks for each Correct Answer and 0 marks in all other cases.

Section V has **2** Matching Type Questions, **2** mark for the correct matching of each row and 0 marks in all other cases.

- You have to evaluate your Response Grids yourself with the help of Solutions.

Section I - Straight Objective Type

This section contains 6 multiple choice questions. Each question has 4 choices (a), (b), (c) and (d), out of which **ONLY ONE** is correct.

1. Which is not the correct order for the stated property.

  (a) $Ba > Sr > Mg$; atomic radius

  (b) $F > O > N$; first ionization enthalpy

  (c) $Cl > F > I$; electron affinity

  (d) $O > Se > Te$; electronegativity

2. The correct decreasing order of first ionisation enthalpies of five elements of the second period is

  (a) $Be > B > C > N > F$ (b) $N > F > C > B > Be$

  (c) $F > N > C > Be > B$ (d) $N > F > B > C > Be$

3. Electron affinity depends on

  (a) atomic size

  (b) nuclear charge

  (c) atomic number

  (d) atomic size and nuclear charge both

RESPONSE GRID   **1.** ⓐⓑⓒⓓ   **2.** ⓐⓑⓒⓓ   **3.** ⓐⓑⓒⓓ

Space for Rough Work

4. Following statements regarding the periodic trends of chemical reactivity of the alkali metals and the halogens are given. Which of these statements gives the correct picture?

(a) Chemical reactivity increases with increase in atomic number down the group in both the alkali metals and halogens

(b) In alkali metals the reactivity increases but in the halogens it decreases with increase in atomic number down the group

(c) The reactivity decreases in the alkali metals but increases in the halogens with increase in atomic number down the group

(d) In both the alkali metals and the halogens the chemical reactivity decreases with increase in atomic number down the group

5. The formation of O^{2-} (g) starting from O(g) is endothermic by 603 kJ mol^{-1}. If electron affinity of O(g) is -141 kJ mol^{-1}, the second electron affinity of oxygen would be

(a) 603 kJ mol^{-1} (b) -603 kJ mol^{-1}

(c) -744 kJ mol^{-1} (d) $+744$ kJ mol^{-1}

6. The van der Waals radii of O, N, Cl, F and Ne increase in the order

(a) F, O, N, Ne, Cl (b) Ne, F, O, N, Cl

(c) F, Cl, O, N, Ne (d) N, O, F, Ne, Cl

Section II - Multiple Correct Answer Type

This section contains 4 multiple correct answer(s) type questions. Each question has 4 choices (a), (b), (c) and (d), out of which **ONE OR MORE** is/are correct.

7. If Aufbau principle and Hund's rule were not followed

(a) Ca would have been d-block element with zero dipole moment

(b) Zn would have been s-block element

(c) Ti would have been diamagnetic

(d) Fe^{3+} ion would have 5 unpaired electrons.

8. Choose the correct statement(s)

(a) The maximum positive oxidation state shown by any element is equal to the total number of electrons (s and p) in valence shell

(b) The maximum oxidation state shown by elements in a group is also known as **group oxidation number**

(c) Group oxidation number is the most common or most stable oxidation state for a particular element

(d) All the elements in a group form some compounds in which they exhibit their group oxidation number.

9. Which of the following trends of electron affinity are correct?

(a) O > S > Se (b) Cl > F > Br

(c) Cl > Br > I (d) O > C > N

10. Which of the following trends of ionic radii are correct.

(a) F$^-$ > Na$^+$ > Mg^{2+} (b) Al^{3+} > O^{2-} > N^{3-}

(c) P^{3-} > S^{2-} > Cl$^-$ (d) H$^-$ > H$^+$ > He

Section III - Integer Type

This section contains 4 questions. The answer to each of the questions is a single digit integer ranging from 0 to 9.

11. How many periods are there in the long form of the periodic table ?

12. What is the total number of elements in the group IB ?

13. What is the number of elements in the third period of the periodic table ?

14. How many elements of the following are electropositive element(s) ?

Sodium, calcium, oxygen and chlorine

Section IV - Comprehension Type

Directions (Qs. 15-18) : Based upon the given paragraphs, 4 multiple choice questions have to be answered. Each question has 4 choices (a), (b), (c) and (d), out of which **ONLY ONE** is correct.

PARAGRAPH-1

The electronegativity of an element is a measure of power of the element to attract electron to itself in **chemical compounds.** It is difficult to assign accurate electronegativities to elements, partly because the precise values may vary in different compounds. Our quantitative estimation of electronegativity is the average of ionization energy and the electron affinity for an element in eV. It is known as **Mulliken's scale.**

The trends in electronegativity values are similar to those in ionization energies.

Various measures of electronegativity have been proposed and all give roughly parallel scales. **Pauling scale** is based upon excess bond energies; **Alfred** and **Rochow's** (R/A) is based upon effective nuclear charges. The % age of ionic character in a bond can be estimated by finding the differences in electronegativity values of atoms forming the bond. The % age ionic character and difference in electronegativity values are given below :

Electronegativity difference	% age ionic character
1.0	20%
1.5	40%
2.0	60%
2.5	80%

Pauling and **Mulliken** values of electronegativity are related as

$$X_{Pauling} = 0.336\left[X_{Mulliken} - 0.615\right]$$

15. In the series carbon, nitrogen, oxygen and fluorine, the electronegativity
    (a) decreases from carbon to fluorine
    (b) increases from carbon to fluorine
    (c) remains constant
    (d) decreases from carbon to oxygen and then increases

16. The electronegativity of the following elements increases in the order
    (a) C, N, Si, P   (b) N, Si, C, P
    (c) Si, P, C, N   (d) P, Si, N, C

PARAGRAPH-2

Lattice energy (U) is defined as change in internal energy when one mole of a solid is converted into one mole of infinitely separated ions in the gas phase at $0\ K$.

The Born-Lande expression for lattice energy may be represented as

$$U_0 = \frac{N_0 A.Z^+.Z^- e^2}{4\pi\varepsilon_0 r_0}\left(1 - \frac{1}{n}\right)$$

where N_0 = Avogadro constant

A = Madelung's constant, which depends upon the geometry of the crystal.

Z^+ and Z^- are charges on positive and negative ions respectively.

e = charge on electron

r_0 = interionic distance

n = A constant called Born exponent (often assumed to be equal to 9)

Σ_0 = permittivity of vacuum

In the above equation first term deals with attraction between the

ions and the second term $\left(\dfrac{1}{n}\right)$ is associated with repulsion.

From the above it becomes clear that lattice energy depends upon
(i) The ionic charges
(ii) The distance between the ions
(iii) Crystal structure

17. Choose the correct statement
    (a) The lattice energy depends upon the reciprocal of the distance between the ions $\dfrac{1}{r_0}$
    (b) For a positive ion, the lattice energy increases as the size of the anion increases.
    (c) For a given anion, the lattice energy increases with increase in the size of positive ion
    (d) For large positive ions, the magnitude of lattice energy is mainly determined by the size of anion.

18. The correct arrangement of compounds in increasing order of their lattice energies is
    (a) $TiF_2 < VF_2 < CrF_2 < MnF_2 < FeF_2$
    (b) $TiF_2 < MnF_2 < VF_2 < CrF_2 < FeF_2$
    (c) $VF_2 < TiF_2 < CrF_2 < FeF_2 < MnF_2$
    (d) $FeF_2 < TiF_2 < MnF_2 < VF_2 < CrF_2$

RESPONSE GRID	15. ⓐⓑⓒⓓ	16. ⓐⓑⓒⓓ	17. ⓐⓑⓒⓓ	18. ⓐⓑⓒⓓ

Section V - Matrix-Match Type

This section contains 2 questions. It contains statements given in two columns, which have to be matched. Statements in column I are labelled as A, B, C and D whereas statements in column II are labelled as p, q, r and s. The answers to these questions have to be appropriately bubbled as illustrated in the following example. If the correct matches are A-p, A-r, B-p, B-s, C-r, C-s and D-q, then the correctly bubbled matrix will look like the following:

19. **Match the elements listed in column I with the period/group listed in column II :**

	Column I		Column II
(A)	Element having At. No. 47	p.	4th period
(B)	Element with lowest At. No. having configuration $(n-1)\,d^{10}\,n\,s^2\,np^3$	q.	5th period
(C)	Element with At No. 34	r.	15th group
(D)	Element with lowest At. No. having configuration $(n-1)\,d^{10}\,n\,s^1$	s.	16th group

20. **The values of IE_1 and IE_2 (kJ mol^{-1}) of few elements designated by A, B, C, and D are shown below in column I. Match their characteristics listed in column II.**

	Column I		Column II
(A)	IE_1 2372, IE_2 5251	p.	A reactive metal
(B)	IE_1 520, IE_2 7300	q.	A reactive non-metal
(C)	IE_1 900, IE_2 1760	r.	A noble gas
(D)	IE_1 1680, IE_2 3380	s.	A metal that forms an halide of formula AX_2

RESPONSE GRID	
19. A - ⓟⓠⓡⓢ; B - ⓟⓠⓡⓢ; C - ⓟⓠⓡⓢ; D - ⓟⓠⓡⓢ	
20. A - ⓟⓠⓡⓢ; B - ⓟⓠⓡⓢ; C - ⓟⓠⓡⓢ; D - ⓟⓠⓡⓢ	

DAILY PRACTICE PROBLEM DPP CHAPTERWISE 3 - CHEMISTRY

Total Questions	20	Total Marks	74
Attempted		Correct	
Incorrect		Net Score	
Cut-off Score	30	Qualifying Score	60
Success Gap = Net Score – Qualifying Score			
Net Score = (Correct × 4) – (Incorrect × 1)			

DPP - Daily Practice Problems

Chapter-wise Sheets

Date : | Start Time : | End Time :

CHEMISTRY CC04

SYLLABUS : Chemical Bonding and Molecular Structure

Max. Marks : 74

Time : 60 min.

GENERAL INSTRUCTIONS

- The Daily Practice Problem Sheet contains 20 Questions divided into 5 sections.
  Section I has **5** MCQs with ONLY 1 Correct Option, **3** marks for each correct answer and **−1** for each incorrect answer.
  Section II has **4** MCQs with ONE or MORE THAN ONE Correct options.
  For each question, marks will be awarded in one of the following categories:
  Full marks: **+4** If only the bubble(s) corresponding to all the correct option(s) is (are) darkened.
  Partial marks: **+1** For darkening a bubble corresponding to each correct option provided NO INCORRECT option is darkened.
  Zero marks: If none of the bubbles is darkened.
  Negative marks: **−2** In all other cases.
  Section III has **5** Single Digit Integer Answer Type Questions, **3** marks for each Correct Answer and 0 marks in all other cases.
  Section IV has Comprehension/Matching Cum-Comprehension Type Questions having **5** MCQs with ONLY ONE correct option, **3** marks for each Correct Answer and 0 marks in all other cases.
  Section V has **1** Matching Type Questions, **2** mark for the correct matching of each row and 0 marks in all other cases.
- You have to evaluate your Response Grids yourself with the help of Solutions.

Section I - Straight Objective Type

This section contains 5 multiple choice questions. Each question has 4 choices (a), (b), (c) and (d), out of which **ONLY ONE** is correct.

1. Which of the following is the wrong statement

    (a) ONCl and ONO⁻ are isoelectronic.

    (b) O_3 molecule is bent

    (c) Ozone is violet-black in solid state

    (d) Ozone is diamagnetic gas.

2. Bond order normally gives idea of stability of a molecular species. All the molecules viz. H_2, Li_2 and B_2 have the same bond order yet they are not equally stable. Their stability order is

    (a) $H_2 > B_2 > Li_2$ (b) $Li_2 > H_2 > B_2$

    (c) $H_2 > Li_2 > B_2$ (d) $B_2 > H_2 > Li_2$

3. The dipole moment of m-dichlorobenzene is 1.5 D. The value of dipole moment of o-dichlorobenzene is :

    (a) 0.0 D   (b) 1.50 D

    (c) 2.60 D   (d) 2.12 D

Space for Rough Work

4. On changing N_2 to N_2^+, the dissociation energy of N–N bond ..... and on changing O_2 to O_2^+ the dissociation energy of O–O bond....
(a) increases, decreases
(b) decreases, increases
(c) decreases in both cases
(d) increases in both cases

5. Which of the following ions does not involve $p\pi - d\pi$ bonding?
(a) SO_3^{2-}
(b) PO_4^{3-}
(c) NO_3^-
(d) $XeOF_4$

Section II - Multiple Correct Answer Type
This section contains 4 multiple correct answer(s) type questions. Each question has 4 choices (a), (b), (c) and (d), out of which **ONE OR MORE** is/are correct.

6. In which of the following change(s), hybridisation of the underlined atom is not affected?
(a) $\underline{P}H_3 + H^+ \longrightarrow PH_4^+$
(b) $\underline{B}F_3 + H_2S \longrightarrow H_2S \rightarrow BF_3$
(c) $H_3\underline{B}O_3 \longrightarrow HBO_2 + H_2O$
(d) $2H\underline{Cl}O_2 \longrightarrow HClO + HClO_3$

7. Amongst the following, the correct statement(s) is/are:
(a) NO has one unpaired electron in the antibonding molecular orbital
(b) NO^+ is more stable than O_2^+
(c) OF^+ is more paramagnetic than Ne_2^+
(d) A pi bond is concentrated along the bond axis.

8. Which of the following have identical bond order?
(a) CN^-
(b) O_2^-
(c) NO^+
(d) CN^+

9. Point out the correct statement(s) amongst the following
(a) Sodium salts are much more soluble than ammonium salts
(b) $SnCl_2$ is ionic but $SnCl_4$ is covalent
(c) NH_3 has lesser polar character than BF_3
(d) Calcium fluoride is more ionic than calcium iodide.

Section III - Integer Type
This section contains 5 questions. The answer to each of the questions is a single digit integer ranging from 0 to 9.

10. The experimental value of the dipole moment of H–X molecule is 1.2 D. The H–X bond length is 0.1nm. If the percent ionic character of the bond is $5x$ then what will be the value of x?

11. Find out the total number of lone pair of electrons in $XeOF_4$.

12. HI is a covalent compound in which small positive charge is present on H and a small negative charge on I, and the molecule is represented as $H^{\delta+} - I^{\delta-}$. The dipole moment of HI is 0.38D and the bond length. H–I is 1.61A°. What fraction of charge is present on I ?

13. Find the maximum number of water molecules that one water molecule can hold through hydrogen bonding.

14. How many of the following compounds violate octet rule?
(i) BrF_5
(ii) SF_6
(iii) IF_7
(iv) $XeOF_4$
(v) ClF_2
(vi) $PCl_4^{\oplus}$

RESPONSE GRID

4. (a)(b)(c)(d) 5. (a)(b)(c)(d) 6. (a)(b)(c)(d) 7. (a)(b)(c)(d) 8. (a)(b)(c)(d)
8. (a)(b)(c)(d) 9. (a)(b)(c)(d) 10. (0)(1)(2)(3)(4)(5)(6)(7)(8)(9)
11. (0)(1)(2)(3)(4)(5)(6)(7)(8)(9) 12. (0)(1)(2)(3)(4)(5)(6)(7)(8)(9)
13. (0)(1)(2)(3)(4)(5)(6)(7)(8)(9) 14. (0)(1)(2)(3)(4)(5)(6)(7)(8)(9)

Section IV - Comprehension Type

Directions (Qs. 15-19) : Based upon the given paragraphs, 5 multiple choice questions have to be answered. Each question has 4 choices (a), (b), (c) and (d), out of which **ONLY ONE** is correct.

PARAGRAPH-1

Column I contains compound and Column II & III contains their geometry and shape respectively.

Column I		Column II		Column III
Compound		Geometry		Shape
(I) XeF_4	(i)	Trigonal bipyramidal	(P)	Tetrahedral
(II) XeO_2F_2	(ii)	Octahedral	(Q)	Octahedral
(III) XeF_6	(iii)	Tetrahedral	(R)	See-saw
(IV) XeO_4	(iv)	Trigonal planar	(S)	Square planar

15. Find suitable combination for Xenon dioxydifluoride

   (a) (II) (iv) (P)   (b) (II) (iii) (S)

   (c) (II) (iii) (Q)   (d) (II) (i) (R)

16. Find appropriate combination which has same shape and geometry

   (a) (I) (iii) (P)   (b) (IV) (ii) (Q)

   (c) (II) (iv) (S)   (d) (IV) (iii) (P)

17. Incorrect combination is

   (a) (I) (ii) (S)   (b) (IV) (iii) (P)

   (c) (III) (iv) (S)   (d) (II) (i) (R)

PARAGRAPH-2

The shapes of molecules can be predicted by VSEPR theory, hybridization and dipole moment. Total number of hybrid orbitals (H) on the central atom of a molecule can be calculated by using the following relation :

H = [Total no. of valence electron pairs (p) – 3 × (no. of atoms surrounding the central atom, excluding hydrogen atoms)]

One can also calculate total no. of bond pairs (n) around central atom as n = total number of atoms surrounding the central atom

also, total no. of lone pairs (m) = H – n

Thus, VSEPR notation of a molecule can be written as AX_nE_m.

Where, A denotes central atom of the molecule.

X denotes bond pairs on central atom of the molecule.

E denotes lone pairs on central atom of the molecule.

In a polar molecule, the net dipole moment of the molecule $\propto$ m

18. VSEPR notation of chlorine trifluoride molecule is –

   (a) AX_5 (b) AX_3

   (c) AX_2E_3 (d) AX_3E_2

19. Some molecules are given below :

CO_2, SO_2, H_2O

   I   II   III

The correct increasing order of dipole moments of given species is –

   (a) I < II < III   (b) II < I < III

   (c) III < II < I   (d) III < I < II

RESPONSE GRID	15. ⓐⓑⓒⓓ	16. ⓐⓑⓒⓓ	17. ⓐⓑⓒⓓ	18. ⓐⓑⓒⓓ	19. ⓐⓑⓒⓓ

Section V - Matrix-Match Type

This section contain 1 question. It contains statements given in two columns, which have to be matched. Statements in column I are labelled as A, B, C and D whereas statements in column II are labelled as p, q, r and s. The answers to these questions have to be appropriately bubbled as Illustrated in the following example. If the correct matches are A-p, A-r, B-p, B-s, C-r, C-s and D-q, then the correctly bubbled matrix will look like the following:

20. Match the columns.

Column-I		**Column-II**	
(A)	Hydrogen bonding	p.	Depend on temperature
(B)	Dispersion forces	q.	Do not depend on temperature
(C)	Dipole-dipole force	r.	This type of forces are involved is solidification of I_2
(D)	Dipole-induced dipole forces	s.	All molecular forces involved in solution of HBr in carbon tetrachloride

RESPONSE GRID   20. A - ⓟⓠⓡⓢ; B - ⓟⓠⓡⓢ; C - ⓟⓠⓡⓢ; D - ⓟⓠⓡⓢ

DAILY PRACTICE PROBLEM DPP CHAPTERWISE 4 - CHEMISTRY			
Total Questions	20	Total Marks	74
Attempted		Correct	
Incorrect		Net Score	
Cut-off Score	24	Qualifying Score	35
Success Gap = Net Score – Qualifying Score			
Net Score = (Correct × 4) – (Incorrect × 1)			

DPP - Daily Practice Problems

Chapter-wise Sheets

Date :   Start Time :   End Time :

CHEMISTRY $\boxed{\text{CC05}}$

SYLLABUS : States of Matter

Max. Marks : 74   **Time : 60 min.**

GENERAL INSTRUCTIONS

- The Daily Practice Problem Sheet contains 20 Questions divided into 5 sections.

  Section I has **6** MCQs with ONLY 1 Correct Option, **3** marks for each correct answer and **−1** for each incorrect answer.

  Section II has **4** MCQs with ONE or MORE THAN ONE Correct options.

  For each question, marks will be awarded in one of the following categories:

  Full marks: **+4** If only the bubble(s) corresponding to all the correct option(s) is (are) darkened.

  Partial marks: **+1** For darkening a bubble corresponding to each correct option provided NO INCORRECT option is darkened.

  Zero marks: If none of the bubbles is darkened.

  Negative marks: **−2** In all other cases.

  Section III has **4** Single Digit Integer Answer Type Questions, **3** marks for each Correct Answer and 0 marks in all other cases.

  Section IV has Comprehension/Matching Cum-Comprehension Type Questions having **5** MCQs with ONLY ONE correct option, **3** marks for each Correct Answer and 0 marks in all other cases.

  Section V has **2** Matching Type Questions, **2** mark for the correct matching of each row and 0 marks in all other cases.

- You have to evaluate your Response Grids yourself with the help of Solutions.

Section I - Straight Objective Type

This section contains 6 multiple choice questions. Each question has 4 choices (a), (b), (c) and (d), out of which **ONLY ONE** is correct.

1. If P_c, V_c and T_c are critical constants, then the value of R will be

(a) $R = \dfrac{P_c V_c}{T_c}$ (b) $R = \dfrac{5}{3} \cdot \dfrac{P_c V_c}{T_c}$

(c) $R = \dfrac{3}{2} \cdot \dfrac{P_c V_c}{T_c}$ (d) $R = \dfrac{8}{3} \dfrac{P_c V_c}{T_c}$

2. 14 g of N_2 and 36 g of ozone are at the same pressure and temperature. Their volumes will be related as

(a) $2V_{N_2} = 3V_{O_3}$

(b) $3V_{N_2} = 2V_{O_3}$

(c) $3V_{N_2} = 4V_{O_3}$

(d) $4V_{N_2} = 3V_{O_3}$

RESPONSE GRID	**1.** ⓐⓑⓒⓓ	**2.** ⓐⓑⓒⓓ

Space for Rough Work

3. A perfect gas is found to obey the relation $PV^{3/2} = $ constant. If the gas is compressed to half of its volume at temperature T adiabatically, the final temperature of the gas will be

(a) $2T\sqrt{2}$ (b) $4T$ (c) $T\sqrt{2}$ (d) $2T$

4. When $CO_2(g)$ is passed over red hot coke it partially gets reduced to $CO(g)$. Upon passing 0.5 L of $CO_2(g)$ over red hot coke, the total volume of the gases increased to 700 mL. The composition of the gaseous mixture at STP is

(a) $CO_2 = 300\,mL; CO = 400\,mL$
(b) $CO_2 = 0.0\,mL; CO = 700\,mL$
(c) $CO_2 = 200\,mL; CO = 500\,mL$
(d) $CO_2 = 350\,mL; CO = 350\,mL$

5. The ratio between most probable velocity, mean velocity and r.m.s velocity is :

(a) $\sqrt{2} : \sqrt{8/\pi} : \sqrt{3}$ (b) $\sqrt{2} : \sqrt{3} : \sqrt{8/\pi}$

(c) $1 : 2 : 3$ (d) $1 : \sqrt{2} : \sqrt{3}$

6. Virial equation of state can be written as follows to express the compressibility factor (Z).

$$Z = 1 + \frac{B}{V} + \frac{C}{V^2} + \frac{D}{V^3} + ...$$

The correct relationship for van der Waal's constant 'b' is

(a) $B = b$ (b) $B = b - \dfrac{a}{RT}$

(c) $b = D^3$ (d) $b = C^2$

Section II - Multiple Correct Answer Type

This section contains 4 multiple correct answer(s) type questions. Each question has 4 choices (a), (b), (c) and (d), out of which **ONE OR MORE** is/are correct.

7. A car tyre has a volume of 10 litre when inflated. The tyre is inflated to a pressure of 3 atm at 17°C with air. Due to driving the temperature of tyre increases to 47°C. Choose the correct options –

(a) Pressure at this temperature is 2.3103 atm.
(b) 3.1029 L of air should be let out at 1 atm to restore the tyre to 3 atm at 47°C.

(c) Pressure at this temperature is 3.3103 atm.
(d) 2.1029 L of air should be let out at 1 atm to restore the tyre to 3 atm at 47°C.

8. The van der Waal's constants for HCl are 371.843 KPa and $b = 40.8\ cm^3mol^{-1}$. Choose the correct options–

(a) The critical pressure is 8.273 MPa
(b) The critical temperature is 224.8 K
(c) The critical volume is 122.4 cm^3
(d) The critical temperature is 324.8 K

9. A gas described by van der Waal's equation –
(a) behave similar to an ideal gas in the limit of large molar volumes
(b) behaves similar to an ideal gas is in limit of large pressures
(c) is characterised by van der Waal's coefficients that are dependent on the identity of the gas but are independent of the temperature.
(d) has the pressure that is lower than the pressure exerted by the same gas behaving ideally

10. Select the correct statements of the following :
(a) Ideal gas can be liquefied by cooling it to a very low temperature and applying a very high pressure
(b) Helium can be liquefied by cooling it to a characteristic temperature and compressing
(c) At ordinary temperatures compressed helium gas get heated up when passed through an orifice into vacuum under adiabatic conditions
(d) At ordinary temperatures hydrogen is less compressible than an ideal gas

Section III - Integer Type

This section contains 4 questions. The answer to each of the questions is a single digit integer ranging from 0 to 9.

11. A 10 L box contains 41.4 g of a mixture of gases C_xH_8 and C_xH_{12}. The total pressure at 44°C in flask is 1.56 atm. Analysis revealed that the gas mixture has 87% total C and 13% total H. Find out the value of x.

12. A gas diffuse 1/5 times as fast as hydrogen. If its molecular weight is 10y. What will be the value of y?

13. The rate of diffusion of methane at a given temperature is twice that of a gas X. If the molecular weight of X is $8y$ then what will be the value of y?

14. At 400 K, the root mean square (rms) speed of a gas X (molecular weight = 40) is equal to the most probable speed of gas Y at 60 K. The molecular weight of the gas Y is

---

Section IV - Comprehension Type

Directions (Qs. 15-18) : Based upon the given paragraphs, 4 multiple choice questions have to be answered. Each question has 4 choices (a), (b), (c) and (d), out of which **ONLY ONE** is correct.

PARAGRAPH-1

In the Figure-1 below, isotherms of CO_2 at several temperatures near the critical point are shown. At the critical point (critical state), the distinction between the liquid and gaseous states disappears and the density of the gaseous substance is equal to that in the liquid state. For every gas this occurs at specific values of temperature and pressure, called critical temperature and critical pressure respectively. At temperatures and pressures above the critical point value, a gas is said be in a supercritical state. The supercritical fluid has the density and ability to dissolve other substances similar to values expected for liquids.

Figure-2 depicts the phase diagram of CO_2. Various curves in the diagram show the equilibrium between two phases and the areas represent different phases. The point, called triple point, describing the equilibrium between three phases has specific values of temperature and pressure.

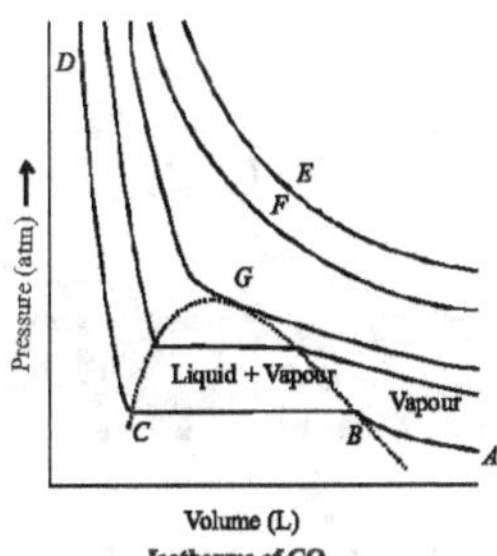

Figure 1

15. According to Figure-2 what is the critical temperature and pressure of CO_2?

  (a) $-42°$ C and 10 atm   (b) $-38°C$ and 80 atm

  (c) $31.1°$ C and 75.3 atm   (d) $31.1°C$ and 1 atm

16. According to Fig.-1, which of the following is correct when CO_2 is compressed at a temperature corresponding to the isotherm ABCD?

  (a) Liquefaction of CO_2 is complete at the point B

  (b) Liquefaction of CO_2 is complete at the point C

  (c) Volume of CO_2 system remains constant along BC

  (d) Proportions of liquid and gaseous CO_2 do not change along BC.

PARAGRAPH-2

The ideal gas equation, $PV = nRT$ is not obeyed by real gases under certain conditions. The deviation from ideal behaviour was attributed to the fact that P_{ideal} is related to P_{real} by the equation

$$P_{ideal} = P_{real} + \frac{an^2}{V^2}$$

In this 'a' is a measure of intermolecular interaction between gaseous molecules that gives rise to non-ideal behaviour.

Again the volume correction was introduced by taking into account the volume occupied by gaseous molecules and the effective volume is $(V - nb)$, where nb represents the volume occupied by n moles of molecules of real gas.

van der Waals equation of real gases is written as

$$\left(P + \frac{an^2}{V^2} \right)(V - nb) = nRT$$

17. The van der Waals equation for real gases will reduce to which one of the following forms under conditions of relatively high pressure?

  (a) $PV = RT - Pb$ (b) $PV = RT + Pb$

  (c) $PV = RT - \dfrac{a}{V^2}$ (d) $PV = RT - \dfrac{a}{V^2}$

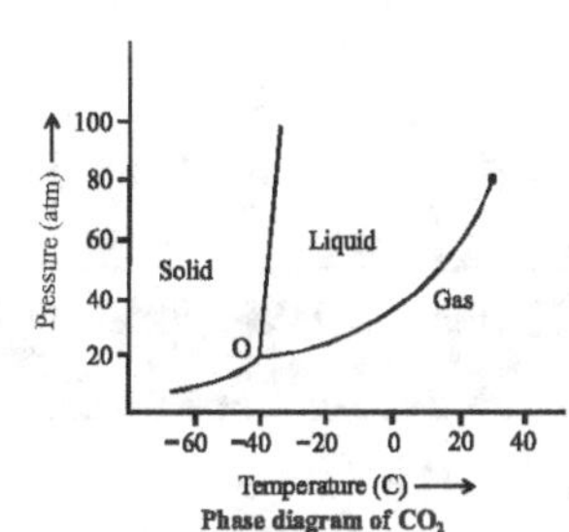

Figure 2

<table>
<tr><td rowspan="2">RESPONSE
GRID</td><td>13. ⓪①②③④⑤⑥⑦⑧⑨</td><td>14. ⓪①②③④⑤⑥⑦⑧⑨</td><td>15. ⓐⓑⓒⓓ</td></tr>
<tr><td>16. ⓐⓑⓒⓓ</td><td>17. ⓐⓑⓒⓓ</td><td></td></tr>
</table>

18. The van der Waals equation for a gas that has non-zero value of force of attraction between molecules but has the molecules to be point masses, will become

(a) $PV = nRT + nbP$

(b) $P(V - nb) = nRT$

(c) $PV = nRT$

(d) $PV = nRT - \dfrac{an^2}{V}$

Section V - Matrix-Match Type

This section contains 2 questions. It contains statements given in two columns, which have to be matched. Statements in column I are labelled as A, B, C and D whereas statements in column II are labelled as p, q, r and s. The answers to these questions have to be appropriately bubbled as illustrated in the following example. If the correct matches are A-p, A-r, B-p, B-s, C-r, C-s and D-q, then the correctly bubbled matrix will look like the following:

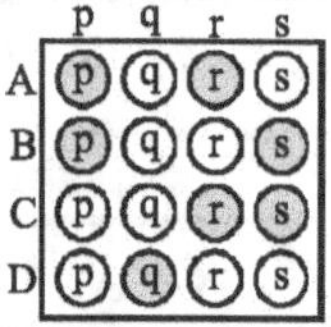

19. T_b and T_i are the Boyle's and inversion temperatures respectively for a real gas. Match the following characteristics with appropriate temperatures.

Column I (Gas Characteristics)		Column II (Temperature)
(A) Attractive intermolecular forces become dominant over repulsive forces when	p.	$> T_i$
(B) Repulsive forces become dominant	q.	$< T_i$
(C) Gas becomes more or less ideal gas when	r.	Any value of temperature
(D) $\mu_{J.T.}$ for ideal gas is zero at	s.	$= T_b$

20. The van der waal's constants a and b of a real gas are $3.6 \, L^2 \, atm \, mol^{-2}$ and $0.05 \, L \, mol^{-1}$ respectively. If 200 g of gas (molecular mass 40) is placed in 10 L vessel at 300 K, then match the following:

Column I		Column II
(A) Pressure correction (atm)	p.	0.25
(B) Free space for the molecules to move about (L)	q.	0.06
(C) Actual volume occupied by gas molecules (L)	r.	0.9
(D) Effective volume occupied by gas molecules (L)	s.	9.75

RESPONSE GRID	
18. (a)(b)(c)(d) ; 19. A - (p)(q)(r)(s); B - (p)(q)(r)(s); C - (p)(q)(r)(s); D - (p)(q)(r)(s)	
20. A - (p)(q)(r)(s); B - (p)(q)(r)(s); C - (p)(q)(r)(s); D - (p)(q)(r)(s)	

DAILY PRACTICE PROBLEM DPP CHAPTERWISE 5 - CHEMISTRY

Total Questions	20	Total Marks	74
Attempted		Correct	
Incorrect		Net Score	
Cut-off Score	26	Qualifying Score	37
Success Gap = Net Score – Qualifying Score			
Net Score = (Correct × 4) – (Incorrect × 1)			

Date :   **Start Time :**   **End Time :**

CHEMISTRY $\boxed{\text{CC06}}$

SYLLABUS : Thermodynamics

Max. Marks : 74   **Time : 60 min.**

GENERAL INSTRUCTIONS

- The Daily Practice Problem Sheet contains 20 Questions divided into 5 sections.
  Section I has **5** MCQs with ONLY 1 Correct Option, **3** marks for each correct answer and **−1** for each incorrect answer.
  Section II has **4** MCQs with ONE or MORE THAN ONE Correct options.
  For each question, marks will be awarded in one of the following categories:
  Full marks: **+4** If only the bubble(s) corresponding to all the correct option(s) is (are) darkened.
  Partial marks: **+1** For darkening a bubble corresponding to each correct option provided NO INCORRECT option is darkened.
  Zero marks: If none of the bubbles is darkened.
  Negative marks: **−2** In all other cases.
  Section III has **5** Single Digit Integer Answer Type Questions, **3** marks for each Correct Answer and 0 marks in all other cases.
  Section IV has Comprehension/Matching Cum-Comprehension Type Questions having **5** MCQs with ONLY ONE correct option, **3** marks for each Correct Answer and 0 marks in all other cases.
  Section V has **1** Matching Type Questions, **2** mark for the correct matching of each row and 0 marks in all other cases.
- You have to evaluate your Response Grids yourself with the help of Solutions.

Section I - Straight Objective Type

This section contains 5 multiple choice questions. Each question has 4 choices (a), (b), (c) and (d), out of which **ONLY ONE** is correct.

1. The $\Delta_f H^\circ$ for $CO_2(g)$, $CO(g)$ and $H_2O(g)$ are −393.5, −110.5 and −241.8 kJ/mol respectively, the standard enthalpy change (in kJ) for the reaction
$$CO_2(g) + H_2(g) \rightarrow CO(g) + H_2O(g) \text{ is :}$$
   (a) 524.1   (b) 41.2   (c) −262.5   (d) −41.2

2. The heats of atomization of $PH_3(g)$ and $P_2H_4(g)$ are 954 kJ mol^{-1} and 1485 kJ mol^{-1} respectively. The P−P bond energy in kJ mol^{-1} is
   (a) 213   (b) 426   (c) 318   (d) 1272

3. 2 mole of an ideal gas at 27°C temperature is expanded reversibly from 2L to 20L. Find the entropy change $(R = 2 \text{ cal/mol K})$
   (a) 92.1   (b) 0   (c) 4   (d) 9.2

4. The molar heat capacity (C_p) of CD_2O is 10 cals at 1000 K. The change in entropy associated with cooling of 32 g of CD_2O vapour from 1000 K to 100 K at constant pressure will be: (D = deuterium, atomic mass = 2 u)
   (a) 23.03 cal deg^{-1} (b) −23.03 cal deg^{-1}
   (c) 2.303 cal deg^{-1} (d) −2.303 cal deg^{-1}

RESPONSE GRID	1. ⓐⓑⓒⓓ	2. ⓐⓑⓒⓓ	3. ⓐⓑⓒⓓ	4. ⓐⓑⓒⓓ

5. Given :

(I) $H_2(g) + \dfrac{1}{2}O_2(g) \rightarrow H_2O(l)$;

$\Delta H^\circ_{298K} = -285.9 \text{ kJ mol}^{-1}$

(II) $H_2(g) + \dfrac{1}{2}O_2(g) \rightarrow H_2O(g)$;

$\Delta H^\circ_{298K} = -241.8 \text{ kJ mol}^{-1}$

The molar enthalpy of vapourisation of water will be :

(a) $241.8 \text{ kJ mol}^{-1}$ (b) 22.0 kJ mol^{-1}

(c) 44.1 kJ mol^{-1} (d) $527.7 \text{ kJ mol}^{-1}$

Section II - Multiple Correct Answer Type

This section contains 4 multiple correct answer(s) type questions. Each question has 4 choices (a), (b), (c) and (d), out of which **ONE OR MORE** is/are correct.

6. The value of enthalpy change (ΔH) for the reaction

$C_2H_5OH(l) + 3O_2(g) \rightarrow 2CO_2(g) + 3H_2O(l)$

at 27° C is $-1366.5 \text{ kJ mol}^{-1}$. The value of internal energy change for the above reaction at this temperature will be :

(a) -1369.0 kJ (b) -1364.0 kJ

(c) -1361.5 kJ (d) -1371.5 kJ

7. On the basis of the following graph (*P–V* graph), choose the correct statements.

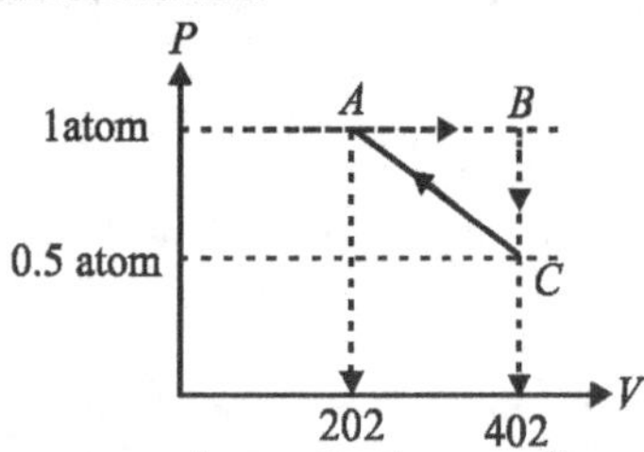

(a) The entropy change for the over all process is zero.

(b) For the over all process $\Delta H > \Delta E$.

(c) Total work done, $W = q$

(d) Total work $= -620.77 \text{ J}$

8. Which of the following are correct for an isothermal reversible expansion of an ideal gas

(a) $\Delta E = 0$ (b) $\Delta H = 0$

(c) $W = nRT ln \dfrac{P_1}{P_2}$ (d) $W = -q$

9. Enthapy of atomization of $C_2H_6(g)$ and $C_3H_8(g)$ are 620 and 880 kJmol^{-1} respectively. The C – C and C – H bond energies are respectively

(a) 80 and 60 kJmol^{-1} (b) 80 and 90 kJmol^{-1}

(c) 70 and 90 kJmol^{-1} (d) 100 and 80 kJmol^{-1}

Section III - Integer Type

This section contains 5 questions. The answer to each of the questions is a single digit integer ranging from 0 to 9.

10. $\Delta_f H^\ominus$ of hypothetical MgCl is -125 kJ mol^{-1} and for $MgCl_2$ is -642 kJ mol^{-1}. The enthalpy of disproportionation of MgCl is $-49x$. Find the value of x.

11. The lattice energy of solid KCl is $181 \text{ kcal mol}^{-1}$ and the enthalpy of solution of KCl in H_2O is $1.0 \text{ kcal mol}^{-1}$. If the hydration enthalpies of K^+ and Cl^- ions are in the ratio of 2 : 1 then the enthalpy of hydration of K^+ is $-20x \text{ k cal mol}^{-1}$. Find the value of x.

12. A heated iron block at 127°C loses 300 J of heat to the surroundings which are at a temperature of 27°. This process is $0.05x \text{ JK}^{-1}$. Find the value of x.

13. An intimate mixture of ferric oxide, Fe_2O_3, and aluminium, Al, is used in solid fuel rockets. Calculate the fuel value per gram and fuel value per cc of the mixture. Heats of formation and densities are as follows :

$H_f(Al_2O_3) = 399 \text{ kcal/mol}$;

$H_f(Fe_2O_3) = 199 \text{ kcal/mol}$;

Density of $Fe_2O_3 = 5.2 \text{ g/cc}$;

Density of Al $= 2.7 \text{ g/cc}$.

14. An insulated container contains 1 mole of a liquid, molar volume 100 mL, at 1 bar. When liquid is steeply pressed to 100 bar, volume decreases to 99 mL. Find the value of

$\dfrac{\Delta H + \Delta U}{1000} - 2$.

RESPONSE GRID	**5.** ⓐⓑⓒⓓ	**6.** ⓐⓑⓒⓓ	**7.** ⓐⓑⓒⓓ	**8.** ⓐⓑⓒⓓ	**9.** ⓐⓑⓒⓓ

RESPONSE GRID

5. ⓐⓑⓒⓓ   6. ⓐⓑⓒⓓ   7. ⓐⓑⓒⓓ   8. ⓐⓑⓒⓓ   9. ⓐⓑⓒⓓ

10. ⓪①②③④⑤⑥⑦⑧⑨   11. ⓪①②③④⑤⑥⑦⑧⑨

12. ⓪①②③④⑤⑥⑦⑧⑨   13. ⓪①②③④⑤⑥⑦⑧⑨

14. ⓪①②③④⑤⑥⑦⑧⑨

Section IV - Comprehension Type

Directions (Qs. 15-19) : Based upon the given paragraphs, 5 multiple choice questions have to be answered. Each question has 4 choices (a), (b), (c) and (d), out of which **ONLY ONE** is correct.

PARAGRAPH-1

For an ideal gas, four different paths A, D (B + C) and D + E, from an initial state P_1, V_1, T_1 to a final state P_2, V_2, T_1 is shown in the given figure.

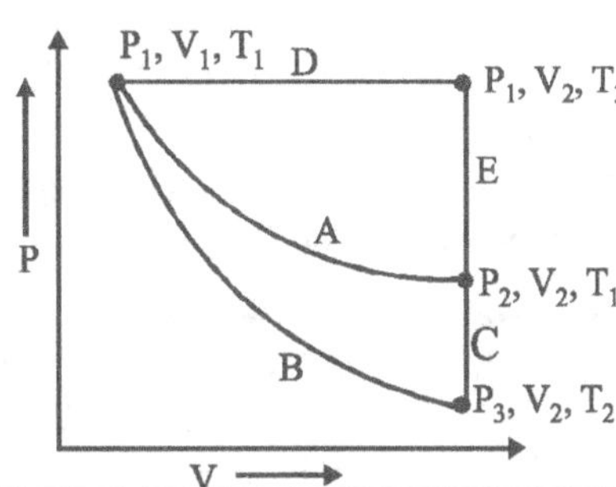

	Column I Path		Column II Path presentation		Column III $q_{reversible}$
(I)	A	(i)	Reversible adiabatic expansion followed by reversible heating at constant volume	(P)	Zero
(II)	B+C	(ii)	Reversible expansion at constant pressure followed by a reversible cooling at constant volume	(Q)	$P_1 (V_2 - V_1)$
(III)	D+E	(iii)	Reversible expansion at constant pressure	(R)	$-nRT_1, \ln \dfrac{V_2}{V_1}$
(IV)	D	(iv)	Reversible isothermal expansion	(S)	$-nR, \ln \dfrac{V_2}{V_1}$

15. Find combination, which represents the q_{rev}, for path (a)

(a) (I)(iii)(S) (b) (I)(iv)(R)

(c) (I)(i)(Q) (d) (I)(ii)(P)

16. q_{rev}, for path (B + C) represented by

(a) (II)(ii)(R) (b) (II)(iv)(S)

(c) (IV)(i)(Q) (d) (II)(i)(S)

17. What is q_{rev}, for path (D + E) ?

(a) (IV)(iii)(S) (b) (III)(i)(P)

(c) (III)(ii)(Q) (d) (III)(iv)(R)

PARAGRAPH-2

Entropy changes for ideal gas are as follows:

(i) Entropy change is terms of temperature and volume is given by

<table><tr><td>RESPONSE
GRID</td><td>15. ⓐⓑⓒⓓ   16. ⓐⓑⓒⓓ   17. ⓐⓑⓒⓓ</td></tr></table>

———————————————— *Space for Rough Work* ————————————————

$$\Delta S = nC_v ln \frac{T_2}{T_1} + nR ln \frac{V_2}{V_1}$$

It is for n moles of an ideal gas from V_1 to V_2 when temperature changes from T_1 to T_2. C_v is the heat capacity at constant volume.

(ii) Entropy change in terms of temperature and pressure:

$$\Delta S = nC_p ln \frac{T_2}{T_1} + nR ln \frac{P_2}{P_1} \quad \text{(For } n \text{ moles of gas)}$$

C_p is the molar heat capacity at constant pressure.

18. The entropy change for expansion of 14 g of nitrogen when heated from 27°C to 127°C at constant volume and constant pressure will be (in cal/degree) respectively.
(Given, $C_v = 4.94$ cal/mol in this temperature range)
(a) 0.70, 0.99   (b) 0.99, 0.70
(c) 0.50, 0.70   (d) 0.70, 0.50

19. When two moles of an ideal gas $\left(C_{p,m} = \frac{5}{2}R \right)$ is heated from 300K to 600K at constant pressure, the value of ΔS is
(a) $\frac{3}{2}R ln2$ (b) $-\frac{3}{2}R ln2$
(c) $5 R ln2$ (d) $\frac{5}{2}R ln2$

Section V - Matrix-Match Type

This section contains 1 questions. It contains statements given in two columns, which have to be matched. Statements in column I are labelled as A, B, C and D whereas statements in column II are labelled as p, q, r and s. The answers to these questions have to be appropriately bubbled as illustrated in the following example. If the correct matches are A-p, A-r, B-p, B-s, C-r, C-s and D-q, then the correctly bubbled matrix will look like the following:

	p	q	r	s
A	ⓟ	ⓠ	ⓡ	ⓢ
B	ⓟ	ⓠ	ⓡ	ⓢ
C	ⓟ	ⓠ	ⓡ	ⓢ
D	ⓟ	ⓠ	ⓡ	ⓢ

20. **Match the following:**

Column I	Column II
(A) $\Delta S_{Total} = 0$	p. Adiabatic
(B) $\Delta S_{System} = R \ln \frac{V_2}{V_1}$	q. Reversible Process
(C) $\mu_{J.T.} = 0$	r. Perfect gas
(D) $PV^\gamma = $ a constant	s. Isothermal process

<table>
<tr><td rowspan="2">RESPONSE GRID</td><td>18. ⓐⓑⓒⓓ   19. ⓐⓑⓒⓓ</td></tr>
<tr><td>20. A - ⓟⓠⓡⓢ; B - ⓟⓠⓡⓢ; C - ⓟⓠⓡⓢ; D - ⓟⓠⓡⓢ</td></tr>
</table>

DAILY PRACTICE PROBLEM DPP CHAPTERWISE 6 - CHEMISTRY

Total Questions	20	Total Marks	74
Attempted		Correct	
Incorrect		Net Score	
Cut-off Score	24	Qualifying Score	35
Success Gap = Net Score – Qualifying Score			
Net Score = (Correct × 4) – (Incorrect × 1)			

DPP - Daily Practice Problems

Chapter-wise Sheets

Date :   Start Time :   End Time :

CHEMISTRY $\boxed{\text{CC07}}$

SYLLABUS : Equilibrium

Max. Marks : 74   **Time : 60 min.**

Section I - Straight Objective Type

This section contains 5 multiple choice questions. Each question has 4 choices (a), (b), (c) and (d), out of which **ONLY ONE** is correct.

1. The degree of hydrolysis in hydrolytic equilibrium

$$A^- + H_2O \rightleftharpoons HA + OH^-$$

at salt concentration of 0.001 M is : $(K_a = 1 \times 10^{-5})$

(a) 1×10^{-3} (b) 1×10^{-4} (c) 5×10^{-4} (d) 1×10^{-6}

2. The equilibrium constants K_{p_1} and K_{p_2} for the reactions $X \rightleftharpoons 2Y$ and $Z \rightleftharpoons P + Q$, respectively are in the ratio of $1 : 9$. If the degree of dissociation of X and Z be equal then the ratio of total pressures at these equilibria is

(a) $1:36$ (b) $1:1$
(c) $1:3$ (d) $1:9$

RESPONSE GRID	1. ⓐⓑⓒⓓ 2. ⓐⓑⓒⓓ

Space for Rough Work

3. K_1, K_2 and K_3 are the equilibrium constants of the following reactions (I), (II) and (III) respectively:

(I) $N_2 + 2O_2 \rightleftharpoons 2NO_2$

(II) $2NO_2 \rightleftharpoons N_2 + 2O_2$

(III) $NO_2 \rightleftharpoons \dfrac{1}{2}N_2 + O_2$

The correct relation from the following is

(a) $K_1 = \dfrac{1}{K_2} = \dfrac{1}{K_3}$ (b) $K_1 = \dfrac{1}{K_2} = \dfrac{1}{(K_3)^2}$

(c) $K_1 = \sqrt{K_2} = K_3$ (d) $K_1 = \dfrac{1}{K_2} = K_3$

4. Which one of the following arrangements represents the correct order of solubilities of sparingly soluble salts Hg_2Cl_2, $Cr_2(SO_4)_3$, $BaSO_4$ and $CrCl_3$ respectively?

(a) $BaSO_4 > Hg_2Cl_2 > Cr_2(SO_4)_3 > CrCl_3$

(b) $BaSO_4 > Hg_2Cl_2 > CrCl_3 > Cr_2(SO_4)_3$

(c) $BaSO_4 > CrCl_3 > Hg_2Cl_2 > Cr_2(SO_4)_3$

(d) $Hg_2Cl_2 > BaSO_4 > CrCl_3 > Cr_2(SO_4)_3$

5. For the decomposition of the compound, represented as

$$NH_2COONH_4(s) \rightleftharpoons 2NH_3(g) + CO_2(g)$$

the $K_p = 2.9 \times 10^{-5}\,atm^3$.

If the reaction is started with 1 mole of the compound, the total pressure at equilibrium would be :

(a) $1.94 \times 10^{-2}\,atm$ (b) $5.82 \times 10^{-2}\,atm$

(c) $7.66 \times 10^{-2}\,atm$ (d) $38.8 \times 10^{-2}\,atm$

Section II - Multiple Correct Answer Type

This section contains 4 multiple correct answer(s) type questions. Each question has 4 choices (a), (b), (c) and (d), out of which **ONE OR MORE** is/are correct.

6. Which of the following solutions will be neutral?

(a)   50 mL of 0.1 M CH_3COOH + 50 mL of 0.1 M NaOH

(b)   100 mL of 0.1M CH_3COOH + 50 mL of 0.2 M NH_3

(c)   100 mL of 0.1M HCl + 50 mL of 0.2 M KOH

(d)   50 mL of 0.1 M HCl + 50 mL of 0.1 M NH_3

7. In which of the following solutions the use of equilibrium constant(s), mentioned in each case, permits the calculation of pH?

(a)   0.1 M each of NH_3 and NH_4Cl in the mixture : K_b of NH_3

(b)   0.1 M NH_3 : K_b of NH_3, K_w

(c)   A solution 0.1 M in CH_3COOH and 0.2 M CH_3COONa : K_a of CH_3COOH

(d)   0.1 M CH_3COONa : K_a of CH_3COOH, K_w

8. For the following equilibrium :

$$NH_2COONH_{4(s)} \rightleftharpoons 2NH_{3(g)} + CO_{2(g)}$$

partial pressure of NH_3 will increase if

(a) $NH_2COONH_{4(s)}$ is added to the system at equilibrium

(b) $NH_{3(g)}$ is added to the system

(c) $CO_{2(g)}$ is added to the system

(d)   temperature of the system is raised

9. If α is neglible as compared to 1 for the following reaction $XY_2(g) \rightleftharpoons XY(g) + Y(g)$

The degree of dissociation (α) for the above reaction is

(a)   directly proportional to square root of V.

(b)   inversely proportional to V.

(c)   inversely proportional to P.

(d)   inversely proportional to square root of P.

Section III - Integer Type

This section contains 5 questions. The answer to each of the questions is a single digit integer ranging from 0 to 9.

10. For the reaction : $SnO_2(s) + 2H_2(g) \rightleftharpoons 2H_2O(g) + Sn(s)$
Calculate $2 \times K_p$ at 900 K where the equilibrium steam hydrogen mixture was 45% H_2 by volume.

11. 16 moles of H_2 and 4 moles of N_2 are sealed in a one litre vessel. The vessel is heated at a constant temperature until the equilibrium is established, it is found that the pressure in the vessel has fallen to 9/10 of its original value. If K_C for the reaction

$$N_2(g) + 3H_2(g) \rightleftharpoons 2NH_3(g)$$

will be $y \times 10^{-z}$ what will be the value of z?

Space for Rough Work

12. 0.1 M NaOH is titrated with 0.1 M HA till the end point; K_a for HA is 5.6×10^{-6} and degree of hydrolysis is less compared to 1. Calculate pH of the resulting solution at the end point.

13. If the approximate pH of a 1×10^{-3} M NaOH solution is $15 - x$ then what will be the value of x?

14. Calculate the pOH of a solution at 25°C that contains 1×10^{-10} M of hydronium ions, i.e. H_3O^+.

Section IV - Comprehension Type

Directions (Qs. 15-19) : Based upon the given paragraphs, 4 multiple choice questions have to be answered. Each question has 4 choices (a), (b), (c) and (d), out of which **ONLY ONE** is correct.

PARAGRAPH-1

Column I, II & III contain different salts, hydrolysis constant and pH of solution respectively.

Column I		Column II		Column III
(I) KCl, NaNO$_2$, Na$_2$SO$_4$, BaCl$_2$ etc	(i)	$K_h = \dfrac{K_w}{K_b}$	(P)	pH $= 7 + \dfrac{1}{2}(pK_a + \log C)$
(II) CH$_3$COONa, Na$_2$CO$_3$, KCN etc	(ii)	do not undergo hydrolysis	(Q)	pH $= 7 + \dfrac{1}{2}(pK_a - pK_b)$
(III) NH$_4$Cl, ZnCl$_2$, FeCl$_3$ etc	(iii)	$K_h = \dfrac{K_w}{K_a}$	(R)	pH $= 7$
(IV) CH$_3$COONH$_4$, NH$_4$CN etc	(iv)	$K_h = \dfrac{h^2}{(1-h)^2}$	(S)	pH $= 7 - \dfrac{1}{2}(pK_b + \log C)$

15. For the salts of strong acid and strong base the only correct combination is
- (a) (III)(ii)(Q)
- (b) (IV)(ii)(P)
- (c) (I)(ii)(R)
- (d) (I)(iv)(S)

16. For the salts of weak base and strong acid the only correct combination is
- (a) (III)(i)(S)
- (b) (I)(i)(Q)
- (c) (IV)(ii)(P)
- (d) (III)(iv)(Q)

17. For the salts of weak acid and weak base the only correct combination is
- (a) (II)(i)(R)
- (b) (III)(ii)(S)
- (c) (IV)(iii)(R)
- (d) (IV)(iv)(Q)

PARAGRAPH-2

There are three different ways of expressing the equilibrium constant for a system of ideal gases.

(i) in terms of partial pressure (K_p)

(ii) in terms of concentration (K_c)

(iii) in terms of mole fracion (K_x)

For the general equilibrium reaction

$$n_1A + n_2B \rightleftharpoons m_1C + m_2D$$

$$K_p = \frac{P_C^{m_1} \times P_D^{m_2}}{P_A^{n_1} \times P_B^{n_2}} \qquad K_c = \frac{[C]^{m_1} \times [D]^{m_2}}{[A]^{n_1} \times [B]^{n_2}}$$

Space for Rough Work

$$K_x = \frac{X_c^{m_1} \times X_D^{m_2}}{X_A^{n_1} \times X_B^{n_2}}$$

Relationship between K_p, K_c and K_x

$$K_p = K_c (RT)^{\Delta n} \qquad K_x = K_p . P^{-\Delta n}$$

or $K_p = K_x (P)^{\Delta n}$

[Δn = difference in number of moles of gaseous products and gaseous reactants]

18. A and B were mixed in a vessel at 25°C. The following equilibrium was established

$$A + B \rightleftharpoons C + D$$

The initial concentration of A was twice the initial concentration of B. At equilibrium, the concentration of C was three times the concentration of B. The value of K for this reaction is

(a) 1.5   (b) 1.8

(c) 2.1   (d) 2.4

19. 0.02 g of hydrogen and 2.54 g of iodine are allowed to react to equilibrium at 460°C. On analysis the equilibrium mixture is found to contain 0.0021 moles of iodine. The value of K_c for the reaction is

(a) 46   (b) 128

(c) 56.6   (d) 21

Section V - Matrix-Match Type

This section contains 1 question. It contains statements given in two columns, which have to be matched. Statements in column I are labelled as A, B, C and D whereas statements in column II are labelled as p, q, r and s. The answers to these questions have to be appropriately bubbled as illustrated in the following example. If the correct matches are A-p, A-r, B-p, B-s, C-r, C-s and D-q, then the correctly bubbled matrix will look like the following:

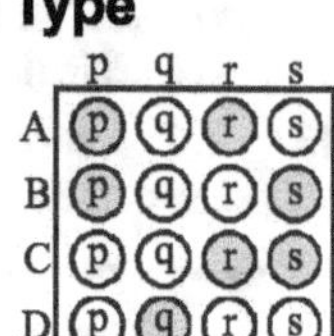

20. K_a and K_b are the dissociation constants of weak acid and weak base and K_w is the ionic product of water. Match the pH stated in column II with the solutions listed in column I at 25°C.

Column I - (Solution)	Column II - (pH)
(A) 0.1 M KCN	p. 7
(B) 0.1 M $C_6H_5NH_3Cl$	q. $6.5 + \frac{1}{2}pK_a$
(C) 0.1 M KCl	r. $7.5 - \frac{1}{2}pK_b$
(D) 0.1 M CH_3COONH_4	s. $7 + \frac{1}{2}pK_a - \frac{1}{2}pK_b$

DAILY PRACTICE PROBLEM DPP CHAPTERWISE 7 - CHEMISTRY

Total Questions	20	Total Marks	74
Attempted		Correct	
Incorrect		Net Score	
Cut-off Score	24	Qualifying Score	35
Success Gap = Net Score – Qualifying Score			
Net Score = (Correct × 4) – (Incorrect × 1)			

Space for Rough Work

DPP - Daily Practice Problems

Chapter-wise Sheets

Date :	Start Time :	End Time :

CHEMISTRY $\boxed{\text{CC08}}$

SYLLABUS : Hydrogen and s-Block Elements

Max. Marks : 74 **Time : 60 min.**

Section I - Straight Objective Type

This section contains 6 multiple choice questions. Each question has 4 choices (a), (b), (c) and (d), out of which **ONLY ONE** is correct.

1. Gradual addition of potassium iodide solution to $Bi(NO_3)_3$ solution initially produces a dark brown precipitate which dissolves in excess of KI to give a clear yellow solution. Identify the yellow precipitate.

   (a) I_2 (b) KI_3
   (c) $Bi(OH)_2$ (d) $Bi(OH)(NO_3)_2$

2. Which of the following is neither deliquescent nor efflorescent and is used for wool washing ?

   (a) NaOH (b) KOH
   (c) $NaHCO_3$ (d) $Na_2CO_3.NaHCO_3.2H_2O$

3. A metal M on heating in nitrogen gas gives Y. Y on treatment with H_2O gives a colourless gas which when passed through $CuSO_4$ solution gives a blue colour. Y is

   (a) NH_3 (b) $Mg(NO_3)_2$
   (c) Mg_3N_2 (d) MgO

RESPONSE GRID	1. ⓐⓑⓒⓓ	2. ⓐⓑⓒⓓ	3. ⓐⓑⓒⓓ

Space for Rough Work

4. An unknown inorganic compound (X) loses its water of crystallization on heating and its aqueous solution gives the following reactions :

(a) It gives a white turbidity with dilute HCl solution

(b) It decolourises a solution of iodine in potassium iodide

(c) It gives a white precipitate with silver nitrate solution which turns black on standing.

Identify the compound (X)

(a) $Na_2CO_3.10H_2O$ (b) $Na_2S_2O_3.5H_2O$

(c) $Na_2SO_4.10H_2O$ (d) None of these

5. On being placed in water, sodium peroxide not only produces an alkaline solution but also some bubbles. If we assume that the peroxide ion picks up two protons from water to produce a compound that can be seen as the dibasic conjugate acid of peroxide ion and then this compound undergoes a redox disproportion.

Using the above information complete the following equation.

$$Na_2O_2(s) + H_2O(l) \longrightarrow (A) + (B)$$

(A) and (B) are

(a) H_2O_2 and NaOH   (b) H_2O and O_2

(c) NaOH and O_2 (d) Na_2O and NaOH

6. The solubilities of carbonates decrease down the group due to a decrease in

(a) hydration energies of cations

(b) inter-ionic attraction

(c) entropy of solution formation

(d) lattice energies of solids

Section II - Multiple Correct Answer Type

This section contains 4 multiple correct answer(s) type questions. Each question has 4 choices (a), (b), (c) and (d), out of which **ONE OR MORE** is/are correct.

7. Select the correct statement.

(a) Microcosmic salt is $Na(NH_4).HPO_4.4H_2O$

(b) Microcosmic salt is prepared by dissolving molecular proportion of Na_2HPO_4 and NH_4Cl in water and crystallizing the contents.

(c) Microcosmic salt is used for detecting coloured ions in qualitative inorganic analysis

(d) Microcosmic salt is a blue crystalline salt.

8. x g of H_2O_2 requires 100 mL of M/5 $KMnO_4$ in a titration in a solution having pOH = 1.0

Which of the following is/are correct?

(a) The value of x is 1.7 g.

(b) The value of x is 0.34 g.

(c) MnO_4^- changes to MnO_4^{2-}.

(d) H_2O_2 changes to O_2.

9. 20 mL of H_2O_2 is reacted completely with acidified $K_2Cr_2O_7$ solution. 40 mL of $K_2Cr_2O_7$ solution is required to oxidise the H_2O_2 completely. Also, 2.0 mL of the same $K_2Cr_2O_7$ solution is required to oxidise 5.0 mL of a 1.0M $H_2C_2O_4$ solution to reach equivalence point. Which of the following statements is/are correct?

(a) The H_2O_2 solution is 5M.

(b) The volume strength of H_2O_2 is 56V.

(c) The volume strength of H_2O_2 is 112V.

(d) If 40 mL more 5M/8 H_2O_2 is further added to the 10 mL more H_2O_2 solution, the volume strength of the resulting solution is changed to 16.8 V.

<table>
<tr><td rowspan="2">**RESPONSE GRID**</td><td>**4.** ⓐⓑⓒⓓ</td><td>**5.** ⓐⓑⓒⓓ</td><td>**6.** ⓐⓑⓒⓓ</td><td>**7.** ⓐⓑⓒⓓ</td><td>**8.** ⓐⓑⓒⓓ</td></tr>
<tr><td>**9.** ⓐⓑⓒⓓ</td><td></td><td></td><td></td><td></td></tr>
</table>

10. Anhydrous barium nitrate when heated decomposes and oxygen and NO_2 gas is evolved. Similarly magnesium nitrate when heated decomposes to give out NO_2 gas and oxygen. In both cases corresponding oxides are also formed. Select the correct answer(s) :

   (a) The lattice energy value is higher for magnesium nitrate than that of barium nitrate

   (b) NO_2 will be evolved at a lower temperature in case of $Mg(NO_3)_2$ as compared to that $Ba(NO_3)_2$

   (c) NO_2 will be evolved at a lower temperature in case of $Ba(NO_3)_2$ as compared to that of $Mg(NO_3)_2$

   (d) In both cases [i.e., heating of $Mg(NO_3)_2$] the ratio of volume of NO_2 and O_2 evolved is 4 : 1

Section III - Integer Type

This section contains 4 questions. The answer to each of the questions is a single digit integer ranging from 0 to 9.

11. Copper sulphate reacts with NaCN to form a cyanide complex. Write the balanced equation and find the number of NaCN molecules involved in the equation for one mole of $CuSO_4$.

12. Calculate heat of solution of NaCl from the following data:

   Hydration energy of $Na^+ = -389\ kJ\ mol^{-1}$

   Hydration energy of $Cl^- = -382\ kJ\ mol^{-1}$

   Lattice energy of NaCl $= -776\ kJ\ mol^{-1}$

13. On heating 8 moles each of Li_2CO_3 and K_2CO_3, how many moles of CO_2 evolved?

14. Calcium carbide reacts with nitrogen and forms an important fertiliser, calcium cyanamide. How much calcium cyanamide is formed when 6.4 g of calcium carbide is completely converted into cyanamide?

Section IV - Comprehension Type

Directions (Qs. 15-18) : Based upon the given paragraphs, 4 multiple choice questions have to be answered. Each question has 4 choices (a), (b), (c) and (d), out of which **ONLY ONE** is correct.

PARAGRAPH-1

The thermal stability of the salts of the s-block elements is dependent upon three main factors. Firstly, the greater the charge of the ions involved, the stronger the interionic attraction and the more stable the salt. Also, the smaller the ions become in terms of their ionic radii the closer they approach each other in the crystal lattice of their salts and the more stable the salt. Thirdly, if the ions in the lattice are of comparable size, the crystal lattice is arranged in a more uniform fashion and thus possesses greater thermal stability. There is one other factor that affects thermal stability. The larger the anions in the crystal become, for example CO_3^{2-}, unless the cation is of comparable size, the anions decompose on heating to give smaller anions such as O^{2-}. This point is especially important when considering the thermal stability of the carbonates, nitrates and hydroxides of the s-block elements.

An unknown s-block salt was uncovered at the landing site of a meteor. When converted to its hydroxide, it was found that the K_b of the salt was 1.0×10^{-6}. It did not decompose to the oxide. The metal obtained exhibited the typical properties of most s-block metals:- ductile, malleable, lustre, good electrical and thermal conductivity and a high reactivity. The original salt obtained from the meteor possessed a complex formula and the metal itself had a high molecular weight.

15. When s-block carbonates decompose, a gas is obtained which is heavier than air and does not support a lighted splint. What gas is it?
   (a) O_2 (b) CO   (c) CO_2 (d) CO_3

16. What would be the pH of a 1.0 M solution of the unknown salt hydroxide given that the metal is monovalent?
   (a) 11   (b) 8.0   (c) 7.5   (d) 13.0

RESPONSE GRID	10. ⓐⓑⓒⓓ 11. ⓪①②③④⑤⑥⑦⑧⑨ 12. ⓪①②③④⑤⑥⑦⑧⑨	
	13. ⓪①②③④⑤⑥⑦⑧⑨ 14. ⓪①②③④⑤⑥⑦⑧⑨ 15. ⓐⓑⓒⓓ	
	16. ⓐⓑⓒⓓ	

PARAGRAPH-2

'A' burns in nitrogen and forms 'B'
(Element)   (Ionic Compound)

$'B' + H_2O \longrightarrow 'C' + 'D'$
(Ionic Compound)

$'C'(aq) + CO_2 \longrightarrow$ milkiness appears.

Consider the above information and answer the following questions

17. The element 'A' is
   (a) Alkali metal
   (b) alkaline earth metal
   (c) Magnesium
   (d) Barium

18. The compound 'C' is
   (a) Mg_3N_2
   (b) $Mg(OH)_2$
   (c) $Ca(OH)_2$
   (d) $Ba(OH)_2$

Section V - Matrix-Match Type

This section contains 2 questions. It contains statements given in two columns, which have to be matched. Statements in column I are labelled as A, B, C and D whereas statements in column II are labelled as p, q, r and s. The answers to these questions have to be appropriately bubbled as illustrated in the following example. If the correct matches are A-p, A-r, B-p, B-s, C-r, C-s and D-q, then the correctly bubbled matrix will look like the following:

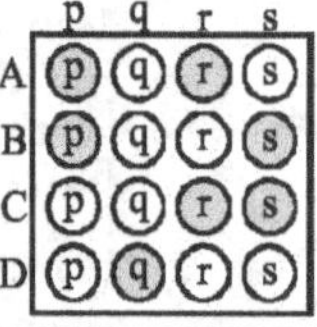

19. **Column I**   **Column II**
   (A) Complex Formation   p. Be
   (B) Formation of covalent compounds   q. Mg
   (C) High solubility of salts   r. Ca
   (D) Explosive reaction with acids   s. Sr

20. **Column - I**   **Column - II**
   (A) It is amphoteric in nature   p. BeC_2
   (B) Liberate methane on reaction with water q. Al_2O_3
   (C) Behaves as Lewis acid   r. $BeCl_2$
   (D) In solid state it has a polymeric chain structure and contains three centred bonds   s. Al_4C_3

RESPONSE GRID	17. (a)(b)(c)(d) 18. (a)(b)(c)(d)
	19. A - (p)(q)(r)(s); B - (p)(q)(r)(s); C - (p)(q)(r)(s); D - (p)(q)(r)(s)
	20. A - (p)(q)(r)(s); B - (p)(q)(r)(s); C - (p)(q)(r)(s); D - (p)(q)(r)(s)

DAILY PRACTICE PROBLEM DPP CHAPTERWISE 8 - CHEMISTRY

Total Questions	20	Total Marks	74
Attempted		Correct	
Incorrect		Net Score	
Cut-off Score	27	Qualifying Score	37
Success Gap = Net Score – Qualifying Score			
Net Score = (Correct × 4) – (Incorrect × 1)			

Date :   **Start Time :**   **End Time :**

CHEMISTRY $\boxed{\text{CC09}}$

SYLLABUS : The p-Block Elements (Group 13 and 14)

Max. Marks : 74   **Time : 60 min.**

GENERAL INSTRUCTIONS

- The Daily Practice Problem Sheet contains 20 Questions divided into 5 sections.

Section I has **6** MCQs with ONLY 1 Correct Option, **3** marks for each correct answer and **−1** for each incorrect answer.

Section II has **4** MCQs with ONE or MORE THAN ONE Correct options.

For each question, marks will be awarded in one of the following categories:

Full marks: **+4** If only the bubble(s) corresponding to all the correct option(s) is (are) darkened.

Partial marks: **+1** For darkening a bubble corresponding to each correct option provided NO INCORRECT option is darkened.

Zero marks: If none of the bubbles is darkened.

Negative marks: **−2** In all other cases.

Section III has **4** Single Digit Integer Answer Type Questions, **3** marks for each Correct Answer and 0 marks in all other cases.

Section IV has Comprehension/Matching Cum-Comprehension Type Questions having **4** MCQs with ONLY ONE correct option, **3** marks for each Correct Answer and 0 marks in all other cases.

Section V has **2** Matching Type Questions, **2** mark for the correct matching of each row and 0 marks in all other cases.

- You have to evaluate your Response Grids yourself with the help of Solutions.

Section I - Straight Objective Type

This section contains 6 multiple choice questions. Each question has 4 choices (a), (b), (c) and (d), out of which **ONLY ONE** is correct.

1. A certain salt (X) gives the following tests :
   (i) Its aqueous solution is alkaline to litmus.
   (ii) On strongly heating it swells to give a glassy bead
   (iii) When concentrated sulphuric acid is added to a hot concentrated solution of (X), crystals of H_3BO_3 separate out. Identify the colour of these crystals.

    (a) White   (b) Blue
    (c) Brown   (d) Violet

2. H_3BO_3 is
   (a) monobasic and weak Lewis acid
   (b) monobasic and weak Bronsted acid
   (c) monobasic and strong Lewis acid
   (d) tribasic and weak Bronsted acid

RESPONSE GRID   1. ⓐⓑⓒⓓ   2. ⓐⓑⓒⓓ

Space for Rough Work

3. Be_2C and Al_4C_3 are called
   (a) ethanides   (b) methanides
   (c) carbonides   (d) acetylides

4. On addition of excess of sodium hydroxide solution to stannous chloride solution, we obtain
   (a) $Sn(OH)_2$ (b) $SnO_2.H_2O$
   (c) Na_2SnO_2 (d) None of these

5. Among the following substituted silanes the one which will give rise to cross linked silicone polymer on hydrolysis is
   (a) R_4Si (b) R_2SiCl_2
   (c) $RSiCl_3$ (d) R_3SiCl

6. In the following sets of reactants which two sets best exhibit the amphoteric characters of $Al_2O_3. xH_2O$?

   Set 1: $Al_2O_3.xH_2O$ (s) and OH^- (aq)

   Set 2: $Al_2O_3.xH_2O$ (s) and H_2O (l)

   Set 3: $Al_2O_3.xH_2O$ (s) and H^+ (aq)

   Set 4: $Al_2O_3.xH_2O$ (s) and NH_3 (aq)

   (a) 1 and 2   (b) 1 and 3
   (c) 2 and 4   (d) 3 and 4

Section II - Multiple Correct Answer Type

This section contains 4 multiple correct answer(s) type questions. Each question has 4 choices (a), (b), (c) and (d), out of which **ONE OR MORE** is/are correct.

7. Which of the following statement(s) is/are correct ?
   (a) Boranes are volatile and decompose to boron and hydrogen at red heat
   (b) They are decomposed by water or aqueous alkali
   (c) All the boranes react with ammonia, depending on the conditions
   (d) None of the above is correct

8. Which of the following statement(s) is/are correct ?
   (a) Lead salts are slow poisons
   (b) Lead metal is used in accumulators
   (c) Plumbo-solvency increases by the presence of carbonates, sulphates, phosphates, etc.
   (d) Lead is a soft metal

9. The correct reason(s) for the acidic nature of an aqueous solution of aluminium chloride is that
   (a) for aluminium ions the, $\dfrac{\text{charge}}{\text{surface area}}$, ratio is large
   (b) the O–H bonds in $[Al(H_2O)_6]^{3+}$ are weaker as compared to the O–H bonds in water.
   (c) aluminium chloride is covalent compound and its aqueous solution is acidic.
   (d) chloride ions (Cl^-) react with water to form hydrochloric acid.

10. Which of the following statement(s) is/are correct for CO ?
    (a) CO is an important fuel
    (b) CO is poisonous gas and a neutral oxide
    (c) It can be prepared by dehydrating formic acid with conc. H_2SO_4
    (d) None of the above is correct

Section III - Integer Type

This section contains 4 questions. The answer to each of the questions is a single digit integer ranging from 0 to 9.

11. In aluminates, the coordination number of Al is

12. How many oxides of the following are non-amphoteric in nature?

    CO_2, SiO_2, SnO_2 and CaO

13. How many of the following ions does not have S – S linkage?

    $S_2O_8^{2-}$, $S_2O_6^{2-}$, $S_2O_4^{2-}$ and $S_2O_3^{2-}$

14. How much nitrogen is evolved when one gram of ammonium chloride is heated with borax strongly?

Section IV - Comprehension Type

Directions (Qs. 15-18) : Based upon the given paragraphs, 4 multiple choice questions have to be answered. Each question has 4 choices (a), (b), (c) and (d), out of which **ONLY ONE** is correct.

PARAGRAPH-1

Silicones are synthetic polymers containing repeated R_2SiO units. Since the empirical formula is that of a ketone (R_2CO), the name silicone has been given to these materials. Silicones can be made into oils, rubbery elastomers and resins. They find a variety of applications bcause of their chemical inertness, water repelling nature, heat resistance and good electrical insulating property. Commercial silicon plymers are usually methyl derivatices and to a lesser extent phenyl derivateives and are synthesised by the hydrolysis of

R_2SiCl_2 [R = Methyl (Me) or phenyl (ϕ)]

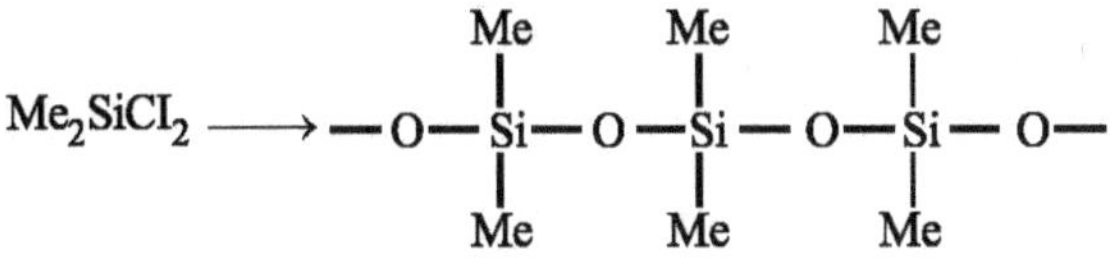

$$Me_2SiCl_2 \longrightarrow -O-\overset{\overset{\displaystyle Me}{|}}{\underset{\underset{\displaystyle Me}{|}}{Si}}-O-\overset{\overset{\displaystyle Me}{|}}{\underset{\underset{\displaystyle Me}{|}}{Si}}-O-\overset{\overset{\displaystyle Me}{|}}{\underset{\underset{\displaystyle Me}{|}}{Si}}-O-$$

15. If we mix $SiMe_3Cl$ with $SiMe_2Cl_2$, we get silicones of the type:

(a) 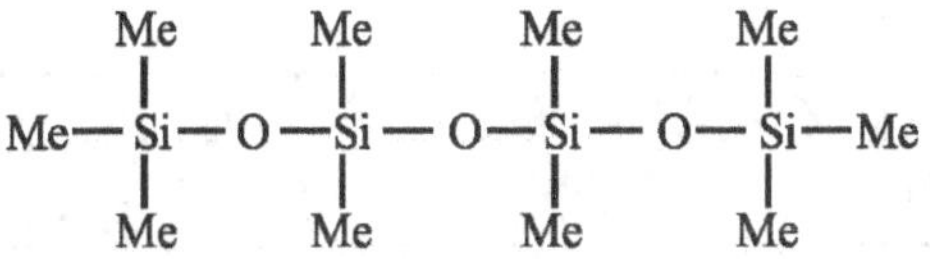 $Me-\overset{Me}{\underset{Me}{Si}}-O-\overset{Me}{\underset{Me}{Si}}-O-\overset{Me}{\underset{Me}{Si}}-O-\overset{Me}{\underset{Me}{Si}}-Me$

(b)

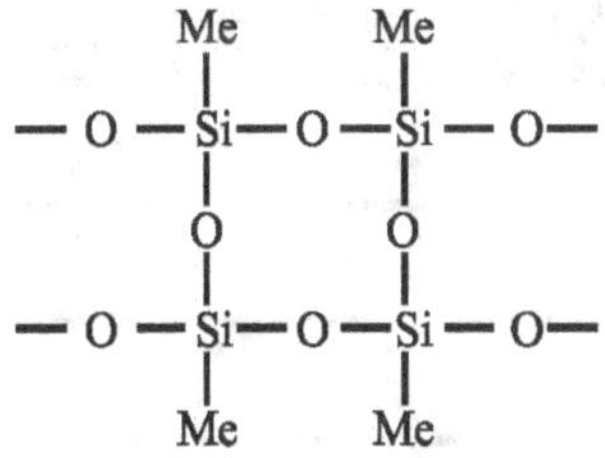

(c) Both of the above

(d) None of the above

16. If we start with $SiMeCl_3$ as the starting material, silicones formed is:

(a) 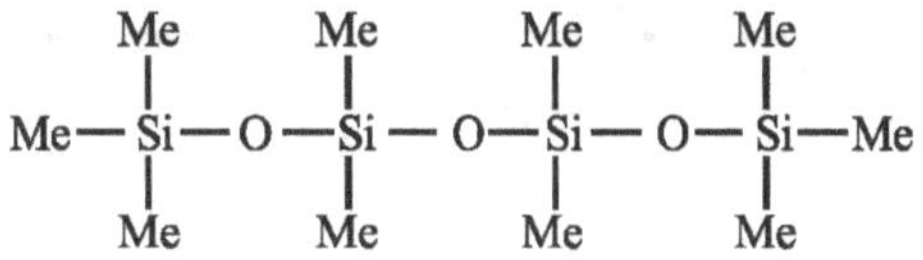 $Me-\overset{Me}{\underset{Me}{Si}}-O-\overset{Me}{\underset{Me}{Si}}-O-\overset{Me}{\underset{Me}{Si}}-O-\overset{Me}{\underset{Me}{Si}}-Me$

(b)

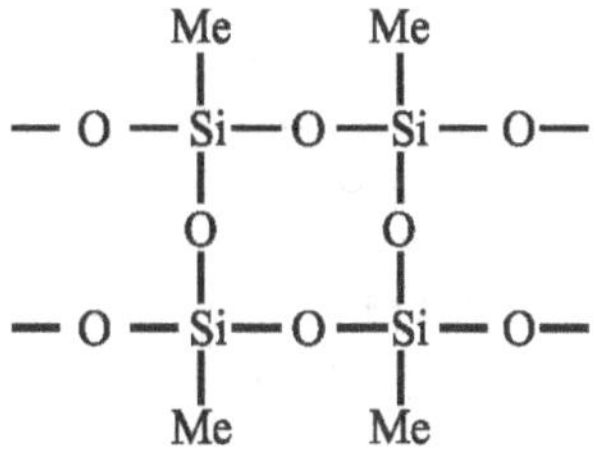

(c) Both of the above

(d) None of the above

PARAGRAPH-2

The heavier members of 13 and 14 groups besides the group oxidation state also show another oxidation state which is two units less than the group oxidation state. Down the group ($\downarrow$), the stability of higher oxidation state decreases and that of lower oxidation state increases. This concept which is commonly called inert pair effect has been used to explain many physical and chemical properties of the element of these groups.

17. Which among the following is the strongest oxidising agent?

(a) SiO_2 (b) GeO_2

(c) SnO_2 (d) PbO_2

18. The strongest reductant among the following is

(a) $SnCl_2$ (b) $SnCl_4$

(c) $PbCl_2$ (d) $GeCl_2$

Space for Rough Work

Section V - Matrix-Match Type

This section contains 2 questions. It contains statements given in two columns, which have to be matched. Statements in column I are labelled as A, B, C and D whereas statements in column II are labelled as p, q, r and s. The answers to these questions have to be appropriately bubbled as illustrated in the following example. If the correct matches are A-p, A-r, B-p, B-s, C-r, C-s and D-q, then the correctly bubbled matrix will look like the following:

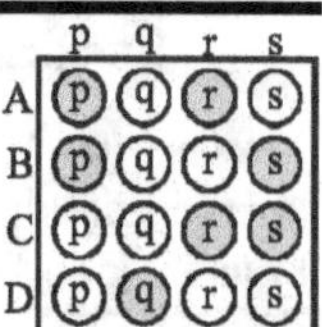

19.

	Column I		Column II
(A)	Corundum	p.	$Ca_2B_6O_{11}.5H_2O$
(B)	Cryolite	q.	$Al_2O_3.2H_2O$
(C)	Colemanite	r.	Sodium aluminium fluoride
(D)	Bauxite	s.	Al_2O_3
		t.	$Na_2B_4O_7.10H_2O$

20.

	Column I		Column II
(A)	Shows $p\pi$–$p\pi$ back bonding	p.	Graphite
(B)	Shows $p\pi$–$d\pi$ back bonding	q.	BCl_3
(C)	Lewis acid	r.	$N(SiH_3)_3$
(D)	Shows inert pair effect	s.	BF_3
		t.	Gallium

RESPONSE GRID	19. A - (p)(q)(r)(s)(t); B - (p)(q)(r)(s)(t); C - (p)(q)(r)(s)(t); D - (p)(q)(r)(s)(t)
	20. A - (p)(q)(r)(s)(t); B - (p)(q)(r)(s)(t); C - (p)(q)(r)(s)(t); D - (p)(q)(r)(s)(t)

DAILY PRACTICE PROBLEM DPP CHAPTERWISE 9 - CHEMISTRY

Total Questions	20	Total Marks	74
Attempted		Correct	
Incorrect		Net Score	
Cut-off Score	25	Qualifying Score	37
Success Gap = Net Score − Qualifying Score			
Net Score = (Correct × 4) − (Incorrect × 1)			

DPP - Daily Practice Problems

Chapter-wise Sheets

Date :   Start Time :   End Time :

CHEMISTRY $\boxed{CC10}$

SYLLABUS : Organic Chemistry : Some Basic Principles and Techniques

Max. Marks : 74   **Time : 60 min.**

GENERAL INSTRUCTIONS

- The Daily Practice Problem Sheet contains 20 Questions divided into 5 sections.

  Section I has **6** MCQs with ONLY 1 Correct Option, **3** marks for each correct answer and **−1** for each incorrect answer.

  Section II has **4** MCQs with ONE or MORE THAN ONE Correct options.

  For each question, marks will be awarded in one of the following categories:

  Full marks: **+4** If only the bubble(s) corresponding to all the correct option(s) is (are) darkened.

  Partial marks: **+1** For darkening a bubble corresponding to each correct option provided NO INCORRECT option is darkened.

  Zero marks: If none of the bubbles is darkened.

  Negative marks: **−2** In all other cases.

  Section III has **4** Single Digit Integer Answer Type Questions, **3** marks for each Correct Answer and 0 marks in all other cases.

  Section IV has Comprehension/Matching Cum-Comprehension Type Questions having **4** MCQs with ONLY ONE correct option, **3** marks for each Correct Answer and 0 marks in all other cases.

  Section V has **2** Matching Type Questions, **2** mark for the correct matching of each row and 0 marks in all other cases.

- You have to evaluate your Response Grids yourself with the help of Solutions.

Section I - Straight Objective Type

This section contains 6 multiple choice questions. Each question has 4 choices (a), (b), (c) and (d), out of which **ONLY ONE** is correct.

1.
$$\underset{\text{meso}}{C_6H_5\overset{\overset{Br}{|}}{C}H\overset{\overset{Br}{|}}{C}HC_6H_5} \xrightarrow[\text{(E2 reaction)}]{CH_3ONa,\ CH_3OH}$$

$$\underset{X}{C_6H_5CBr = CHC_6H_5}$$

and

$$\underset{\text{racemic}}{C_6H_5\overset{\overset{Br}{|}}{C}H\overset{\overset{Br}{|}}{C}HC_6H_5} \xrightarrow[\text{(E2 reaction)}]{CH_3ONa,\ CH_3OH}$$

$$\underset{Y}{C_6H_5CBr = CHC_6H_5}$$

The alkenes X and Y respectively are

(a) Z and E   (b) E and Z

(c) Z in both cases   (d) E in both cases

Space for Rough Work

2. In which of the following two carbon atoms are differently hybridised?

$\overset{+}{CH_2} = CH$ (i) $CH_3 \overset{-}{CH}CH_3$ (ii) $\overset{-}{CH_2} = CH$ (iii)

$CH \equiv \overset{-}{C}$ (iv) $C(CH_3)_3$ (v)

(a) (i)   (b) (ii)   (c) (v)   (d) (i) and (v)

3.

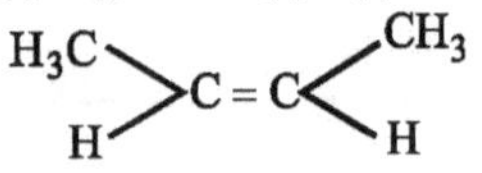

$$\underset{H}{\overset{H_3C}{>}}C=C\underset{H}{\overset{CH_3}{<}}$$

$$+ Cl_2(H_2O) \longrightarrow H_3C - \underset{[X]}{\overset{OH}{\underset{|}{CH}}} - \overset{Cl}{\underset{|}{CH}}CH_3$$

$$\underset{H_3C}{\overset{H}{>}}C=C\underset{H}{\overset{CH_3}{<}}$$

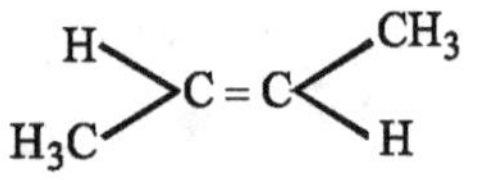

$$+ Cl_2(H_2O) \longrightarrow H_3C - \underset{[Y]}{\overset{OH}{\underset{|}{CH}}} - \overset{Cl}{\underset{|}{CH}}CH_3$$

Products X and Y respectively are

(a) Racemic-threo-chlorohydrin

(b) Racemic-erythro-chlorohydrin

(c) Racemic-threo-chlorohydrin and racemic-erythro-chlorohydrin

(d) Racemic-erythro-chlorohydrin and racemic-threo-chlorohydrin

4. Structure of the compound whose IUPAC name is 3-ethyl-2-hydroxy-4-methylhex-3-en-5-ynoic acid is :

(a) 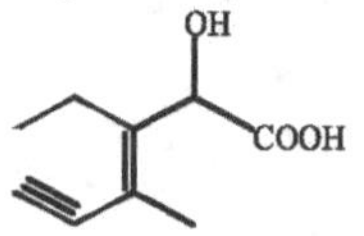 [structure]   (b) 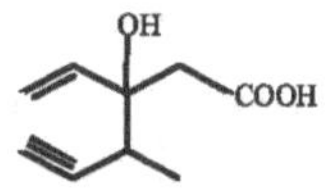 [structure]

(c) 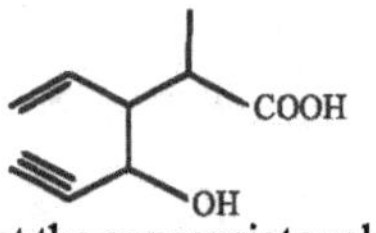 [structure]   (d) 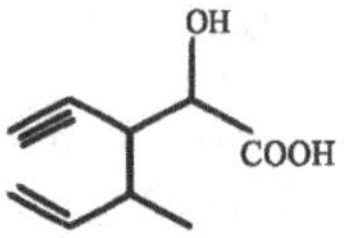 [structure]

5. Select the appropriate relation with respect to acidity of X, Y, Z for the given compound, with increasing order.

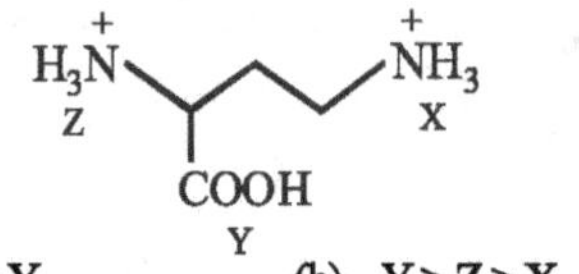

$$\underset{Z}{\overset{+}{H_3N}}\text{—}\underset{\underset{Y}{COOH}}{}\text{—}\underset{X}{\overset{+}{NH_3}}$$

(a) Z > X > Y   (b) Y > Z > X

(c) Z < X > Y   (d) X > Y > Z

6. A sample of 0.5 g of an organic compound was treated according to Kjeldahl's method. The ammonia evolved was absorbed in 50 mL of 0.5 M H_2SO_4. The remaining acid after neutralisation by ammonia consumed 80 mL of 0.5 M NaOH. The percentage of nitrogen in the organic compound is

(a) 14   (b) 28   (c) 42   (d) 56

Section II - Multiple Correct Answer Type

This section contains 4 multiple correct answer(s) type questions. Each question has 4 choices (a), (b), (c) and (d), out of which **ONE OR MORE** is/are correct.

7. The correct statement(s) about the compound $H_3C(HO)HC–CH=CH–CH(OH)CH_3$ **(X)** is(are)

(a) the total number of stereoisomers possible for **X** is 6

(b) the total number of diastereomers possible for **X** is 3

(c) if the stereochemistry about the double bond in **X** is *trans*, the number of enantiomers possible for **X** is 4

(d) if the stereochemistry about the double bond in **X** is *cis*, the number of enantiomers possible for **X** is 2

8. Purine has four nitrogens, which one you expect to be basic?

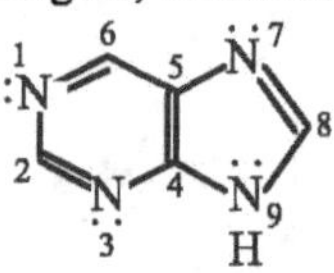

(a) N_1 (b) N_3 (c) N_7 (d) N_9

9. Guanidine, $(NH_2)_2 C = NH$, is said to be the strongest nitrogen containing organic base because

(a) it has two —NH_2 groups

(b) it has three nitrogen atoms that can be protonated

(c) its imino group is first protonated

(d) its conjugate acid is very much stable due to three equivalent structures.

10. Which of the following compounds are chiral and resolvable?

(a) $[C_6H_5N^+(CH_2CH_2CH_3)(C_2H_5)(CH_3)]Br^-$

(b) $C_6H_5N(CH_3)(C_2H_5)$

(c) $CH_3CH_2\underset{\underset{CH_3}{|}}{CH} N (CH_3) (C_2H_5)$

(d) 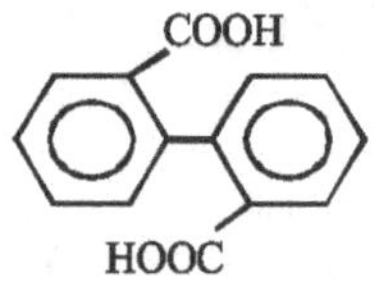 [structure: biphenyl with COOH and HOOC groups]

Section III - Integer Type

This section contains 4 questions. The answer to each of the questions is a single digit integer ranging from 0 to 9.

11. Amongst the following compounds the total number of compounds which gives coloured test with both ceric ammonium nitrate (CAN) and neutral $FeCl_3$ solution.

I. Phenol **II.** Benzyl alcohol

III. Benzaldehyde **IV.** Aniline

V. $HO{-}\langle O \rangle{-}CH_2OH$

VI. $HO{-}\langle O \rangle{-}CH_2OH$ **VII.** $HO{-}\langle O \rangle{-}$, HOH_2C

VIII. $PhCH_2CH(OH)CH_3$ **IX.** Urea **X.** Thiourea

12. The maximum number of isomers (including stereoisomers) that are possible on monochlorination of the following compound is

$$CH_3{-}\underset{H}{\overset{|}{C}}{-} \quad CH_3H_2C \quad CH_2CH_3$$

13. How many hydrogens in the compound below are replced by deuterium when it is shaken in D_2O containing trace of hydroxide ion?

(cyclopentanone with two Br substituents; Br Br)

14. The number of resonance structures for N is

(2-naphthol) $\xrightarrow{NaOH}$ N

Section IV - Comprehension Type

Directions (Qs. 15-18) : Based upon the given paragraphs, 4 multiple choice questions have to be answered. Each question has 4 choices (a), (b), (c) and (d), out of which **ONLY ONE** is correct.

PARAGRAPH-1

Amines are derivatives of ammonia and are classified as 1°, 2°, and 3°. Primary and secondary (but not tertiary amines) form intermolecular hydrogen bonds and thus they boil at higher temperatures than expected. Like ammonia, all amines are basic, although they differ in their basic nature. As amines are considered as derivatives of ammonia, quaternary ammonium salts are considered as derivatives of ammonium salts. Only the quaternary ammonium salts can show optical activity.

15. Which of the following statement is correct?
   (a) All classes of amines form hydrogen bonds with each other
   (b) Only primary and secondary amines form hydrogen bonds with water
   (c) All classes of amines can form hydrogen bonds with water
   (d) All amines are completely soluble in water

16. Which of the following statement is false about $NR_1R_2R_3$ molecule?
   (a) The molecule is optically inactive
   (b) N is tetrahedrally hybridised
   (c) The molecule is not superimposable on its mirror image
   (d) None of the three

PARAGRAPH-2

Although the carboxyl group consists of $C{=}O$ and $-OH$, it is the $-OH$ that undergoes change, either loss of H^+ or replacement by another group. However, the carbonyl group markedly influences the reactions of carboxylic acids. The presence of the $C{=}O$ part is also responsible for nucleophilic substitution reactions in acid derivatives.

Presence of an electron withdrawing group increases the acidity of aliphatic as well as aromatic acids. On the other hand, electron releasing groups imparts opposite effect.

17. Which statement is correct when an acid weakening group is present in benzoic acid?
   (a) Acid weakening groups activate the ring towards electrophilic substitution
   (b) Acid weakening groups deactivate the ring towards electrophilic substitution
   (c) Acid weakening groups activate the ring toward nucleophilic substitution
   (d) None of the above

18. Aldehydes and ketones react with nucleophiles to give addition product rather substituion because
   (a) They are more acidic
   (b) They are less acidic
   (c) They are sterically hindered
   (d) The $C-H$ and $C-C$ bonds do not break easily

<table>
<tr><td rowspan="3">RESPONSE GRID</td><td>11. ⓪①②③④⑤⑥⑦⑧⑨</td><td>12. ⓪①②③④⑤⑥⑦⑧⑨</td></tr>
<tr><td>13. ⓪①②③④⑤⑥⑦⑧⑨</td><td>14. ⓪①②③④⑤⑥⑦⑧⑨</td></tr>
<tr><td colspan="2">15. ⓐⓑⓒⓓ 16. ⓐⓑⓒⓓ 17. ⓐⓑⓒⓓ 18. ⓐⓑⓒⓓ</td></tr>
</table>

Section V - Matrix-Match Type

This section contains 2 questions. It contains statements given in two columns, which have to be matched. Statements in column I are labelled as A, B, C and D whereas statements in column II are labelled as p, q, r and s. The answers to these questions have to be appropriately bubbled as illustrated in the following example. If the correct matches are A-p, A-r, B-p, B-s, C-r, C-s and D-q, then the correctly bubbled matrix will look like the following:

19. **Column-I**

A. $N_2CHCOOC_2H_5 \xrightarrow{heat}$

B. $CH_2N_2 \xrightarrow{heat}$

C. $CH_3N = NCH_3 \xrightarrow{heat}$

D. $C_6H_5N_2Cl \xrightarrow{heat}$

Column-II

p. Free radical

q. Carbene

r. Carbocations

s. Neutral species

20. **Column-I**

A. $CH_3 - \overset{\overset{O}{\|}}{C} - COOH \xrightarrow{NaBH_4}$ (product: H—C(COOH)(CH_3)—OH, (+) – (100%))

B. $CH_3(H)C = C(H)CH_3 \xrightarrow{Br_2}$ (product: meso (100%))

C. (bromo compound) $\xrightarrow[KOH]{alc.}$ $C_6H_5(H)C = C(H)C_6H_5$

D. $H_3CC \equiv C\,CH_3 \xrightarrow[BaSO_4]{H_2/Pd.}$ $(CH_3)(H)C = C(CH_3)(H)$ (95%)

Column-II

p. Stereospecific

q. Stereoselective

r. *anti*-Addition

s. *anti*-Elimination

RESPONSE GRID	19. A - p q r s ; B - p q r s ; C - p q r s ; D - p q r s
	20. A - p q r s ; B - p q r s ; C - p q r s ; D - p q r s

DAILY PRACTICE PROBLEM DPP CHAPTERWISE 10 - CHEMISTRY

Total Questions	20	Total Marks	74
Attempted		Correct	
Incorrect		Net Score	
Cut-off Score	24	Qualifying Score	35
Success Gap = Net Score – Qualifying Score			
Net Score = (Correct × 4) – (Incorrect × 1)			

Date : **Start Time :** **End Time :**

CHEMISTRY [CC11]

SYLLABUS : Hydrocarbons

Max. Marks : 74   **Time : 60 min.**

GENERAL INSTRUCTIONS

- The Daily Practice Problem Sheet contains 20 Questions divided into 5 sections.

  Section I has **6** MCQs with ONLY 1 Correct Option, **3** marks for each correct answer and **−1** for each incorrect answer.

  Section II has **4** MCQs with ONE or MORE THAN ONE Correct options.

  For each question, marks will be awarded in one of the following categories:

  Full marks: **+4** If only the bubble(s) corresponding to all the correct option(s) is (are) darkened.

  Partial marks: **+1** For darkening a bubble corresponding to each correct option provided NO INCORRECT option is darkened.

  Zero marks: If none of the bubbles is darkened.

  Negative marks: **−2** In all other cases.

  Section III has **4** Single Digit Integer Answer Type Questions, **3** marks for each Correct Answer and 0 marks in all other cases.

  Section IV has Comprehension/Matching Cum-Comprehension Type Questions having **4** MCQs with ONLY ONE correct option, **3** marks for each Correct Answer and 0 marks in all other cases.

  Section V has **2** Matching Type Questions, **2** mark for the correct matching of each row and 0 marks in all other cases.

- You have to evaluate your Response Grids yourself with the help of Solutions.

Section I - Straight Objective Type

This section contains 6 multiple choice questions. Each question has 4 choices (a), (b), (c) and (d), out of which **ONLY ONE** is correct.

1. The final product Z in the following reaction is

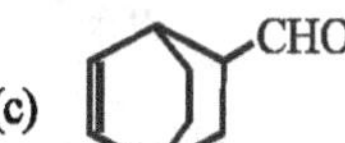

$$\xrightarrow[\text{CCl}_4]{\text{NBS}} [\ ] \xrightarrow{(CH_3)_3COK} [\ ] \xrightarrow{} Z$$

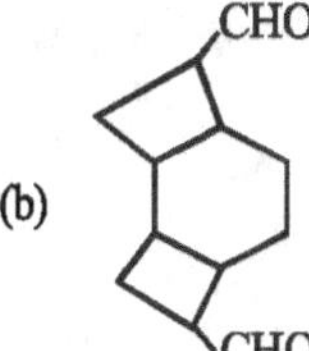

(a)   (b)

(c)   (d)

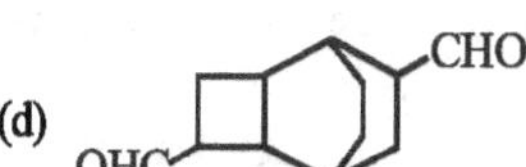

RESPONSE GRID   **1.** ⓐⓑⓒⓓ

Space for Rough Work

2. Methane can be chlorinated by
  (i) treating with chlorine in presence of UV light
  (ii) heating with chlorine in presence of tetraethyl lead
  (iii) treating with tert-butyl hypochlorite in presence of UV light
  (a) only method (i)
  (b) by methods (i) and (ii)
  (c) by methods (i) and (iii)
  (d) by methods (i), (ii) and (iii)

3. The gas liberated by the electrolysis of Dipotassium succinate solution is
  (a) Ethane
  (b) Ethyne
  (c) Ethene
  (d) Propene

4. Choose the correct alkyne and reagents for the preparation of

  (a) $HgSO_4$, H_2SO_4, H_2O
  (b) $HgSO_4$, H_2SO_4, H_2O
  (c) BH_3, H_2O_2, $NaOH$
  (d) BH_3, H_2O_2, $NaOH$

5. n-Propylbenzene can be obtained in quantitative yield by following method :
  (i) By treating benzene with n-propyl chloride in presence of $AlCl_3$
  (ii) By treating excess of benzene with n-propyl chloride in presence of $AlCl_3$
  (iii) By treating benzene with allyl chloride in presence of $AlCl_3$ followed by reduction
  (iv) By treating benzene with propinoyl chloride in presence of $AlCl_3$ followed by Clemmensen reduction.
  (a) By (ii), (iii) and (iv)
  (b) By (i), (iii) and (iv)
  (c) By (iii) and (iv)
  (d) By (ii) only

6. The final product in the following series of reactions should be

H_3CO—〈 〉—$CH = CHCH_3$ $\xrightarrow{HBr}$ [ ] $\xrightarrow[\text{(ii) HBr}]{\text{(i) Na}}$ Product

(a) H_3CO—〈 〉—$CH_2 - \underset{CH_3}{CH} - \underset{CH_3}{CH} - CH_2$—〈 〉—$OCH_3$

(b) HO—〈 〉—$CH_2 - \underset{CH_3}{CH} - \underset{CH_3}{CH} - CH_2$—〈 〉—$OCH_3$

(c) HO—〈 〉—$\underset{C_2H_5}{CH} - \underset{C_2H_5}{CH}$—〈 〉—$OH$

(d) H_3CO—〈 〉—$\underset{C_2H_5}{CH} - \underset{C_2H_5}{CH}$—〈 〉—$OCH_3$

Section II - Multiple Correct Answer Type

This section contains 4 multiple correct answer(s) type questions. Each question has 4 choices (a), (b), (c) and (d), out of which **ONE OR MORE** is/are correct.

7. Which of the following statements are correct?
  (a) Monochlorination of ethane gives C_2H_5Cl only
  (b) Thermal or photochemical chlorination of C_2H_5Cl gives, 1, 1-dichloroethane and 1,2-dichloroethane
  (c) Chlorination of isobutane gives tertiary butyl chloride and isobutyl chloride in the ratio of 2 : 1 even though there are nine 1° H atoms in the compound in comparison to only one 3° H atom
  (d) Monochlorination of CH_4 is not possible

8. Which of the following method can not be used for preparation of $CH_3 - CH_3$?
  (a) $CH_3Cl \xrightarrow{Zn / dust}$
  (b) $CH_3CH_2Cl \xrightarrow{LiAlH_4}$
  (c) $Al_4C_3 \xrightarrow{H_2O/HCl}$
  (d) $CaC_2 \xrightarrow{H_2O/H^+}$

9. Propene (I), 2-methylpropene (II), and ethene (III), each containing one carbon-carbon double bond, is separately treated with HI under the same set of conditions. The order of reactivity for the three alkenes should be
  (a) I is more reactive than II as well as III
  (b) I is more reactive than III, but less than II
  (c) II is more reactive than both I and III
  (d) III is more reactive than I which is more reactive than II

| RESPONSE | **2.** ⓐⓑⓒⓓ | **3.** ⓐⓑⓒⓓ | **4.** ⓐⓑⓒⓓ | **5.** ⓐⓑⓒⓓ | **6.** ⓐⓑⓒⓓ |
| GRID | **7.** ⓐⓑⓒⓓ | **8.** ⓐⓑⓒⓓ | **9.** ⓐⓑⓒⓓ | | |

10. The possible compounds formed in the following reaction is

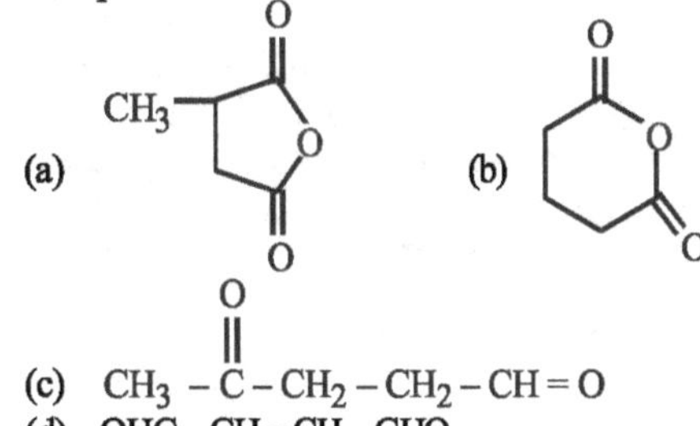

(a)   (b)

Br   Br

(c)   (d)

Br   Br

Section III - Integer Type

This section contains 4 questions. The answer to each of the questions is a single digit integer ranging from 0 to 9.

11. Number of monochloro derivatives (excluding stereoisomers), dichloro derivatives and trichloro derivatives of cyclopentane are n_1, n_2 and n_3 then $(n_1 + n_2)/n_3$ is equal to

12. How many stereoisomers are possible for dichlorocyclobutane?

13. On conversion into the Grignard reagent followed by treatment with water, how many alkyl bromides would yield isopentane?

14. Total no. of alkynes that on catalytic reduction gives 3-ethyl-4-methylheptane.

Section IV - Comprehension Type

Directions (Qs. 15-18) : Based upon the given paragraphs, 4 multiple choice questions have to be answered. Each question has 4 choices (a), (b), (c) and (d), out of which **ONLY ONE** is correct.

PARAGRAPH-1

A hydrocarbon (X) of the formula C_6H_{12} does not react with bromine water but reacts with bromine in presence of light, forming compound (Y). Compound (Y) on treatment with alc. KOH gives compound [Z] which on ozonolysis gives (T) of the formula $C_6H_{10}O_2$. Compound (T) reduces Tollen's reagent and gives compound (W). (W) gives iodoform test and produces compound (U) which when heated with P_2O_5 forms a cyclic anhydride (V).

15. Compound V is –

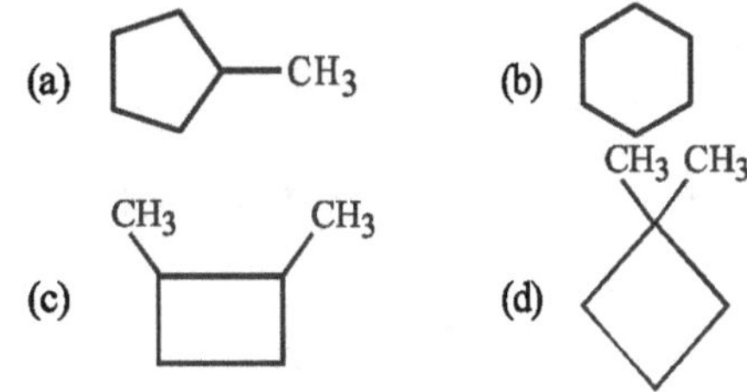

(a)   (b)

(c) $CH_3 - \overset{\overset{O}{\|}}{C} - CH_2 - CH_2 - CH = O$

(d) $OHC - CH = CH - CHO$

16. Compound X is –

(a)   cyclopentane–CH_3 (b) cyclohexane

(c)   1,2-dimethyl (CH_3, CH_3) cyclobutane

(d)   1,1-dimethyl (CH_3 CH_3) cyclobutane

PARAGRAPH-2

Chlorination of methane involves three steps : chain-initiating, chain-propagating and chain-terminating.

$$Cl_2 \xrightarrow{\text{Heat or light}} 2\overset{\bullet}{Cl} \qquad \text{Chain initiating}$$

$$CH_4 + \overset{\bullet}{Cl} \longrightarrow \overset{\bullet}{CH_3} + HCl$$

$$\overset{\bullet}{CH_3} + Cl_2 \longrightarrow CH_3Cl + \overset{\bullet}{Cl} \qquad \text{Chain propagating}$$

When oxygen is passed through the reaction mixture, chlorination of methane slows down temporarily.

17. Although chlorination of methane is an exothermic, the reaction requires high temperature because
(a) Activation energy is low
(b) Heat of reaction is negative
(c) Chain-initiating step is endothermic
(d) Chain-terminating step is endothermic

18. Temporary slow down of chlorination of methane in presence of oxygen in due to the formation of

(a) $CH_3OO^{\bullet}$ which is highly unstable and decomposes easily

(b) $CH_3OO^{\bullet}$ which is less reactive than $^{\bullet}CH_3$

(c) $ClO^{\bullet}$ which is highly reactive

(d) a diradical $Cl\overset{\bullet}{O}^{\bullet}$

RESPONSE GRID		
10. ⓐⓑⓒⓓ	**11.** ⓪①②③④⑤⑥⑦⑧⑨	**12.** ⓪①②③④⑤⑥⑦⑧⑨
13. ⓪①②③④⑤⑥⑦⑧⑨	**14.** ⓪①②③④⑤⑥⑦⑧⑨	
15. ⓐⓑⓒⓓ	**16.** ⓐⓑⓒⓓ **17.** ⓐⓑⓒⓓ	**18.** ⓐⓑⓒⓓ

Section V - Matrix-Match Type

This section contains 2 questions. It contains statements given in two columns, which have to be matched. Statements in column I are labelled as A, B, C and D whereas statements in column II are labelled as p, q, r and s. The answers to these questions have to be appropriately bubbled as Illustrated in the following example. If the correct matches are A-p, A-r, B-p, B-s, C-r, C-s and D-q, then the correctly bubbled matrix will look like the following:

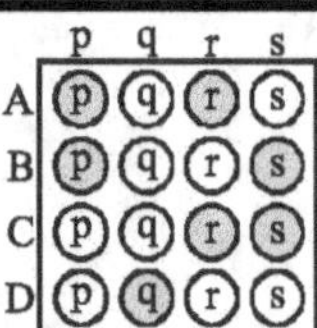

19.

Column-I

Reaction

(A) $CH_3CH_2CH = CHCH_3$ on reaction with HCl gives two products

(B) $CH_2 = CH–CH = CH_2$ reacts with HCl to form 1, 2- and 1, 4-addition products

(C) $C_6H_5CH=CHCH_3 + HBr$ gives only one product

(D) $C_6H_5CH_2CH = CH_2 + HBr$ forms a compound identical to that obtained in (C).

Column-II

Factor responsible for the reaction

p. Rearrangement

q. Inductive effect

r. Hyperconjugation

s. Resonance

20.

Column-I

(A) $CH_2 = CHCN + (CH_3)_2 NH \longrightarrow$

(B) $CH_2 = CHCN \xrightarrow{\text{catalyst}}$

(C) $CH_3 - \overset{\overset{\displaystyle O}{\|}}{C} - Cl + (CH_3)_2 NH \longrightarrow$

(D) $ClCH_2CH=CHCN + (CH_3)_2NH \longrightarrow$

Column-II

p. Transition state involves pentavalent carbon

q. Nucleophilic substitution

r. Nucleophilic addition

s. Free radical addition

RESPONSE GRID	
19. A - (p)(q)(r)(s)(t); B - (p)(q)(r)(s)(t); C - (p)(q)(r)(s)(t); D - (p)(q)(r)(s)(t)	
20. A - (p)(q)(r)(s)(t); B - (p)(q)(r)(s)(t); C - (p)(q)(r)(s)(t); D - (p)(q)(r)(s)(t)	

DAILY PRACTICE PROBLEM DPP CHAPTERWISE 11 - CHEMISTRY

Total Questions	20	Total Marks	74
Attempted		Correct	
Incorrect		Net Score	
Cut-off Score	24	Qualifying Score	35
Success Gap = Net Score – Qualifying Score			
Net Score = (Correct × 4) – (Incorrect × 1)			

Space for Rough Work

DPP - Daily Practice Problems

Chapter-wise Sheets

Date : | Start Time : | End Time :

CHEMISTRY $\boxed{\text{CC12}}$

SYLLABUS : The Solid State

Max. Marks : 74　　　　　　　　　　　　　　　　　**Time : 60 min.**

GENERAL INSTRUCTIONS

- The Daily Practice Problem Sheet contains 20 Questions divided into 5 sections.
  Section I has **6** MCQs with ONLY 1 Correct Option, **3** marks for each correct answer and **−1** for each incorrect answer.
  Section II has **4** MCQs with ONE or MORE THAN ONE Correct options.
  For each question, marks will be awarded in one of the following categories:
  Full marks: **+4** If only the bubble(s) corresponding to all the correct option(s) is (are) darkened.
  Partial marks: **+1** For darkening a bubble corresponding to each correct option provided NO INCORRECT option is darkened.
  Zero marks: If none of the bubbles is darkened.
  Negative marks: **−2** In all other cases.
  Section III has **4** Single Digit Integer Answer Type Questions, **3** marks for each Correct Answer and 0 marks in all other cases.
  Section IV has Comprehension/Matching Cum-Comprehension Type Questions having **4** MCQs with ONLY ONE correct option, **3** marks for each Correct Answer and 0 marks in all other cases.
  Section V has **2** Matching Type Questions, **2** mark for the correct matching of each row and 0 marks in all other cases.
- You have to evaluate your Response Grids yourself with the help of Solutions.

Section I - Straight Objective Type

This section contains 6 multiple choice questions. Each question has 4 choices (a), (b), (c) and (d), out of which **ONLY ONE** is correct.

1. The pyknometric density of sodium chloride crystal is $2.165 \times 10^3 \, \text{kg m}^{-3}$ while its X-ray density is $2.178 \times 10^3 \, \text{kg m}^{-3}$. The fraction of unoccupied sites in sodium chloride crystal is

    (a) 5.96×10^{-3}
    (b) 5.96×10^{4}
    (c) 5.96×10^{-2}
    (d) 5.96×10^{-1}

2. The number of atoms in 100 g of an 'fcc' crystal with density, $d = 10 \, \text{g/cm}^3$ and cell edge equal to 100 pm, is equal to

    (a) 1×10^{25}
    (b) 2×10^{25}
    (c) 3×10^{25}
    (d) 4×10^{25}

3. KCl crystallises in the same type of lattice as does NaCl. Given that $r_{Na^+}/r_{Cl^-} = 0.55$ and $r_{K^+}/r_{Cl^-} = 0.74$. Calculate the ratio of the edge length of the unit cell for KCl to that of NaCl.

    (a) 1.123
    (b) 0.891
    (c) 1.414
    (d) 0.414

RESPONSE GRID	1. ⓐⓑⓒⓓ	2. ⓐⓑⓒⓓ	3. ⓐⓑⓒⓓ

Space for Rough Work

4. A solid has a 'bcc' structure. If the distance of nearest approach between two atoms is 1.73Å, the edge length of the cell is

(a) 314.20 pm   (b) 1.41 pm

(c) 200 pm   (d) 216 pm

5. Ammonium chloride crystallizes in a body centred cubic lattice with edge length of unit cell of 390 pm. If the size of chloride ion is 180 pm, the size of ammonium ion would be

(a) 174 pm   (b) 158 pm

(c) 142 pm   (d) 126 pm

6. The total number of octahedral void (s) per atom present in a cubic close packed structure is:

(a) 2   (b) 4

(c) 1   (d) 3

Section II - Multiple Correct Answer Type

This section contains 4 multiple correct answer(s) type questions. Each question has 4 choices (a), (b), (c) and (d), out of which **ONE OR MORE** is/are correct.

7. In case of ionic crystals which of the following are **correct**?

(a) They are hard and brittle

(b) The heats of evaporation are very high

(c) They are soluble in water but not in other polar solvents

(d) all the above are correct

8. Select the correct statement(s)

(a) When two formes of a solid exist together in equilibrium with each other at a particular temperature which depends only on pressure, the property is known as enantiotropy

(b) The temperature, at which two forms of a solid exist in equilibrium with each other which depends only on pressure, is called transition temperature

(c) In case of monotropy, the transition point lies below the m.p.

(d) In case of Enantiotropy, the transition temperature lies above m.p.

9. Select the covalent crystal(s)

(a) Diamond   (b) Graphite

(c) Zinc sulphide   (d) Silver iodide

10. Choose the correct statements–

(a) Vacancy defects lower the density of the substance

(b) Interstitial defects increase the density of the substance

(c) Schottsky defects, preserve the electrical neutrality of the crystal.

(d) Frenkel defects do not affect the density of the crystal.

Section III - Integer Type

This section contains 4 questions. The answer to each of the questions is a single digit integer ranging from 0 to 9.

11. Cesium atoms are the largest naturally occurring atoms. The radius of Cs atom is 2.6Å. The number of moles of Cs atoms to be laid side by side to give a row of Cs atoms 2.50 cm long is $x \times 10^{-17}$. Find the value of x.

12. A solid has a structure in which X atoms are located at cubic corners of unit cell, O atom are at the edge centres and Y atoms at cube centre.

Then the formula of compound is $X_a Y_b O_c$.

If two atoms of O are missing from any of two edge centres per unit cell, then the molecular formula is $X_x Y_y O_z$.

Then, find the value of $(x + y + z) - (a + b + c)$.

13. Iron cystallizes in several modifications. At about 910°C, α-form having 'bcc' lattice undergoes transition to form γ-form with 'fcc' lattice. Assuming that the distance between the nearest neighbours is the same in the two forms at the transition temperature, compute the ratio of the density of γ-form to that of α-form of iron at the transition temperature.

<table>
<tr><td rowspan="3">RESPONSE GRID</td><td>4. ⓐⓑⓒⓓ</td><td>5. ⓐⓑⓒⓓ</td><td>6. ⓐⓑⓒⓓ</td><td>7. ⓐⓑⓒⓓ</td><td>8. ⓐⓑⓒⓓ</td></tr>
<tr><td>9. ⓐⓑⓒⓓ</td><td>10. ⓐⓑⓒⓓ</td><td colspan="3">11. ⓪①②③④⑤⑥⑦⑧⑨</td></tr>
<tr><td colspan="2">12. ⓪①②③④⑤⑥⑦⑧⑨</td><td colspan="3">13. ⓪①②③④⑤⑥⑦⑧⑨</td></tr>
</table>

14. KCl crystallizes in the same type of lattice as does NaCl. Given that

$$\frac{r_{Na^+}}{r_{Cl^-}} = 0.5 \qquad \frac{r_{Na^+}}{r_{K^+}} = 0.7$$

Calculate the ratio of the side of the unit cell for KCl to that of NaCl.

Section IV - Comprehension Type

Directions (Qs. 15-18) : Based upon the given paragraphs, 4 multiple choice questions have to be answered. Each question has 4 choices (a), (b), (c) and (d), out of which **ONLY ONE** is correct.

PARAGRAPH-1

Density (ρ) of a crystal $= \dfrac{n \times A}{N_A \times a^3}$ g cm^{-3}

where n = number of atoms per unit cell

   A = Mass of structural unit (atomic weight/Formula wt.)

   N_A = Avogadro's number = 6.023×10^{23}

   a = edge length of the cell

15. An element crystallizes in a structure having fcc unit cell of an edge length 200 pm. What will be the density of this element if 200 g of it contains 24×10^{23} atoms ?
    (a) 24×10^{23} g cm^{-3} (b) 41.6 g cm^{-3}
    (c) 2.46 g cm^{-3} (d) none of these

16. Copper crystal has fcc structure. Atomic radius of copper is 128 pm. The edge length of copper crystal is
    (a) 36.2 pm   (b) 362 nm
    (c) 3.62×10^{-10} cm   (d) 362×10^{-10} cm

PARAGRAPH-2

It has been found that the angles between corresponding faces on various crystals of the same substance are constant. However the shapes of crystals may differ because of the fact that the crystal faces are unequally developed. Here we have represented two crystals **A** and **B** in two dimensions which have different shapes but the angles between corresponding faces of them are same.

The shape or the external form of a crystal depends upon the rate of deposition of atoms or ions on the different faces. During crystallization of sodium chloride, the crystals obtained by crystallization from aqueous solution are cubic while those obtained by crystallization from urea solution are octahedral.

17. The angle of intersection between the corresponding faces in crystals "**A**" and "**B**" above will be
    (a) same   (b) constant
    (c) equal   (d) all these are correct

18. The crystals of NaCl are found to be cubic when crystallisation is done from an aqueous solution of sodium chloride but have an octahedral shape if crystallized from urea solution. In view of the above observations, what about the law of constancy of interfacial angle?
    (a) The law is still valid
    (b) The law is not always valid
    (c) It is an exception to the law
    (d) None of these is correct

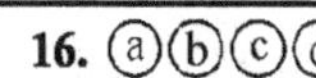

RESPONSE GRID
14. ⓪①②③④⑤⑥⑦⑧⑨   15. ⓐⓑⓒⓓ   16. ⓐⓑⓒⓓ   17. ⓐⓑⓒⓓ
18. ⓐⓑⓒⓓ

Section V - Matrix-Match Type

This section contains 2 questions. It contains statements given in two columns, which have to be matched. Statements in column I are labelled as A, B, C and D whereas statements in column II are labelled as p, q, r and s. The answers to these questions have to be appropriately bubbled as Illustrated in the following example. If the correct matches are A-p, A-r, B-p, B-s, C-r, C-s and D-q, then the correctly bubbled matrix will look like the following:

19. If a is the edge length of unit cell of CsCl, match the following lattice planes with appropriate chracteristics.

Column I		Column II
(A) d_{100} plane spacings	p.	Only Cs^+ or Cl^- ions
(B) d_{110} plane spacings	q.	Both Cs^+ and Cl^- ions
(C) (100) plane consists of	r.	$a/2$
(D) (110) plane consists of	s.	$a\sqrt{2}/2$

20.

Column I		Column II
(A) Schottky defect	p.	NaCl
(B) Frenkel defect	q.	KCl
(C) Its yellow colour is due to non-stoichiometric defects.	r.	No effect on density but an increase in dielectric constant.
(D) Its blue-lilac colour is due to Berthollide defects	s.	Observed in silver halides

RESPONSE GRID

19. A - (p)(q)(r)(s); B - (p)(q)(r)(s); C - (p)(q)(r)(s); D - (p)(q)(r)(s)

20. A - (p)(q)(r)(s); B - (p)(q)(r)(s); C - (p)(q)(r)(s); D - (p)(q)(r)(s)

DAILY PRACTICE PROBLEM DPP CHAPTERWISE 12 - CHEMISTRY

Total Questions	20	Total Marks	74
Attempted		Correct	
Incorrect		Net Score	
Cut-off Score	24	Qualifying Score	35
Success Gap = Net Score – Qualifying Score			
Net Score = (Correct × 4) – (Incorrect × 1)			

Date :   Start Time :   End Time :

CHEMISTRY $\boxed{CC13}$

SYLLABUS : Solutions

Max. Marks : 74   **Time : 60 min.**

GENERAL INSTRUCTIONS

- The Daily Practice Problem Sheet contains 20 Questions divided into 5 sections.

Section I has **6** MCQs with ONLY 1 Correct Option, **3** marks for each correct answer and **−1** for each incorrect answer.

Section II has **4** MCQs with ONE or MORE THAN ONE Correct options.

For each question, marks will be awarded in one of the following categories:

Full marks: **+4** If only the bubble(s) corresponding to all the correct option(s) is (are) darkened.

Partial marks: **+1** For darkening a bubble corresponding to each correct option provided NO INCORRECT option is darkened.

Zero marks: If none of the bubbles is darkened.

Negative marks: **−2** In all other cases.

Section III has **4** Single Digit Integer Answer Type Questions, **3** marks for each Correct Answer and 0 marks in all other cases.

Section IV has Comprehension/Matching Cum-Comprehension Type Questions having **4** MCQs with ONLY ONE correct option, **3** marks for each Correct Answer and 0 marks in all other cases.

Section V has **2** Matching Type Questions, **2** mark for the correct matching of each row and 0 marks in all other cases.

- You have to evaluate your Response Grids yourself with the help of Solutions.

Section I - Straight Objective Type

This section contains 6 multiple choice questions. Each question has 4 choices (a), (b), (c) and (d), out of which **ONLY ONE** is correct.

1. Two liquids X and Y form an ideal solution. At 300 K, vapour pressure of the solution containing 1 mol of X and 3 mol of Y is 550 mmHg. At the same temperature, if 1 mol of Y is further added to this solution, vapour pressure of the solution increases by 10 mmHg. Vapour pressure (in mmHg) of X and Y in their pure states will be, respectively:

(a)   300 and 400   (b)   400 and 600
(c)   500 and 600   (d)   200 and 300

2. Liquids A and B form an ideal solution. At 30°C, the total vapour pressure of a solution containing 1 mol of A and 2 mol of B is 250 mm Hg. The total vapour pressure becomes 300 mm Hg when 1 more mol of A is added to the first solution. The vapour pressures of pure A and B at the same temperature are

(a)   150, 450 mm Hg   (b)   125, 150 mm Hg
(c)   450, 150 mm Hg   (d)   250, 300 mm Hg

RESPONSE GRID   **1.** ⓐⓑⓒⓓ   **2.** ⓐⓑⓒⓓ

Space for Rough Work

3. A molecule M associates in a given solvent according to the equation $M \rightleftharpoons (M)_n$. For a certain concentration of M, the van't Hoff factor was found to be 0.9 and the fraction of associated molecules was 0.2. The value of n is:
(a) 3   (b) 5   (c) 2   (d) 4

4. A solution of $Al_2(SO_4)_3$ {d=1.253 gm / ml} contain 22% salt by weight. The molarity, normality and molality of the solution is
(a) 0.805 M, 4.83 N, 0.825 m
(b) 0.825 M, 48.3 N, 0.805 m
(c) 4.83 M, 4.83 N, 4.83 m
(d) None of these

5. When a gas is bubbled through water at 298 K, a very dilute solution of the gas is obtained. Henry's law constant for the gas at 298 K is 100 kbar. If the gas exerts a partial pressure of 1 bar, the number of millimoles of the gas dissolved in one litre of water is
(a) 0.555   (b) 5.55   (c) 0.0555   (d) 55.5

6. Equal masses of a solute are dissolved in equal amount of two solvents A and B, respective molecular masses being M_A and M_B. The relative lowering of vapour pressure of solution in solvent A is twice that of the solution in solvent B. If the solutions are dilute, M_A and M_B are related as
(a) $M_A = M_B$ (b) $2M_A = M_B$
(c) $M_A = 2M_B$ (d) $M_A = 4M_B$

Section II - Multiple Correct Answer Type

This section contains 4 multiple correct answer(s) type questions. Each question has 4 choices (a), (b), (c) and (d), out of which **ONE OR MORE** is/are correct.

---

7. The total vapour pressure of a binary solution is given by the relation
$P_s = (110.X_A + 125 X_B)$ mm of Hg
where x_A = mole fraction of component A in solution
x_B = mole fraction of component B in solution
From the above, we can say that
(a) the V.P. of solution (P_s) containing equal number of mole of both the components (i.e., $x_A = x_B$) is less than the vapour pressure of pure component B (i.e, P_B°)
(b) the V.P. of solution (P_s) containing equal number of moles of both the components (i.e., $x_A = x_B$) is more than the V.P. of pure component A (i.e. P_A°)

(c) $P_A^\circ = 110$ mm of Hg and $P_B^\circ = 125$ mm of Hg

(d) $P_A^\circ = 125$ mm of Hg and $P_B^\circ = 110$ mm of Hg

8. For a 0.1 m solutions each of two solutes X and Y in which solute X behaves as a univalent electrolyte and Y dimerises in solution. The correct statement (s) are
(a) The b.p. of solution of solute X will be higher than that of Y.
(b) The osmotic pressure of the solution of solute Y will be lower than that of X.
(c) The freezing point of solution of solute X will be lower than that of Y.
(d) The relative lowering of V.P. of solution of solute X will be same as that of Y.

9. Which of the following represents the behaviour of ideal binary liquid solution? (X_A = mole fraction of A)
(a) Plot of P_{Total} vs X_A is linear passing through the origin
(b) Plot of P_{Total} vs X_A is linear having an intercept P_B°
(c) Plot of P_{Total} vs X_A is linear having an intercept P_A°
(d) Plot of P_{Total} vs X_A is non-linear

10. Vapour pressure – temperature curves of pure solvent and a solution cantaining a non-volatile solute are depicted in the figure aside. Select the correct statements(s) of the following

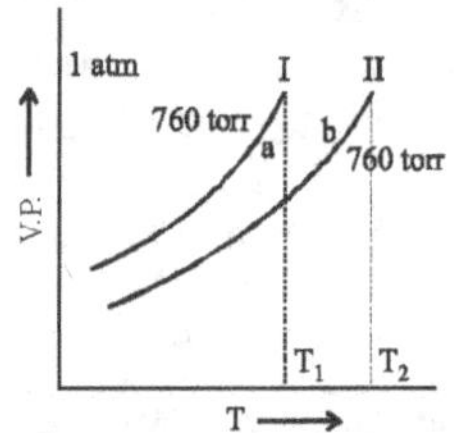

(a) Curve I represents variation vapour pressure of solution and II that of solvent with temperature
(b) Curves I and II represent the variation of vapour pressures of solvent and solution respectively with temperature
(c) Gap ab represents $K_b m$ for the solution
(d) Gap ab represents $K_c m$ for the solution

<table>
<tr><td rowspan="2">RESPONSE GRID</td><td>3. ⓐⓑⓒⓓ</td><td>4. ⓐⓑⓒⓓ</td><td>5. ⓐⓑⓒⓓ</td><td>6. ⓐⓑⓒⓓ</td><td>7. ⓐⓑⓒⓓ</td></tr>
<tr><td>8. ⓐⓑⓒⓓ</td><td>9. ⓐⓑⓒⓓ</td><td>10. ⓐⓑⓒⓓ</td><td></td><td></td></tr>
</table>

Section III - Integer Type

This section contains 4 questions. The answer to each of the questions is a single digit integer ranging from 0 to 9.

11. An element X (Atomic mass = 25) exists as X_4 is benzene. 51g of saturated solution of X in benzene was added to 50.0 g of pure benzene. The resulting solution showed a depression of freezing point of 0.55 K. Calculate the solubility of X per 100 g of benzene. (K_f for benzene = 5.5 K kg mol^{-1})

12. Compound $PdCl_4 \cdot 6H_2O$ is a hydrated complex; 1 m aqueous solution of it has freezing point 269.28 K. Assuming 100% ionization of complex, calculate the number of ions furnished by complex in the solution.

13. The osmotic pressure of urea solution at 10°C is 200 mm. becomes 105.3 mm when it is diluted and temperature raised to 25°C. How many times the solution gets diluted?

14. What will be the osmotic pressure of a solution containing 40 g of solute (molecular mass 246) per litre at 27°C ($R = 0.0822$ atm L mol^{-1})?

Section IV - Comprehension Type

Directions (Qs. 15-18) : Based upon the given paragraphs, 4 multiple choice questions have to be answered. Each question has 4 choices (a), (b), (c) and (d), out of which **ONLY ONE** is correct.

PARAGRAPH-1

Properties such as boiling point, freezing point and vapour pressure of pure solvent change when solute molecules are added to get solution. The changes in these properties are called colligative properties. Applications of colligative properties are very useful in day-to-day life. One of its examples is the use of ethylene glycol and water mixture as anti-freezing mixture in the radiater of automobiles.

A solution M is prepared by mixing ethanol and water. The mole fraction of ethanol in the mixture is 0.9.

Given : K_f for water = 1.86 K Kg mol^{-1}; K_f for ethanol = 2.0 K Kg mol^{-1}; K_b for water = 0.52 K Kg mol^{-1}; K_b for ethanol = 1.2 K Kg mol^{-1}; standard freezing point and boiling point of water = 273 K and 373 K; standard freezing point and boiling point of ethanol = 155.7 K and 351.5 K respectively; vapour pressure of pure ethanol = 40 mm Hg, molecular weight of water = 18 g mol^{-1}, molecular weight of ethanol = 46 g mol^{-1}

15. The freezing point of the solution M is
    (a) 268.7 K (b) 268.5 K
    (c) 234.2 K (d) 150.9 K

16. The vapour pressure of the solution M is
    (a) 39.3 mm Hg (b) 36.0 mm Hg
    (c) 29.5 mm Hg (d) 28.8 mm Hg

PARAGRAPH-2

To account for all abnormal cases (i.e., those of association or dissociation of solute molecules when dissolved in a solvent), van't Hoff introduced a factor, i, known as van't Hoff factor.

$$i = \frac{\text{Number of particles after association or dissociation}}{\text{Number of normal solute particles}}$$

The ratio of van't Hoff factor (i) to the number of ions furnished by one molecule of solute is known as osmotic coefficient 'g'

$$\text{i.e., } g = \frac{i}{n} = \frac{\text{van't Hoff factor}}{n}$$

Consider 0.5% aqueous soluion of potassium chloride which was found to freeze at 272.76 K. [Given K_f of water = 1.86 K kg mol^{-1}) and answer the following questions.

17. The van't Hoff factor for it is approximately
    (a) 1 (b) 2
    (c) $\dfrac{1}{2}$ (d) Can't be predicted

18. What is the degree of dissociation (α) in this case?
    (a) 100% (b) 95%
    (c) 92.0% (d) 90%

Section V - Matrix-Match Type

This section contains 2 questions. It contains statements given in two columns, which have to be matched. Statements in column I are labelled as A, B, C and D whereas statements in column II are labelled as p, q, r and s. The answers to these questions have to be appropriately bubbled as illustrated in the following example. If the correct matches are A-p, A-r, B-p, B-s, C-r, C-s and D-q, then the correctly bubbled matrix will look like the following:

19. **Solubility of a solid solute into water increases as the temperature is raised. Match the processes listed in Column I with the changes in appropriate properties listed in Column II. (m = molality)**

    Column I

    (A) Gas + water $\rightarrow$ Solution

    (B) Solid + water $\rightarrow$ Solution

    (C) Saturated solution
    + Solid solute

    (D) Super saturated solution
    + Solid solute

    Column II

    p. $\Delta H > 0, \Delta S > 0$

    q. $\Delta H = 0, \Delta m = 0$

    r. $\Delta H < 0, \Delta m < 0$

    s. $\Delta H < 0, \Delta S < 0$

20. ΔH_f = Molar heat of fusion of ice; L_f = Latent heat of fusion of ice (g^{-1})

    ΔH_v = Molar heat of vaporisation of water; L_v = Latent heat of vaporisation of water (g^{-1})

    Match the following appropriately :

    Column I

    (A) Molal depression
    constant of water

    (B) Molal elevation
    constant of water

    (C) ΔT_f of solution containing
    9.0 g of glucose in 50 g of water

    (D) ΔT_b of solution containing
    3.0g of urea in 50g of water

    Column II

    p. $\dfrac{18 \times 373 \times 373 \times R}{1000 \, \Delta H_v}$

    q. $\dfrac{373 \times 373 \times R}{1000 \, L_v}$

    r. $\dfrac{18 \times 273 \times 273 \times R}{1000 \, \Delta H_f}$

    s. $\dfrac{273 \times 273 \times R}{1000 \, L_f}$

RESPONSE GRID	
19. A - p q r s ; B - p q r s ; C - p q r s ; D - p q r s	
20. A - p q r s ; B - p q r s ; C - p q r s ; D - p q r s	

DAILY PRACTICE PROBLEM DPP CHAPTERWISE 13 - CHEMISTRY

Total Questions	20	Total Marks	74
Attempted		Correct	
Incorrect		Net Score	
Cut-off Score	26	Qualifying Score	37
Success Gap = Net Score – Qualifying Score			
Net Score = (Correct × 4) – (Incorrect × 1)			

Date : [ ]   **Start Time :** [ ]   **End Time :** [ ]

CHEMISTRY $\boxed{\text{CC14}}$

SYLLABUS : Electrochemistry

Max. Marks : 74   **Time : 60 min.**

GENERAL INSTRUCTIONS

- The Daily Practice Problem Sheet contains 20 Questions divided into 5 sections.
  Section I has **5** MCQs with ONLY 1 Correct Option, **3** marks for each correct answer and **−1** for each incorrect answer.
  Section II has **4** MCQs with ONE or MORE THAN ONE Correct options.
  For each question, marks will be awarded in one of the following categories:
  Full marks: **+4** If only the bubble(s) corresponding to all the correct option(s) is (are) darkened.
  Partial marks: **+1** For darkening a bubble corresponding to each correct option provided NO INCORRECT option is darkened.
  Zero marks: If none of the bubbles is darkened.
  Negative marks: **−2** In all other cases.
  Section III has **5** Single Digit Integer Answer Type Questions, **3** marks for each Correct Answer and 0 marks in all other cases.
  Section IV has Comprehension/Matching Cum-Comprehension Type Questions having **5** MCQs with ONLY ONE correct option, **3** marks for each Correct Answer and 0 marks in all other cases.
  Section V has **1** Matching Type Questions, **2** mark for the correct matching of each row and 0 marks in all other cases.
- You have to evaluate your Response Grids yourself with the help of Solutions.

Section I - Straight Objective Type

This section contains 5 multiple choice questions. Each question has 4 choices (a), (b), (c) and (d), out of which **ONLY ONE** is correct.

1. In a fuel cell methanol is used as fuel and oxygen gas is used as an oxidizer. The reaction is

   $$CH_3OH(l) + 3/2O_2(g) \longrightarrow CO_2(g) + 2H_2O(l)$$

   At 298 K standard Gibb's energies of formation for $CH_3OH(l)$, $H_2O(l)$ and and $CO_2(g)$ are −166.2 −237.2 and −394.4 kJ mol^{-1} respectively. If standard enthalpy of combustion of methanol is − 726 kJ mol^{-1}, efficiency of the fuel cell will be:

   (a) 87%   (b) 90%   (c) 97%   (d) 80%

2. Resistance of 0.2 M solution of an electrolyte is 50 Ω. The specific conductance of the solution is 1.4 S m^{-1}. The resistance of 0.5 M solution of the same electrolyte is 280 Ω. The molar conductivity of 0.5 M solution of the electrolyte in S m^{2}mol^{-1} is:

   (a) 5×10^{-4} (b) 5×10^{-3}
   (c) 5×10^{3} (d) 5×10^{2}

RESPONSE GRID	1. ⓐⓑⓒⓓ 2. ⓐⓑⓒⓓ

———— Space for Rough Work ————

3. Given:

$$E^{\circ}_{Fe^{3+}/Fe} = -0.036 \text{ V}, \quad E^{\circ}_{Fe^{2+}/Fe} = -0.439 \text{ V}$$

The value of standard electrode potential for the change,

$Fe^{3+}(aq) + e^- \longrightarrow Fe^{2+}(aq)$ will be:

(a) 0.385 V (b) -0.770 V (c) -0.270 V (d) 0.072 V

4. Which of the following statements are correct concerning redox properties?

(i) A metal M for which E° for the half life reaction $M^{n+} + ne^- \rightleftharpoons M$ is very negative will be a good reducing agent.

(ii) The oxidizing power of the halogens decreases from chlorine to iodine.

(iii) The reducing power of hydrogen halides increases from hydrogen chloride to hydrogen iodide

(a) (i), (ii) and (iii)   (b) (i) and (ii)

(c) (i) only   (d) (ii) and (iii)

5. A current of 10.0 A flows for 2.00 h through an electrolytic cell containing a molten salt of metal X. This results in the decomposition of 0.250 mole of metal X at the cathode. The oxidation state of X in the molten salt is: (F = 96,500 C)

(a) $1+$ (b) $2+$ (c) $3+$ (d) $4+$

Section II - Multiple Correct Answer Type

This section contains 4 multiple correct answer(s) type questions. Each question has 4 choices (a), (b), (c) and (d), out of which **ONE OR MORE** is/are correct.

6. On passing 0.5 mole of electrons through $CuSO_4$ and $Hg_2(NO_3)_2$ solutions in series using inert electrodes:

(a) 0.5 mole of Cu deposited

(b) 0.5 mole of Hg deposited

(c) 0.125 mole of O_2 produced in each solution

(d) 0.5 mole of O_2 produced in each solution

7. Which of the following statements is/are correct?

(a) In the reaction $MnO_4^{2-} + H^+ \longrightarrow Mn^{2-} + ?$ the missing product is MnO_4^-.

(b) In the above reaction (a), the missing product is MnO_2.

(c) In the reaction $NO_2 + H_2O \longrightarrow No + ?$ the missing product is NO_3^-.

8. Which of the following cells give the cell potentials to be their standard values ?

(a) $Zn(s) \,|\, Zn^{2+}(aq)(0.01M) \,\|\, H_3O^+(aq)(0.1M) \,|\, H_2(g)(1\,atm),Pt$

(b) $Cu(s) \,|\, Cu^{2+}(aq)(0.25M) \,\|\, Ag^+(aq)(0.5M) \,|\, Ag$

(c) $Cd(s) \,|\, Cd^{2+}(aq)(0.01M) \,\|\, pH = 1 \,|\, H_2(g)(1\,atm), Pt$

(d) $Zn(s) \,|\, Zn^{2+}(aq)(0.1M) \,\|\, pH = 1 \,|\, H_2(g)(1\,atm), Pt$

9. Which of the following expression(s) represent the voltage of cell at 298 K :

$$Ag(s)| \underset{\substack{\text{Saturated (1)}\\\text{solution}}}{AgI} \,\|\, \underset{\substack{\text{Saturated (2)}\\\text{solution}}}{Ag_2C_2O_4} | Ag(s)$$

(a) $E_{cell} = 0.0592 \log \dfrac{[Ag^+]_1}{[Ag^+]_2}$

(b) $E_{cell} = 0.0592 \log \dfrac{[Ag^+]_2}{[Ag^+]_1}$

(c) $E_{cell} = 0.0592 \log \dfrac{K_{sp}(Ag_2C_2O_4)}{K_{sp}(AgI)}$

(d) $E_{cell} = 0.0592 \log \dfrac{[2K_{sp}(Ag_2C_2O_4)]^{1/3}}{[K_{sp}(AgI)]^{1/2}}$

Section III - Integer Type

This section contains 5 questions. The answer to each of the questions is a single digit integer ranging from 0 to 9.

10. During the electrolysis of conc. H_2SO_4, it was found that $H_2S_2O_8$ and O_2 were liberated in a molar ratio of 3 : 1. How many moles of H_2 were found in terms of moles of $H_2S_2O_8$? (Express your answer as: $3 \times$ moles of H_2; integer answer is between 0 and 9).

11. CN^- ion is oxidised by a powerful oxidising agent to NO_3^- and CO_2 or CO_3^{2-} depending on the acidity of the reaction mixture.

$$CN^- \longrightarrow CO_2 + NO_3^- + H^+ + ne^-$$

What is the number (n) of electrons involved in the process, divided by 10?

12. During the discharge of a lead storage battery, the density of 40% H_2SO_4 by weight fell from 1.225 to 0.98 (which is 20% by weight). What is the change in molarities of H_2SO_4?

13. When electrolysis of KCl is done in alkaline medium, 10 g of $KClO_3$ is produed as follows:

$$Cl^- + 6OH^- \rightarrow ClO_3^- + 3H_2O + 6e^-$$

A current of 2A is passed for 10.941 hours. Calculate the

$$\left(\frac{\text{Percentage current efficiency}}{10} \right) \text{used in the process.}$$

(Mw of $KClO_3 = 122.5$)

<table>
<tr><td rowspan="4">RESPONSE
GRID</td><td>3. ⓐⓑⓒⓓ</td><td>4. ⓐⓑⓒⓓ</td><td>5. ⓐⓑⓒⓓ</td><td>6. ⓐⓑⓒⓓ</td><td>7. ⓐⓑⓒⓓ</td></tr>
<tr><td>8. ⓐⓑⓒⓓ</td><td>9. ⓐⓑⓒⓓ</td><td colspan="3">10. ⓪①②③④⑤⑥⑦⑧⑨</td></tr>
<tr><td colspan="2">11. ⓪①②③④⑤⑥⑦⑧⑨</td><td colspan="3">12. ⓪①②③④⑤⑥⑦⑧⑨</td></tr>
<tr><td colspan="5">13. ⓪①②③④⑤⑥⑦⑧⑨</td></tr>
</table>

14. What is the total score for the correct statement(s) from the following.

Given: $MnO_4^- + 8H^+ + 5e^- \rightarrow Mn^{2+} + 4H_2O$; $E° = 1.51$ V

$Fe^{3+} + e^- \rightarrow Fe^{2+}$; $E° = 0.77$ V

$Cl_2 + 2e^- \rightarrow 2Cl^-$; $E° = 1.36$ V

$Ce^{4+} + e^- \rightarrow Ce^{3+}$; $E° = 1.76$ V

	Statement	Score
a.	MnO_4^- is a sufficiently strong oxidant in acidic solution (pH = 0) to oxidize Fe^{2+} ion.	1
b.	Fe^{2+} ion cannot be titrated against standard $KMnO_4$ solution if the medium is made acidic (pH = 0) by adding HCl.	2
c.	MnO_4^- ion cannot oxidize Ce^{3+} in acidic medium (pH = 0)	3
d.	Fe^{2+} cannot be titrated against standard $KMnO_4$ solution in acidic medium (pH = 0) in the presence of Ce^{3+} ion.	4

Section IV - Comprehension Type

Directions (Qs. 15-19): Based upon the given paragraphs, 4 multiple choice questions have to be answered. Each question has 4 choices (a), (b), (c) and (d), out of which **ONLY ONE** is correct.

PARAGRAPH-1

Column I, II & III contains, cell representation, type of reaction and electrode potential respectively.

	Column I		Column II		Column III
(I)	Pt, H_2 (1 atm) $\mid H^+$ (10^{-3} M) $\parallel H^+$ (10^{-6} M) $\mid H_2$ (1 atm) $\mid$ Pt	(i)	Spontaneous	(P)	$E_{cell} = -0.13$ V
(II)	Pt, F_2(g) (1 atm) $\mid F^-$ (10^{-2} M) $\parallel F^-$ (10^{-3} M) $\mid F_2$(g) (2 atm) $\mid$ Pt	(ii)	Non-spontaneous	(Q)	$E_{cell} = -0.177$ V
(III)	Hg, Hg_2Cl_2(s) $\mid$ KCl saturated solution $\parallel H^+$ (pH = 10) $\mid$ Q, $QH_2 \mid$ Pt $\left(\begin{array}{l} E_{Q\mid H_2O} = 0.7 \text{ V} \\ E_{SCE} = 0.24 \text{ V} \end{array} \right)$	(iii)	Exergonic	(R)	$E_{cell} = 0.582$ V
(IV)	$Q + 2H^+ (pH = 2) + 2e^- \longrightarrow H_2O(aq)$ $E^o_{cell} = 0.7$ V	(iv)	Endergonic	(S)	$E_{cell} = 0.069$ V

15. For the cell given in column I, the only correct combination is

(a) (I)(ii)(P)   (b) (I)(ii)(Q)

(c) (I)(iv)(R)   (d) (I)(iv)(S)

16. For the cell given in column I, the only correct combination is

(a) (III)(iv)(P)   (b) (III)(iv)(Q)

(c) (III)(ii)(R)   (d) (III)(ii)(S)

17. For the cell given in column I, the only correct combination is

(a) (IV)(iii)(S)   (b) (IV)(iii)(R)

(c) (IV)(i)(Q)   (d) (IV)(ii)(P)

PARAGRAPH-2

Consider a cell which operates revesibly at constant temperature and pressure. The electrical work done by the system per mole of reactant consumed (i.e electrical energy supplied by the cell) is nFE, where n is the number of electrons liberated at one electrode or valency of the metal, F is Faraday (i.e. 96500 coulombs) and E is the emf of the cell. At the same time free energy of the system decreases by an amount ΔG. Therefore

$$-\Delta G = nFE$$

Also $\Delta G = \Delta H + T \left(\dfrac{\partial(\Delta G)}{\partial T} \right)_P$ ... (Gibbs-Helmholtz equn.)

From the above two equations, we see

$$nFE = -\Delta H + nFT \left(\dfrac{\partial E}{\partial T} \right)_P$$

This equation gives heat of chemical reaction occurring within the cell as a function of EMF and temperature.

$\left(\dfrac{\partial E}{\partial T} \right)_P$ is known as temperature coefficient of the cell.

18. At 25° the values of E for the reversible cells, $Pb \mid PbCl_2(s)$ $KCl(aq), AgCl(s) \mid Ag$ and $Pb \mid PbI_2(s), KI(aq); AgI(s) \mid Ag$

are 0.4902 V and 0.2111 V, and the values of $\left(\dfrac{\partial E}{\partial T}\right)_p$ are -0.000186 volt degree^{-1} and -0.000127 volt degree^{-1} respectively. In both cases, the silver electrode is the positive pole of the cell. The ΔH in calories at 25°C for the reaction

$PbI_2(s) + 2AgCl(s) + \rightleftharpoons PbCl_2(s) + 2AgI(s)$ is

(a) -25160 cal   (b) 11480 cal
(c) -13680 cal   (d) -11480 cal.

19. The EMF of Daniels's cell at 15°C is 1.0934 volt and temperature coeffficeint of emf is -4.29×10^{-4} Volt/degree. The heat of reaction for the cell is

(a) -56187 cal   (b) $+44702$ cal
(c) -47402 cal   (d) $+56187$ cal

Section V - Matrix-Match Type

This section contains 1 questions. It contains statements given in two columns, which have to be matched. Statements in column I are labelled as A, B, C and D whereas statements in column II are labelled as p, q, r and s. The answers to these questions have to be appropriately bubbled as illustrated in the following example. If the correct matches are A-p, A-r, B-p, B-s, C-r, C-s and D-q, then the correctly bubbled matrix will look like the following:

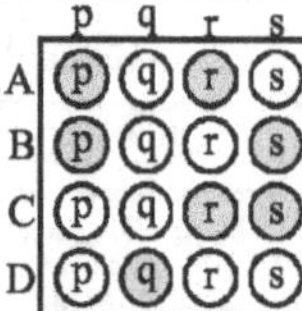

20. Match the following :

Column I		Column II
(A) Maximum potential for H-electrode at $p_{H_2} = 1$ atm	p.	-0.414 V
(B) Minimum potential for H-electrode at $p_{H_2} = 1$ atm	q.	-0.018 V
(C) Potential of H-electrode set up in 1 M KCl and $p_{H_2} = 1$ atm	r.	-0.827 V
(D) Potential of H-electrode set up in 1.0 M HCl and $p_{H_2} = 4$ atm	s.	0.0 V

RESPONSE GRID	
18. (a)(b)(c)(d) 19. (a)(b)(c)(d)	
20. A - (p)(q)(r)(s); B - (p)(q)(r)(s); C - (p)(q)(r)(s); D - (p)(q)(r)(s)	

DAILY PRACTICE PROBLEM DPP CHAPTERWISE 14 - CHEMISTRY

Total Questions	20	Total Marks	74
Attempted		Correct	
Incorrect		Net Score	
Cut-off Score	24	Qualifying Score	35
Success Gap = Net Score – Qualifying Score			
Net Score = (Correct × 4) – (Incorrect × 1)			

Date :   **Start Time :**   **End Time :**

CHEMISTRY [CC15]

SYLLABUS : Chemical Kinetics

Max. Marks : 74   **Time : 60 min.**

GENERAL INSTRUCTIONS

- The Daily Practice Problem Sheet contains 20 Questions divided into 5 sections.
  Section I has **5** MCQs with ONLY 1 Correct Option, **3** marks for each correct answer and **−1** for each incorrect answer.
  Section II has **4** MCQs with ONE or MORE THAN ONE Correct options.
  For each question, marks will be awarded in one of the following categories:
  Full marks: **+4** If only the bubble(s) corresponding to all the correct option(s) is (are) darkened.
  Partial marks: **+1** For darkening a bubble corresponding to each correct option provided NO INCORRECT option is darkened.
  Zero marks: If none of the bubbles is darkened.
  Negative marks: **−2** In all other cases.
  Section III has **5** Single Digit Integer Answer Type Questions, **3** marks for each Correct Answer and 0 marks in all other cases.
  Section IV has Comprehension/Matching Cum-Comprehension Type Questions having **5** MCQs with ONLY ONE correct option, **3** marks for each Correct Answer and 0 marks in all other cases.
  Section V has **1** Matching Type Questions, **2** mark for the correct matching of each row and 0 marks in all other cases.
- You have to evaluate your Response Grids yourself with the help of Solutions.

Section I - Straight Objective Type

This section contains 5 multiple choice questions. Each question has 4 choices (a), (b), (c) and (d), out of which **ONLY ONE** is correct.

1. Reaction rate between two substance A and B is expressed as following:
rate $= k[A]^n[B]^m$
If the concentration of A is doubled and concentration of B is made half of initial concentration, the ratio of the new rate to the earlier rate will be:

(a) $m+n$ (b) $n-m$

(c) $\dfrac{1}{2^{(m+n)}}$ (d) $2^{(n-m)}$

2. The rate coefficient (k) for a particular reactions is $1.3 \times 10^{-4}\,M^{-1}\,s^{-1}$ at $100°C$, and $1.3 \times 10^{-3}\,M^{-1}\,s^{-1}$ at $150°C$. What is the energy of activation (E_a) (in kJ) for this reaction? (R = molar gas constant = $8.314\,JK^{-1}\,mol^{-1}$)

(a) 16   (b) 60

(c) 99   (d) 132

3. The rate constant, the activation energy and the arrhenius parameter of a chemical reaction at $25°C$ are $3.0 \times 10^{-4}\,s^{-1}$, $104.4\,kJ\,mol^{-1}$ and $6.0 \times 10^{14}\,s^{-1}$ respectively. The value of the rate constant as $T \to \infty$ is

(a) $2.0 \times 10^{18}\,s^{-1}$ (b) $6.0 \times 10^{14}\,s^{-1}$

(c) Infinity   (d) $3.6 \times 10^{30}\,s^{-1}$

RESPONSE GRID	1. ⓐⓑⓒⓓ	2. ⓐⓑⓒⓓ	3. ⓐⓑⓒⓓ

Space for Rough Work

4. For the non-stoichiometric reaction $2A + B \rightarrow C + D$, the following kinetic data were obtained in three separate experiments, all at 298 K.

Initial Concentration (A)	Initial Concentration (B)	Initial rate of formation of C (mol L^{-1} s^{-1})
0.1 M	0.1 M	1.2×10^{-3}
0.1 M	0.2 M	1.2×10^{-3}
0.2 M	0.1 M	2.4×10^{-3}

The rate law for the formation of C is:

(a) $\dfrac{dC}{dt} = k[A][B]$ (b) $\dfrac{dC}{dt} = k[A]^2[B]$

(c) $\dfrac{dC}{dt} = k[A][B]^2$ (d) $\dfrac{dC}{dt} = k[A]$

5. The initial rates of reaction
$3A + 2B + C \longrightarrow$ Products, at different initial concentrations are given below:

Initial rate, Ms^{-1}	$[A]_0$, M	$[B]_0$, M	$[C]_0$, M
5.0×10^{-3}	0.010	0.005	0.010
5.0×10^{-3}	0.010	0.005	0.015
1.0×10^{-2}	0.010	0.010	0.010
1.25×10^{-3}	0.005	0.005	0.010

The order with respect to the reactants, A, B and C are respectively

(a) 3, 2, 0   (b) 3, 2, 1   (c) 2, 2, 0   (d) 2, 1, 0

Section II - Multiple Correct Answer Type

This section contains 4 multiple correct answer(s) type questions. Each question has 4 choices (a), (b), (c) and (d), out of which **ONE OR MORE** is/are correct.

6. Hydrolysis of an ester is catalysed by H$^+$ ion. Using equimolar concentrations of two acids HX and HY, both being strong acids, the rate constants of the reaction are found to be 3×10^{-3} min^{-1} and 5×10^{-3} min^{-1} respectively at a fixed temperature. It can be concluded that

(a) Rate constant may be taken as the measure of degree of ionization of the acid used as catalyst

(b) HX is a stronger acid than HY, their relative strength being 1.7

(c) HX is a weaker acid than HY, their relative strength being 0.6

(d) none is correct

7. Hydrolysis of a sugar is catalysed by H$^+$ ion. Half-life of the reaction is independent of initial concentration of sugar at a particular pH. At a constant concentration of sugar rate increases 10 times when pH is decreased by one unit. Pick out the correct statements of the following :

(a) Rate α [sugar]

(b) Rate α [H$^+$]

(c) Rate law : rate $= k$ [sugar]

(d) Rate law : rate $= k$ [sugar] [H$^+$]

8. The rate law of gaseous reaction : $A_{(g)} + B_{(g)} \rightarrow$ Products is given by $k[A]^2[B]$. If the volume of the reaction vessel is suddenly doubled, which of the following will happen?

(a) The rate w.r.t. A will decrease two times

(b) The rate w.r.t. A will decrease four times

(c) The rate w.r.t. B will decrease two times

(d) The overall rate will decrease 8 times of the original value

9. The reaction $2A + B \longrightarrow C + D$ goes to completion and follows the following rate law
$$-\frac{d}{dt}[A] = k[A]^2[B]$$
For this reaction the values of x and y in the following table are

Set	$[A]_0 \times 10^6$ (mol dm^{-3})	$[B]_0 \times 10^6$ (mol dm^{-3})	Half-life $(t_{1/2})$ (sec)
1	300	40	62.6
2	300	60	x
3	5	300	625
4	10	300	y

(a) 62.6 and 625   (b) 62.6 and 312.5

(c) 31.3 and 625   (d) 31.3 and 312.5

Section III - Integer Type

This section contains 5 questions. The answer to each of the questions is a single digit integer ranging from 0 to 9.

10. If one starts with 1 Curie (Ci) of radioactive substance $(t_{1/2} = 15$ hr$)$, the activity left after a period of two weeks will be about $0.02x$ μCi. Find the value of x.

11. Hydrolysis of an alkyl halide (RX) by dilute alkali [$\overset{\ominus}{\text{OH}}$] takes place simultaneously by S$_N$2 and S$_N$1 pathways. A plot of $-\dfrac{1}{[RX]}\dfrac{d[R-X]}{dt}$ vs [$\overset{\ominus}{\text{OH}}$] is a straight line of the slope equal to 2×10^3 mol^{-1} L h^{-1} and intercept equal to 1×10^2 h^{-1}. Calculate the initial rate (mol L^{-1} min^{-1}) of consumption of RX when the reaction is carried out taking 1 mol L^{-1} of RX and 0.1 mol L^{-1} of [$\overset{\ominus}{\text{OH}}$] ions.

12. In the case of a first order reaction. The time required for 93.75% of reaction to take place is x times that required for half of the reaction. Find the value of x.

13. A second order reaction requires 70 min to change the concentration of reactants from 0.08 M to 0.01 M. The time required to become 0.04 M $= 2x$ min. Find the value of x.

14. What is the order of reaction for which rate becomes half if volume of the container having same amount of reactant is doubled? Assume gaseous phase reaction.

Section IV - Comprehension Type

Directions (Qs. 15-19) : Based upon the given paragraphs, 4 multiple choice questions have to be answered. Each question has 4 choices (a), (b), (c) and (d), out of which **ONLY ONE** is correct.

PARAGRAPH-1

Column I, II and III contains order of reaction, integral equation and nature of plot respectively.

Column I	Column II	Column III
(I) $A \xrightarrow{k} Product, order = \dfrac{3}{2}$	(i) $k = \dfrac{1}{t} \times \left(\dfrac{1}{(a-x)} - \dfrac{1}{a} \right)$	(P) 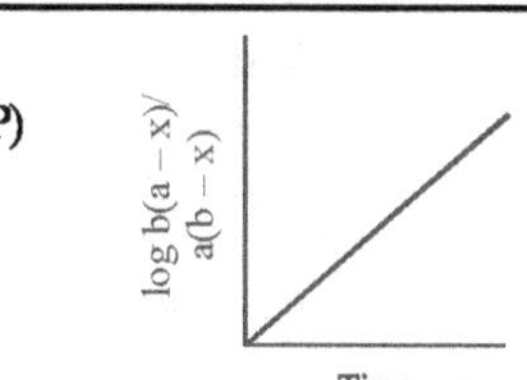 Slope $= \dfrac{k(a-b)}{2.303}$
(II) $A \xrightarrow{k} Product, order = \dfrac{1}{2}$	(ii) $k = \dfrac{2}{t} \times \left(\dfrac{1}{(a-x)^{1/2}} - \dfrac{1}{a^{1/2}} \right)$	(Q) 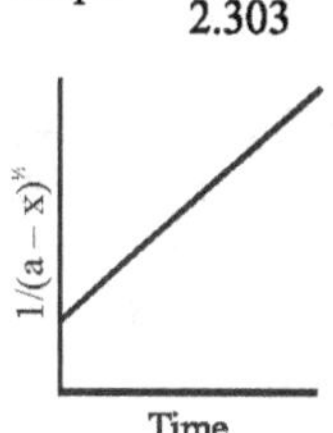 Slope $= k/2$, intercept $= \dfrac{1}{a^{1/2}}$
(III) $\begin{array}{cc} A + B \xrightarrow{k} Product, order = 2 \\ (a) \quad (a) \end{array}$	(iii) $k = \dfrac{2.303}{t(a-b)} \times \log \dfrac{b(a-x)}{a(b-x)}$	(R) 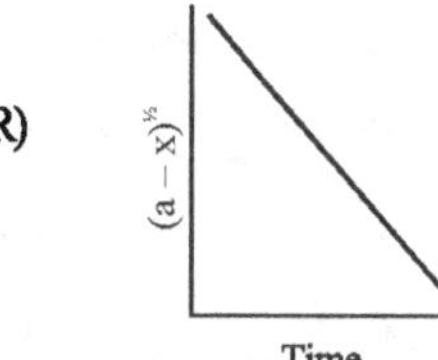 Slope $= k/2$, intercept $= a/2$
(IV) $\begin{array}{cc} A + B \xrightarrow{k} Product \\ (a) \quad (b) \end{array}$	(iv) $k = \dfrac{2}{t} \times \left[a^{1/2} - (a-x)^{1/2} \right]$	(S) 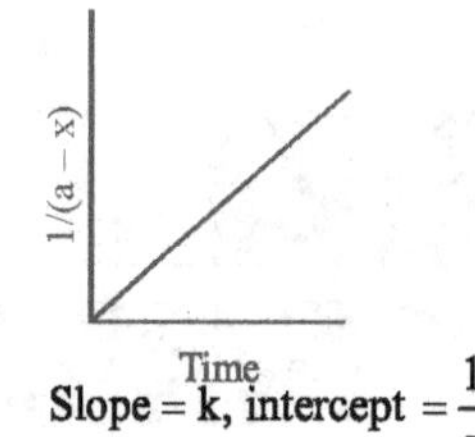 Slope $= k$, intercept $= \dfrac{1}{a}$

15. For reaction given in column I, the only correct combination is
  (a) (I) (iv) (S)   (b) (I) (iv) (Q)
  (c) (I) (ii) (Q)   (d) (I) (i) (P)

16. For reaction given in column II, the only correct combination is
  (a) (II) (iv) (R)   (b) (II) (iv) (Q)
  (c) (II) (i) (Q)   (d) (II) (ii) (S)

17. For reaction given in column III, the only correct combination is
  (a) (III) (ii) (P)   (b) (III) (i) (Q)
  (c) (III) (i) (S)   (d) (III) (iv) (R)

PARAGRAPH-2

Chemical reactions such as

$$A \xrightarrow{k_1} B \xrightarrow{k_2} C$$

proceed from reactants to products through one or more intermediate steps are called consecutive reactions. In these reactions each stage has its own rate and own rate constants.

The simplest case is one in which there are only two consecutive stages and the two reactions are of first order with specific reaction rates k_1 and k_2.

RESPONSE GRID	15. ⓐⓑⓒⓓ	16. ⓐⓑⓒⓓ	17. ⓐⓑⓒⓓ

The rate equation for A is readily integrated to obtain

$$[A]_t = [A]_0 .e^{-k_1 t}; \text{ and } [B] = \frac{k_1[A]_0}{k_2 - k_1}(e^{-k_1 t} - e^{-k_2 t})$$

18. The above equation shows that
(a) concentration of A falls exponentially and the amount of C will rise until it approaches that of B.
(b) concentration of A falls exponentially but the concentration of B slowly goes on increasing till it becomes constant at certain concentrations.
(c) The concentration of B will first increase and rises to a maximum and then decreases.
(d) all the above are correct.

19. If C_0 is the initial concentration of A and C_1, C_2 and C_3 are concentrations of A, B and C respectively at any time t, then the values of k_1 and k_2 can be determined using the equations

(a) $C_2 = \dfrac{k_1 . C_0 .}{k_2 - k_1}[e^{-k_1 t} - e^{-k_2 t}]$

(b) $C_2 = \dfrac{k_1 . C_1 .}{k_2 - k_1}[e^{-k_1 t} - e^{-k_2 t}]$

(c) $C_2 = \dfrac{k_1 . C_0 .}{k_1 - k_2}[e^{-k_1 t} - e^{-k_2 t}]$

(d) none of these

Section V - Matrix-Match Type

This section contains 1 questions. It contains statements given in two columns, which have to be matched. Statements in column I are labelled as A, B, C and D whereas statements in column II are labelled as p, q, r and s. The answers to these questions have to be appropriately bubbled as illustrated in the following example. If the correct matches are A-p, A-r, B-p, B-s, C-r, C-s and D-q, then the correctly bubbled matrix will look like the following:

	p	q	r	s
A	⬤	q	⬤	s
B	⬤	q	r	⬤
C	p	q	⬤	⬤
D	p	⬤	r	s

20. Match the appropriate experimental methods used to study the kinetics of the following reactions :

Reactions

(A) $2N_2O_5(g) \rightarrow 4NO_2(g) + O_2(g)$

(B) $CH_3COOC_2H_5(aq) + H_2O \xrightarrow{[H^+]}$
$CH_3COOH(aq) + C_2H_5OH(aq)$

(C) $C_6H_5N = N - Cl(aq) \rightarrow C_6H_5Cl(l) + N_2(g)$

(D) $C_{12}H_{22}O_{11}(aq) + H_2O \xrightarrow{[H^+]}$
$C_6H_{12}O_6(aq) + C_6H_{12}O_6(aq)$
  Glucose   Fructose

Experimental Methods

p. Measurement of optical activity

q. Measurement of volume of gas at constant P and T

r. Titration of an aliquot of reaction mixture with alkali

s. Measurement of pressure of reaction mixture at constant V and T

RESPONSE GRID	18. (a)(b)(c)(d) 19. (a)(b)(c)(d)
	20. A - (p)(q)(r)(s); B - (p)(q)(r)(s); C - (p)(q)(r)(s); D - (p)(q)(r)(s)

DAILY PRACTICE PROBLEM DPP CHAPTERWISE 15 - CHEMISTRY

Total Questions	20	Total Marks	74
Attempted		Correct	
Incorrect		Net Score	
Cut-off Score	24	Qualifying Score	35
Success Gap = Net Score − Qualifying Score			
Net Score = (Correct × 4) − (Incorrect × 1)			

Date : | **Start Time :** | **End Time :**

CHEMISTRY $\boxed{\text{CC16}}$

SYLLABUS : Surface Chemistry

Max. Marks : 74   **Time : 60 min.**

GENERAL INSTRUCTIONS

- The Daily Practice Problem Sheet contains 20 Questions divided into 5 sections.
- **Section I** has **6** MCQs with ONLY 1 Correct Option, **3** marks for each correct answer and **−1** for each incorrect answer.
- **Section II** has **4** MCQs with ONE or MORE THAN ONE Correct options.
- For each question, marks will be awarded in one of the following categories:
- Full marks: **+4** If only the bubble(s) corresponding to all the correct option(s) is (are) darkened.
- Partial marks: **+1** For darkening a bubble corresponding to each correct option provided NO INCORRECT option is darkened.
- Zero marks: If none of the bubbles is darkened.
- Negative marks: **−2** In all other cases.
- **Section III** has **4** Single Digit Integer Answer Type Questions, **3** marks for each Correct Answer and 0 marks in all other cases.
- **Section IV** has Comprehension/Matching Cum-Comprehension Type Questions having **4** MCQs with ONLY ONE correct option, **3** marks for each Correct Answer and 0 marks in all other cases.
- **Section V** has **2** Matching Type Questions, **2** mark for the correct matching of each row and 0 marks in all other cases.
- You have to evaluate your Response Grids yourself with the help of Solutions.

Section I - Straight Objective Type

This section contains 6 multiple choice questions. Each question has 4 choices (a), (b), (c) and (d), out of which **ONLY ONE** is correct.

1. The ion that is more effective for the coagulation of As_2S_3 sol is
   (a) Ba^{2+} (b) Na^+ (c) PO_4^{3-} (d) Al^{3+}

2. Which of the following ions will have the minimum coagulating value for the sol obtained by adding $FeCl_3$ solution to slight excess of NaOH
   (a) SO_4^{2-} (b) $[Fe(CN)_6]^{3-}$
   (c) Ba^{2+} (d) Al^{3+}

3. When 6.0×10^{-5} g of a protective colloid was added to 20 mL of a standard gold sol, the precipitation of latter was just prevented on addition of 2 mL of 10% NaCl solution. The gold number of the protective colloid is
   (a) 3   (b) 3×10^{-5}
   (c) 0.06   (d) 0.03

RESPONSE GRID   **1.** (a)(b)(c)(d)   **2.** (a)(b)(c)(d)   **3.** (a)(b)(c)(d)

Space for Rough Work

4. Which of the following when dissolved in water to get their sol lower the surface tension of water?

(a) Al_2O_3 (b) Silica

(c) Protein   (d) Stannic oxide

5. The volume of a colloidal particle, V_C as compared to the volume of a solute particle in a true solution V_S, could be

(a) $\dfrac{V_C}{V_S} \simeq 10^3$ (b) $\dfrac{V_C}{V_S} \simeq 10^{-3}$

(c) $\dfrac{V_C}{V_S} \simeq 10^{23}$ (d) $\dfrac{V_C}{V_S} \simeq 1$

6. If x is the mass of the gas adsorbed on mass m of the adsorbent at pressure p, Freundlich adsorption isotherm gives a straight line on plotting

(a) x/m vs p (b) x/m vs $1/p$

(c) $\log x/m$ vs $\log p$ (d) $\log x/m$ vs p

Section II - Multiple Correct Answer Type

This section contains 4 multiple correct answer(s) type questions. Each question has 4 choices (a), (b), (c) and (d), out of which **ONE OR MORE** is/are correct.

7. When a hydrophilic sol like gelatin is subjected to electric field, the sol particles move

(a) towards cathode at pH less than the isoelectric point

(b) towards anode at pH greater than the isoelectric point

(c) in both directions at isoelectric pH

(d) in neither direction at isoelectric pH

8. Following diagram shows the dependence of coagulation value on concentration of sol in case of hydrophobic sol.

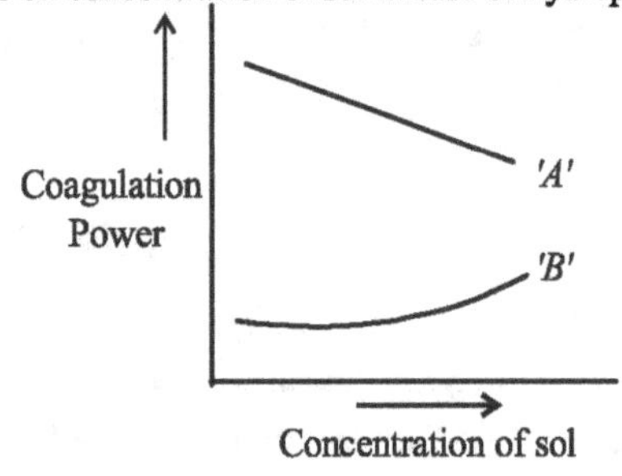

(a) Curve 'A' is for univalent electrolyte

(b) Curve 'A' is for polyvalent electrolyte

(c) Curve 'B' is for univalent electrolyte

(d) Curve 'B' is for polyvalent electrolyte

9. Which of the following statement(s) is/are correct ?

(a) Colloidal electrolytes are those electrolytes that are partially associated and that form conducting micelles when dissolved in water.

(b) Dyes, soap belong to colloidal electrolytes.

(c) The solutions of colloidal electrolytes have higher osmotic pressure than expected.

(d) Colloidal electrolytes can be regarded as macromolecules.

10. Which of the following is/are correct statement(s)

(a) Spontaneous adsorption of gases on solid surface is an exothermic process as entropy decreases during adsorption

(b) Formation of micelles takes place when temperature is below Kraft Temperature (T_k) and concentration is above critical micelle concentration (CMC)

(c) A colloid of $Fe(OH)_3$ is prepared by adding a little excess (required to completely precipitate Fe^{3+} ions as $Fe(OH)_3$) of NaOH in $FeCl_3$ solution. The particles of this sol will move towards cathode during electrophoresis.

(d) According to Hardy-Schulze rules the coagulation (flocculating) value of Fe^{3+} ion will be more than Ba^{2+} or Na^+.

Section III - Integer Type

This section contains 4 questions. The answer to each of the questions is a single digit integer ranging from 0 to 9.

11. For the coagulation of 500 mL of arsenious sulphide sol, 2 mL of 1 M NaCl is required. What is the flocculation value of NaCl?

12. The gold number of gelatin is 0.01. Calculate the amount of gelatin to be added to 1000 mL of a colloidal sol of gold to prevent its coagulation, before adding 1 mL of 10% NaCl solution.

13. 526.3 mL of 0.5 m HCl is shaken with 0.5 g of activated charcoal and filtered. The concentration of the filtrate is reduced to 0.4 m. Calculate the amount of adsorption (x/m)?

14. In an adsorption experiment, a graph between $\log (x/m)$ versus $\log P$ was found to be linear with a slope of $45°$. The intercept on the y axis was found to be 0.301. Calculate the amount of the gas adsorbed per gram of charcoal under a pressure of 3.0 atm.

Section IV - Comprehension Type

Directions (Qs. 15-18) : Based upon the given paragraphs, 4 multiple choice questions have to be answered. Each question has 4 choices (a), (b), (c) and (d), out of which **ONLY ONE** is correct.

PARAGRAPH-1

The Colloidal particles are electrically charged as is indictated by their migration towards cathode or anode under the applied electric field. In a particular colloidal system, all particles carry either positive or negative charge.

The electric charge on colloidal particles originate in several ways. According to preferential adsorption theory, the freshly obtained precipitate particles adsorb ions from the dispersion medium, which are common to their lattice and acquire the charge of adsorbed ions.

In some cases the colloidal particles are aggregates of cations or anions having ampiphilic character. When the ions possess hydrophobic part (hydrocarbon end) as well as hydrophilic part (polar end group), they undergo association in aqueous solution to form particles having colloidal size. The formation of such particles, called micelles, plays a very important role in the solubilization of water insoluble substances, (hydrocarbons, oils, fats, grease etc.). In micelles, the polar end groups are directed towards water and the hydrocarbon ends into the centre. The charge on sol particles of proteins depends on the pH. At low pH, the basic group of protein molecule is ionized (protonated) and at higher pH (alkaline medium), the acidic group is ionized. At isoelectric pH, characteristic to the protein, both basic and acidic groups are equally ionized.

15. When 9.0 mL of arsenius sulphide sol and 1.0 mL of 1.0×10^{-4} M $BaCl_2$ are mixed, turbidity due to precipitation just appears after 2 hours. The effective ion and its coagulating value are respectively

  (a) Cl^-, 10 m mol/L   (b) Cl^-, 20 m mol/L

  (c) Ba^{2+}, 10 m mol/L   (d) Ba^{2+}, 20 m mol /L

16. How are the osmotic pressures (π) of 1.0 M KCl (1) and 0.1 M potassium oleate (2) are related, temperature being the same?

  (a) $\pi_1 = \pi_2$ (b) $\pi_1 < \pi_2$

  (c) $\pi_1 > \pi_2$ (d) Can't be predicted

PARAGRAPH-2

The stability of a colloidal solution is attributed largely to the electric charge of dispersed particles. Removal of this charge causes the separation of dispersed phase and dispersion medium. On addition of small amount of electrolytes, the ions carrying opposite charge are adsorbed by sol particles resulting in the neutralization of their charge. The sol particles with no charge or reduced charge aggregate and separate from the dispersion medium. The coagulating power of the effective ion is expressed in terms of its coaguluting value, defined as its minimum concentration (milli moles per litre) needed to precipitate a given sol.

In case sol particles are extensively hydrated the sol has extra stability due the charge and solvation of the particles.

17. Which of the following ions would have the maximum coagulating power for a sol prepared from freshly obtained SnO_2 on peptization by little NaOH solution

(a) Cl^- (b) PO_4^{3-} (c) K^+ (d) Ba^{2+}

18. A sodium oleate sol can be precipitated more easily by adding

(a) NaCl only

(b) Na_2SO_4 only

(c) NaCl and C_2H_5OH

(d) KCl

Section V - Matrix-Match Type

This section contains 2 questions. It contains statements given in two columns, which have to be matched. Statements in column I are labelled as A, B, C and D whereas statements in column II are labelled as p, q, r and s. The answers to these questions have to be appropriately bubbled as illustrated in the following example. If the correct matches are A-p, A-r, B-p, B-s, C-r, C-s and D-q, then the correctly bubbled matrix will look like the following:

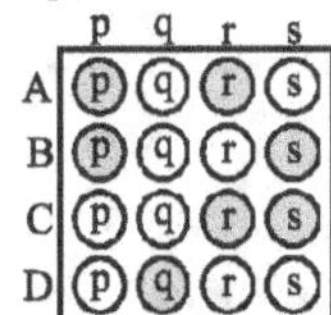

19. Match the items given in Column I and Column II.

Column-I	Column-II
(A) Protective colloid	p. $FeCl_3 + NaOH$
(B) Liquid-liquid colloid	q. Lyophilic colloids
(C) Positively charged colloid	r. Emulsion
(D) Negatively charged colloid	s. $FeCl_3 +$ hot water

20. Match the items of Column I and Column II.

Column-I	Column-II
(A) Dialysis	p. Cleansing action of soap
(B) Peptisation	q. Coagulation
(C) Emulsification	r. Colloidal sol formation
(D) Electrophoresis	s. Purification

RESPONSE GRID	
	17. ⓐⓑⓒⓓ **18.** ⓐⓑⓒⓓ
	19. A - ⓟⓠⓡⓢ; B - ⓟⓠⓡⓢ; C - ⓟⓠⓡⓢ; D - ⓟⓠⓡⓢ
	20. A - ⓟⓠⓡⓢ; B - ⓟⓠⓡⓢ; C - ⓟⓠⓡⓢ; D - ⓟⓠⓡⓢ

DAILY PRACTICE PROBLEM DPP CHAPTERWISE 16 - CHEMISTRY

Total Questions	20	Total Marks	74
Attempted		Correct	
Incorrect		Net Score	
Cut-off Score	26	Qualifying Score	36
Success Gap = Net Score – Qualifying Score			
Net Score = (Correct × 4) – (Incorrect × 1)			

Space for Rough Work

Date :   **Start Time :**   **End Time :**

CHEMISTRY $\boxed{\text{CC17}}$

SYLLABUS : General Principles and Processes of Isolation of Elements

Max. Marks : 74   **Time : 60 min.**

GENERAL INSTRUCTIONS

- The Daily Practice Problem Sheet contains 20 Questions divided into 5 sections.

  Section I has **5** MCQs with ONLY 1 Correct Option, **3** marks for each correct answer and **−1** for each incorrect answer.

  Section II has **4** MCQs with ONE or MORE THAN ONE Correct options.

  For each question, marks will be awarded in one of the following categories:

  Full marks: **+4** If only the bubble(s) corresponding to all the correct option(s) is (are) darkened.

  Partial marks: **+1** For darkening a bubble corresponding to each correct option provided NO INCORRECT option is darkened.

  Zero marks: If none of the bubbles is darkened.

  Negative marks: **−2** In all other cases.

  Section III has **5** Single Digit Integer Answer Type Questions, **3** marks for each Correct Answer and 0 marks in all other cases.

  Section IV has Comprehension/Matching Cum-Comprehension Type Questions having **5** MCQs with ONLY ONE correct option, **3** marks for each Correct Answer and 0 marks in all other cases.

  Section V has **1** Matching Type Questions, **2** mark for the correct matching of each row and 0 marks in all other cases.

- You have to evaluate your Response Grids yourself with the help of Solutions.

Section I - Straight Objective Type

This section contains 5 multiple choice questions. Each question has 4 choices (a), (b), (c) and (d), out of which **ONLY ONE** is correct.

1. Which of the following factors is of no significance for roasting sulphide ores to the oxides and not subjecting the sulphide ores to carbon reduction directly?

   (a) Metal sulphides are thermodynamically more stable than CS_2

   (b) CO_2 is thermodynamically more stable than CS_2

   (c) Metal sulphides are less stable than the corresponding oxides

   (d) CO_2 is more volatile than CS_2

2. In the electrolysis of alumina to obtain aluminium metal, cryolite is added mainly to

   (a) lower the melting point of alumina

   (b) dissolve alumina in molten cryolite

   (c) remove the impurities of alumina

   (d) increase the electrical conductivity

RESPONSE GRID   **1.** ⓐⓑⓒⓓ   **2.** ⓐⓑⓒⓓ

Space for Rough Work

3. Calcination is the process in which
   (a) ore is heated above its melting point to expel H_2O or CO_2 or SO_2
   (b) ore is heated below its melting point to expel volatile impurities
   (c) ore is heated above its melting point to remove S, As and Sb as SO_2, As_2O_3 and Sb_2O_3 respectively
   (d) ore is heated below its melting point to expel H_2O or CO_2

4. Identity x, y, z for the following metallurgical process.

   $$\text{Metal sulphide} \xrightarrow{x} \text{Metal oxide} \xrightarrow{y} \text{Impure metal}$$
   $$\xrightarrow{z} \text{Pure metal.}$$

   x, y and z are respectively
   (a) roasting, smelting, electrolysis
   (b) roasting, calcination, smelting
   (c) calcination, auto-reduction, bassemerisation
   (d) None of the above is correct

5. Consider the following statements –
   (A) In the Aluminothermite process, aluminium acts as reducing agent.
   (B) 'Slag' formed during smelting in the extraction of copper is $FeSiO_3$.
   (C) In the extractive metallurgy of zinc, partial fusion of ZnO with coke is called sintering and reduction of ore to the molten metal is called smelting.
   (D) Extractive metallurgy of silver from its ore argentine involves complex formation and displacement by more electropositive metal.
   Choose the correct options –
   (a) A and B
   (b) B and C
   (c) A, B and C
   (d) A, B, C and D

Section II - Multiple Correct Answer Type
This section contains 4 multiple correct answer(s) type questions. Each question has 4 choices (a), (b), (c) and (d), out of which **ONE OR MORE** is/are correct.

6. In the process of extraction of gold

   $$\text{Roasted gold ore} + CN^- + H_2O \xrightarrow{O_2} [X] + OH^-$$
   $$[X] + Zn \longrightarrow [Y] + Au$$

   Identify the complexes [X] and [Y].
   (a) $X = [Au(CN)_2]^-$
   (b) $Y = [Zn(CN)_4]^{2-}$
   (c) $Y = [Zn(CN)_6]^{4+}$
   (d) $X = [Au(CN)_4]^{3-}$

7. Which of the following is/are false ?
   (a) All minerals are ores
   (b) Mercury is transported in containers made of iron
   (c) Calcination is the process of heating the ore strongly in the presence of air
   (d) Cassiterite is an ore of iron

8. Magnesium and aluminium can be extracted
   (a) by electrolysis of their fused salts
   (b) Mg from fused $MgCl_2$ and aluminium from alumina
   (c) by electrolysis of aqueous solution of their salts
   (d) by reduction of their oxides with carbon

9. Select the statement(s) that are true about reduction during smelting
   (a) It may be carried out using carbon
   (b) It may be carried out using aluminium
   (c) It may be carried out using hydrogen
   (d) It may be carried out using silver

Section III - Integer Type
This section contains 5 questions. The answer to each of the questions is a single digit integer ranging from 0 to 9.

10. How many cyanide ions are involved in the following chemical equation?

    $$Au + CN^{\ominus} + H_2O + O_2 \rightarrow [Au(CN)_2]^{\ominus} + \overset{\ominus}{O}H$$

11. Amongst the following, how many ores can be concentrated by froth flotation process:

    Galena, sphalerite, cassiterite, calamine, chalcocite, haematite, argentite

12. How many of the following are oxide ores:

    Calamine, cuprite, zincite, chalcocite, haematite, bauxite, magnetite, cassiterite

<table>
<tr><td rowspan="3">RESPONSE GRID</td><td>3. ⓐⓑⓒⓓ</td><td>4. ⓐⓑⓒⓓ</td><td>5. ⓐⓑⓒⓓ</td><td>6. ⓐⓑⓒⓓ</td><td>7. ⓐⓑⓒⓓ</td></tr>
<tr><td>8. ⓐⓑⓒⓓ</td><td>9. ⓐⓑⓒⓓ</td><td colspan="3">10. ⓪①②③④⑤⑥⑦⑧⑨</td></tr>
<tr><td colspan="2">11. ⓪①②③④⑤⑥⑦⑧⑨</td><td colspan="3">12. ⓪①②③④⑤⑥⑦⑧⑨</td></tr>
</table>

13. Find the number of following reactions which are involved in roasting process:

   i. $S_8 + 8O_2 \xrightarrow{\Delta} 8SO_2 \uparrow$

   ii. $P_4 + 5O_2 \xrightarrow{\Delta} P_4O_{10} \uparrow$

   iii. $4As + 3O_2 \xrightarrow{\Delta} 2As_2O_3 \uparrow$

   iv. $2ZnS + 3O_2 \xrightarrow{\Delta} 2ZnO + 2SO_2 \uparrow$

   v. $ZnCO_3 \xrightarrow{\Delta} 4ZnO + CO_2 \uparrow$

14. How many metallic ores are concentrated by magnetic separation method from the given ores?

Cassiterite, pyrolusite, rutile, magnetite, galena, cinnabar.

Section IV - Comprehension Type

Directions (Qs. 15-19) : Based upon the given paragraphs, 5 multiple choice questions have to be answered. Each question has 4 choices (a), (b), (c) and (d), out of which **ONLY ONE** is correct.

PARAGRAPH-1

Column I contains compound and Column II & III contains their formula and uses respectively.

	Column I		Column II		Column III
(I)	Glauber's salt	(i)	$FeSO_4.(NH_4)_2SO_4.6H_2O$	(P)	Efflorescent
(II)	Washing soda	(ii)	$NaHCO_3$	(Q)	Iron plating
(III)	Baking soda	(iii)	$Na_2CO_3.10H_2O$	(R)	Deliquescent
(IV)	Mohr's salt	(iv)	$Na_2SO_4.10H_2O$	(S)	Gives CO_2 on heating

15. Which combination represents such materials which are used as a laxative in medical field

  (a) (III)(ii)(Q)   (b) (IV)(ii)(P)

  (c) (I)(iv)(R)   (d) (I)(iii)(R)

16. Find the combination which loses water spontaneously

  (a) (I)(iv)(S)   (b) (II)(ii)(Q)

  (c) (IV)(iii)(R)   (d) (II)(iii)(P)

17. Correct combination is

  (a) (I)(iv)(S)   (b) IV(i)(Q)

  (c) (III)(iii)(S)   (d) (II)(ii)(Q)

PARAGRAPH-2

Standard Electrode Potentials and Metallurgy : The method employed for extracting a metal from its ore depends on the nature of the metal, that of the ore and may be related to the position of the metal in the electrochemical series. In general, metals with reduction potential less than − 0.5 volt yield compounds which are very difficult to reduce. Such metals are isolated by electrolysis. On the other hand noble metals with reduction potential + 0.5 volt form easily reducible compounds.

The standard electrode potential of a metal is a measure of its tendency to go into solution as hydrated ion. On the other hand, in metallurgical extractions we generally come across ores which are to be reduced to the metallic state. Thus, it may be said that a metal higher up in the electrochemical series should be more difficult to reduce to metallic form. As we move down, the reduction becomes more and more easy. However, it must be borne in mind that this is a very general statement and cannot be strictly applied because metals are seldom extracted from aqueous solutions.

Energy Factors and Electrode Potentials – The heat of sublimation (S) of solid metal, the ionization energy (I) of gaseous metal atom and the heat of hydration (H) of gaseous ion are the contributory factors towards electrode potential (E). These factors may be consolidated in a Born-Haber type of cycle.

$$M_{(solid)} \xrightarrow{\ E\ } M^+_{(aq)} + e^-$$
$$\Big\downarrow S \qquad\qquad \Big\uparrow H$$
$$M_{(gaseous)} \xrightarrow{\ I\ } M^+_{(gaseous)} + e^-$$

Thus, $E = +S + I - H$

S and *I* are positive because energy is supplied while *H* is negative as the process of hydration is an exothermic one liberating heat. As expected, ionization energies of alkali metals follow the trend :
Li > Na > K > Rb > Cs
It means Li has the least tendency to lose electron among alkali metals. However, from electrochemical series we find that lithium is the most reducing in character (E° for $\dfrac{Li^+}{Li}$ = – 3.05 volt). The anomalous behaviour of Li is understandable from the fact that heat of hydration of its ion is highest because of small size. The contribution of this hydration factor towards electrode potential makes Li even more reducing than Na or K.

18. The incorrect statement among the following is
- (a) the first ionisation potential of Al is less than the first ionisation potential of Mg
- (b) the second ionisation potential of Mg is greater than the second ionisation potential of Na
- (c) the first ionisation potential of Na is less than the first ionisation potential of Mg
- (d) the third ionisation of Mg is greater than third ionisation potential of Al.

19. How can alkali metals be extracted?
- (a) Reduction of their oxides
- (b) Displacement from their salt solution by any other element
- (c) Electrolysis of their fused salts
- (d) Electrolysis of their aqueous salt solutions

Section V - Matrix-Match Type

This section contains 1 question. It contains statements given in two columns, which have to be matched. Statements in column I are labelled as A, B, C and D whereas statements in column II are labelled as p, q, r and s. The answers to these questions have to be appropriately bubbled as illustrated in the following example. If the correct matches are A-p, A-r, B-p, B-s, C-r, C-s and D-q, then the correctly bubbled matrix will look like the following:

20. Match the following :

Column I		Column II	
(A)	Carbon monoxide	p.	Cu
(B)	Liquation	q.	Ag
(C)	Cupellation	r.	Ni
(D)	Hydrometallurgy	s.	Pb

Response Grid	18. ⓐⓑⓒⓓ 19. ⓐⓑⓒⓓ
	20. A - ⓟⓠⓡⓢ; B - ⓟⓠⓡⓢ; C - ⓟⓠⓡⓢ; D - ⓟⓠⓡⓢ

DAILY PRACTICE PROBLEM DPP CHAPTERWISE 17 - CHEMISTRY

Total Questions	20	Total Marks	74
Attempted		Correct	
Incorrect		Net Score	
Cut-off Score	28	Qualifying Score	38
Success Gap = Net Score – Qualifying Score			
Net Score = (Correct × 4) – (Incorrect × 1)			

Date :   Start Time :   End Time :

CHEMISTRY $\boxed{\text{CC18}}$

SYLLABUS : The p-Block Elements (Group 15, 16, 17 and 18)

Max. Marks : 74   **Time : 60 min.**

GENERAL INSTRUCTIONS

- The Daily Practice Problem Sheet contains 20 Questions divided into 5 sections.
  Section I has **6** MCQs with ONLY 1 Correct Option, **3** marks for each correct answer and **−1** for each incorrect answer.
  Section II has **4** MCQs with ONE or MORE THAN ONE Correct options.
  For each question, marks will be awarded in one of the following categories:
  Full marks: **+4** If only the bubble(s) corresponding to all the correct option(s) is (are) darkened.
  Partial marks: **+1** For darkening a bubble corresponding to each correct option provided NO INCORRECT option is darkened.
  Zero marks: If none of the bubbles is darkened.
  Negative marks: **−2** In all other cases.
  Section III has **5** Single Digit Integer Answer Type Questions, **3** marks for each Correct Answer and 0 marks in all other cases.
  Section IV has Comprehension/Matching Cum-Comprehension Type Questions having **5** MCQs with ONLY ONE correct option, **3** marks for each Correct Answer and 0 marks in all other cases.
  Section V has **1** Matching Type Questions, **2** mark for the correct matching of each row and 0 marks in all other cases.
- You have to evaluate your Response Grids yourself with the help of Solutions.

Section I - Straight Objective Type

This section contains 5 multiple choice questions. Each question has 4 choices (a), (b), (c) and (d), out of which **ONLY ONE** is correct.

1. Excess of KI reacts with $CuSO_4$ solution and then $Na_2S_2O_3$ solution is added to it. Which of the statements is incorrect for this reaction ?

    (a) $Na_2S_2O_3$ is oxidised   (b) CuI_2 is formed

    (c) Cu_2I_2 is formed   (d) Evolved I_2 is reduced

2. Which of the following xenon-oxo compounds may not be obtained by hydrolysis of xenon fluorides?

    (a) XeO_2F_2 (b) $XeOF_4$ (c) XeO_3 (d) XeO_4

3. A yellow metallic powder when burnt in a stream of fluorine produced a colourless, thermally stable and chemically inert gas 'X'. A gas 'Y', which is colourless and consists of the same elements as are present in gas 'X', is obtained by heating together sulphur dichloride and sodium fluoride. Gases 'X' and 'Y' respectively are

    (a) SF_4 and SF_6 (b) SF_4 and S_2F_2

    (c) SF_6 and SF_4 (d) None of these

RESPONSE GRID   **1.** ⓐⓑⓒⓓ   **2.** ⓐⓑⓒⓓ   **3.** ⓐⓑⓒⓓ

Space for Rough Work

4. If Cl_2 gas is passed into aqueous solution of KI containing some CCl_4 and the mixture is shaken then
   (a) upper layer becomes violet
   (b) lower layer becomes violet
   (c) homogenous violet layer is formed
   (d) None of these

5. The formation of $O_2^+[PtF_6]^-$ is the basis for the formation of xenon fluorides. This is because
   (a) O_2 and Xe have comparable sizes
   (b) both O_2 and Xe are gases
   (c) O_2 and Xe have comparable ionisation energies
   (d) Both (a) and (c)

Section II - Multiple Correct Answer Type

This section contains 4 multiple correct answer(s) type questions. Each question has 4 choices (a), (b), (c) and (d), out of which **ONE OR MORE** is/are correct.

6. Which of the following cannot be used as dehydrating agents for ammonia?
   (a) Conc. H_2SO_4 (b) anhydrous $CaCl_2$
   (c) P_4O_{10} (d) CaO

7. Sodium nitrate decomposes above $800°$ C to give
   (a) N_2 (b) O_2
   (c) NO_2 (d) Na_2O

8. Which of the following is/are correct for the characteristics indicated against each ?

(a) $HClO < HClO_2 < HClO_3 < HClO_4$ (oxidising power)
(b) $ClO_4^- < BrO_4^- < IO_4^-$ (oxidising power)
(c) $ClO^- < BrO^- < IO^-$ (disproportionation)
(d) $HClO < HClO_2 < HClO_3 < HClO_4$ (Acidic strength)

9. It is not suitable to add conc. H_2SO_4 to KI (s) for preparation of HI because
   (a) I^- (iodide ions) are oxidized to I_2
   (b) The product formed gets contaminated by compounds of sulphur.
   (c) Both the acids (i.e., H_2SO_4 and HI) are strong acids
   (d) H_2SO_4 is a strong acid and HI is a weak acid.

Section III - Integer Type

This section contains 5 questions. The answer to each of the questions is a single digit integer ranging from 0 to 9.

10. How many P–O–P bonds are present in P_4O_8?

11. Among the oxides given below, how many are acidic?
    $CrO_3, Mn_2O_7, CuO, CO, SO_2$

12. In the molecule ICl_3, how many lone pairs of electrons are associated with iodine?

13. How many $d\pi–p\pi$ bonds are there in XeO_4?

14. What is the total number of lone pair of electrons present in Xe in XeF_2?

<table>
<tr><td rowspan="4">RESPONSE GRID</td><td>4. (a)(b)(c)(d)</td><td>5. (a)(b)(c)(d)</td><td>6. (a)(b)(c)(d)</td><td>7. (a)(b)(c)(d)</td><td>8. (a)(b)(c)(d)</td></tr>
<tr><td>9. (a)(b)(c)(d)</td><td colspan="2">10. (0)(1)(2)(3)(4)(5)(6)(7)(8)(9)</td><td colspan="2">11. (0)(1)(2)(3)(4)(5)(6)(7)(8)(9)</td></tr>
<tr><td colspan="2">12. (0)(1)(2)(3)(4)(5)(6)(7)(8)(9)</td><td colspan="3">13. (0)(1)(2)(3)(4)(5)(6)(7)(8)(9)</td></tr>
<tr><td colspan="5">14. (0)(1)(2)(3)(4)(5)(6)(7)(8)(9)</td></tr>
</table>

Space for Rough Work

Section IV - Comprehension Type

Directions (Qs. 15-19) : Based upon the given paragraphs, 5 multiple choice questions have to be answered. Each question has 4 choices (a), (b), (c) and (d), out of which **ONLY ONE** is correct.

PARAGRAPH-1

Column I contains different acids & Column II & III contains their molecular formula and No. of σ & π bonds respectively

	Column I		Column II		Column III
	Compound		**Molecular Formula**		**No. of σ and π bonds**
(I)	Thiosulfuric acid	(i)	$H_2S_2O_6$	(P)	$6\,\sigma$ and 2π
(II)	Persulfuric acid	(ii)	$H_2S_2O_8$	(Q)	$11\,\sigma$ and 4π
(III)	Peroxydisulfuric acid	(iii)	H_2SO_5	(R)	$9\,\sigma$ and 4π
(IV)	Dithionic acid	(iv)	$H_2S_2O_3$	(S)	$7\,\sigma$ and 2π

15. Find appropriate combination for caro's acid

(a) (IV)(iii)(R)   (b) (II)(iv)(P)

(c) (II)(iii)(S)   (d) (I)(iii)(Q)

16. Find appropriate combination for marshall's acid

(a) (III)(i)(R)   (b) (IV)(iii)(S)

(c) (I)(ii)(P)   (d) (III)(ii)(Q)

17. The only correct combination among the following is

(a) (I)(iv)(R)   (b) (II)(iii)(Q)

(c) (IV)(i)(R)   (d) (III)(i)(S)

PARAGRAPH-2

In all the oxyacids of phosphorous, each phosphorous atom is in sp^3 hybrid state, i.e., it is tetrahedrally bonded to neighbouring four atoms. All these acids contain P – OH bonds, the hydrogen atom of which are ionisable imparting acidic nature to the compound. The *ous acids* (oxidation state of P = +1 or +3) also have P – H bonds in which hydrogens are not ionisable (P and hydrogen have nearly same electronegativity). The presence of P – H group in these acids imparts reducing properties. The structure of the various acids are drawn below (note that the tetrahedral shape of phosphorus is not shown only for convenience of representation).

$$\begin{array}{cc}
\quad\text{O} & \quad\text{O}\\
\quad\|\| & \quad\|\|\\
\text{HO}-\overset{\displaystyle}{\underset{\displaystyle \text{H}}{\text{P}}}-\text{H} & \text{HO}-\overset{\displaystyle}{\underset{\displaystyle \text{H}}{\text{P}}}-\text{OH}
\end{array}$$

(A) Hypophosphorous acid   (B) Phosphorous acid

RESPONSE GRID	15. ⓐⓑⓒⓓ	16. ⓐⓑⓒⓓ	17. ⓐⓑⓒⓓ

$$HO-\underset{\underset{OH}{|}}{\overset{\overset{O}{\|}}{P}}-\underset{\underset{OH}{|}}{\overset{\overset{O}{\|}}{P}}-OH$$

(C) Hypophosph oric acid

$$HO-\underset{\underset{OH}{|}}{\overset{\overset{O}{\|}}{P}}-OH$$

(D) Phosphoric (Orthphosph oric) acid

$$HO-\overset{\overset{O}{\|}}{P}=O$$

(E) Metaphosphoric acid

$$HO-\underset{\underset{OH}{|}}{\overset{\overset{O}{\|}}{P}}-O-\underset{\underset{OH}{|}}{\overset{\overset{O}{\|}}{P}}-OH$$

(F) Pyrophosph oric acid

18. Among the above acids, the acids having basicity 4 are :

  (a) A & E   (b) C & D

  (c) C & F   (d) D & F

19. Metaphosphoric acid (E) can be prepared by heating

  (a) D & F   (b) C & F

  (c) C & D   (d) B, C & F

Section V - Matrix-Match Type

This section contains 1 question. It contains statements given in two columns, which have to be matched. Statements in column I are labelled as A, B, C and D whereas statements in column II are labelled as p, q, r and s. The answers to these questions have to be appropriately bubbled as illustrated in the following example. If the correct matches are A-p, A-r, B-p, B-s, C-r, C-s and D-q, then the correctly bubbled matrix will look like the following:

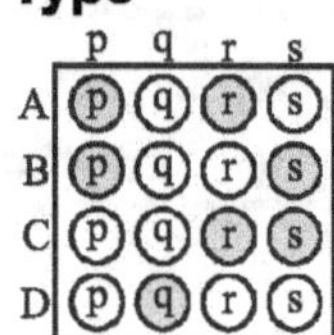

20.

Column I		Column II
(A) H_2S	p.	decolourises acidified soln. of $KMnO_4$
(B) SO_2	q.	Disproportionation reaction
(C) NO_2	r.	Bleaching action
(D) HNO_2	s.	V-shaped structure

RESPONSE GRID	18. (a)(b)(c)(d) 19. (a)(b)(c)(d) 20. A - (p)(q)(r)(s); B - (p)(q)(r)(s); C - (p)(q)(r)(s); D - (p)(q)(r)(s)

DAILY PRACTICE PROBLEM DPP CHAPTERWISE 18 - CHEMISTRY

Total Questions	20	Total Marks	74
Attempted		Correct	
Incorrect		Net Score	
Cut-off Score	24	Qualifying Score	35
Success Gap = Net Score – Qualifying Score			
Net Score = (Correct × 4) – (Incorrect × 1)			

Date :   Start Time :   End Time :

CHEMISTRY $\boxed{\text{CC19}}$

SYLLABUS : The d- and f-Block Elements

Max. Marks : 74   **Time : 60 min.**

GENERAL INSTRUCTIONS

- The Daily Practice Problem Sheet contains 20 Questions divided into 5 sections.

  Section I has **6** MCQs with ONLY 1 Correct Option, **3** marks for each correct answer and **–1** for each incorrect answer.

  Section II has **4** MCQs with ONE or MORE THAN ONE Correct options.

  For each question, marks will be awarded in one of the following categories:

  Full marks: **+4** If only the bubble(s) corresponding to all the correct option(s) is (are) darkened.

  Partial marks: **+1** For darkening a bubble corresponding to each correct option provided NO INCORRECT option is darkened.

  Zero marks: If none of the bubbles is darkened.

  Negative marks: **–2** In all other cases.

  Section III has **4** Single Digit Integer Answer Type Questions, **3** marks for each Correct Answer and 0 marks in all other cases.

  Section IV has Comprehension/Matching Cum-Comprehension Type Questions having 4 MCQs with ONLY ONE correct option, **3** marks for each Correct Answer and 0 marks in all other cases.

  Section V has **2** Matching Type Questions, **1** mark for the correct matching of each row and 0 marks in all other cases.

- You have to evaluate your Response Grids yourself with the help of Solutions.

Section I - Straight Objective Type

This section contains 6 multiple choice questions. Each question has 4 choices (a), (b), (c) and (d), out of which **ONLY ONE** is correct.

1. Calomel (Hg_2Cl_2) on reaction with ammonium hydroxide gives

   (a) HgO (b) Hg_2O

   (c) $NH_2 - Hg - Hg - Cl$ (d) $Hg\,NH_2\,Cl$

2. Which of the following arrangements does not represent the correct order of the property stated against it ?

   (a) $V^{2+} < Cr^{2+} < Mn^{2+} < Fe^{2+}$: paramagnetic behaviour

   (b) $Ni^{2+} < Co^{2+} < Fe^{2+} < Mn^{2+}$: ionic size

   (c) $Co^{3+} < Fe^{3+} < Cr^{3+} < Sc^{3+}$: stability in aqueous solution

   (d) $Sc < Ti < Cr = Mn$: number of oxidation states

RESPONSE GRID   **1.** ⓐⓑⓒⓓ   **2.** ⓐⓑⓒⓓ

Space for Rough Work

3. Which series of reactions correctly represents chemical reactions related to iron and its compound?

(a) $Fe \xrightarrow{dil.\,H_2SO_4} FeSO_4 \xrightarrow{H_2SO_4,\,O_2}$

$\qquad\qquad\qquad Fe_2(SO_4)_3 \xrightarrow{heat} Fe$

(b) $Fe \xrightarrow{O_2,\,heat} FeO \xrightarrow{dil.\,H_2SO_4}$

$\qquad\qquad\qquad FeSO_4 \xrightarrow{heat} Fe$

(c) $Fe \xrightarrow{Cl_2,\,heat} FeCl_3 \xrightarrow{heat,\,air} FeCl_2 \xrightarrow{Zn} Fe$

(d) $Fe \xrightarrow{O_2,\,heat} Fe_3O_4 \xrightarrow{CO,\,600°C}$

$\qquad\qquad\qquad FeO \xrightarrow{CO,\,700°C} Fe$

4. Which of the following is not formed when H_2S reacts with acidic $K_2Cr_2O_7$ solution?

(a) $CrSO_4$ (b) $Cr_2(SO_4)_3$

(c) K_2SO_4 (d) S

5. An excess of $Na_2S_2O_3$ reacts with aqueous $CuSO_4$ to give

(a) CuS_2O_3 (b) $Cu_2S_2O_3$

(c) $Na_2[Cu(S_2O_3)_2]$ (d) $Na_4[Cu_6(S_2O_3)_5]$

6. Which of the following lanthanoid ions is diamagnetic ? (At nos. Ce = 58, Sm = 62, Eu = 63, Yb = 70)

(a) Sm^{2+} (b) Eu^{2+}

(c) Yb^{2+} (d) Ce^{2+}

Section II - Multiple Correct Answer Type
This section contains 4 multiple correct answer(s) type questions. Each question has 4 choices (a), (b), (c) and (d), out of which **ONE OR MORE** is/are correct.

7. Which of the following statements is/are correct?

(a) Anhydrous ferric chloride can be obtained by heating hydrated ferric chloride

(b) A solution of ferric oxalate in dilute H_2SO_4 will decolorise $KMnO_4$

(c) Ferric salts are more stable than ferrous salts

(d) The Mohr's salt is resistant to oxidation by atmospheric oxygen

8. Which of the following statements is/are correct?

(a) Fe^{2+} and Fe^{3+} form octahedral complexes with NH_3

(b) A ferric chloride solution gives a brown turbidity on standing

(c) A pale yellow precipitate is formed when H_2S is passed through acidic solution of Fe(III)

(d) Mercury can not be transported in iron containers.

9. Which of the following statements is/are true?

(a) Both Hg^{2+} and Hg_2^{2+} ions show the divalency

(b) The ionization potentials of 12 group metals are fairly greater then those of coinage metals yet more reactive than the latter

(c) Ionization potential of Hg is smaller than that of Cd

(d) Zn, Cd and Hg exhibit positive oxidation potentials.

10. Which of the following statements is/are *not* correct about corrosive sublimate?

(a) Its aqueous solution gives red precipitate with KI (not in excess)

(b) Its aqueous solution gives white precipitate with excess of $SnCl_4$

(c) It forms grey precipitate with excess of $SnCl_2$ solution

(d) It decomposes on heating to give Hg_2Cl_2 and Cl_2.

RESPONSE GRID					
3. ⓐⓑⓒⓓ	**4.** ⓐⓑⓒⓓ	**5.** ⓐⓑⓒⓓ	**6.** ⓐⓑⓒⓓ	**7.** ⓐⓑⓒⓓ
8. ⓐⓑⓒⓓ	**9.** ⓐⓑⓒⓓ	**10.** ⓐⓑⓒⓓ		

Section III - Integer Type

This section contains 4 questions. The answer to each of the questions is a single digit integer ranging from 0 to 9.

11. What is the oxidation states of Cr in butterfly structure.

12. Out of the following, how many oxides are acidic.

MnO, Mn_2O_3, MnO_2, MnO_3, Mn_2O_7

13. What is the value of x in the Wilkinson's catalyst $[RhCl (Ph_3P)x]$ which is used as a homogenous catalyst in the hydrogenation of alkene.

14. How many of the transition elements are called platinum metals.

Section IV - Comprehension Type

Directions (Qs. 15-18) : Based upon the given paragraphs, 4 multiple choice questions have to be answered. Each question has 4 choices (a), (b), (c) and (d), out of which **ONLY ONE** is correct.

PARAGRAPH-1

A water insoluble solid "A" turns yellow on heating and becomes white again on cooling. When "A" is treated with HCl (aq) it forms a clear solution "B". "A" when treated with NaOH (aq) also gives a clear solution "C". When H_2S (g) is bubbled through clear solution "B" no change is observed but when H_2S is bubbled through clear solution "C", a white precipitate of compound "D" is observed.

15. The compound "A" is

(a) ZnO (b) PbO

(c) MnO (d) CdO

16. The compound "B" is

(a) $ZnCl_2$ (b) $PbCl_2$

(c) $MnCl_2$ (d) $NiCl_2$

17. The change of colour from green to purple is due to

(a) conversion of Mn^{+6} to Mn^{+7}

(b) conversion of Mn^{+6} to Mn^{+4}

(c) conversion of Mn^{+4} to Mn^{+7}

(d) conversion of Mn^{+4} to Mn^{+6}

PARAGRAPH-2

When we pass carbon dioxide gas through a green coloured solution of potassium manganate, the colour of solution changes to purple and a brown coloured solid gets precipitated.

The green colour of potassium manganate solution also becomes purple when it is subjected to electrolysis using iron rods as cathodes as well as anode.

18. In following reaction

$$3K_2MnO_4 + 2H_2O + 4CO_2 \longrightarrow$$
$$\text{(green)}$$
$$2KMnO_4 + MnO_2 + 4KHCO_3$$
$$\text{(purple)}$$

the function of CO_2 is

(a) to make solution acidic by formation of $KHCO_3$

(b) to make solution basic by formation of CO_3^{2-}

(c) to act only as a medium of reaction

(d) none of the above

Space for Rough Work

Section V - Matrix-Match Type

This section contains 2 questions. It contains statements given in two columns, which have to be matched. Statements in column I are labelled as A, B, C and D whereas statements in column II are labelled as p, q, r and s. The answers to these questions have to be appropriately bubbled as illustrated in the following example. If the correct matches are A-p, A-r, B-p, B-s, C-r, C-s and D-q, then the correctly bubbled matrix will look like the following:

19.

Column-I		Column-II
(A)	Left behind as waste in Kipp's apparatus	p. Mohr's salt
(B)	It is green in colour	q. Green vitriol
(C)	On heating it leaves a residue that is brown in colour	r. Basic copper carbonate
(D)	On heating it leaves a residue that is black in colour	s. Hydrated cupric chloride

20. Match each of the reactions given in Column-I with the corresponding product(s) given in Column-II.

Column-I		Column-II
(A)	$Cu + dil. HNO_3$	p. NO
(B)	$Cu + conc. HNO_3$	q. NO_2
(C)	$Zn + dil. HNO_3$	r. N_2O
(D)	$Zn + conc. HNO_3$	s. $Cu(NO_3)_2$
		t. $Zn(NO_3)_2$

RESPONSE GRID	
19. A - p q r s; B - p q r s; C - p q r s; D - p q r s
20. A - p q r s; B - p q r s; C - p q r s; D - p q r s

DAILY PRACTICE PROBLEM DPP CHAPTERWISE 19 - CHEMISTRY

Total Questions	20	Total Marks	74
Attempted		Correct	
Incorrect		Net Score	
Cut-off Score	26	Qualifying Score	36
Success Gap = Net Score – Qualifying Score			
Net Score = (Correct × 4) – (Incorrect × 1)			

Date :   Start Time :   End Time :

CHEMISTRY [CC20]

SYLLABUS : Coordination Compounds

Max. Marks : 74   **Time : 60 min.**

GENERAL INSTRUCTIONS

- The Daily Practice Problem Sheet contains 20 Questions divided into 5 sections.
- **Section I** has **5** MCQs with ONLY 1 Correct Option, **3** marks for each correct answer and **–1** for each incorrect answer.
- **Section II** has **4** MCQs with ONE or MORE THAN ONE Correct options.
- For each question, marks will be awarded in one of the following categories:
- Full marks: **+4** If only the bubble(s) corresponding to all the correct option(s) is (are) darkened.
- Partial marks: **+1** For darkening a bubble corresponding to each correct option provided NO INCORRECT option is darkened.
- Zero marks: If none of the bubbles is darkened.
- Negative marks: **–2** In all other cases.
- **Section III** has **5** Single Digit Integer Answer Type Questions, **3** marks for each Correct Answer and 0 marks in all other cases.
- **Section IV** has Comprehension/Matching Cum-Comprehension Type Questions having **5** MCQs with ONLY ONE correct option, **3** marks for each Correct Answer and 0 marks in all other cases.
- **Section V** has **1** Matching Type Questions, **2** mark for the correct matching of each row and 0 marks in all other cases.
- You have to evaluate your Response Grids yourself with the help of Solutions.

Section I - Straight Objective Type

This section contains 5 multiple choice questions. Each question has 4 choices (a), (b), (c) and (d), out of which **ONLY ONE** is correct.

1. A solution containing 2.675 g of $CoCl_3 \cdot 6\,NH_3$ (molar mass = 267.5 g mol^{-1}) is passed through a cation exchanger. The chloride ions obtained in solution were treated with excess of $AgNO_3$ to give 4.78 g of AgCl (molar mass = 143.5 g mol^{-1}). The formula of the complex is

(At. mass of Ag = 108 u)

2. The d-electron configurations of Cr^{2+}, Mn^{2+}, Fe^{2+} and Co^{2+} are d^4, d^5, d^6 and d^7 respectively. Which one of the following will exhibit the lowest paramagnetic behaviour?

(Atomic no. Cr = 24, Mn = 25, Fe = 26, Co = 27).

(a) $[Co(NH_3)_6]Cl_3$ (b) $[CoCl_2(NH_3)_4]Cl$

(c) $[CoCl_3(NH_3)_3]$ (d) $[CoCl(NH_3)_5]Cl_2$

(a) $[Co(H_2O)_6]^{2+}$ (b) $[Cr(H_2O)_6]^{2+}$

(c) $[Mn(H_2O)_6]^{2+}$ (d) $[Fe(H_2O)_6]^{2+}$

RESPONSE GRID   **1.** ⓐⓑⓒⓓ   **2.** ⓐⓑⓒⓓ

Space for Rough Work

3. The complex ion $[Pt(NO_2)(Py)(NH_3)(NH_2OH)]^+$ will give

(a) 2 isomers (Geometrical)

(b) 3 isomers (Geometrical)

(c) 6 isomers (Geometrical)

(d) 4 isomers (Geometrical)

4. Which of the following complex species is not expected to exhibit optical isomerism ?

(a) $[Co(en)_3]^{3+}$

(b) $[Co(en)_2 Cl_2]^+$

(c) $[Co(NH_3)_3 Cl_3]$

(d) $[Co(en)(NH_3)_2 Cl_2]^+$

5. Nickel $(Z = 28)$ combines with a uninegative monodentate ligand to form a diamagnetic complex $[NiL_4]^{2-}$. The hybridisation involved and the number of unpaired electrons present in the complex are respectively:

(a) sp^3, two   (b) dsp^2, zero

(c) dsp^2, one   (d) sp^3, zero

Section II - Multiple Correct Answer Type

This section contains 4 multiple correct answer(s) type questions. Each question has 4 choices (a), (b), (c) and (d), out of which **ONE OR MORE** is/are correct.

---

6. Amongst the following which are *not* true ?

(a) EAN of iron in $Fe(C_5H_5)_2$ is 36.

(b) $[Fe(H_2O)_6]^{2+}$ has paramagnetism due to 4 unpaired electrons.

(c) $[Cr(NH_3)_6]^{3+}$ is diamagnetic.

(d) $[CoI_4]^{2-}$ has square planar geometry.

7. Point out the correct statements amongst the following

(a) $[Cu(CN)_4]^{3-}$ has square planar geometry and sp^2d hybridization

(b) $[Ni(CN)_6]^{4-}$ is octahedral and Ni has d^2sp^3 hybridization

(c) $[ZnBr_4]^{2-}$ is tetrahedral and diamagnetic

(d) $[Cr(NH_3)_6]^{3+}$ has octahedral geometry and sp^3d^2 hybridization

8. In which of the following cases, the complex ion will migrate towards anode under the applied electric field?

(a) formed by adding $NH_3(aq)$ to AgCl

(b) formed by mixing $FeSO_4(aq)$ and KCN(aq)

(c) formed by mixing $CuSO_4(aq)$ and $NH_3(aq)$

(d) formed by mixing KCl(aq) and $PtCl_4(aq)$

9. Select the correct statement(s) about the stability of chelates.

(a) A chelate having five membered ring is more stable if it contains double bonds.

(b) For formation of a chelate the ligands involved must be at least bidentate.

(c) With increasing number of rings in a chelate, there is an increase in the stability of the chelate

(d) A chelate having six membered ring is more stable if it does not contain any double bonds.

Section III - Integer Type

This section contains 5 questions. The answer to each of the questions is a single digit integer ranging from 0 to 9.

---

10. Give the number of ligands which are negative as well as flexidentate.

$$CO_3^{2-}, CH_3COO^{\ominus}, X^{\ominus}, H^{\ominus}, SO_4^{2-}$$

11. How many pairs of enantiomers are possible for $[M(AA)(BC)de]$?

<table>
<tr><td rowspan="3">RESPONSE GRID</td><td>3. ⓐⓑⓒⓓ</td><td>4. ⓐⓑⓒⓓ</td><td>5. ⓐⓑⓒⓓ</td><td>6. ⓐⓑⓒⓓ</td><td>7. ⓐⓑⓒⓓ</td></tr>
<tr><td>8. ⓐⓑⓒⓓ</td><td>9. ⓐⓑⓒⓓ</td><td colspan="3">10. ⓪①②③④⑤⑥⑦⑧⑨</td></tr>
<tr><td colspan="5">11. ⓪①②③④⑤⑥⑦⑧⑨</td></tr>
</table>

---

12. Give the ratio of trans-isomers in $[M(AA)b_2c_2]$ (A) and $[Ma_4b_2]$, (B) respectively.

13. Give the number of unpaired electron present in the d-orbitals (whose lobes are present along the axis) for the complex $[Co(SCN)_4]^{2-}$

14. How many maximum atom (s) is/are present in same plane of $Cr(CO)_6$?

Section IV - Comprehension Type

Directions (Qs. 15-19) : Based upon the given paragraphs, 5 multiple choice questions have to be answered. Each question has 4 choices (a), (b), (c) and (d), out of which **ONLY ONE** is correct.

PARAGRAPH-1

Column I contains compound and Column II & III contains their CFSE value and dipule moment respectively.

Column I	Column II CFSE (Δ°)		Column III μ spin (B.M)
(I) d^3 (high spin)	(i)–1.6	(P)	1.73
(II) d^4 (low spin)	(ii)–1.8	(Q)	4.90
(III) d^6 (high spin)	(iii)–1.2	(R)	2.83
(IV) d^7 (low spin)	(iv)–0.4	(S)	3.87

15. Find suitable combination which has highest dipole moment

   (a) (I)(ii)(Q)   (b) (IV)(iii)(S)

   (c) (III)(iv)(Q)   (d) (II)(i)(Q)

16. e_g^0 configuration is shown by which combination

   (a) (III)(i)(P)   (b) (III)(iii)(R)

   (c) (IV)(i)(P)   (d) (I)(iii)(S)

17. Correct combination is

   (a) (I)(ii)(S)   (b) (I)(iii)(Q)

   (c) (IV)(ii)(P)   (d) (IV)(iv)(R)

PARAGRAPH-2

An exchange reaction is one in which ligands in the coordination sphere of a metal ion are interchanged for other ligands. Exchange reactions are observed at relatively slow rates between Co^{2+} and Co^{3+} ions. For hexaamine cobalt (III), the exchange reaction is given by Equation-1.

Equation - 1 : $Co(NH_3)_6^{3+} + Co(NH_3)_6^{2+} \rightleftharpoons$

$$Co(NH_3)_6^{2+} + Co(NH_3)_6^{3+}$$

This reaction is believed to p proceed via the following mechanism

$$Co(NH_3)_6^{3+} + H_2O \rightleftharpoons Co(NH_3)_6^{3+} + OH^- + H^+ \text{ (Fast)}$$

$$OH^- + Co(NH_3)_6^{3+} \longrightarrow Co(NH_3)_6OH^{2+} \text{ (Slow)}$$

$$H^+ + Co(NH_3)_6OH^{2+} + Co(NH_3)_6^{2+} \longrightarrow$$

$$Co(NH_3)_6^{2+} + H_2O + Co(NH_3)_6^{3+} \text{ (fast)}$$

The rates of reaction for this type of process are often elucidated using isotopic labeling.

Figure-1 shows how changes in pH affect the relative rate of Equaiton - 1

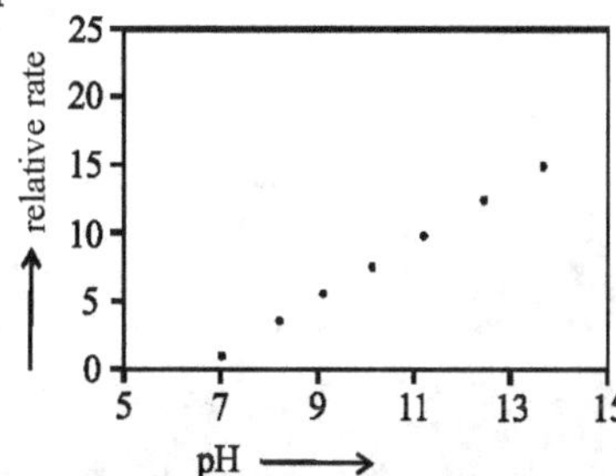

Figure - 1 Effect of pH change on Relative Rate

A chemist prepares a new solution for observation by placing 6.7 g of $Co(NH_3)_6Cl_3$ and 5.5 g of $Co(NH)_6Cl_2$ in a beaker containing 1L of water. The pH of the solution is adjusted to 9.

Mol. wt. $Co(NH_3)_6Cl_3 = 268$ g

Mol. wt. $Co(NH)_6Cl_2 = 232$ g

RESPONSE GRID	12. ⓪①②③④⑤⑥⑦⑧⑨ 13. ⓪①②③④⑤⑥⑦⑧⑨
	14. ⓪①②③④⑤⑥⑦⑧⑨ 15. ⓐⓑⓒⓓ 16. ⓐⓑⓒⓓ 17. ⓐⓑⓒⓓ

18. Sodium oxide hydrolyzes in aqueous solution as follows : $Na_2O + H_2O \longrightarrow 2NaOH$. If the chemist adds 0.0307 g Na_2O to this cobalt ammonium chloride solution, how is the relative reaction rate affected?

   (a) It remians unchanged   (b) It increases by a factor of 4

   (c) It increases by a factor of 2   (d) It decreases by a factor of 2

19. If the chemist now dissolves 27 g of $[Co(NH_3)_6]Cl_3$ and 22 g of $[Co(NH)_6]Cl_2$ in 1 L of water, what will be the molality of the solution?

   (a) 0.2m   (b) 0.7m   (c) 1.0m   (d) 2.0m

Section V - Matrix-Match Type

This section contains 1 question. It contains statements given in two columns, which have to be matched. Statements in column I are labelled as A, B, C and D whereas statements in column II are labelled as p, q, r and s. The answers to these questions have to be appropriately bubbled as illustrated in the following example. If the correct matches are A-p, A-r, B-p, B-s, C-r, C-s and D-q, then the correctly bubbled matrix will look like the following:

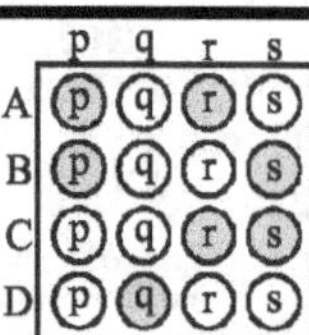

20. Match the magnetic moments listed in column II with the electronic configurations of the complexes listed in column I :

Column I	Column II
(A) d^3 (octahedral)	p. 0.0 B.M.
(B) d^5 (octahedral, low spin)	q. $2\sqrt{6}$ B.M.
(C) d^6 (octahedral, low spin)	r. $\sqrt{15}$ B.M.
(D) d^6 (octahedral, outer orbital)	s. $\sqrt{3}$ B.M.

RESPONSE GRID   18. (a)(b)(c)(d)   19. (a)(b)(c)(d)   20. A - (p)(q)(r)(s); B - (p)(q)(r)(s); C - (p)(q)(r)(s); D - (p)(q)(r)(s)

DAILY PRACTICE PROBLEM DPP CHAPTERWISE 20 - CHEMISTRY

Total Questions	20	Total Marks	74
Attempted		Correct	
Incorrect		Net Score	
Cut-off Score	24	Qualifying Score	35
Success Gap = Net Score − Qualifying Score			
Net Score = (Correct × 4) − (Incorrect × 1)			

CHEMISTRY $\boxed{CC21}$

SYLLABUS : Haloalkanes and Haloarenes

Max. Marks : 74 **Time : 60 min.**

GENERAL INSTRUCTIONS

- The Daily Practice Problem Sheet contains 20 Questions divided into 5 sections.

  Section I has **5** MCQs with ONLY 1 Correct Option, **3** marks for each correct answer and **−1** for each incorrect answer.

  Section II has **4** MCQs with ONE or MORE THAN ONE Correct options.

  For each question, marks will be awarded in one of the following categories:

  Full marks: **+4** If only the bubble(s) corresponding to all the correct option(s) is (are) darkened.

  Partial marks: **+1** For darkening a bubble corresponding to each correct option provided NO INCORRECT option is darkened.

  Zero marks: If none of the bubbles is darkened.

  Negative marks: **−2** In all other cases.

  Section III has **5** Single Digit Integer Answer Type Questions, **3** marks for each Correct Answer and 0 marks in all other cases.

  Section IV has Comprehension/Matching Cum-Comprehension Type Questions having **5** MCQs with ONLY ONE correct option, **3** marks for each Correct Answer and 0 marks in all other cases.

  Section V has **1** Matching Type Questions, **2** mark for the correct matching of each row and 0 marks in all other cases.

- You have to evaluate your Response Grids yourself with the help of Solutions.

Section I - Straight Objective Type

This section contains 5 multiple choice questions. Each question has 4 choices (a), (b), (c) and (d), out of which **ONLY ONE** is correct.

1. Identify Z in

$$CH_3CH_2CH_2Br \xrightarrow{\text{aq. NaOH}} X$$
$$\xrightarrow{Al_2O_3} Y \xrightarrow{Cl_2/H_2O} Z$$

- (a) Mixture of $CH_3CHClCH_2Cl$ and $CH_3CHOHCH_2Cl$
- (b) $CH_3CHOHCH_2Cl$
- (c) $CH_3CHClCH_2OH$
- (d) $CH_3CHClCH_2Cl$

2. The compound

$$C_7H_8 \xrightarrow{3Cl_2/\Delta} A \xrightarrow{Br_2/Fe} B \xrightarrow{Zn/HCl} C$$

The compound C is
- (a) *o*-Bromotoluene
- (b) *m*-Bromotoluene
- (c) *p*-Bromotoluene
- (d) 3-Bromo-2, 4, 6-trichlorotoluene

3. Identify the product of the following reaction

$$\text{(o-chlorotoluene)} \xrightarrow[{-33\,°C}]{NaNH_2, NH_3}$$

- (a) only ortho-methyl aniline
- (b) ortho-methyl aniline and meta-methyl aniline
- (c) ortho-methyl aniline and para-methyl aniline
- (d) meta-and para-methyl aniline

RESPONSE GRID	1. ⓐⓑⓒⓓ	2. ⓐⓑⓒⓓ	3. ⓐⓑⓒⓓ

Space for Rough Work

4.
$$C_6H_5- \xrightarrow[\text{Anhy. AlCl}_3]{(CH_3)_2CH-CH_2Cl} A$$
$$\xrightarrow[\text{Anhy. AlCl}_3]{(CH_3)_2CH-Cl} B$$

A and B are
(a) tert.-butyl benzene, *n*-propyl benzene
(b) iso-butyl benzene, iso-propyl benzene
(c) *t*-butyl benzene, isopropyl benzene
(d) iso-butyl benzene, *n*-propyl benzene

5. An alkyl halide with molecular formula $C_6H_{13}Br$ on dehydrohalogenation gave two isomeric alkenes X and Y with molecular formula C_6H_{12}. On reductive ozonolysis, X and Y gave four compounds CH_3COCH_3, CH_3CHO, CH_3CH_2CHO and $(CH_3)_2CHCHO$. The alkyl halide is
(a) 2-bromohexane
(b) 2, 2-dimethyl-1-bromobutane
(c) 4-bromo-2-methylpentane
(d) 3-bromo-2-methylpentane

Section II - Multiple Correct Answer Type

This section contains 4 multiple correct answer(s) type questions. Each question has 4 choices (a), (b), (c) and (d), out of which **ONE OR MORE** is/are correct.

6. Which of the following statement(s) is/are false regarding following reaction ?

$$\text{(Cl, NO}_2\text{-benzene ring)} + NH_3 \xrightarrow[\text{pressure}]{\text{heat}}$$

(a) No reaction is possible because —Cl is present on benzene ring.
(b) A nucleophilic substitution will take place in which both —Cl will be replaced by two —NH_2 groups.
(c) A nucleophilic substitution will take place in which only —Cl attached on C_1 will be replaced by —NH_2.
(d) A nucleophilic substitution will take place in which only —Cl attached on C_4 will be replaced by —NH_2.

7. Aryl halides are less reactive towards nucleophilic substitution reaction as compared to alkyl halides due to
(a) the formation of less stable carbonium ion
(b) resonance stabilization
(c) longer carbon-halogen bond
(d) sp^2 hybridized carbon attached to the halogen.

8.

$$\xrightarrow{\text{MeI/THF}} (I)$$

$$\xrightarrow{\text{Me}_3\text{C}-\text{Br/THF}} (II)$$

The products (I) and (II) are:

(a) (I) is 2-methyl cyclohexanone.

(b) (II) is a mixture of cyclohexanone and 2-methyl propene.

(c) (I) is 1-methoxy cyclohexene.

(d) (II) is *t*-butoxy cyclohexene.

9.

$$\text{(A)} \xrightarrow[\text{Liq.NH}_2]{\text{NaNH}_2} \text{Products.}$$

Which of the following statements are correct for the above reaction?

(a) The product is a mixture of (I) and (II).

(b) The product (II) is a cine-substitution product.
(c) The reaction proceeds *via* benzyne intermediate.
(d) The reaction is ArSN (addition-elimination).

Section III - Integer Type

This section contains 5 questions. The answer to each of the questions is a single digit integer ranging from 0 to 9.

10.

$$\xrightarrow{\text{(a) alc. KOH}}$$

Moles of alc. KOH consumed are:

11. How many isomer of C_4H_9Br when reacts with $NaNH_2$ diastereomers will form? (excluding stereoisomer)

12.

$$\text{(cyclohexane structure with methylene and CH}_2\text{CHO)} \xrightarrow{\text{a-PCl}_5} \xrightarrow{\text{b-NaNH}_2} \xrightarrow{\text{CH}_2\text{I}} \text{(product with Cl and C≡C–CH)}$$

Sum of $a + b =$

13.

$$\text{(cyclohexane with CH}_3 \text{ and Cl)} \xrightarrow{\text{CH}_3\text{OH}} ?$$

X = Total number of substitution and elimination product(s). Find the value of X.

14. 1, 2-Dibromopropane on treatment with X moles of $NaNH_2$ followed by treatment with C_2H_5Br gives a pentyne. The value of X is:

Section IV - Comprehension Type

Directions (Qs. 15-19) : Based upon the given paragraphs, 5 multiple choice questions have to be answered. Each question has 4 choices (a), (b), (c) and (d), out of which **ONLY ONE** is correct.

PARAGRAPH-1

Column I contains some reactions and Column II & III contains reagents and intermediates involved in corresponding reactions respectively.

Column I (Reaction)		Column II (Reagent)		Column III (Intermediate)
(I) $Ph\text{-CH=CH-CH}_3 \longrightarrow Ph\text{-CHCl-CH}_2\text{-CH}_3$	(i)	$Cl_2 + h\nu$	(P)	Carbene
(II) $Ph\text{-CH=CH-Ph} \longrightarrow$ (cyclopropane with Ph, H, Br, Cl)	(ii)	$CHBrClI /$ —ONa	(Q)	Free radical
(III) (isobutane) $\longrightarrow$ (tert-butyl chloride)	(iii)	$NBS + h\nu / HBr$	(R)	Carbanion
(IV) (cyclopentene) $\longrightarrow$ (3-bromocyclopentene)	(iv)	HCl/Peroxide	(S)	Carbocation

15. For the given reactions in column I, the only correct combination for carbene addition is

(a) (IV)(iii)(P) (b) (III)(iv)(P)
(c) (II)(ii)(P) (d) (I)(ii)(S)

16. For allylic bromination, the correct combination is

(a) (IV)(ii)(R) (b) (IV)(iii)(Q)
(c) (III)(iii)(Q) (d) (III)(ii)(R)

17. Which combination proceeds via carbocation intermediate

(a) (I)(iv)(S) (b) (IV)(i)(S)
(c) (III)(i)(S) (d) (I)(iv)(S)

PARAGRAPH-2

Isopropyl bromide was treated separately with sodium tert-butoxide and sodium ethoxide under two different conditions.
Reaction I : Treatment of isopropyl bromide with sodium tert-butoxide at 40°C gave almost exclusively compound **A** (C_3H_6).

<table>
<tr><td rowspan="3">RESPONSE
GRID</td><td>11. ⓪①②③④⑤⑥⑦⑧⑨</td><td>12. ⓪①②③④⑤⑥⑦⑧⑨</td></tr>
<tr><td>13. ⓪①②③④⑤⑥⑦⑧⑨</td><td>14. ⓪①②③④⑤⑥⑦⑧⑨</td></tr>
<tr><td>15. ⓐⓑⓒⓓ　　16. ⓐⓑⓒⓓ</td><td>17. ⓐⓑⓒⓓ</td></tr>
</table>

Space for Rough Work

Reaction - II : Treatement of isopropyl bromide with sodium ethoxide at 30°C yielded compound *A* along with small amount of an ether **B** ($C_5H_{12}O$).

Compound A was readily oxidized by a neutral solution of cold dilute potassium permangnate to give a brown precipitate.

18. Formation of A and B can best be explained by
    (a) S_N2 reaction and E_2 reacion respectively
    (b) E2 reaction and S_N2 reaction respectively
    (c) E1 reaction and S_N1 reaction respectively
    (d) E2 reaction and S_N1 reaction respectively

19. Which of the following most accurately represents the activated complex formed in reaction II that leads to compound A?

(a) $\underset{\underset{CH_3}{|}}{\overset{\overset{CH_3}{|}}{H-C}}\cdots\cdots Br$ (b) $\underset{\underset{CH_3}{|}}{\overset{\overset{CH_3}{|}}{H-C^+}}$

(c) $C_2H_5O^{\delta-}\cdots\underset{\underset{CH_3}{|}}{\overset{\overset{CH_3}{|}}{C}}\cdots\cdots Br^{\delta-}$ with H

(d) $C_2H_5O^{\delta-}\cdots H\cdots \underset{\underset{H}{|}}{\overset{\overset{H}{|}}{C}}=\!=\!=\underset{\underset{H}{|}}{\overset{\overset{CH_3}{|}}{C}}\cdots Br^{\delta-}$

Section V - Matrix-Match Type

This section contains 1 question. It contains statements given in two columns, which have to be matched. Statements in column I are labelled as A, B, C and D whereas statements in column II are labelled as p, q, r and s. The answers to these questions have to be appropriately bubbled as

	p	q	r	s
A	ⓟ	ⓠ	ⓡ	Ⓢ
B	ⓟ	ⓠ	ⓡ	Ⓢ
C	ⓟ	ⓠ	ⓡ	Ⓢ
D	ⓟ	ⓠ	ⓡ	ⓢ

illustrated in the following example. If the correct matches are A-p, A-r, B-p, B-s, C-r, C-s and D-q, then the correctly bubbled matrix will look like the following:

20. Observe the following columns :

Column-I		Column-II

(A) $(CH_3)_2\overset{\overset{Br}{|}}{C}-CH_2CH_3$ $+OC_2H_5^- \longrightarrow$ p. Saytzeff elimination

(B) $(CH_3)_2\overset{\overset{Br}{|}}{C}-CH_2CH_3$ $+Me_3CO^- \longrightarrow$ q. Hoffmann elimination

(C) $CH_3CH_2\overset{\overset{F}{|}}{C}HCH_3$ $+OCH_3^- \longrightarrow$ r. $CH_3CH=CHCH_3$ is the major product

(D) $CH_3CH_2\overset{\overset{Cl}{|}}{C}HCH_3$ $+OCH_3^- \longrightarrow$ s. $CH_3CH_2CH=CH_2$ is the major product

RESPONSE GRID	18. ⓐⓑⓒⓓ 19. ⓐⓑⓒⓓ
	20. A - ⓟⓠⓡⓢ; B - ⓟⓠⓡⓢ; C - ⓟⓠⓡⓢ; D - ⓟⓠⓡⓢ

DAILY PRACTICE PROBLEM DPP CHAPTERWISE 21 - CHEMISTRY

Total Questions	20	Total Marks	74
Attempted		Correct	
Incorrect		Net Score	
Cut-off Score	27	Qualifying Score	38
Success Gap = Net Score – Qualifying Score			
Net Score = (Correct × 4) – (Incorrect × 1)			

Date :   Start Time :   End Time :

CHEMISTRY $\boxed{CC22}$

SYLLABUS : Alcohols, Phenols and Ethers

Max. Marks : 74   **Time : 60 min.**

GENERAL INSTRUCTIONS

- The Daily Practice Problem Sheet contains 20 Questions divided into 5 sections.
  Section I has **6** MCQs with ONLY 1 Correct Option, **3** marks for each correct answer and **−1** for each incorrect answer.
  Section II has **4** MCQs with ONE or MORE THAN ONE Correct options.
  For each question, marks will be awarded in one of the following categories:
  Full marks: **+4** If only the bubble(s) corresponding to all the correct option(s) is (are) darkened.
  Partial marks: **+1** For darkening a bubble corresponding to each correct option provided NO INCORRECT option is darkened.
  Zero marks: If none of the bubbles is darkened.
  Negative marks: **−2** In all other cases.
  Section III has **4** Single Digit Integer Answer Type Questions, **3** marks for each Correct Answer and 0 marks in all other cases.
  Section IV has Comprehension/Matching Cum-Comprehension Type Questions having **4** MCQs with ONLY ONE correct option, **3** marks for each Correct Answer and 0 marks in all other cases.
  Section V has **2** Matching Type Questions, **2** mark for the correct matching of each row and 0 marks in all other cases.
- You have to evaluate your Response Grids yourself with the help of Solutions.

Section I - Straight Objective Type

This section contains 6 multiple choice questions. Each question has 4 choices (a), (b), (c) and (d), out of which **ONLY ONE** is correct.

1. *p*-cresol reacts with chloroform in alkaline medium to give the compound A which adds hydrogen cyanide to form, the compound B. The latter on acidic hydrolysis gives chiral carboxylic acid. The structure of the carboxylic acid is

   (a) [structure: CH_3 ring with CH_2COOH and OH]

   (b) [structure: CH_3 ring with CH_2COOH and OH]

   (c) [structure: CH_3 ring with $CH(OH)COOH$ and OH]

   (d) [structure: CH_3 ring with $CH(OH)COOH$ and OH]

2. In the Victor-Meyer's test, the colour given by 1°, 2° and 3° alcohols are respectively:
   (a) Red, colourless, blue
   (b) Red, blue, colourless
   (c) Colourless, red, blue
   (d) Red, blue, violet

RESPONSE GRID	1. ⓐⓑⓒⓓ 2. ⓐⓑⓒⓓ

Space for Rough Work

3. The main product of the following reaction is

$$C_6H_5CH_2CH(OH)CH(CH_3)_2 \xrightarrow{conc.H_2SO_4} ?$$

(a) $\underset{H}{\overset{H_5C_6}{>}}C=C\underset{CH(CH_3)_2}{\overset{H}{<}}$

(b) $\underset{H}{\overset{C_6H_5CH_2}{>}}C=C\underset{CH_3}{\overset{CH_3}{<}}$

(c) $\underset{H_3C}{\overset{H_5C_6CH_2CH_2}{>}}C=CH_2$

(d) $\underset{H}{\overset{C_6H_5}{>}}C=C\underset{H}{\overset{CH(CH_3)_2}{<}}$

4. An ether (A), $C_5H_{12}O$, when heated with excess of hot concentrated HI produced two alkyl halides which when treated with NaOH yielded compounds (B) and (C). Oxidation of (B) and (C) gave a propanone and an ethanoic acid respectively. The IUPAC name of the ether (A) is :

(a) 2-ethoxypropane   (b) ethoxypropane

(c) methoxybutane   (d) 2-methoxybutane

5. Sodium phenoxide when heated with CO_2 under pressure at 125°C yields a product which on acetylation produces C

$$\text{C}_6\text{H}_5\text{ONa} + CO_2 \xrightarrow[5\ atm]{125°} B \xrightarrow[Ac_2O]{H^+} C$$

The major product C would be

(a) (ortho OCOCH₃, COOH substituted benzene)

(b) (OH, with COCH₃ ortho and COCH₃ para substituted benzene)

(c) (OH, COOCH₃ ortho substituted benzene)

(d) (OCOCH₃, COOH meta substituted benzene)

6. Which one of the following statements is not correct?

(a) Alcohols are weaker acids than water

(b) Acid strength of alcohols decreases in the following
$$RCH_2OH > R_2CHOH > R_3COH$$

(c) Carbon-oxygen bond length in methanol (CH_3OH) is shorter than that of C – O bond length in phenol.

(d) The bond angle $\overset{O}{\underset{C\ \ \ H}{\wedge}}$ in methanol is 108.9°.

<hr>

Section II - Multiple Correct Answer Type

This section contains 4 multiple correct answer(s) type questions. Each question has 4 choices (a), (b), (c) and (d), out of which **ONE OR MORE** is/are correct.

<hr>

7. Pick up the correct statements in the following reaction

(structure: 2-(but-3-enyl)phenol) $\xrightarrow{H^+} P$

(a) protonation occurs at –OH

(b) protonation occurs at C=C linkage

(c) P is (chromane/benzopyran structure)

(d) P is (2-methyl chromane structure)

8.

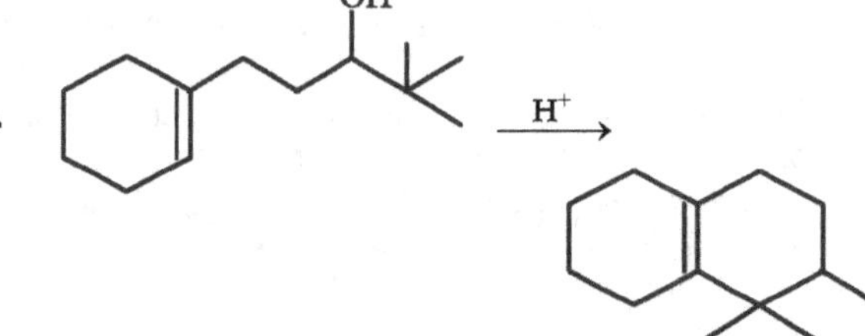

The above transformation involves

(a) protonation at the C=C linkage

(b) protonation at –OH group

(c) formation of 2° carbocation

(d) formation of 3° carbocation

Space for Rough Work

9. Which of the following combination(s) can't be used for preparing an ether ?

    (a) $C_6H_5OH + (CH_3)_2SO_4$

    (b) $C_6H_5Br + CH_3CH_2OH$

    (c) $p\text{-}NO_2C_6H_4Br + CH_3CH_2OH$

    (d) $C_6H_5OH + (CH_3)_3CBr$

10. Which of the following can't be prepared by the typical Williamson reaction ?

    (a) R_3COCR_3

    (b) ArOAr

    (c) $RCH = CHOCH = CHR'$

    (d) $C_6H_5CH_2OC_2H_5$

Section III - Integer Type

This section contains 4 questions. The answer to each of the questions is a single digit integer ranging from 0 to 9.

11. How many isomeric alcohols (including stereo isomers if any) are possible for the compound with molecular formula $C_5H_{12}O$

12. How many cyclic (including stereo isomers) alcohols are possible for the compound with molecular formula C_4H_7OH

13. In Zeisel's method for the determination of methoxyl groups, a sample of 2.68 gm of a compound (A) gave 14.08 gm of AgI. If the molecular weight of compound (A) is 134. Find the number of $(-OCH_3)$ group(s) in the compound (A).

14. If $(d\ell)$ or $(\pm)$ 2-methyl butanoic acid were esterified by reaction with $(d\ell)$ or $(\pm)$ 2-butanol, how many optically active compounds would be present in the final equilibrium reaction mixture?

Section IV - Comprehension Type

Directions (Qs. 15-18) : Based upon the given paragraphs, 4 multiple choice questions have to be answered. Each question has 4 choices (a), (b), (c) and (d), out of which **ONLY ONE** is correct.

PARAGRAPH-1

Alkyl halides and alcohols easily undergo nucleophilic substitution either through S_N1 or S_N2 mechanism. The relative ease of these two processes depends upon the nature of the substrate (alkyl group as well as leaving group), nature of nucleophile and also upon the nature of solvent.

S_N1 mechanism involves the formation of carbocation as intermediate while S_N2 mechanism involves the formation of a transition pentavlent state. S_N1 is the main mechanism in 3° alkyl halides and alcohols, while S_N2 mechanism is the path adopted by most of the 1° alkyl halides; 2° alkyl halides may follow S_N1 as well as S_N2.

15. Rearrangement of alkyl groups occur when hydrogen halides react with alcohols except with most primary alcohols. The best explanation is that

    (a) The 1° carbocations are unstable and hence not formed

    (b) The 1° carbocations are unable to undergo rearrangement

    (c) Both are true

    (d) Both are false

16. Neopentyl alcohol, Me_3CCH_2OH, reacts with HX according to

    (a) S_N1 mechanism

    (b) S_N2 mechanism

    (c) Both

    (d) None

PARAGRAPH-2

Alcohols are isomeric to ethers and the two differ in their reactivity. Alcohols are very reactive while ethers are comparatively very inert; however ethers react with HI at high temperature to form alkyl halides. Higher alcohols from C-3 onwards can exist 1°, 2° or 3° alcohols which can be distinguished by their oxidation, dehydrogenation and behaviour of their respective nitro derivatives toward nitrous acid.

Observe the following series of reactions carefully and answer the questions listed below the series :

17. In the above series of reactions, A and B respectively are

    (a) $n\text{-}C_4H_9OH$ and $CH_3\overset{\overset{\displaystyle OH}{|}}{C}HCH_2CH_3$

    (b) $n\text{-}C_4H_9OH$ and $(CH_3)_3COH$

    (b) $CH_3CHOHCH_2CH_3$ and $CH_3CH_2OCH_2CH_3$

    (d) $n\text{-}C_4H_9OH$ and $CH_3CH_2OCH_2CH_3$

<table>
<tr><td rowspan="3">**RESPONSE GRID**</td><td>**9.** ⓐⓑⓒⓓ   **10.** ⓐⓑⓒⓓ</td><td>**11.** ⓪①②③④⑤⑥⑦⑧⑨</td></tr>
<tr><td>**12.** ⓪①②③④⑤⑥⑦⑧⑨</td><td>**13.** ⓪①②③④⑤⑥⑦⑧⑨</td></tr>
<tr><td>**14.** ⓪①②③④⑤⑥⑦⑧⑨</td><td>**15.** ⓐⓑⓒⓓ **16.** ⓐⓑⓒⓓ **17.** ⓐⓑⓒⓓ</td></tr>
</table>

18. At which step, the above series of reactions first differs
   (a) step 1   (b) step 2
   (c) step 3   (d) step 4

Section V - Matrix-Match Type

This section contains 2 questions. It contains statements given in two columns, which have to be matched. Statements in column I are labelled as A, B, C and D whereas statements in column II are labelled as p, q, r and s. The answers to these questions have to be appropriately bubbled as illustrated in the following example. If the correct matches are A-p, A-r, B-p, B-s, C-r, C-s and D-q, then the correctly bubbled matrix will look like the following:

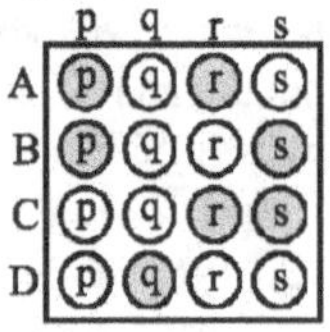

19.   **Column I**   **Column II**
   (A) Hemiacetal   p. Hydrolysed by acids
   (B) Acetal   q. Hydrolysed by bases
   (C) Glycosides   r. Carbohydrates
   (D) Ether   s. Ziesel method

20.   **Column I**   **Column II**

(A) 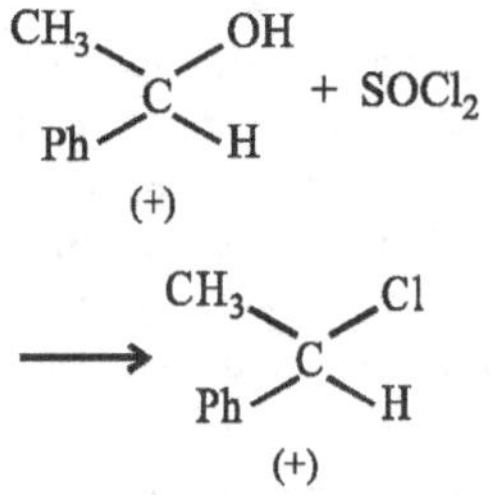
$$CH_3 \underset{Ph}{\overset{OH}{\underset{\big|}{C}}} H \; + SOCl_2 \xrightarrow{\hspace{1cm}} CH_3 \underset{Ph}{\overset{Cl}{\underset{\big|}{C}}} H$$
(+)   (+)

p. S_N1

(B) 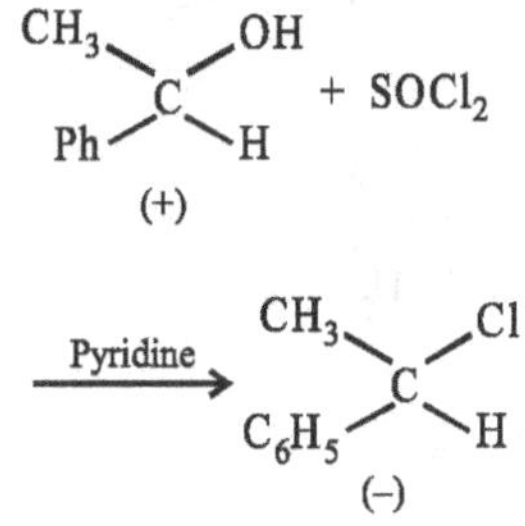
$$CH_3 \underset{Ph}{\overset{OH}{\underset{\big|}{C}}} H \; + SOCl_2 \xrightarrow{\text{Pyridine}} C_6H_5 \underset{}{\overset{CH_3 \quad Cl}{C}} H$$
(+)   (−)

q. S_N2

(C) $CH_3CH = CHCH_2OH + SOCl_2 \longrightarrow$
$$CH_3\overset{Cl}{\underset{\big|}{C}}HCH = CH_2$$

r. S_Ni

(D) 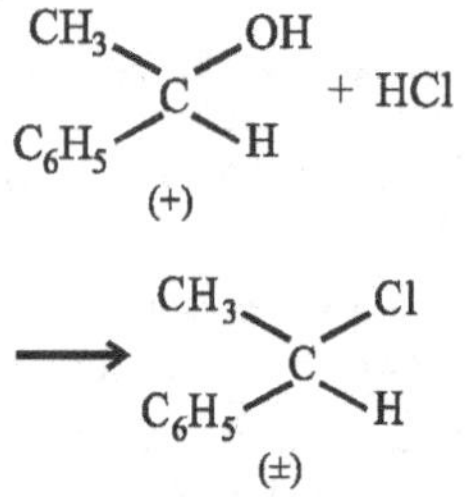
$$CH_3 \underset{C_6H_5}{\overset{OH}{\underset{\big|}{C}}} H \; + HCl \xrightarrow{\hspace{1cm}} C_6H_5 \underset{}{\overset{CH_3 \quad Cl}{C}} H$$
(+)   (±)

s. S_Ni

DAILY PRACTICE PROBLEM DPP CHAPTERWISE 22 - CHEMISTRY

Total Questions	20	Total Marks	74
Attempted		Correct	
Incorrect		Net Score	
Cut-off Score	24	Qualifying Score	35
Success Gap = Net Score − Qualifying Score			
Net Score = (Correct × 4) − (Incorrect × 1)			

Date : | Start Time : | End Time :

CHEMISTRY $\boxed{\text{CC23}}$

SYLLABUS : Aldehydes, Ketones and Carboxylic acids

Max. Marks : 74   **Time : 60 min.**

GENERAL INSTRUCTIONS

- The Daily Practice Problem Sheet contains 20 Questions divided into 5 sections.
  Section I has **5** MCQs with ONLY 1 Correct Option, **3** marks for each correct answer and **−1** for each incorrect answer.
  Section II has **4** MCQs with ONE or MORE THAN ONE Correct options.
  For each question, marks will be awarded in one of the following categories:
  Full marks: **+4** If only the bubble(s) corresponding to all the correct option(s) is (are) darkened.
  Partial marks: **+1** For darkening a bubble corresponding to each correct option provided NO INCORRECT option is darkened.
  Zero marks: If none of the bubbles is darkened.
  Negative marks: **−2** In all other cases.
  Section III has **5** Single Digit Integer Answer Type Questions, **3** marks for each Correct Answer and 0 marks in all other cases.
  Section IV has Comprehension/Matching Cum-Comprehension Type Questions having **5** MCQs with ONLY ONE correct option, **3** marks for each Correct Answer and 0 marks in all other cases.
  Section V has **1** Matching Type Questions, **2** mark for the correct matching of each row and 0 marks in all other cases.
- You have to evaluate your Response Grids yourself with the help of Solutions.

Section I - Straight Objective Type

This section contains 5 multiple choice questions. Each question has 4 choices (a), (b), (c) and (d), out of which **ONLY ONE** is correct.

1. In the given transformation, which of the following is the most appropriate reagent ?

2. An organic compound A upon reacting with NH_3 gives B. On heating B gives C. C in presence of KOH reacts with Br_2 to given $CH_3CH_2NH_2$. A is :

(a) $NH_2NH_2, \overset{-}{O}H$ (b) $Zn - Hg/HCl$

(c) $Na, Liq. NH_3$ (d) $NaBH_4$

(a) CH_3COOH

(b) $CH_3CH_2CH_2COOH$

(c) $CH_3 - \underset{\underset{CH_3}{|}}{CH} - COOH$

(d) CH_3CH_2COOH

RESPONSE GRID   **1.** ⓐⓑⓒⓓ   **2.** ⓐⓑⓒⓓ

Space for Rough Work

3. An organic compound A, C_5H_8O; reacts with H_2O, NH_3 and CH_3COOH as described below:

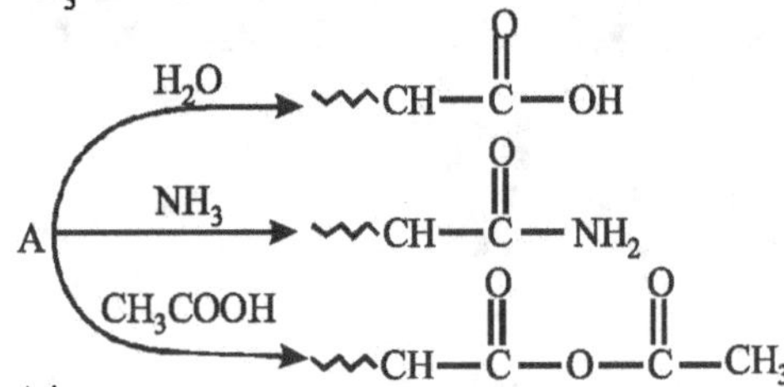

A is:

(a) $CH_3CH=\underset{\underset{\displaystyle CH_3}{|}}{C}-CHO$

(b) $CH_2=CH\underset{\underset{\displaystyle CH_3}{|}}{CH}-CHO$

(c) $CH_3-CH_2-\underset{\underset{\displaystyle CH_3}{|}}{C}=C=O$

(d) $CH_3-CH_2-\underset{\underset{\displaystyle CH_2}{||}}{C}-\overset{\overset{\displaystyle O}{||}}{C}-H$

4. An ester (A) with molecular fomula, $C_9H_{10}O_2$ was treated with excess of CH_3MgBr and the complex so formed was treated with H_2SO_4 to give an olefin (B). Ozonolysis of (B) gave a ketone with molecular formula C_8H_8O which shows positive iodoform test. The structure of (A) is

(a) $C_6H_5COOC_2H_5$
(b) $C_2H_5COOC_6H_5$
(c) $H_3CCOOCH_2C_6H_5$
(d) $p-H_3C-C_6H_4-COCH_3$

5. Which of the following reagent(s) used for the conversion?

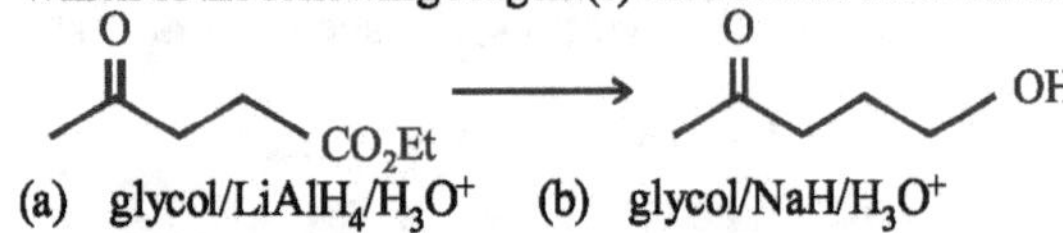

(a) glycol/$LiAlH_4$/H_3O^+ (b) glycol/NaH/H_3O^+
(c) $LiAlH_4$ (d) $NaBH_4$

Section II - Multiple Correct Answer Type

This section contains 4 multiple correct answer(s) type questions. Each question has 4 choices (a), (b), (c) and (d), out of which **ONE OR MORE** is/are correct.

6. $2C_6H_5CHO \xrightarrow[H_2O]{OH^-} C_6H_5CH_2OH + C_6H_5COO^-$

Which of the following statement(s) is/are correct regarding the above reduction of benzaldehyde to benzyl alcohol?

(a) One hydrogen is coming from H_2O as H^+ and another from C_6H_5CHO as H^-
(b) One hydrogen is coming from H_2O as H^- and another from C_6H_5CHO as H^+
(c) One hydrogen from H_2O and another from C_6H_5CHO, both in the form of H^-

(d) The reduction is an example of disproportionation reaction

7. 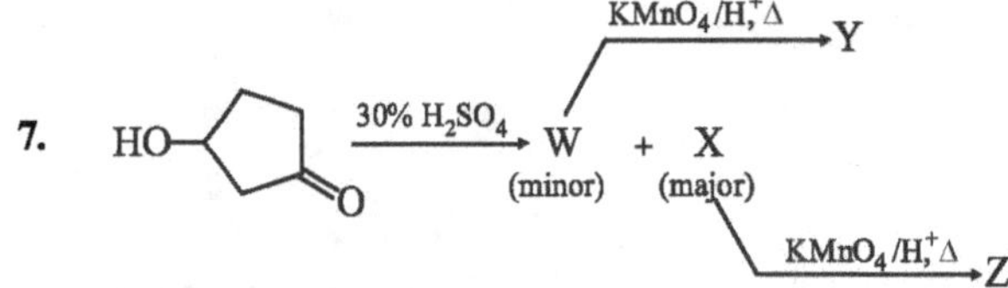

Of the 4 compounds listed above, more than one will :
(a) exhibit resonance due to conjugation in their structure
(b) show $NaHCO_3$ test
(c) have a cyclic structure
(d) show 2, 4-DNPh precipitation

8. One mole of $C_6H_5COCH_2CH_3$ is treated with one mole of Br_2 in basic solution, the product(s) formed is (are)

(a) 1 mole of $C_6H_5COCBr_2CH_3$
(b) 1 mole of $C_6H_5COCHBrCH_2Br$
(c) 0.5 mole of $C_6H_5COCBr_2CH_3$
(d) 0.5 mole of unreacted $C_6H_5COCH_2CH_3$.

9. $R-\overset{\overset{\displaystyle O}{||}}{C}-R+CH_2N_2 \longrightarrow$ Product(s) is/are

(a) $RCOCH_2R$ (b) $R\underset{\underset{\displaystyle OCH_3}{|}}{CH}R$

(c) $\underset{R_2C-CH_2}{\overset{O}{\diagup\diagdown}}$ (d) All the three

Section III - Integer Type

This section contains 5 questions. The answer to each of the questions is a single digit integer ranging from 0 to 9.

10. $CH_3\overset{\overset{\displaystyle O}{||}}{C}CH_3 + CH_3CH_2\overset{\overset{\displaystyle O}{||}}{C}CH_3 \xrightarrow[\Delta]{KOH(aq)} (A)$

(A) = number of aldol condensation product (including stereoisomer).

11. In the scheme given below, the total number of intramolecular aldol condensation products formed from (Y) is

$\xrightarrow[\text{2. } Zn, H_2O]{\text{1. } O_3} (Y) \xrightarrow[\text{2. Heat}]{\text{1. NaOH(aq.)}}$

12. Total number of enol possible for the compound formed during given reaction will be (including stereoisomer):

$CH_3MgBr + CH_3CH_2\overset{\overset{\displaystyle O}{||}}{C}Cl \rightarrow$

13. The total number of carboxylic acid groups in the product P is

$\xrightarrow[\text{2. } O_3 \atop \text{3. } H_2O_2]{\text{1. } H_3O^{\oplus},\, \Delta} P$

14. Among the following, the number of reaction(s) that product(s) benzaldehyde is

I.

$$\xrightarrow[\text{Anhydrous AlCl}_3/\text{CuCl}]{\text{CO, HCl}}$$

II. (CHCl$_2$)

$$\xrightarrow[100°C]{H_2O}$$

III.

$$\xrightarrow[\text{Pd-BaSO}_4]{H_2}$$

IV. (CO$_2$Me)

$$\xrightarrow[\substack{\text{Toluene, } -78°C \\ H_2O}]{\text{DIBAL}-H}$$

Section IV - Comprehension Type

Directions (Qs. 15-19) : Based upon the given paragraphs, 4 multiple choice questions have to be answered. Each question has 4 choices (a), (b), (c) and (d), out of which **ONLY ONE** is correct.

PARAGRAPH-1

Column I contains some reaction and Column II & Column III contains Reagent used and Products formed respectively.

Column I (Reaction)	Column II (Reagent)	Column III (Product)
(I) cyclohexanone with CHO	(i) (i) BH$_3$/THF (ii) H$_2$O$_2$/$\overset{\ominus}{O}$H	(P) ring with CHO, CHO
(II) benzaldehyde with CHO and COOH	(ii) (i) NaBH$_4$/EtOH	(Q) ring with CHO, CHO
(III) $=$cyclohexane$=$O $\longrightarrow$	(iii) (i) Glycol + HCl (ii) SOCl$_2$ (iii) DIBAL$-$H	(R) decalin with OH, H and $=$CH$_2$
(IV) decalone with $=$CH$_2$	(iv) H$_3$O$^{\oplus}$	(S) HO and O cyclohexane
	(iv) (i) LAH (ii) Conc. H$_2$SO$_4$/Δ (iii) O$_3$/Zn or Me$_2$S	

15. Find the correct combination
  (a) (I)(iii)(P)   (b) (II)(iv)(Q)
  (c) (I)(iv)(P)   (d) (IV)(i)(R)

16. Find the combination where acid group is converting into aldehyde group
  (a) (I)(iv)(Q)   (b) (I)(iii)(S)
  (c) (II)(iii)(P)   (d) (II)(iii)(Q)

17. Find suitable combination which follows hydroboration-oxidation reaction
  (a) (III)(i)(R)   (b) (IV)(iv)(S)
  (c) (III)(i)(S)   (d) (I)(iii)(S)

PARAGRAPH-2

Methanoic acid, the first member of carboxylic acid series, when warmed with concentrated sulphuric acid decomposes in the following way and evolves carbon monoxide.

$$H-\overset{\overset{O}{\|}}{C}-OH \xrightarrow{H^+} H-\overset{\overset{O}{\|}}{C}-\overset{+}{O}H_2 \xrightarrow{-H_2O}$$

$$\left[H-\overset{\overset{O}{\|}}{\underset{+}{C}} \longleftrightarrow H-\overset{\overset{O^+}{\||}}{C} \right] \xrightarrow{-H^-} C \equiv O + H^+$$

The driving force for this reaction lies in the fact that the HC $\equiv$ O$^+$ ion is very unstable acid and thus easily loses H$^+$.

Space for Rough Work

18. What happens when acetic acid is treated with conc. H_2SO_4?
  (a) $CO + H_2O$ (b) $CH_4 + CO_2$
  (c) $CO + CH_4$ (d) No reaction

19. If formic acid is replaced by benzoylformic acid, $C_6H_5COCOOH$ the product formed will be

  (a) $C_6H_5COOH + CO + CO_2$
  (b) $C_6H_5COOH + CO_2$
  (c) $C_6H_5COOH + CO$
  (d) $C_6H_5CHO + CO_2$

Section V - Matrix-Match Type

This section contains 1 questions. It contains statements given in two columns, which have to be matched. Statements in column I are labelled as A, B, C and D whereas statements in column II are labelled as p, q, r and s. The answers to these questions have to be appropriately bubbled as illustrated in the following example. If the correct matches are A-p, A-r, B-p, B-s, C-r, C-s and D-q, then the correctly bubbled matrix will look like the following:

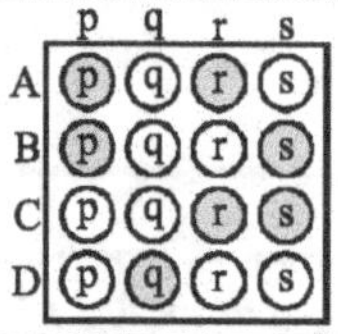

20. Match the columns.

Column-I

(A) $\xrightarrow{aq.NaOH}$

(B) $CH_2CH_2CH_2Cl \xrightarrow{CH_3MgI} CH_3$

(C) $^{18}CH_2CH_2CH_2OH \xrightarrow{H_2SO_4}$

(D) $CH_2CH_2CH_2C(CH_3)_2 , OH \xrightarrow{H_2SO_4}$ $H_3C \quad CH_3$

Column-II

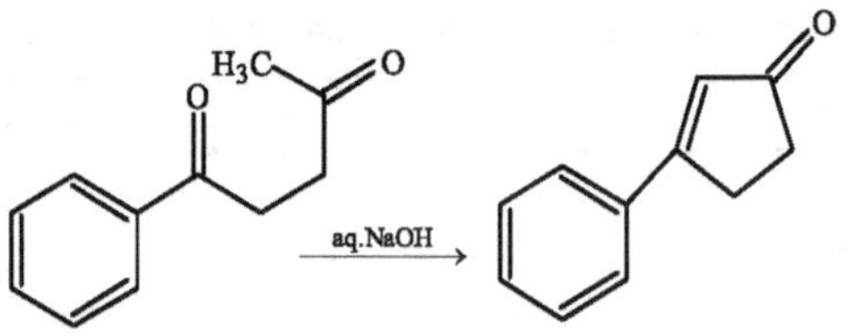

p.   Nucleophilic substitution

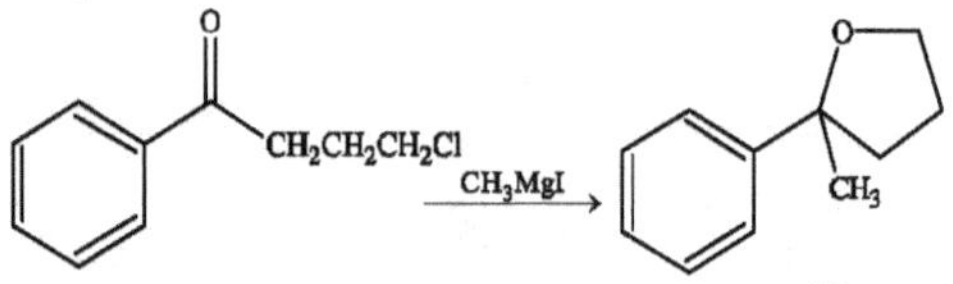

q.   Electrophilic substitution

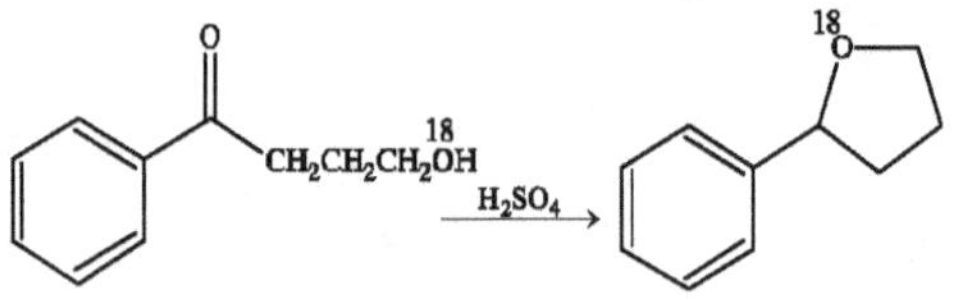

r.   Dehydration

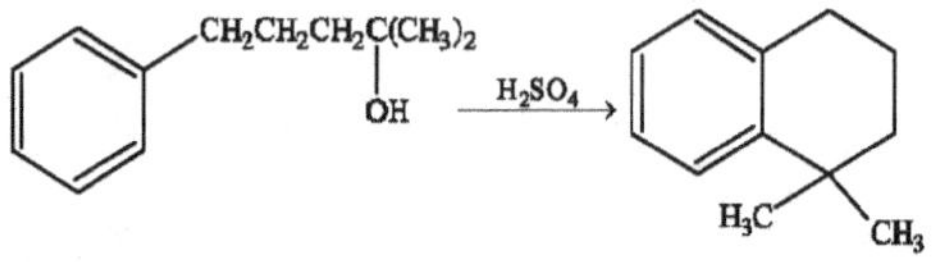

s.   Nucleophilic addition

RESPONSE GRID	18. (a)(b)(c)(d) 19. (a)(b)(c)(d)
	20. A - (p)(q)(r)(s); B - (p)(q)(r)(s); C - (p)(q)(r)(s); D - (p)(q)(r)(s)

DAILY PRACTICE PROBLEM DPP CHAPTERWISE 23 - CHEMISTRY

Total Questions	20	Total Marks	74
Attempted		Correct	
Incorrect		Net Score	
Cut-off Score	24	Qualifying Score	35
Success Gap = Net Score – Qualifying Score			
Net Score = (Correct × 4) – (Incorrect × 1)			

Date :   Start Time :   End Time :

CHEMISTRY $\boxed{CC24}$

SYLLABUS : Amines

Max. Marks : 74   **Time : 60 min.**

GENERAL INSTRUCTIONS

- The Daily Practice Problem Sheet contains 20 Questions divided into 5 sections.

Section I has **6** MCQs with ONLY 1 Correct Option, **3** marks for each correct answer and **−1** for each incorrect answer.

Section II has **4** MCQs with ONE or MORE THAN ONE Correct options.

For each question, marks will be awarded in one of the following categories:

Full marks: **+4** If only the bubble(s) corresponding to all the correct option(s) is (are) darkened.

Partial marks: **+1** For darkening a bubble corresponding to each correct option provided NO INCORRECT option is darkened.

Zero marks: If none of the bubbles is darkened.

Negative marks: **−2** In all other cases.

Section III has **4** Single Digit Integer Answer Type Questions, **3** marks for each Correct Answer and 0 marks in all other cases.

Section IV has Comprehension/Matching Cum-Comprehension Type Questions having **4** MCQs with ONLY ONE correct option, **3** marks for each Correct Answer and 0 marks in all other cases.

Section V has **2** Matching Type Questions, **2** mark for the correct matching of each row and 0 marks in all other cases.

- You have to evaluate your Response Grids yourself with the help of Solutions.

Section I - Straight Objective Type

This section contains 6 multiple choice questions. Each question has 4 choices (a), (b), (c) and (d), out of which **ONLY ONE** is correct.

1. $[A] \xrightarrow{\text{reduction}} [B] \xrightarrow{CHCl_3 + KOH}$

    $[C] \xrightarrow{\text{reduction}} N - \text{Methylanil ine}$, A is

    (a) Formaldehyde
    (b) Trichloromethane
    (c) Nitrobenzene
    (d) Toluene

2. Choose the amide which on reduction with $LiAlH_4$ yields a secondary amine
    (a) Ethanamide
    (b) N-Methylethanamide
    (c) N, N-dimethylethanamide
    (d) Phenylmethanamide

RESPONSE GRID   **1.** (a)(b)(c)(d)   **2.** (a)(b)(c)(d)

Space for Rough Work

3. Aniline is reacted with bromine water and the resulting product is treated with an aqueous solution of sodium nitrite in presence of dilute hydrochloric acid. The compound so formed is converted into a tetrafluoroborate which is subsequently heated dry. The final product is

(a) 1,3,5-tribromobenzene
(b) *p*-bromofluorobenzene
(c) *p*-bromoaniline
(d) 2,4,6-tribromofluorobenzene

4. The order of basicity of the compounds

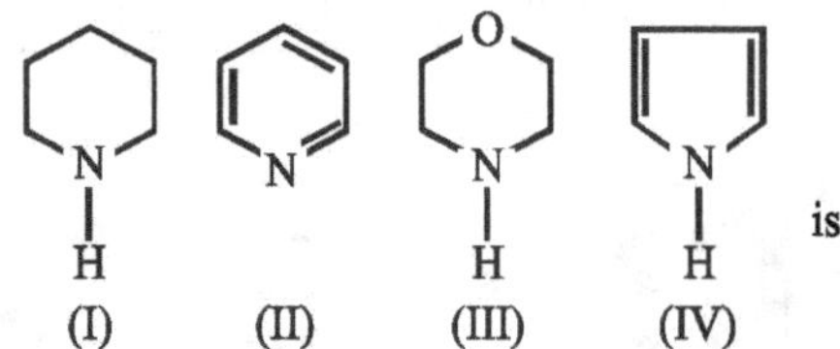

is

   (I)   (II)   (III)   (IV)

(a) IV > I > III > II
(b) I > III > II > IV
(c) III > I > IV > II
(d) II > I > III > IV

5. Considering the basic strength of amines in aqueous solution, which one has the smallest pK_b value?

(a) $(CH_3)_2NH$
(b) CH_3NH_2
(c) $(CH_3)_3N$
(d) $C_6H_5NH_2$

6. In a set of reactions *p*-nitrotoluene yielded a product E.

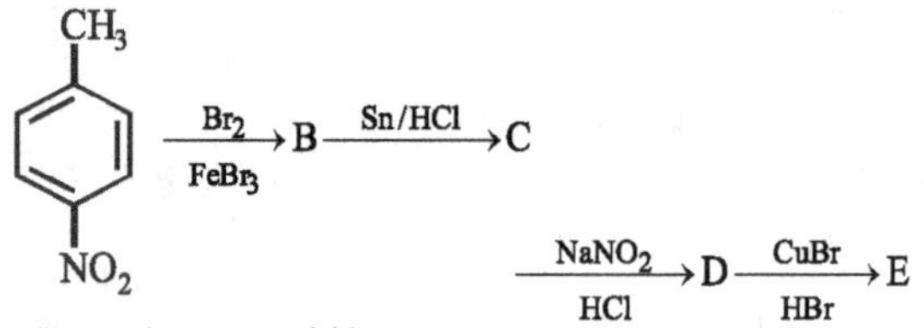

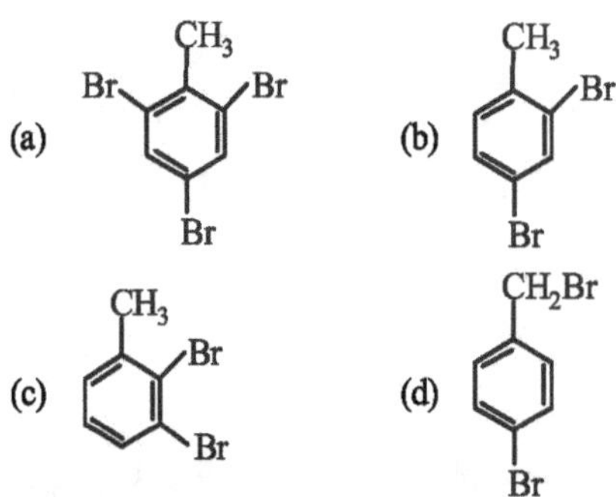

The product E would be:

(a) (2,4,6-tribromotoluene structure)
(b) (2-methyl-5-bromo... 2,4-dibromotoluene structure)
(c) (2,3-dibromotoluene structure)
(d) (4-bromobenzyl bromide structure)

Section II - Multiple Correct Answer Type

This section contains 4 multiple correct answer(s) type questions. Each question has 4 choices (a), (b), (c) and (d), out of which **ONE OR MORE** is/are correct.

7. Which of the following can't be used as an alkylating agent for an amine ?

(a) CH_3CH_2Cl
(b) $CH_2=CHCl$
(c) C_6H_5Cl
(d) $(CH_3)_3CCl$

8. Which of the following reacts with nitrous acid ?

(a) Acetamide
(b) 2-Nitrobutane
(c) 2-Methyl-2-nitropropane
(d) Diethylamine

9. Which of the following reaction can be used for preparing aniline ?

(a) $C_6H_5COOH \xrightarrow{N_3H,\ conc.\ H_2SO_4}$

(b) $C_6H_5NC \xrightarrow{H_3O^+}$

(c) $C_6H_5NC \xrightarrow{LiAlH_4}$

(d) $C_6H_5CONH_2 \xrightarrow{Br_2\ /\ NaOH}$

10. 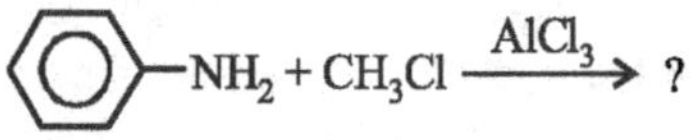 —$NH_2 + CH_3Cl \xrightarrow{AlCl_3}$?

Which of the following statement is false regarding above reaction?

(a) 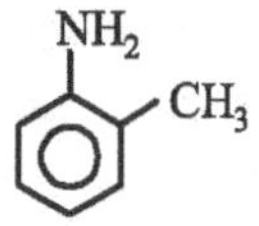 (*o*-toluidine) is major product

(b)  (*p*-toluidine) is major product

(c) 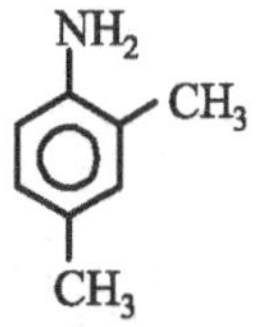 (2,4-dimethylaniline) is major product

(d) No substitution

Section III - Integer Type

This section contains 4 questions. The answer to each of the questions is a single digit integer ranging from 0 to 9.

11. How many of the following can be used to reduce nitrobenzene to aniline?

$\underset{I}{H_2/Ni}$, $\underset{II}{Sn/HCl}$, $\underset{III}{Zn/NaOH}$ and $\underset{IV}{LiAlH_4}$

12. How many of the following method(s) is/ are used for eliminating nitrogen of an amine present outside the ring? Hofmann elimination, Cope elimination and Emde degradation

13. How many structural isomers of a Grignard reagent are possible for preparing *n*-butane by reaction with ethyl amine?

14. How many of the following compounds can be methylated by diazomethane?
C_2H_5COOH, $C_2H_5NH_2$, C_6H_5OH and $CH_3COCH_2COOC_2H_5$

Section IV - Comprehension Type

Directions (Qs. 15-18) : Based upon the given paragraphs, 4 multiple choice questions have to be answered. Each question has 4 choices (a), (b), (c) and (d), out of which **ONLY ONE** is correct.

PARAGRAPH-1

Understand carefully the following two reactions and answer the questions mentioned below.

Reaction (i)

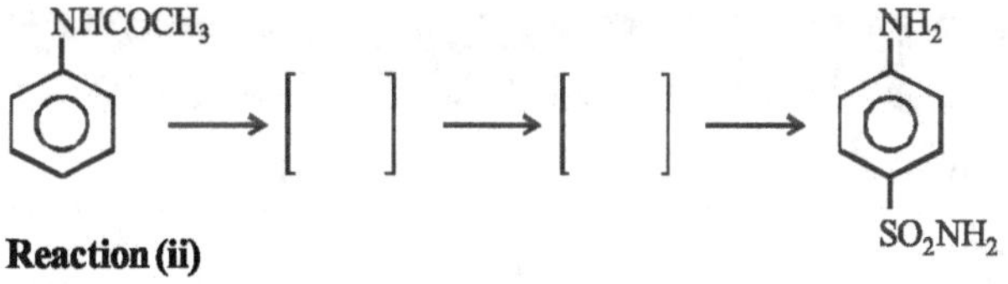

Reaction (ii)

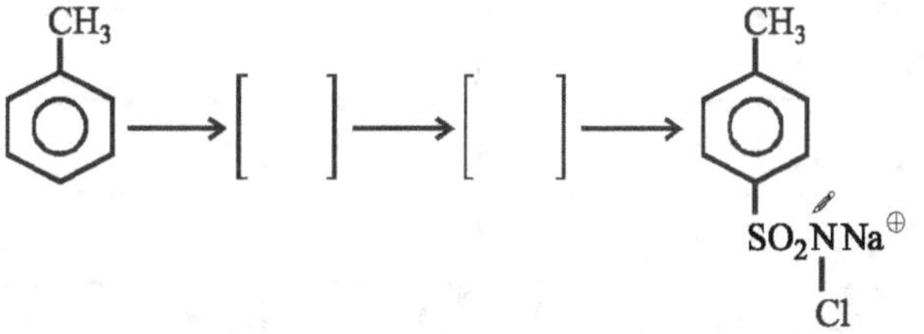

15. Which one of the following reagent can be used for the introduction of Cl and Na in reaction (ii)?
(a) Cl_2/Na_2CO_3 (b) $HCl/NaOH$
(c) $NaCl/NaOH$ (d) $NaOCl/NaOH$

16. Saccharin, an important sweetening agent, of the following structure is prepared by one of the products of the reaction (ii), that product should be

(a) (b)

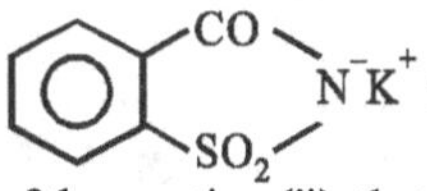

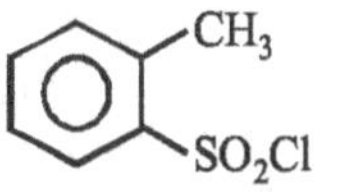

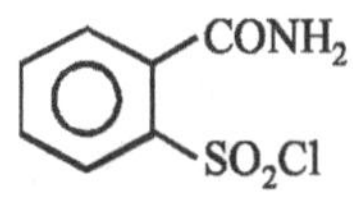

(c) (d)

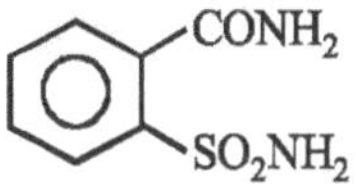

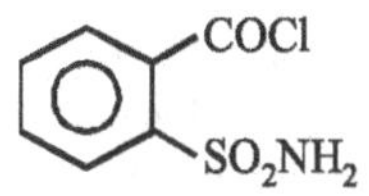

PARAGRAPH-2

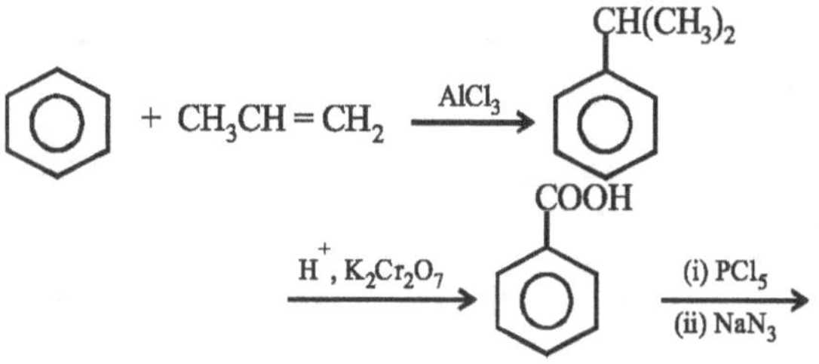

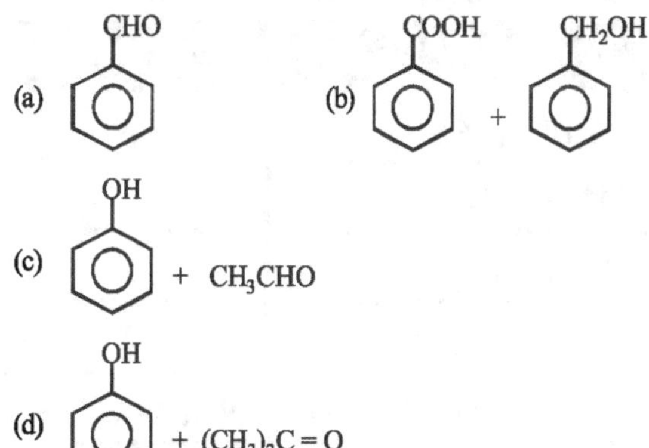

$C_6H_5CON_3 \xrightarrow{heat} C_6H_5NCO \xrightarrow{C_2H_5OH} \text{Product}$

17. What will be the product(s) when isopropylbenzene is oxidised with oxygen and product is acidified

(a) (b)

(c) + CH_3CHO

(d) + $(CH_3)_2C=O$

RESPONSE GRID	
11. ⓪①②③④⑤⑥⑦⑧⑨	12. ⓪①②③④⑤⑥⑦⑧⑨
13. ⓪①②③④⑤⑥⑦⑧⑨	14. ⓪①②③④⑤⑥⑦⑧⑨
15. ⓐⓑⓒⓓ 16. ⓐⓑⓒⓓ	17. ⓐⓑⓒⓓ

Space for Rough Work

18. Conversion of $C_6H_5CON_3$ to C_6H_5NCO is an example of rearrangement where an alkyl group migrates to
   (a) electron deficient carbon atom
   (b) electron deficient oxygen atom
   (c) electron deficient nitrogen atom
   (d) electron rich nitrogen atom

Section V - Matrix-Match Type

This section contains 2 questions. It contains statements given in two columns, which have to be matched. Statements in column I are labelled as A, B, C and D whereas statements in column II are labelled as p, q, r and s. The answers to these questions have to be appropriately bubbled as illustrated in the following example. If the correct matches are A-p, A-r, B-p, B-s, C-r, C-s and D-q, then the correctly bubbled matrix will look like the following:

19.

	Column-I		**Column-II**

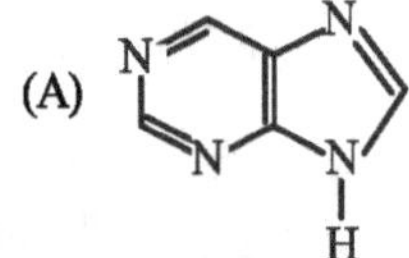

(A)   p.   One type of N

(B) $H_2N - \overset{\overset{\textstyle NH}{\|}}{C} - NH_2$ q.   Two types of N

(C) 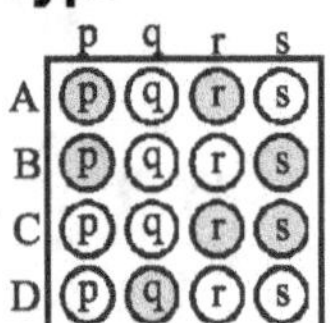   r.   Aromatic

(D) $C_6H_5N^+ \equiv NCl^-$ s.   Non-aromatic

20. Match each of the compounds in **Column I** with its characteristic reaction(s) in **Column II**.

Column I		**Column II**
(A) $CH_3CH_2CH_2CN$	(p)	Reduction with Pd–C/H$_2$
(B) $CH_3CH_2OCOCH_3$	(q)	Reduction with SnCl$_2$/ HCl
(C) $CH_3–CH=CH–CH_2OH$	(r)	Development of foul smell on treatment with chloroform and alcoholic KOH
(D) $CH_3CH_2CH_2CH_2NH_2$	(s)	Reduction with diisobutylaluminium hydride(DIBAL-H)
	(t)	Alkaline hydrolysis

<table>
<tr><td rowspan="3">Response Grid</td><td>18. ⓐⓑⓒⓓ</td></tr>
<tr><td>19. A - ⓟⓠⓡⓢ; B - ⓟⓠⓡⓢ; C - ⓟⓠⓡⓢ; D - ⓟⓠⓡⓢ</td></tr>
<tr><td>20. A - ⓟⓠⓡⓢ; B - ⓟⓠⓡⓢ; C - ⓟⓠⓡⓢ; D - ⓟⓠⓡⓢ</td></tr>
</table>

DAILY PRACTICE PROBLEM DPP CHAPTERWISE 24 - CHEMISTRY

Total Questions	20	Total Marks	74
Attempted		Correct	
Incorrect		Net Score	
Cut-off Score	24	Qualifying Score	35
Success Gap = Net Score – Qualifying Score			
Net Score = (Correct × 4) – (Incorrect × 1)			

DPP - Daily Practice Problems

Chapter-wise Sheets

Date :   Start Time :   End Time :

CHEMISTRY $\boxed{\text{CC25}}$

SYLLABUS : Biomolecules

Max. Marks : 74   **Time : 60 min.**

GENERAL INSTRUCTIONS

- The Daily Practice Problem Sheet contains 20 Questions divided into 5 sections.

  Section I has **6** MCQs with ONLY 1 Correct Option, **3** marks for each correct answer and **−1** for each incorrect answer.

  Section II has **4** MCQs with ONE or MORE THAN ONE Correct options.

  For each question, marks will be awarded in one of the following categories:

  Full marks: **+4** If only the bubble(s) corresponding to all the correct option(s) is (are) darkened.

  Partial marks: **+1** For darkening a bubble corresponding to each correct option provided NO INCORRECT option is darkened.

  Zero marks: If none of the bubbles is darkened.

  Negative marks: **−2** In all other cases.

  Section III has **4** Single Digit Integer Answer Type Questions, **3** marks for each Correct Answer and 0 marks in all other cases.

  Section IV has Comprehension/Matching Cum-Comprehension Type Questions having **4** MCQs with ONLY ONE correct option, **3** marks for each Correct Answer and 0 marks in all other cases.

  Section V has **2** Matching Type Questions, **2** mark for the correct matching of each row and 0 marks in all other cases.

- You have to evaluate your Response Grids yourself with the help of Solutions.

Section I - Straight Objective Type

This section contains 6 multiple choice questions. Each question has 4 choices (a), (b), (c) and (d), out of which **ONLY ONE** is correct.

1. In both DNA and RNA, heterocylic base and phosphate ester linkages are at –

(a) C_5' and C_1' respectively of the sugar molecule

(b) C_1' and C_5' respectively of the sugar molecule

(c) C_2' and C_5' respectively of the sugar molecule

(d) C_5' and C_2' respectively of the sugar molecule

2. The term anomers of glucose refers to

(a) enantiomers of glucose

(b) isomers of glucose that differ in configuration at carbon one (C-1)

(c) isomers of glucose that differ in configurations at carbons one and four (C-1 and C-4)

(d) a mixture of (D)-glucose and (L)-glucose

3. Which of the following compounds can be detected by Molisch's Test ?

(a) Nitro compounds   (b) Sugars

(c) Amines   (d) Primary alcohols

RESPONSE GRID	1. ⓐⓑⓒⓓ	2. ⓐⓑⓒⓓ	3. ⓐⓑⓒⓓ

4. Synthesis of each molecule of glucose in photosynthesis involves :

  (a) 18 molecules of ATP   (b) 10 molecules of ATP

  (c) 8 molecules of ATP   (d) 6 molecules of ATP

5. Which of the following structures represents thymine ?

(a)   (b)

(c)   (d)

6. Among the following organic acids, the acid present in rancid butter is:

  (a) Pyruvic acid   (b) Lactic acid

  (c) Butyric acid   (d) Acetic acid

Section II - Multiple Correct Answer Type

This section contains 4 multiple correct answer(s) type questions. Each question has 4 choices (a), (b), (c) and (d), out of which **ONE OR MORE** is/are correct.

---

7. The correct statement(s) about the following sugars **X** and **Y** is(are)

X

Y

(a) **X** is a reducing sugar and **Y** is a non-reducing sugar

(b) **X** is a non-reducing sugar and **Y** is a reducing sugar

(c) The glucosidic linkages in **X** and **Y** are α and β, respectively

(d) The glucosidic linkages in **X** and **Y** are β and α, respectively

8. Which of the statement(s) given below is/are true regarding following structures?

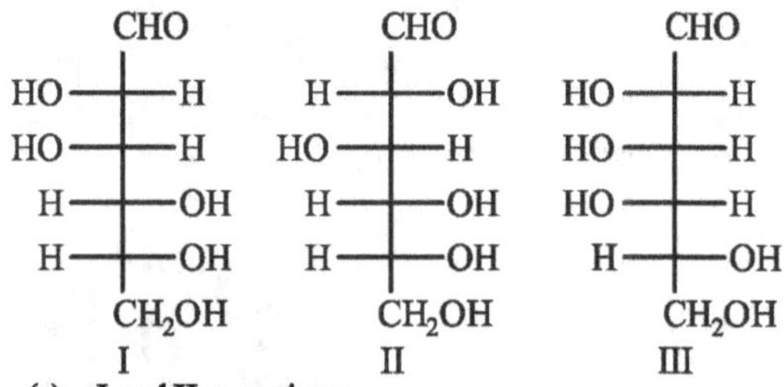

(a) I and II are epimers

(b) II and III are epimers

(c) I and III are epimers

(d) All are epimers to each other

9. Which of the following statement(s) is/are correct ?

(a) Fruit mainly contains glucose as carbohydrate

(b) Honey mainly contains invert sugar

(c) Blood sugar and grape sugar mainly contain glucose

(d) Sucrose is an oligosaccharide.

10. Which of the following carbohydrates on treatment with excess of phenylhydrazine give the same osazone?

  (a) Glucose   (b) Fructose

  (c) Mannose   (d) Galactose

Section III - Integer Type

This section contains 4 questions. The answer to each of the questions is a single digit integer ranging from 0 to 9.

11.

D-sorbose

Number of stereoisomer of product (P) is:

---

12. Glucose molecule reacts with 'X' number of molecule of phenylhydrazine to yield osazone. The value of X is:

13. How many chiral centers are there in a 2-ketohexose?

14. $OHC(CHOH)_4CH_2OH \rightarrow HIO_4$

16-isomer of above compound when reacts with periodic acid (HIO_4), calculate the value of X, when X is:

$$X = \frac{\text{No. of moles of } HIO_4 \text{ consumed}}{10}$$

Section IV - Comprehension Type

Directions (Qs. 15-18) : Based upon the given paragraphs, 4 multiple choice questions have to be answered. Each question has 4 choices (a), (b), (c) and (d), out of which **ONLY ONE** is correct.

PARAGRAPH-1

Monosaccharides have –CHO (or C = O) and –OH groups, so they undergo usual oxidation and reduction. Further, monosaccharides form osazone when treated with excess of phenylhydrazine (3 equivalents). In osazone formation only the first two carbon atoms are involved. Thus monosaccharides having identical configuration on rest of C atoms except first two will form same osazone, as is the case with glucose and fructose.

A, B and C are three hexoses and form same osazone D. Compounds A to D behave as below :

(i) $D \xrightarrow[CH_3COOH]{HCl} \xrightarrow{Zn} D - Fructose$

(ii) $A \xrightarrow{Ni, H_2} \xrightarrow{HNO_3} \xrightarrow[H_3O^+]{Na-Hg} B + C$

(iii) $B \xrightarrow{HNO_3}$ Optically active glycaric acid

(iv) $C \xrightarrow{HNO_3}$ Optically inactive glycaric acid

15. Compound A should be
   (a) D-glucose   (b) D-fructose
   (c) L-glucose   (d) L-fructose

16. Compound B and C, respectively, are
   (a) D-glucose and D-mannose
   (b) D-mannose and D-glucose
   (c) D-glucose and L-glucose
   (d) D-glucose and L-mannose

PARAGRAPH-2

Refer the following scheme of reactions and answer the questions that follows :

17. The reagent in the first step is
   (a) 1 mole of NH_3 (b) NH_4OH
   (c) 2 moles of NH_3 (d) (i) $SOCl_2$ (ii) NH_3

18. Reaction at step 4 is
   (a) S_N1 (b) S_N2
   (c) E2   (d) E1

Section V - Matrix-Match Type

This section contains 2 questions. It contains statements given in two columns, which have to be matched. Statements in column I are labelled as A, B, C and D whereas statements in column II are labelled as p, q, r and s. The answers to these questions have to be appropriately bubbled as illustrated in the following example. If the correct matches are A-p, A-r, B-p, B-s, C-r, C-s and D-q, then the correctly bubbled matrix will look like the following:

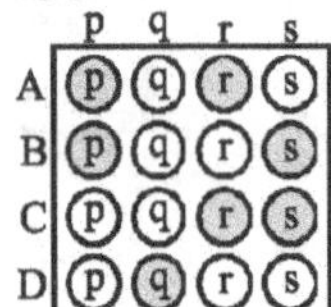

19.

	Column-I		Column-II
(A)	Natural glucose	p.	Optically active
(B)	Natural amino acids	q.	Optically inactive
(C)	Honey	r.	L-series
(D)	Glucose as synthetic sweetner	s.	Invert sugar

20.

	Column-I		Column-II
(A)	α-D-Glucopyranose	p.	Mutarotation
(B)	β-D-Methylglucopyranoside	q.	No mutarotation
(C)	Glucose pentacetate	r.	Anomerism
(D)	β-D-Glucopyranose	s.	Reducing character

RESPONSE GRID	17. ⓐⓑⓒⓓ 18. ⓐⓑⓒⓓ 19. A - ⓟⓠⓡⓢ; B - ⓟⓠⓡⓢ; C - ⓟⓠⓡⓢ; D - ⓟⓠⓡⓢ 20. A - ⓟⓠⓡⓢ; B - ⓟⓠⓡⓢ; C - ⓟⓠⓡⓢ; D - ⓟⓠⓡⓢ

DAILY PRACTICE PROBLEM DPP CHAPTERWISE 25 - CHEMISTRY

Total Questions	20	Total Marks	74
Attempted		Correct	
Incorrect		Net Score	
Cut-off Score	27	Qualifying Score	38
Success Gap = Net Score – Qualifying Score			
Net Score = (Correct × 4) – (Incorrect × 1)			

Date :   Start Time :   End Time :

CHEMISTRY $\boxed{\text{CC26}}$

SYLLABUS : Polymers

Max. Marks : 74   **Time : 60 min.**

GENERAL INSTRUCTIONS

- The Daily Practice Problem Sheet contains 20 Questions divided into 5 sections.
  Section I has **14** MCQs with ONLY 1 Correct Option, **3** marks for each correct answer and **−1** for each incorrect answer.
  Section II has **8** MCQs with ONE or MORE THAN ONE Correct options.
  For each question, marks will be awarded in one of the following categories:
  Full marks: **+4** If only the bubble(s) corresponding to all the correct option(s) is (are) darkened.
  Partial marks: **+1** For darkening a bubble corresponding to each correct option provided NO INCORRECT option is darkened.
  Zero marks: If none of the bubbles is darkened.
  Negative marks: **−2** In all other cases.

Section I - Straight Objective Type

This section contains 14 multiple choice questions. Each question has 4 choices (a), (b), (c) and (d), out of which **ONLY ONE** is correct.

1. Which one of the following statement is *not true*?

  (a) In vulcanization the formation of sulphur bridges between different chains make rubber harder and stronger.

  (b) Natural rubber has the *trans* -configuration at every double bond.

  (c) Buna-S is a copolymer of butadiene and styrene.

  (d) Natural rubber is a 1, 4 - polymer of isoprene.

2. The condensation of hexamethylenediamine with sebacoyl chloride at 525 K gives

  (a) nylon-6,20   (b) nylon-6,01

  (c) nylon-6,10   (d) None of these

3. The polymer used in orthopaedic devices and in controlled drug release is

  (a) Orlon   (b) PTFE

  (c) SBR   (d) PHBV

RESPONSE GRID   1. ⓐⓑⓒⓓ   2. ⓐⓑⓒⓓ   3. ⓐⓑⓒⓓ

Space for Rough Work

4. Which of the following is not correctly matched?

(a) Terylene $\left[OCH_2\text{-}CH_2\text{-}\overset{O}{\overset{\|}{C}}\text{-}\langle C_6H_4\rangle\text{-}\overset{O}{\overset{\|}{C}}\text{-}\right]_n$

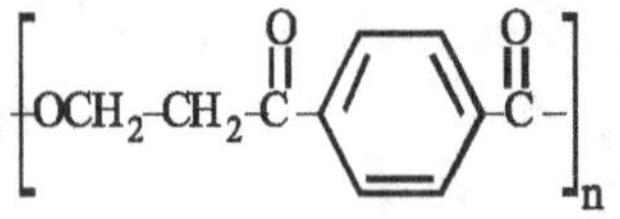

(b) Neoprene $\left[CH_2\text{—}\underset{\underset{Cl}{|}}{C}=CH\text{—}CH_2\right]_n$

(c) Nylon-66 $\left[NH\text{-}(CH_2)_6\text{-}NH\text{-}\overset{O}{\overset{\|}{C}}\text{-}(CH_2)_4\text{-}\overset{O}{\overset{\|}{C}}\text{-}O\right]_n$

(d) PMMA $\left[CH_2\text{-}\underset{\underset{COOCH_3}{|}}{\overset{\overset{CH_3}{|}}{C}}\text{—}\right]_n$

5. Mark out the most unlike form of polymerization of $CH_2=CH\text{-}CH=CH_2$

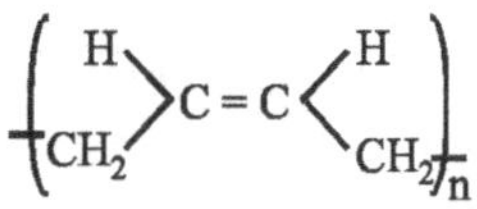

(a) 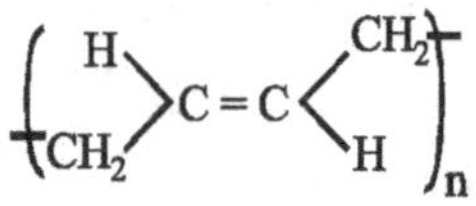 $\left[\overset{H}{\underset{CH_2}{>}}C=C\overset{CH_2}{\underset{H}{<}}\right]_n$

(b) $\left(\overset{H}{\underset{CH_2}{>}}C=C\overset{H}{\underset{CH_2}{<}}\right)_n$

(c) $\left[CH_2\text{-}\underset{\underset{CH=CH_2}{|}}{CH}\text{-}CH_2\text{-}\underset{\underset{CH=CH_2}{|}}{CH}\right]_n$

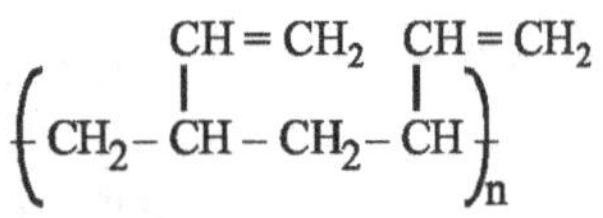

(d) 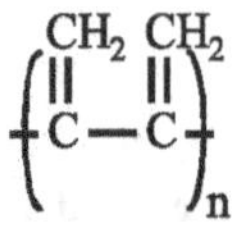 $\left[\underset{\underset{C}{\|}}{\overset{\overset{CH_2}{\|}}{C}}\text{—}\underset{\underset{C}{\|}}{\overset{\overset{CH_2}{\|}}{C}}\right]_n$

6. Ebonite is
(a) Natural rubber
(b) Synthetic rubber
(c) Highly vulcanized rubber
(d) Polypropene

7. Structure of some important polymers are given. Which one represents Buna-S?

(a) $(-CH_2-\underset{\underset{CH_3}{}}{\overset{\overset{CH_3}{|}}{C}}=CH-CH_2-)_n$

(b) $(-CH_2-CH=CH-CH_2-\underset{\underset{C_6H_5}{|}}{CH}-CH_2-)_n$

(c) $(-CH_2-CH=CH-CH_2-\underset{\underset{CN}{|}}{CH}-CH_2-)_n$

(d) $(-CH_2-\underset{\underset{Cl}{|}}{C}=CH-CH_2-)_n$

8. What is the percentage of sulphur used in vulcanization of rubber
(a) 05% to 30%   (b) 03% to 25%
(c) 10% to 20%   (d) 05% to 25%

9. Which one of the following is not a condensation polymer?
(a) Melamine   (b) Glyptal
(c) Dacron   (d) Neoprene

10. Which of the following is not an example of addition polymer ?
(a) Polystyrene   (b) Nylon
(c) PVC   (d) Polypropylene

11. Which one of the following sets forms the biodegradable polymer?

    (a) $CH_2=CH-CN$ and $CH_2=CH-CH=CH_2$

    (b) H_2N-CH_2-COOH and $H_2N-(CH_2)_5-COOH$

    (c) $HO-CH_2-CH_2-OH$ and

$$HOOC-\langle\bigcirc\rangle-COOH$$

    (d) $\langle\bigcirc\rangle-CH=CH_2$ and $CH_2=CH-CH=CH_2$

12. Among the following a natural polymer is

    (a) cellulose   (b) PVC

    (c) teflon   (d) polyethylene

13. Which of the following polymer is a polyamide ?

    (a) Terylene   (b) Nylon

    (b) Rubber   (d) Vulcanised rubber

14. Which of the following polymers do not involve cross linkages?

    (a) Melmac   (b) Bakelite

    (c) Polythene   (d) Vulcanised rubber

Section II - Multiple Correct Answer Type

This section contains 8 multiple correct answer(s) type questions. Each question has 4 choices (a), (b), (c) and (d), out of which **ONE OR MORE** is/are correct.

15. Which of the following polymers can be made by free radical addition polymerisation mechanism?

    (a) PE   (b) HDPE

    (c) LDPE   (d) Teflon

16. Which of the following polymers can be made by condensation polymerisation reaction?

    (a) Dacron   (b) Nylon-6, 6

    (c) Bakelite   (d) PE

17. Nylon-5, 10 can be prepared by:

    (a) $H_2N(CH_2)_5NH_2$ + Decanoic acid (Sebacic acid)

    (b) $HOOC(CH_2)_3COOH + H_2N(CH_2)_{10}NH_2$

    (c) $H_2N(CH_2)_6NH_2 + HOOC(CH_2)_8COOH$

    (d) $H_2N(CH_2)_{10}NH_2 + HOOC(CH_2)_4COOH$

18. By which of the following reaction sequence can nylon-5 be prepared?

    (a) (cyclopentanone) $\xrightarrow{NH_2OH}$? $\xrightarrow[H_3O^+]{H^\oplus}$? $\xrightarrow[H_3O^\oplus]{\Delta}$ Nylon-5

    (b) (cyclohexanone) $\xrightarrow{NH_2OH}$? $\xrightarrow[H_3O^\oplus]{H^\oplus}$? $\xrightarrow[H_3O^\oplus]{\Delta}$ Nylon-5

    (c) Diethyl adipate $\xrightarrow{NaOEt}$? $\xrightarrow[(ii)\ \Delta]{(i)\ H_3O^\oplus}$?

    $\xrightarrow[(ii)\ H^\oplus]{(i)\ NH_2OH}$? $\xrightarrow{\Delta/H_3O^+}$ Nylon-5

    (iii) $H_3O^\oplus$

    (d) All

Response	11. ⓐⓑⓒⓓ	12. ⓐⓑⓒⓓ	13. ⓐⓑⓒⓓ	14. ⓐⓑⓒⓓ
Grid	15. ⓐⓑⓒⓓ	16. ⓐⓑⓒⓓ	17. ⓐⓑⓒⓓ	18. ⓐⓑⓒⓓ

19. Which of the following fibres are made of polyamides?

   (a) Wool   (b) Natural silk

   (c) Rayon   (d) Nylon

20. Which of the following polymers contain 1, 3-butadiene as one of the monomers?

   (a) Butyl rubber   (b) Nitrile rubber

   (c) ABS plastic   (d) SBR

21. Which one of the following statement is/are *true*?

   (a) In vulcanization the formation of sulphur bridges between different chains make rubber harder and stronger.

   (b) Natural rubber has the *trans* -configuration at every double bond

   (c) Buna-S is a copolymer of butadiene and styrene

   (d) Natural rubber is a 1, 4 - polymer of isoprene

22. Structures of some common polymers are given. Which one is correctly presented?

   (a) Neoprene;

$$\left[-CH_2 - \underset{\underset{Cl}{|}}{C} = CH - CH_2 - CH_2 - \right]_n$$

   (b) Terylene;

$$\left(-OC - \bigcirc - COOCH_2 - CH_2 - O- \right)_n$$

   (c) Nylon 6, 6;

$$\left[-NH(CH_2)_6 NH\,CO(CH_2)_4 CO - \right]_n$$

   (d) Teflon; $(-CF_2 - CF_2 -)_n$

RESPONSE GRID	19. ⓐⓑⓒⓓ	20. ⓐⓑⓒⓓ	21. ⓐⓑⓒⓓ	22. ⓐⓑⓒⓓ

DAILY PRACTICE PROBLEM DPP CHAPTERWISE 26 - CHEMISTRY

Total Questions	22	Total Marks	74
Attempted		Correct	
Incorrect		Net Score	
Cut-off Score	30	Qualifying Score	48
Success Gap = Net Score – Qualifying Score			
Net Score = (Correct × 4) – (Incorrect × 1)			

1. **(a)** $\dfrac{E + \text{Eq.mass of } Cl^-}{\text{Eq. mass of } Ag + \text{Eq. mass of } Cl^-} = \dfrac{E + 35.5}{108 + 35.5}$

$= \dfrac{0.2}{0.5} \Rightarrow E = 21.90$

2. **(b)** $H_2SO_4 + 2NaOH \longrightarrow Na_2SO_4 + 2H_2O$;

Mol. of H_2SO_4 required for 1 mol of $NaOH = \dfrac{1}{2} = 0.5$

$H_3PO_4 + 3NaOH \longrightarrow Na_3PO_4 + 3H_2O$;

Mol. of H_3PO_4 required for 1 mol of $NaOH = \dfrac{1}{3}$

Hence, mass of H_2SO_4 : mass of $H_3PO_4 = \dfrac{1}{2} : \dfrac{1}{3}$

$= 3 : 2 \quad (M_{H_2SO_4} = M_{H_3PO_4} = 98)$

3. **(a)** $Cu + 2H_2SO_4(aq) \longrightarrow CuSO_4(aq) + 2H_2O + SO_2(g)$
    1 mole   2 mole   1 mole
    From the above equation we find that 1 mole of
    Cu reacts with 2 mole of H_2SO_4. Since we have only
    1 mole of H_2SO_4 so it is the limiting reagent.
    Now
    Since 2 moles of H_2SO_4 react with Cu to produce SO_2
    $= 1$ mole
    $\therefore$ 1 mole of H_2SO_4 reacts with Cu to produce SO_2

$= \dfrac{1}{2}$ mole

Now one mole of $SO_2 = 6.023 \times 10^{23}$ molecules of SO_2

$\therefore \dfrac{1}{2}$ mole of $SO_2 = \dfrac{6.023 \times 10^{23}}{2}$ molecules of SO_2

$= 3 \times 10^{23}$ molecules of SO_2

4. **(a)** No. of molecules in different cases
    (a) $\because$ 22.4 litre of H_2 at STP contains
    $= 6.023 \times 10^{23}$ molecules of H_2

$\therefore$ 15 litre of H_2 at STP contains $= \dfrac{15}{22.4} \times 6.023 \times 10^{23}$

$= 4.03 \times 10^{23}$ molecules of H_2

(b) $\because$ 22.4 litre of N_2 gas at STP contains
$= 6.023 \times 10^{23}$ molecules of N_2
$\therefore$ 5 litre of N_2 gas at STP contains

$= \dfrac{5}{22.4} \times 6.023 \times 10^{23}$

$= 1.344 \times 10^{23}$ molecules of N_2

(c) $\because$ 2 g of $H_2 = 6.023 \times 10^{23}$ molecules of H_2

$\therefore$ 0.5 g of $H_2 = \dfrac{0.5}{2} \times 6.023 \times 10^{23}$

$= 1.505 \times 10^{23}$ molecules of H_2

(d) Similarly 10 g of O_2 gas

$= \dfrac{10}{32} \times 6.023 \times 10^{23}$ molecules of O_2

$= 1.88 \times 10^{23}$ molecules of O_2

5. **(d)**

Element	Percentage	Atomic mass	Relative no. of atoms	Simplest ratio
C	20%	12	1.66	1
H	6.7%	1	6.7	4
N	46.7%	14	3.33	2
O	26.6%	16	1.66	1

Empirical formula = Molecular formula
$= CH_4N_2O$ or NH_2CONH_2

$H_2NCONH_2 + H_2NCONH_2 \xrightarrow{\Delta}$

$\underset{\text{biuret,}}{H_2NCONHCONH_2} + NH_3$

When an aqueous solution of biuret is treated with
dilute sodium hydroxide and a drop of copper sulphate,
a violet colour is produced. This test is known as biuret
test, is characteristic of compounds having the group
$-CONH$.

6. **(b,c,d)** $2Na_3PO_4(aq) + 3Ba(NO_3)_2(aq)$

$\longrightarrow Ba_3(PO_4)_2(s) + 6NaNO_2(aq)$

Na_3PO_4 is the limiting reactant and is completely
consumed.

Mol of $Ba_3(PO_4)_2$ formed $= \dfrac{0.2}{2} = 0.1$;

mol of $Ba(NO_3)_2$ reacted $= \dfrac{3}{2} \times 0.2 = 0.3$

Mol of unreacted $Ba(NO_3)_2 = 0.5 - 0.3 = 0.2 = $ moL
of Ba^{2+} ion
Mol of Na^+ in solution $= 0.2 \times 3 = 0.6$;
Mol of NO_3^- in solution $= 0.5 \times 2 = 1$

7. **(a,b,d)** $2CO + O_2 \rightarrow 2CO_2$ The residual gas is CO.
    Volume of CO oxidised $= 2 \times 30 = 60$ mL ;
    Volume of CO $= 60 + 10 = 70$ mL
    hence the volume of CO remains
    unreacted $= 70 - 60 = 10$ mL

Volume of CO_2 initially present in the mixture
$= 100 - 70 = 30$ mL
Volume of CO_2 formed $= 60$ mL; Volume of CO_2 absorbed by KOH $= 30 + 60 = 90$ mL
As per reaction O_2 is completely consumed.

8. (a,b,c) Volume strength of an H_2O_2 solution is the volume of O_2 in litres at NTP produced by 1 L of the solution.

$$2H_2O_2 \longrightarrow 2H_2O + O_2$$
$$68\,g \qquad\qquad 22.4\,L\,at\,NTP$$

$\therefore$ Volume produced by 17g H_2O_2 (present in 1 L

solution) $= \dfrac{22.4}{68} \times 17 = 5.6$ L at NTP

So the volume strength is 5.6.
The volume of O_2 given out at NTP by 1 L of solution
$= 5.6$ L
$\therefore$ Volume of O_2 given out at NTP by 1 mL of solution
$= 5.6$ mL
Converting this volume to volume at 2 atmosphere pressure and 273 K temperature, we get

$$\dfrac{P_1 V_1}{T_1} = \dfrac{P_2 V_2}{T_2} \text{ or volume} = \dfrac{5.6}{2} = 2.8 \text{ mL}$$

Moles of H_2O_2 present in 1 L solution $= \dfrac{17}{34}$

$$= 0.5 \text{ moles}$$
$$[\text{Mol wt} = 34]$$

$\because$ Volume strength $= N \times 5.6$
$\therefore$ N $= 5.6 / 5.6 = 1$ N.

9. (c) Let the hydrocarbon be $C_x H_y$. The reaction that occurs can be represented as

$$C_x H_y + \left(x + \dfrac{y}{4}\right) O_2 \longrightarrow x\,CO_2 + \dfrac{y}{2}\,H_2O$$
$$10\,mL \quad 10(x + y/4)\,mL \qquad 10x\,mL$$

1 mole of hydrocarbon reacts with $(x + y/4)$ moles of $O_2(g)$ to produce x mole of CO_2 and $y/2$ moles of H_2O.
Volume of CO_2 produced from 10 mL of hydrocarbon $= 10x$ mL
Volume of O_2 consumed by 10 mL of hydrocarbon
$= 10x(x + y/4)$ mL
At a pressure of 1 atm and room temperature water vapour is condensed to liquid state. The residual gases are CO_2 and unreacted O_2.
Hence, volume of CO_2 and left out $O_2 = 180$ mL
On passing the mixture of gases through aqueous KOH, CO_2 is absorbed leaving behind O_2.
Hence volume of unreacted $O_2 = 100$ mL (given)
Volume of O_2 reacted $= 200 - 100 = 100$ mL
Volume of CO_2 produced $= 180 - 100 = 80$ mL
Then, we have
$\quad 10x = 80 \quad$ or $\quad x = 8$
And $\quad 10 \times (x + y/4) = 100$
or $\quad 8 + y/4 = 10 \Rightarrow y = 8$

Thus the hydrocarbon is $C_8 H_8$

10. 4.
Let a and b cm^3 be the volumes of CO and CH$_4$ respectively in the mixture.

$$CO(g) + \dfrac{1}{2}O_2(g) \longrightarrow CO_2(g)$$
$$1\,vol \quad 1/2\,vol \qquad\quad 1\,vol$$
$$a\,cm^3 \quad a/2\,cm^3 \qquad a\,cm^3$$

$$CH_4(g) + 2O_2(g) \longrightarrow CO_2(g) + 2H_2O(l)$$
$$1\,vol \qquad 2\,vol \qquad\quad 1\,vol$$
$$b\,cm^3 \quad 2b\,cm^3 \qquad b\,cm^3$$

Reactions show that volume contraction after the reaction is due only to the consumption of oxygen.

Volume contraction after reaction, $\dfrac{a}{2} + 2b = 13$ .... (i)

When treated with aqueous KOH, CO_2 is absorbed.
Hence $a + b = 14$ ....(ii)
Solving equation (i) and (ii), $a = 10$, $b = 4$
% of CO $= 50$; % of CH$_4$ = **20**; % of He $= 30$;
According to question
$5x =$ % of CH$_4$ $= 20$
$x = 4$

11. 4.

$$HCOOH \xrightarrow{H_2SO_4} H_2O \;+\; CO$$
$$a\,moles \qquad\qquad\quad a\,moles$$

$$H_2C_2O_4 \xrightarrow{H_2SO_4} H_2O + CO + CO_2$$
$$b\,moles \qquad\qquad b\,moles \; b\,moles$$

Total number of moles of gases formed $= a + 2b$
Moles of gas (CO_2) absorbed by KOH $= b$

Hence, $b = \dfrac{1}{6}(a + 2b)$ [Volume $\propto$ moles)

$$a/b = 4$$

12. 2. Equivalents of A oxidised = Equivalents of A reduced.
Since in acidic medium, A^{n+} is oxidised to AO_3^-, the change in oxidation state from

$$(+5)\,to\,(+n) = 5 - n \qquad [\because \text{O.S. of A in } AO_3^- = +5]$$

$\therefore$ Total number of electrons that have been given out during oxidation of 2.68×10^{-3} moles of A^{n+}
$$= 2.68 \times 10^{-3} \times (5 - n)$$

Thus the number of electrons added to reduce 1.61×10^{-3} moles of MnO_4^- to Mn^{2+}, *i.e.*
$(+7)\,to\,(+2) = 1.61 \times 10^{-3} \times 5$
[Number of electrons involved $= +7 - (+2) = 5$]
$\therefore \quad 1.61 \times 10^{-3} \times 5 = 2.68 \times 10^{-3} \times (5 - n)$

$$5 - n = \dfrac{1.61 \times 5}{2.68} \text{ or } n = 5 - \dfrac{8.05}{2.68} \approx 2$$

13. 6.

Mass of Fe_2O_3 in the sample $= \dfrac{55.2}{100} \times 1 = 0.552$ g

Number of moles of $Fe_2O_3 = \dfrac{0.552}{159.8} = 3.454 \times 10^{-3}$

Number of moles of Fe^{3+} ions $= 2 \times 3.454 \times 10^{-3}$
$$= 6.9 \times 10^{-3} \text{ mol} = 6.90 \text{ mmol}$$

Since its only 1 electron is exchanged in the conversion of Fe^{3+} to Fe^{2+}, the molecular mass is the same as equivalent mass.

$\therefore$ Amount of Fe^{2+} ion in 100 mL. of sol. = 6.90 meq
Volume of oxidant used for 100 mL of Fe^{2+} sol.
$$= 17 \times 4 = 68 \text{ mL.}$$
Amount of oxidant used $= 68 \times 0.0167$ mmol
$$= 1.1356 \text{ mmol}$$
Let the number of electrons taken by the oxidant $= n$
$\therefore$ No. of meq. of oxidant used $= 1.1356 \times n$
Thus $1.1356 \times n = 6.90$

$$n = \dfrac{6.90}{1.1356} = 6$$

14. 7

$$d = \dfrac{\text{mass}}{V} \Rightarrow 10.5 \text{ g/cc means in 1 cc}$$

$\Rightarrow 10.5$ g of Ag is present.

Number of atoms of Ag in 1 cc $\Rightarrow \dfrac{10.5}{108} \times N_A$

In 1 cm, number of atoms of Ag $= \sqrt[3]{\dfrac{10.5}{108}} N_A$

In 1 cm^2, number of atoms of Ag $= \left(\dfrac{10.5}{108} N_A\right)^{2/3}$

In 10^{-12} m^2 or 10^{-8} cm^2, number of atoms of Ag

$$\left(\dfrac{10.5}{108} N_A\right)^{2/3} \times 10^{-8}$$

$$= \left(\dfrac{10.5 \times 6.022 \times 10^{23}}{108}\right)^{2/3} \times 10^{-8} = 1.5 \times 10^7$$

Hence $x = 7$

15. (c) Molarity $= \dfrac{9.8 \times 10 \times 1.8}{98} = 1.8$ M

$$\because d = M\left(\dfrac{\text{Mol.wt.}}{1000} + \dfrac{1}{m}\right)$$

$$1.8 = 1.8\left(\dfrac{98}{1000} + \dfrac{1}{m}\right)$$

$\therefore m = 1.10$

H_2SO_4 is a dibasic acid i.e. it has two replaceable H^+. Hence n-factor for this is 2.

16. (b) $1.8 N_A$ molecules = 1.8 mol of HCl in 500 mL = 1.8 Equiv., n-factor for HCl = 1 (only one replaceable H^+)

17. (a) Molarity $= \dfrac{9.8 \times 10 \times 1.2}{98} = 1.2$ M

n-factor for $H_3PO_4 = 3$

18. (b) In one mole of CO_2 the number of C atom = 1 mole
In one mole of H_2O the number of H atoms = 2 mole
Since the mole ratio of CO_2 and H_2O is 1 : 1
$\therefore$ C : H ratio is 1 : 2

19. (c) It will consists of CO_2, H_2O and hydrocarbon.
Since the hydrocarbon is C_2H_4 (the atomic ratio C : H is 1 : 2 and and so the hydrocarbon is C_2H_4)

$$C_2H_4 + 3O_2 \longrightarrow 2CO_2 + 2H_2O$$
$$\text{1 mole} \quad \text{3 mole} \qquad (28 \text{ g})$$

Since the mole of O_2 required is three times the mole of hydrocarbon so in a mixture containing equal number of moles of hydrocarbon and oxygen, hydrocarbon will be in excess and some of it will remain unreacted while whole of O_2 will be consumed. Thus the mixture in vessel after the completion of reaction will consist of products (i.e., CO_2 and H_2O) and excess of hydrocarbon that has remained unreacted.

20. A - p, q; B - p; C - p, q, r; D - s

1. 5 mole of CO_2 (g) $= 1.5 \times 22400$ mL at NTP
$$= 33600 \text{ mL at NTP}$$
Total number of atoms in one molecule of $CO_2 = 1 + 2 = 3$
Total number of atoms in 1.5 mole of $CO_2 = 1.5 \times 3 \times N_A$
$$= 4.5 \times N_A$$

3.0 g of $H_2 = \dfrac{3}{2} \times 22400$ mL of H_2 at NTP = 33600 mL at NTP

Number of mole of H_2 in 3.0 g $H_2 = \dfrac{3}{2}$ or 1.5 moles

Number of atoms in 1 molecule of $H_2 = 2$
Number of atoms in 1.5 mole $H_2 = 2 \times 1.5 \times N_A$
$$= 3.0 \times N_A$$
Volume of 1.5 moles of ozone at NTP $= 22400 \times 1.5$ mL
$$= 33600 \text{ mL}$$
Number of atoms in one molecule of $O_3 = 3$
Total number of atoms in 1.5 mole of $O_3 = 3 \times 1.5 \times N_A$
$$= 4.5 \times N_A$$
Weight of 1 mole of $O_3 = 48$ g
Weight of 1.5 mole of $O_3 = 48 \times 1.5$ g = 72 g
Weight of 1 mole of oxygen $(O_2) = 32$ g

1. **(b)** de – Broglie wavelength is given by :

$$\lambda = \frac{h}{mv} \qquad \dots (i)$$

$$\text{K.E.} = \frac{1}{2}mv^2$$

$$v^2 = \frac{2KE}{m}$$

$$v = \sqrt{\frac{2KE}{m}}$$

Substituting this in equation (i)

$$\lambda = \frac{h}{m}\sqrt{\frac{m}{2KE}}$$

$$\lambda = h\sqrt{\frac{1}{2m(K.E.)}}$$

i.e. $\lambda \propto \dfrac{1}{\sqrt{KE}}$

∴ when KE become 4 times wavelength become 1/2.

2. **(d)** From the expression of Bohr's theory, we know that

$$m_e v_1 r_1 = n_1 \frac{h}{2\pi}$$

$$\&\ m_e v_2 r_2 = n_2 \frac{h}{2\pi}$$

$$\frac{m_e v_1 r_1}{m_e v_2 r_2} = \frac{n_1}{n_2}\frac{h}{2\pi}\times\frac{2\pi}{h}$$

Given, $r_1 = 5 r_2, n_1 = 5, n_2 = 4$

$$\frac{m_e \times v_1 \times 5r_2}{m_e \times v_2 \times r_2} = \frac{5}{4}$$

$$\Rightarrow \frac{v_1}{v_2} = \frac{5}{4\times 5} = \frac{1}{4} = 1:4$$

3. **(d)** $\dfrac{1}{\lambda} = R_H Z^2 \left(\dfrac{1}{n_1^{\,2}} - \dfrac{1}{n_2^{\,2}}\right)$

To calculate shortest wavelength take $n_2 = \infty$ and longest wavelength take nearest value of n_2.
For H-atom,

$$\frac{1}{\lambda_{\text{shortest}}} \quad n_2 = \infty, Z = 1, n_1 = 1$$

$$\therefore \frac{1}{x} = R_H \text{ (Lyman series)}$$

For $\dfrac{1}{\lambda_{\text{longest}}}$ for Li^{2+}, $Z = 3$, $n_1 = 2$, $n_2 = 3$ (Balmer series)

$$\frac{1}{\lambda_{\text{longest}}} = \frac{1}{x} \times 3^2 \left(\frac{1}{2^2} - \frac{1}{3^2}\right) = \frac{5}{4x}$$

$$\therefore\ \lambda_{\text{longest}} = \frac{4x}{5}$$

4. **(d)** Using the relation, $\lambda \propto \dfrac{1}{\text{K.E.}}$, we get

$\lambda_1 = \lambda$ and $\text{K.E.}_1 = E$ (initial)
$\lambda_2 = 0.9\lambda$

$$[10\% \text{ decrease from } \lambda_1, \lambda_2 = \lambda - \frac{10}{100}\lambda$$
$$= \lambda(1 - 0.1) = 0.9\lambda]$$

We are required to find $\text{K.E.}_2 = ?$

$$\therefore\ \text{K.E.}_2 = \frac{\lambda_1^2}{\lambda_2^2}\times \text{K.E.}_1 = \frac{\lambda^2}{(.9\lambda)^2}\times \text{K.E.}_1$$

$$= \frac{\lambda^2 \times 100}{81\lambda^2}\times E \quad [\text{K.E}_1 = E]$$

$$= \frac{100}{81}E \quad [\text{more than K.E.}_1 \text{ i.e., increase}]$$

Now increase in $\text{K.E.} = \text{K.E.}_2 - \text{K.E.}_1 = \dfrac{100}{81}E - E$

$$\% \text{ increase of K.E.} = \frac{\dfrac{100}{81}E - E}{E}\times 100$$

$$= \frac{19}{81}\times 100 = 23.4\%$$

5. **(d)** Lyman series, $n_1 = 1$
For third line of Lyman series, $n_2 = 4$
For hydrogen, $Z = 1$

$$\upsilon_H = \frac{1}{\lambda} = R_H Z^2\left(\frac{1}{n_1^2} - \frac{1}{n_2^2}\right)$$

$$= R_H (1)^2\left(\frac{1}{1} - \frac{1}{(4)^2}\right) = \frac{15}{16}R_H \qquad \dots(i)$$

For lithium, $Z = 3$
For first line of Balmer series, $n_1 = 2, n_2 = 3$

$$\upsilon_{Li} = R_H (3)^2 \left(\frac{1}{(2)^2} - \frac{1}{(3)^2} \right) = R_H \times 9 \times \frac{5}{56}$$

$$= \frac{5}{4} R_H \qquad \qquad \dots (ii)$$

on dividing equation (i) by (ii), we get

$$\frac{\upsilon_H}{\upsilon_{Li}} = \frac{(15/16)R_H}{(5/4)R_H} = \frac{15}{16} \times \frac{4}{5} = \frac{3}{4}$$

6. **(a,b,c,d)** $E_n = -13.6 \dfrac{Z^2}{n^2}$; for He^+, $Z = 2$

$$K.E. = -E_n = 13.6 \frac{Z^2}{n^2};$$

$$v_n = 2.19 \times 10^6 \, Z / n \text{ ms}^{-1}$$

7. **(b)** $A - 1s^2 2s^2 2p^6 3s^2 3p^5 - Cl$ (17), $11\,p$ electrons

$B - 1s^2 2s^2 2p^6 3s^2 3p^6 4s^2 3d^1$, (Sc - 21), $l = 2$ and $m_l = 2$ for $3d$-electron.

$C - 1s^2 2s^2 2p^6 3s^2 3p^6 4s^2 3d^2$ (Ti - 22), $n = 3$ and $l = 2$ for $3d^2$ electrons.

8. **(a, c)** $\bar{v} = RZ^2 \left(\dfrac{1}{n_1^2} - \dfrac{1}{n_2^2} \right)$

$$x = R \left(\frac{1}{2^2} - \frac{1}{3^2} \right) = \frac{5R}{36}$$

$$\bar{v}_1 = R \times 2^2 \left(1 - \frac{1}{2^2} \right) = 3R = \frac{36}{5} x \times 3 = \frac{108x}{5}$$

For H atom 2nd lyman

$$\frac{1}{\lambda_2} = R \left(1 - \frac{1}{9} \right) = \frac{8}{9} \times \frac{36x}{5} = \frac{32x}{5} \Rightarrow \lambda_2 = \frac{5}{32x}$$

9. **(b, c)** Statements (a) and (d) are incorrect.

(a) The excited electron has a tendency to return back to lower energy state.

(d) Angular momentum $= \dfrac{nh}{2\pi}$

10. **(6)** As the α-particle travelling with velocity, 'u', stops at a distance 10^{-13} m, its K.E. becomes zero and gets converted into P.E.

$$\therefore \frac{1}{2} mu^2 = \frac{1}{4\pi\varepsilon_0} \times \frac{2Ze^2}{r} \text{ or } u^2 = \frac{Ze^2}{\pi\varepsilon_0 . m . r}$$

Here, $Z = 29$ for Cu atom

$$\Rightarrow u^2 = \frac{29 \times (1.6 \times 10^{-19})^2}{3.14 \times 8.85 \times 10^{-12} \times (4 \times 1.672 \times 10^{-27}) \times 10^{-13}}$$

$$\therefore u = 6.3 \times 10^6 \text{ m sec}^{-1}$$

According to question,

$x \times 10^y = 6.3 \times 10^6$

thus, $y = 6$

11. **(2)** $\Delta v = \dfrac{0.001}{100} \times 30{,}000 = 0.3 \text{ cm sec}^{-1}$

According to uncertainty principle,

$$\Delta x . \Delta p \approx \frac{h}{4\pi}; \quad \Delta x . \Delta v \approx \frac{h}{4\pi m}$$

$$\Delta x \times 9.1 \times 10^{-28} \times 0.3 \approx \frac{6.625 \times 10^{-27} \times 7}{4 \times 22}$$

$$\Delta x \approx 1.93 \text{ cm.} \approx 2$$

12. **(2)** Energy of photon, $\qquad E = h\nu = \dfrac{hc}{\lambda}$

Here, $c = 3.0 \times 10^8 \text{ ms}^{-1}$

In first case, $\lambda = 800 \text{ nm} = 800 \times 10^{-9} \text{ m}$

$$\therefore E_1 = \frac{(6.626 \times 10^{-34} \text{ Js}) \times (3 \times 10^8 \text{ ms}^{-1})}{800 \times 10^{-9} \text{ m}}$$

$$= 2.48 \times 10^{-19} \text{ J}$$

In second case, $\lambda = 400 \text{ nm} = 400 \times 10^{-9} \text{ m}$

$$\therefore E_2 = \frac{(6.626 \times 10^{-34} \text{ Js}) \times (3 \times 10^8 \text{ ms}^{-1})}{400 \times 10^{-9} \text{ m}}$$

$$= 4.91 \times 10^{-19} \text{ J}$$

Ratio of energy of first and second radiations,

$$\frac{E_1}{E_2} = \frac{2.48 \times 10^{-19} \text{ J}}{4.97 \times 10^{-19} \text{ J}} = \frac{1}{2}$$

$$E_1 : E_2 = 1 : 2 \text{ or } E_2 = 2E_1$$

Thus, energy of the radiation with wavelength 400 nm is twice that of the radiation of wavelength 800 nm.

13. **(4)** Energy associated with the incident photon $= \dfrac{hc}{\lambda}$

$$i.e., \, E = \frac{(6.6 \times 10^{-34} \text{ Js})(3 \times 10^8 \text{ ms}^{-1})}{(300 \times 10^{-9} \text{ m})}$$

$$= 6.6 \times 10^{-19} \text{ J} = \frac{6.6 \times 10^{-19}}{1.6 \times 10^{-19}} \text{ eV} = 4.12 \text{ eV}$$

$\therefore$ Metals showing photoelectric effect will be Li, Na, K and Mg only i.e., 4 metals (which have work function less than 4.12 eV).

14. **(1)** $n = 3, l = 2$ means $3d$ orbital

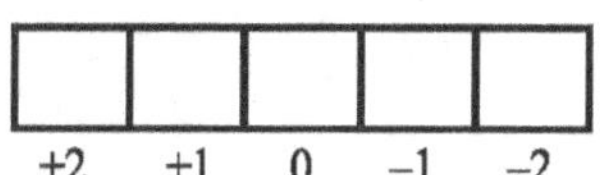

i.e. in an atom only one orbital can have the value $m_l = +2$

15. **(c)** radius $(r_n) = \dfrac{n^2 h^2}{4\pi^2 m Z e^2} = \dfrac{n^2}{Z} \times 0.529 \text{Å}$

$$= \frac{n^2}{Z} = 0.0529 \text{ nm}$$

16. (b) $V_n = \dfrac{2\pi Z e^2}{nh} = \left(\dfrac{Z e^2}{rm}\right)^{1/2}$

17. (d) $E_n = -\dfrac{2\pi^2 m Z^2 e^4}{n^2 h^2} = -\dfrac{Z^2}{n^2} \times 313.6\,\text{kcal}$

18. (d) Given : subsidiary quantum number $(l) = 4$
$\therefore$ number of degenerate orbitals $= 2l + 1 = 2 \times 4 + 1$
$\qquad\qquad\qquad\qquad\qquad\qquad = 8 + 1 = 9$

For this maximum total spins (s) $= 9 \times \dfrac{1}{2}$

For this minimum total spins (s) $= 1 \times \dfrac{1}{2}$

$\therefore$ Maximum total multiplicity $= 2s + 1 = 2 \times \dfrac{9}{2} + 1 = 10$

Minimum total multiplicity $= 2 \times \dfrac{1}{2} + 1 = 2$

19. (c) $Fe(Z = 26)$, Fe^{2+}; $3d^6$, number of d-electrons in $Fe^{2+} = 6$
In Fe, $3d^6 4s^2$, so number of d-electron $= 6$
In $Ne(Z = 10)$; $1s^2\,2s^2\,2p^6$; number of p-electrons $= 6$
In $Cl\,(Z = 17)$; $1s^2 2s^2 p^6 3s^2 p^5$, so number of p-electrons $= 6 + 5 = 11$
In $Mg(Z = 12)$, $1s^2 2s^2 2p^6 3s^2$, so number of s-electrons $= 2 + 2 + 2 = 6$
Thus number of p-electrons in Cl is not equal to number of d-electrons in Fe^{2+}.

20. **A-r, B-s, C-q, D-p**

Wave number $\bar{v} = \dfrac{1}{\lambda} = kZ^2\left[\dfrac{1}{n_1^2} - \dfrac{1}{n_2^2}\right]$

For shortest wavelength ($\bar{v}_{max}$) in Lyman series
$n_1 = 1$, $n_2 = \infty$ and $Z = 1$ (for H-atom)

Hence, $\dfrac{1}{\lambda} = \dfrac{1}{x} = kZ^2 = \left[\dfrac{1}{1^2} - \dfrac{1}{\infty^2}\right] \Rightarrow k = \dfrac{1}{x}$

(A) For shortest wavelength in Lyman series of Li^{2+}
$n = 1$, $n = \infty$, $Z = 3$

Hence $\dfrac{1}{\lambda} = \dfrac{1}{x} \times 3^2 \left[\dfrac{1}{1^2} - \dfrac{1}{\infty^2}\right] = \dfrac{9}{x} \Rightarrow \lambda = \dfrac{x}{9}$

(B) For longest wavelength in Lyman series, $n_1 = 1$, $n_2 = 2$

$\dfrac{1}{\lambda} = \dfrac{1}{x} \times 3^2 \left[\dfrac{1}{1^2} - \dfrac{1}{2^2}\right] = \dfrac{27}{4x} \Rightarrow \lambda = \dfrac{4x}{27}$

(C) For shortest wavelength in Balmer series, $n_1 = 2$, $n_2 = \infty$

Hence, $\dfrac{1}{\lambda} = \dfrac{1}{x} \times 3^2 \left[\dfrac{1}{2^2} - \dfrac{1}{\infty^2}\right] \Rightarrow \lambda = \dfrac{4x}{9}$

(D) For longest wavelength in Balmer series, $n_1 = 2$, $n_2 = 3$

Hence, $\dfrac{1}{\lambda} = \dfrac{1}{x} \times 3^2 \times \left[\dfrac{1}{2^2} - \dfrac{1}{3^2}\right] \Rightarrow \lambda = \dfrac{4x}{5}$

1. (b) On moving along the period, ionization enthalpy increases.

In second period, the order of ionization enthalpy should be as follows :

$$F > O > N.$$

But N has half-filled structure, therefore, it is more stable than O. That is why its ionization enthalpy is higher than O. Thus, the correct order of IE is

$$F > N > O.$$

2. (c) As we move along the period, the atomic size decreases due to increase in nuclear charge. Therefore, it is more difficult to remove electron from an atom. Hence the sequence of first ionization enthalpy in decreasing order is

$$F > N > C > B > Be$$

But ionization enthalpy of boron is less as compared to beryllium because first electron in boron is to be removed from p-orbital while in beryllium, is to be removed from s-orbital.

As s-orbital is closer to nucleus in comparison to p-orbital thus energy required to remove an electron from s-orbital is greater.

3. (d) Greater the effective nuclear charge, more is the attraction of nucleus towards the electron and hence higher will be the value of E.A.

Greater the atomic radius of the atom, less will be the attraction of the nucleus to the electron to be added and hence lower will be the value of E.A.

4. (b) The alkali metals are highly reactive because their first ionisation potential is very low and hence they have great tendency to lose electrons to form unipositive ions. On moving down a group from Li to Cs ionisation enthalpy decreases hence the reactivity increases.

The halogens are most reactive elements due to their low bond dissociation energy, high electron affinity and high enthalpy of hydration of halide ion however their reactivity decreases with increase in atomic number. As the size increases, the attraction for an additional electron by the nucleus becomes less. Thus reactivity decreases.

5. (d) $O(g) + 2e^- \rightarrow O^{2-}(g), \Delta H = 603\,\text{kJ mol}^{-1}$ ......(i);

$O(g) + e^- \rightarrow O^-(g), \Delta H = -141\,\text{kJ mol}^{-1}$ ......(ii)

(i) - (ii) gives :

$O^- + e^- \rightarrow O^{2-}, \Delta H = 603 - (-141) = 744\,\text{kJ mol}^{-1}$

6. (b) van der Waals radii decrease as we move from left to right in a period. It is due to increasing nuclear charge. The given elements belong to second period (except Cl). The van der Waals radius of Cl will be largest.

7. (a, b, c) For no consideration of Aufbau principle and Hund's rule, the electronic configurations will be as:

$Ca(20):[Ar]3d^2$; $Zn(30):[Ar]3d^{10}4s^2$ (filling of $4s$ subshell after $3d$ subshell); Ti (22): $[Ar]\,3d^2$ (both electrons paired up)

$Fe^{3+}[23] = [Ar]3d^3 4s^2$

i.e., -3 unpaired electrons

8. (a,b) Group oxidation number (i.e., maximum oxidation state in a group) need not necessarily be the most common or most stable oxidation state for a particular element, so option (c) is **incorrect.**

In fact some elements may have no compounds at all in the group oxidation number state e.g. in case of flourine, so (d) option is incorrect.

9. (b,c,d) Electron affinity increases as we move from left to right in a period and decreases on moving down a group. However there are many exceptions. The periodic trends are less well defined than those for I.E. partly because of lack of reliable data.

The following graph shows the plot of E.A. values against atomic number for some elements.

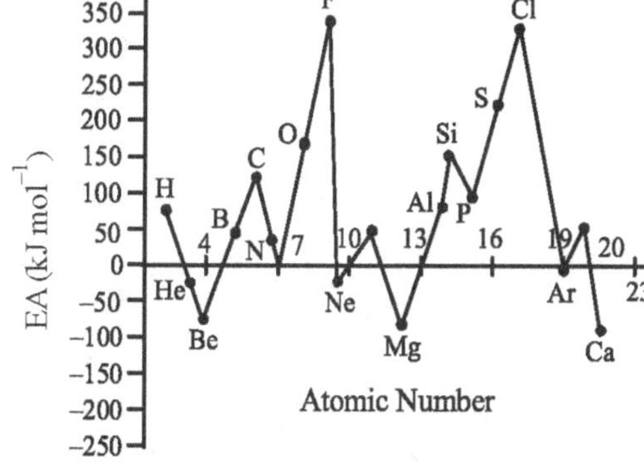

From the graphs we can see that (b), (c), (d) are correct, (a) is incorrect. E.A. of $S > O$

10. (a,c) In option (a), (b) and (c) all the species are isoelectronic 10, 10, 18 electrons in each. In isoelectronic species the ionic radii decrease with increase in atomic number so (a) is correct, (b) is incorrect and (c) is correct.

The size of anion is larger than that of neutral atom and that of cation is smaller than the neutral atom, so $H^- > H^+$. He is a noble gas its ionic radii cannot be measured as the ionic radii are obtained from internuclear distances in ionic compounds. Thus (d) is incorrect.

11. **(7)** Long form of periodic table contains 18 groups and 7 periods.

12. **(3)** Group I B contain Cu, Ag and Au.

13. **(8)** Third period contains total 8 elements

14. **(2)** Two elements sodium and calcium are electropositive metals.

15. **(b)** The electronegativity like ionisation energy increases steadily on moving from left to right in a period.

16. **(c)** Electronegativities increase steadily on moving across a period (N > C) and generally decrease on descending a group (P > Si).

17. **(a)** Both for positive ion and negative ions the lattice energy decreases (and not increases) with increase in the size of the ion, thus statements (b) and (c) are incorrect.

For large positive ion, the magnitude of lattice energy is mainly determined by the size of the positive ion (and not of anion) thus statement (d) is also incorrect.

18. **(b)** The lattice energies of difluorides of first row transition metals increase along the period as would be expected from decrease in ionic radii. However, there is a slight decrease at manganese which is due to d^5 configuration of Mn, which reduces the effective nuclear charge and decreases the lattice energy. Due to this the correct order is (b) and not (a).

The values of the lattice energy for these are

Compound	Lattice energy (kJ mol^{-1})
TiF_2	2749
VF_2	2810
CrF_2	2879
MnF_2	2770
FeF_2	2912

i.e., for MnF_2 it is less than VF_2 but more than TiF_2.

19. **A - q; B - p, r; C - p, s; D - p**

(A) At. No. 47 : $[Kr]4d^9 5s^2$; group : $9 + 2 = 11^{th}$; period : 5th

(B) For lowest At. No. having $(n-1)d^{10}ns^2 np^3$ configuration, $n - 1 = 3 \Rightarrow n = 4$
Hence, group : $10 + 5 = 15^{th}$; period : 4th

(C) At. No. 34 : $[Ar]\ 3d^{10} 4s^2 4p^4$; Group : $10 + 6 = 16^{th}$; period $= 4^{th}$

(D) For lowest At. No. having $(n-1)d^{10}ns^1$ configuration, $n - 1 = 3 \Rightarrow n = 4$
Group $= 10 + 1 = 11^{th}$; Period $= 4^{th}$

20. **A - r; B - p; C - s; D - q**

(A) IE_1 and IE_2 are very high. The element must be inert gas.

(B) IE_1 has low value and IE_2 has very high value. The element must belong to first group (ns^1), hence it is reactive.

(C) IE_1 and IE_2 do not have very high values. The element must belong to 2nd group (ns^2) and must form halide of formula AX_2.

(D) IE_1 and IE_2 values suggest the element to be a non-metal which is not inert.

1. (a)

(a) $ONCl = 8 + 7 + 17 = 32e^-$ ⎫ not isoelectronic
$ONO^- = 8 + 7 + 8 + 1 = 24e^-$ ⎭

(b) 1.278Å ⟋Ö⟍ 1.278Å
O 116.8° O
The central atom is sp^2 hybridized with one lone pair.

(c) It is a pale blue gas. At $-249.7°$, it forms violet black crystals.

(d) It is diamagnetic in nature due to absence of unpaired electrons.

2. (c) The molecular orbital configuration of the given molecules is
$H_2 = \sigma 1s^2$ (no electron anti-bonding)
$Li_2 = \sigma 1s^2 \sigma^* 1s^2 \sigma 2s^2$ (two anti-bonding electrons)
$B_2 = \sigma 1s^2 \sigma^* 1s^2 \sigma 2s^2 \sigma^* 2s^2 \left\{ \pi 2p_x^1 = \pi 2p_y^1 \right\}$
(4 anti-bonding electrons)
Though the bond order of all the species are same (B.O = 1) but stability is different. This is due to the difference in the presence of no. of anti-bonding electron.
Higher the no. of anti-bonding electron lower is the stability hence the correct order is $H_2 > Li_2 > B_2$

3. (c) If x is the dipole moment of chlorobenzene, then its value for m-dichlorobenzene
$$= \sqrt{x^2 + x^2 + 2x \times x \cos 120°} = 1.5\ D.\ x \Rightarrow 1.5\ D$$
(given).
Dipole moment for o-dichlorobenzene
$$= \sqrt{1.5^2 + 1.5^2 + 2 \times 1.5^2 \cos 60°}, = 2.60\ D$$

4. (b) On changing N_2 to N_2^+, B.O. decreases from 3 to 2.5 whereas on changing O_2 to O_2^+, B.O. increases from 2 to 2.5. In former case, the bond dissociation energy decreases and in the latter case, it increases.

5. (c) (a) The S-atom in the excited state $(3s^2 3p^3 3d^1)$ has
sp^3 hybridization- $(sp^3)^2 (sp^3)^1 (sp^3)^1 (sp^3)^1 3d^1$.
The three hybrid orbitals form three (S-O) σ-bonds and the $3d$ pure orbital gives (S-O) π-bond.

(b) In PO_4^{3-}, P-atom in its excited state $(3s^1 3p^3 3d^1)$ is sp^3 hybridized. Four hybrid orbitals forms (P-O) σ-bonds whereas $3d^1$ gives (P-O) π-bond.

(c) In NO_3^-, N-atom is sp^2 hybridized as
$$(sp^2)^2 (sp^2)^1 (sp^2)^1 2p_z^1$$
Completely filled sp^2 hybrid orbital on N-atom donates an electron pair to the vacant $2p$ orbital of O atom to form dative bond. Other two hybrid orbitals form (N-O) σ-bonds. The pure $2p_z^1$ orbital forms (N-O) π-bond.

(d) In $XeOF_4$, Xe-atom in its excited state $(5s^2 5p^3 5d^3)$ is $sp^3 d^2$ hybridized. The singly filled five hybrid orbitals form σ-bonds with 4F atoms and O atom. The pure $5d$ orbital forms π-bond with $2p$ orbital of O-atom.

6. (a,d) (a) sp^3 to sp^3 (b) sp^2 to sp^3
(c) sp^2 to sp (d) sp^3 to sp^3

7. (a,b,c) $NO\,(11) : (\sigma 2s)^2 (\sigma^* 2s)^2 (\sigma 2p_z)^2 (\pi 2p_x^2 = \pi 2p_y)^2 (\pi^* 2p_x)^1$
$NO^+\,(10) : (\sigma 2s)^2 (\sigma^* 2s)^2 (\pi 2p_x^2 = \pi 2p_y)^2; (\sigma 2p_z)^2$
B.O. = 3
$O_2^+\,(11) :$ B.O. = 2.5
$OF^+\,(12) : (\sigma 2s)^2 (\sigma^* 2s)^2 (\sigma 2p_z)^2 (\pi 2p_x^2 = \pi 2p_y)^2 (\pi^* 2p_x)^1 (\pi^* 2p_y)^1;$
$Ne_2^+\,(15) : (\sigma 2s)^2 (\sigma^* 2s)^2 (\sigma 2p_z)^2 (\pi 2p_x^2 = \pi 2p_y)^2 (\pi^* 2p_x)^2 (\pi^* 2p_y)^2 (\sigma^* 2p_z)^1$
In a π bond the electron density is concentrated in the region perpendicular to the bond axis.

8. (a,c) Bond order of various species are
$$\underset{6+7+1=14}{CN^-}\ \text{or}\ \frac{N_b - N_a}{2} = \frac{10-4}{2} = 3$$
$$\underset{8+8+1=17}{O_2^-}\ \text{or}\ \frac{10-7}{2} = 1.5$$
$$\underset{7+8-1=14}{NO^+}\ \text{or}\ \frac{10-4}{2} = 3$$
$$\underset{6+7-1=12}{CN^+}\ \text{or}\ \frac{8-4}{2} = 2$$
Thus CN^- and NO^+ have identical bond order.

9. (b,d) (a) Na^+ ion is solvated by ion-dipole interaction while NH_4^+ ion is solvated by H-bonding which is a stronger force of attraction.

   (b) Sn^{4+} has greater charge and smaller size than Sn^{2+}. Hence due to greater charge density, it distorts the Cl^- ion electron cloud to greater extent. So $SnCl_4$ is covalent.

   (c) NH_3 has greater dipole moment than BF_3.

   (d) I^- ion, being much bigger in size than F^- ion, is distorted to greater extent.

10. (5) For 100% ionic character of H–X, dipole moment
$$= 4.8 \times 10^{-10} \times 0.1 \times 10^{-9} \times 10^2 = 4.8\,D$$
Hence, % ionic character of H–X bond
$$= \frac{1.2}{4.8} \times 100 = 25$$

According to question
$$5x = 25$$
$$x = 5$$

11. (1) sp^3d^2 hybridisation of Xe-atom in the excited state-
$(sp^3d^2)^2$, $(sp^3d^2)^2$ $(sp^3d^2)^1$ $(sp^3d^2)^1$ $(sp^3d^2)^1$ $(sp^3)^1$

12. (5) Using the relation, charge $= \dfrac{\text{Dipole moment}}{\text{bond length}}$

$$= \frac{0.38 \times 10^{-18}\,\text{esu} - \text{cm}}{1.61 \times 10^{-8}\,\text{cm}}$$
$$= 2.44 \times 10^{-11}\,\text{esu}$$

$\therefore$ Percentage of charge $= \dfrac{2.4 \times 10^{-11}\,\text{esu}}{4.8 \times 10^{-10}\,\text{esu}} \times 100$
$$= 5\%$$

13. (4) One water molecule is bonded with 4 other water molecules as shown below.

14. (5) (i) $BrF_5 = 10\,e^-$'s
    (ii) $SF_6 = 12\,e^-$'s
    (iii) $IF_7 = 14\,e^-$'s

   (iv) $XeOF_4 \Rightarrow$ $= 12\,e^-$'s

   (v) $ClF_2 \Rightarrow$ $= 4\,e^-$'s

   (vi) $PCl_4^{\oplus} \Rightarrow$ $= 8\,e^-$'s

Hence (i) to (v) violate octet rule.

15. (d) Xenon dioxydifluoride (XeO_2F_2)

      sp^3d

Trigonal bipyramidal   See-saw shape due to presence of one lone pair of electron

16. (d) XeO_4

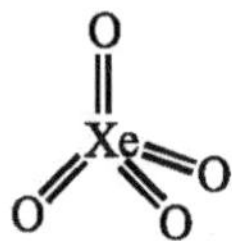

sp^3, {Geometry, shape} Tetrahedral

17. (c) $XeF_6 - sp^3d^3$
Geometry – pentagonal bipyramidal
shape – monocapped octahedral
Thus, option (c) is incorrect.

18. (d) Number of hybrid orbitals, H in ClF_3

$$= \frac{1}{2}\ (\text{valence electrons of Cl} + 3$$
$$\times \text{ valence electrons of F } - 3 \times 3\ \text{F-atoms})$$

$$= \frac{1}{2}\ (7 + 3 \times 7) - 9 = 14 - 9 = 5$$

Number of bond pairs (n) = 3
Total number of lone pairs (m) $= H - n = 5 - 3 = 2$
Hence, VSEPR notation of ClF_3 is AX_3E_2.

19. (a) $CO_2 : H = \dfrac{1}{2}\ (4 + 2 \times 6) - 3 \times 2 = 2$;

$n = 2; m = H - n = 2 - 2 = 0$

$SO_2 : H = \dfrac{1}{2}(6 + 2 \times 6) - 3 \times 2 = 3$;

$n = 2; m = 3 - 2 = 1$

$H_2O : H = \dfrac{1}{2}(2 \times 1 + 6) - 3 \times 0 = 4$;

$n = 2; m = 4 - 2 = 2$

The dipole moment of molecule α m CO_2 (m = 0), SO_2 (m = 1) and H_2O (m = 2)

Hence order is $CO_2 < SO_2 < H_2O$

20. **A → p; B → q, r, s; C → p, s; D → q, s**

Dipole-Dipole forces depend on temperature. Various forces involved in solution of HBr in carbon tetrachloride are :

HBr – HBr ; dipole-dipole

HBr – CCl_4; dipole-induced dipole

CCl_4 – CCl_4; dispersion forces

Dipole-dipole types of forces are found in molecules having dipole moment. In HBr, these is $+\delta$ on H atom and $-\delta$ on Br atom so HBr has dipole moment. There is thus a small dipole-dipole force of attraction between adjacent HBr molecules.

Dipole-induced dipole type of forces are observed in between non-polar molecule and a molecule having dipole moment. e.g. between CCl_4 (non-polar) and HBr (molecule having dipole moment)

Induced dipole-Induced dipole type of forces are found in between molecules having no dipole moment. These are also known as **London** dispersion forces.

1. **(d)** $R = \dfrac{PV}{T}$

At critical point $V = V_c$
and $(V - V_c)^3 = 0$
Expanding this equation, we have

$$V^3 - 3V_c \cdot V^2 + 3V_c^2 \cdot V - V_c^3 = 0 \qquad ..(i)$$

The vander waals equation in critical point is

$$V^3 - \left(b + \dfrac{RT_c}{P_c}\right)V^2 + \left(\dfrac{a}{P_c}\right)V - \dfrac{ab}{P_c} = 0 \qquad ...(ii)$$

Comparing (i) and (ii), we get

$$V_c = 3b, \; P_c = \dfrac{a}{27b^2}, \; T_c = \dfrac{8a}{27Rb}$$

Eliminating constants a and b from the values of critical constants, we obtain

$$R = \dfrac{8P_c V_c}{3T_c}$$

2. **(b)** At the same conditions of T and P, $V \propto n$

$$n_{N_2} = \dfrac{14}{28} = \dfrac{1}{2}; \; V_{N_2} \alpha \dfrac{1}{2} \quad n_{O_3} = \dfrac{36}{48} = \dfrac{3}{4}; \; V_{O_3} \alpha \dfrac{3}{4}$$

Hence, $V_{N_2} / V_{O_3} = \dfrac{2}{3}, \; 3V_{N_2} = 2V_{O_3}$

3. **(c)** $PV^{\frac{3}{2}} = $ constant.

Again $P = \dfrac{nRT}{V}$

$$\therefore \quad \dfrac{nRT}{V} \times V^{\frac{3}{2}} = \text{constant (K)}$$

$$\text{or,} \quad TV^{\frac{1}{2}} = \dfrac{K}{nR} = K' \text{ (constant)}$$

For two states, $T_1 V_1^{\frac{1}{2}} = T_2 V_2^{\frac{1}{2}}$

$$T_2 = T_1 \left(\dfrac{V_1}{V_2}\right)^{\frac{1}{2}}$$

But $V_2 = \dfrac{V_1}{2}$ (given)

$$\therefore \quad T_2 = T_1 \left(\dfrac{V_1}{\frac{V_1}{2}}\right)^{\frac{1}{2}} = T_1 \sqrt{2}$$

4. **(a)** $CO_2 + C \longrightarrow 2CO$
Stoichiometry ratio is 1 : 2
AT STP, $P = 1$ atm, $T = 273$ K, $R = 0.0821$

Initial moles of CO_2, $n(CO_2 \text{initial}) = \dfrac{PV}{RT}$

$$= \dfrac{1 \times 0.5}{0.0821 \times 273} = 0.022 \text{ mole}$$

In final mixture no. of moles; $n(CO_2/CO \text{ mixture})$

$$= \dfrac{1 \times 0.7}{0.0821 \times 273} = 0.031$$

Increase in volume is by $= 0.031 - 0.022$
$$= 0.009 \text{ mole of gas}$$

Final no. of moles of CO i.e. $n_{(CO \; final)}$

$n_{(CO \; final)} = 2n_{(CO2 \; initial)} - n_{(CO2 \; final)}$

$\qquad = 2(0.022 - n_{(CO2 \; final)}) \qquad ...(i)$

$n_{(CO \; final)} = 0.044 - 2n_{(CO2 \; final)} \qquad ...(ii)$

$\therefore$ Now, $n_{(CO \; final)} + n_{(CO2 \; final)} = 0.031$

$\qquad n_{(CO2 \; final)} = 0.031 - n_{(CO \; final)} \qquad ...(ii)$

Substituting (ii) in eq. (i)

$n_{(CO \; final)} = 0.044 - 2[0.031 - n_{(CO \; final)}]$

$n_{(CO \; final)} = 0.044 - 0.062 + 2n_{(CO \; final)}$

$n_{(CO \; final)} = 0.018$ mol.

$$\text{Volume of CO} = V = \dfrac{nRT}{P} = \dfrac{0.018 \times 0.0821 \times 273}{1}$$

$$= 0.40 \text{ Litre}$$

and volume of $CO_2 = 0.7$ litre $- 0.4$ litre
$$= 0.3 \text{ litre}$$

$\therefore \; CO_2 = 300$ mL, CO $= 400$ mL

5. **(a)** Most probable velocity $= \sqrt{\dfrac{2RT}{M}}$

Average velocity $= \sqrt{\dfrac{8RT}{\pi M}}$

Root mean square velocity $= \sqrt{\dfrac{3RT}{M}}$

$\therefore$ Most probable : Average : Root mean square
$\quad$ velocity $\quad$ velocity $\qquad$ velocity

$$= \sqrt{\dfrac{2RT}{M}} : \sqrt{\dfrac{8RT}{\pi M}} : \sqrt{\dfrac{3RT}{M}} = \sqrt{2} : \sqrt{\dfrac{8}{\pi}} : \sqrt{3}$$

6. **(b)** The van der Waals equation is

$$\left(P+\frac{a}{V^2}\right)(V-b)=RT \quad \text{(For one mole)}$$

$$\text{or}\left(P+\frac{a}{V^2}\right)=\frac{RT}{(V-b)}$$

$$\text{or } P=\frac{RT}{V-b}-\frac{a}{V^2}$$

Multiplying throughout by molar volume (V) and dividing by RT, we have

$$\frac{PV}{RT}=\frac{V}{V-b}-\frac{a}{RTV} \quad \text{or} \quad \frac{PV}{RT}=\left(\frac{V-b}{V}\right)^{-1}-\frac{a}{RTV}$$

$$\text{or } \frac{PV}{RT}=\left(1-\frac{b}{V}\right)^{-1}-\frac{a}{RTV}$$

$$\text{or } \frac{PV}{RT}=1+\frac{b}{V}+\frac{b^2}{V^2}+\frac{b^2}{V^3}-\frac{a}{RTV}$$

$$\text{or } \frac{PV}{RT}=1+\left(b-\frac{a}{RT}\right)\times\frac{1}{V}+\frac{b^2}{V^2}+\frac{b^3}{V^3}$$

Comparing this with virial equation we get

$$B=b-\frac{a}{RT}$$

7. **(b, c)** Given $V=10$ litre, $P=3$ atm, $T=290\,K$
After driving $V=10$ litre $\quad P=?$

$$\frac{P_1V_1}{T_1}=\frac{P_2V_2}{T_2} \quad \therefore V_1=V_2=10\,\text{lit,}$$

$$\therefore \frac{P_1}{T_1}=\frac{P_2}{T_2} \quad \text{or} \quad P_2=\frac{P_1}{T_1}\times T_2$$

$$\text{or } P_2=3\times\frac{320}{290}=3.3103\text{ atm.}$$

$\therefore$ Pressure of the gas in the tyre at 47°C = 3.3103 atm.
At pressure 3.103 atm, the volume of tyre is 10 lit.
$\therefore$ Volume of tyre at 3 atm pressure

$$=\frac{3.3103\times10}{3}=11.03433\text{ lit.}$$

$\therefore$ The volume which is to be reduced at 3 atm pressure
$$=11.03433-10=1.03433\text{ lit.}$$
$\therefore$ The volume which is to be reduced at 1 atm pressure

$$=\frac{1.03433\times3}{1}=3.1029\text{ lit.}$$

$\therefore$ 3.1029 lit of air should be let out at 1 atm to restore the tyre to 3 atm at 47°C.

8. **(a,c,d)** The critical pressure,

$$P_C=\frac{a}{27b^2}=\frac{371.843\times10^3}{27\times(40.8)^2\times10^{-6}}$$

$$=\frac{371.843\times10^9}{27\times(40.8)^2}=8.273\times10^6\,\text{Pa}=8.273\text{ MPa}$$

The critical temperature, $T_C=\dfrac{8a}{27Rb}$

$R=8.314\,\text{KPa dm}^3\,\text{K}^{-1}\,\text{mol}^{-1}$

$$T_C=\frac{8a}{27Rb}=\frac{8.371.843}{8.314\times27\times40.8\times10^{-3}}$$
$$=324.79=324.8\text{ K.}$$

The critical volume, $V_C=3b=3\times40.8=122.4\text{ cm}^3$

9. **(a, c)** van der Waal's equation is

$$\left(P+\frac{n^2a}{V^2}\right)(V-nb)=nRT \quad \text{[For n moles of a gas)}$$

a, b are van der Waal's constants
The ideal gas equation is $PV=nRT$ [For n moles of a gas]
where P is pressure excerted by ideal gas and V is volume occupied by ideal gas.

In van der Waal's equation the term $\left(P+\dfrac{n^2a}{V^2}\right)$ represents

the pressure exerted by the gas and ($V-nb$) the volume occupied by the gas. At low pressure, when the gas occoupies large volume the intermolecular distance between gaseous moleculas is quite large and in such case there is no significant role played by intermolecular forces and thus the gas behaves like an ideal gas thus (a) is correct

NOTE: Under high pressure the intermolecular distance decreases and the intermolecular forces play a significant role and the gas shows a devation from ideal behaviour.
Thus (b) is *not* correct.
a, b i.e. the van der Waal's coefficients defined on the nature of gas and are independent of temperature so (c) is correct.

The pressure $\left(P+\dfrac{n^2a}{V}\right)$ is not lower than P so (d) is not

correct.
Hence the correct answer is (a, c).

10. **(b,c,d)** (a) An ideal gas cannot be liquefied at any temperature for any pressure. It is due to the absence of intermolecular forces.
(b) Helium, a real gas, can be liquefied by cooling it to critical temperature or below and applying high pressure.
(c) The inversion temperature of helium is much below the room temperature. Hence, it shows heating effect during Joule-Thompson porous plug streaming of the gas at ordinary temperatures.

(d) Compressibility factor $\left(Z=\dfrac{PV}{RT}\right)$ of hydrogen is

greater than unity

11. **(5)** Given, $P=1.56$ atm; $V=10\,L$
$T=317\,K; R=0.082$

$$\text{Total moles }(n)=\frac{PV}{RT}=\frac{1.56\times10}{0.082\times317}=0.6\text{ mol}$$

Let C_xH_8 be a mol, therefore moles of $C_xH_{12} = (0.6 - a)$ mol; mass of C in a mol of $C_xH_{12} = 12ax$ g; mass of C in $(0.6 - a)$ mol of $C_xH_{12} = 12 \times (0.6 - a)$ g

$\therefore$ Total mass of C in mixture $= 12ax + 12x(0.6 - a)$ g
$$= 41.4 \text{ g}$$

$$\% \text{ of } C \text{ in mixture} = \frac{7.2x}{41.4} \times 100$$

Given % of $C = 87\%$

or $\dfrac{720x}{41.4} = 87$ or $x = 5$

12. (5) $r_g = \dfrac{1}{5} r_{H_2}$

$$\frac{M_g}{M_{H_2}} = \left[\frac{r_{H_2}}{r_g}\right]^2 = (5)^2 = 25; M_g = 2 \times 25 = 50$$
$$10\,y = 50 \Rightarrow y = 5$$

13. (8) $\dfrac{r_{CH_4}}{r_x} = 2 = \sqrt{\dfrac{M_x}{M_{CH_4}}} = \sqrt{\dfrac{M_x}{16}}$, or $M_x = 64$

$$8\,y = 64 \Rightarrow y = 8$$

14. (4) v_{rms} of $X = \sqrt{\dfrac{3RT_x}{M_x}}$; v_{mp} of $Y = \sqrt{\dfrac{2RT_y}{M_y}}$

Given $v_{rms} = v_{mp}$

$$\Rightarrow \sqrt{\frac{3RT_x}{M_x}} = \sqrt{\frac{2RT_y}{M_y}}$$

$$\Rightarrow M_y = \frac{2RT_yM_x}{3RT_x} = \frac{2 \times 60 \times 40}{3 \times 400} = 4$$

15. (c) The curve representing the gas-liquid equilibrium ends at the *dark* point, the critical point. Above the temperature corresponding to this point, CO_2 can not be liquefied for any value of pressure. Temperature and pressure corresponding to the *dark* point are T_c and P_c

16. (b) At point B, liquefaction of CO_2 commences and is complete at the point C. Along the line BC the proportion of gas phase of CO_2 decreases and that of liquid phase increases, and hence the volume of the system decreases along the line BC.

17. (b) For one mole of real gas, we have

$$\left(P + \frac{a}{V^2}\right)(V - b) = RT$$

Under conditions of high pressure

$$P + \frac{a}{V^2} \approx P$$

$\therefore$ The above equation becomes
$P(V - b) = RT$
or $PV - Pb = RT$
or $PV = RT + Pb$

18. (d) Since the value of $b = 0$ in case of molecules to be point masses
$\therefore$ The van der Waals' equation will become

$$\left(P + \frac{an^2}{V^2}\right)(V - 0) = nRT \quad (\because b = 0, \text{ so } nb = 0)$$

or $\left(P + \dfrac{an^2}{V^2}\right)V = nRT$

or $PV + \dfrac{an^2}{V} = nRT$ or $PV = nRT - \dfrac{an^2}{V}$

19. A-q; B-p, C-s; D-r

(A) At temperature $< T_i$, $\mu_{JT} = \left[\left(\dfrac{dT}{dP}\right)_H\right]$ becomes positive, i.e. cooling effect takes place in streaming process. It suggests that the forces between the gas molecules are attractive in nature.

(B) At temperature $> T_i$, μ_{JT} is negative which suggests the existance of repulsive forces between the gas molecules.

(C) At Boyle's temperature and above, a real gas obeys gas laws over a wide range of pressure.

(D) In ideal gas the intermolecular forces do not exist. Hence Joule-Thompson effect is zero.

20. A-r; B-s; C-q; D-p

(A) Pressure correction $= \dfrac{an^2}{V^2}$

$$= \frac{3.6(L^2 atm\, mol^{-2})}{10^2(L^2)} \times \left(\frac{200}{40}\right)^2 (mol^2) = 0.9 \text{L atm}$$

(B) Free space $= V - nb = 10 - 5 \times 0.05 = 9.75L$

(C) Actual volume of gas molecules

$$= \frac{nb}{4} = \frac{5 \times 0.05}{4} = 0.06L$$

(D) Effective volume of gas molecules
$$= nb = 5 \times 0.05 = 0.25L$$

1. **(b)** $\Delta H = \Sigma\left[\Delta H_f^\circ \text{ products}\right] - \Sigma\left[\Delta H_f^\circ \text{ reactants}\right]$

$\Delta H^\circ = [\Delta H_f^\circ(CO)(g) + \Delta H_f^\circ(H_2O)(g)] -$

$$[\Delta H_f^\circ(CO_2)(g) + \Delta H_f^\circ(H_2)(g)]$$

$= [-110.5 + (-241.8)] - [-393.5 + 0] = 41.2$

2. **(a)** In $PH_3(g)$, energy required to break 3 P–H bonds
$= 954\,kJ\,mol^{-1}$

∴ Energy required to break 1 P – H bond

$= \dfrac{954}{3} = 318 \text{ kJ mol}^{-1}$

In $P_2H_4(g)$, energy of 1 P – P bond + 4 P – H bonds
$= 1485\,kJ\,mol^{-1}$

∵ Energy of 1 P – H bond		$= 318\,kJ\,mol^{-1}$
∴ Energy of 4 P – H bond		$= 318 \times 4$
		$= 1272\,kJ\,mol^{-1}$
Thus, the P – P bond energy		$= 1485 - 1272$
		$= 213\,kJ\,mol^{-1}$

3. **(d)** For isothermal reversible expansion

$$w = q = nRT \times 2.303 \log\dfrac{V_2}{V_1}$$

$$= 2RT \times 2.303 \log\dfrac{20}{2}$$

$$= 2 \times 2 \times T \times 2.303 \times 1 = 9.2\,T$$

Entropy change, $\Delta S = \dfrac{q}{T} = \dfrac{9.2T}{T} = 9.2$ cal.

4. **(b)** Given, $C_p = 10$ cals at $1000\,K$
$T_1 = 1000\,K.\ T_2 = 100\,K$
$m = 32\,g$
$\Delta S = ?$
at constant pressure

$$\Delta S = C_p \ln\dfrac{T_2}{T_1}$$

$$= 2.303 \times C_p \log\dfrac{T_2}{T_1}$$

$$= 2.303 \times 10 \log\dfrac{100}{1000}$$

$$= -23.03 \text{ cal deg}^{-1}$$

5. **(c)** Given

$$H_2(g) + \frac{1}{2}O_2(g) \longrightarrow H_2O(l);$$

$\Delta H^\circ = -285.9\,kJ\,mol^{-1}$ ...(1)

$$H_2(g) + \frac{1}{2}O_2(g) \longrightarrow H_2O(g);$$

$\Delta H^\circ = -241.8\,kJ\,mol^{-1}$ ...(2)
We have to calculate
$H_2O(l) \longrightarrow H_2O(g)$; $\Delta H^\circ = ?$
On substracting eqn. (2) from eqn. (1) we get
$H_2O(l) \longrightarrow H_2O(g)$;

$\Delta H^\circ = -241.8 - (-285.9)$

$= 44.1\,kJ\,mol^{-1}$

6. **(b)** $C_2H_5OH(l) + 3O_2(g)$

$$\rightarrow 2CO_2(g) + 3H_2O(l)$$

$\Delta n_g = 2 - 3 = -1$

$\Delta U = \Delta H - \Delta n_g RT$

$= -1366.5 - (-1)\,RT$

$= -1366.5 - (1) \times \dfrac{8.314}{10^3} \times 300$

$= -1366.5 + 0.8314 \times 3 = -1364\,kJ$

7. **(a,d)** The over all process can be depicted as

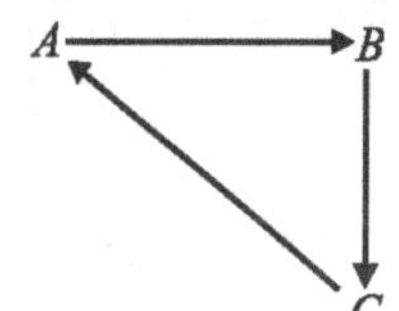

Thus it is a cyclic process.
Hence, $\Delta E = 0,\ \Delta H = 0,\ \Delta S = 0$ (cyclic process)
and $\Delta E = q + W$ (Ist law)
∴ $0 = q + W$
or $q = -W$
Total work done $= W_{A \to B} + W_{B \to C} + W_{C \to A}$

∴ $W = -P(V_B - V_A) + 0 + 2.303\,nRT\log\dfrac{V_C}{V_A}$

$= -(40 - 20) + 0 + 2.303 \times 1 \times 0.082 \times \log\dfrac{V_C}{V_A}$

$= -6.13$ litre-atmosphere
$= -620.77\,J$

8. **(a,b,d)** For such a process ,

$$W = -nRT\ln\dfrac{P_1}{P_2}$$

9. **(b)** $C_2H_6(g) \longrightarrow 2C(g) + 6H(g)$

$\Delta H_{C-C} + 6\Delta H_{C-H} = 620\,kJ\,mol^{-1}$

$C_3H_8(g) \longrightarrow 3C(g) + 8H(g)$;

$$2\Delta H_{C-C} + 8\Delta H_{C-H} = 880 \, kJ \, mol^{-1}$$

Hence, $\Delta H_{C-C} = 80 \, kJ \, mol^{-1}$;

$$\Delta H_{C-H} = 90 \, kJ \, mol^{-1}$$

10. (8) $2MgCl \rightarrow Mg + MgCl_2 \qquad \Delta H = ?$

$$Mg(s) + 1/2 \, Cl_2(g) \rightarrow MgCl \qquad \Delta H_1 = -125 \, kJ \, mol^{-1}$$

$$Mg(s) + Cl_2(g) \rightarrow MgCl_2 \qquad \Delta H_2 = -642 \, kJ \, mol^{-1}$$

$$\Delta H = \Delta H_2 - 2\Delta H_1 = -642 - (2 \times -125) = -392 \, kJ \, mol^{-1}$$

$$\therefore -49x = -392$$

$$x = 8$$

11. (6) $KCl(s) \longrightarrow K^+(g) + Cl^-(g), \Delta H_1 = 181 \, kcal \, mol^{-1}$

$$KCl(s) + H_2O(l) \longrightarrow K^+(aq) + Cl^-(aq),$$

$$\Delta H_2 = 1.0 \, kcal \, mol^{-1}$$

Let the enthalpy of hydration of K^+ is $2a \, kcal \, mol^{-1}$

$$K^+(g) + H_2O(l) \longrightarrow K^+(aq), \Delta H_3 = 2a$$

$$Cl^-(g) + H_2O(l) \longrightarrow Cl^-(aq), \qquad \Delta H_4 = a$$

$$\therefore \Delta H_3 = -\Delta H_1 + \Delta H_2 - \Delta H_4$$

$$2a = -181 + 1 - a$$

$$3a = -180, a = -60$$

$$\therefore \Delta_{hyd}H \text{ of } K^+ = 2a = -60 \times 2 = -120$$

$$\therefore -20x = -120$$

$$x = 6$$

12. (5) $\therefore \Delta_{sys}S = \dfrac{q_{sys}}{T_{sys}} = -\dfrac{300}{273 + 127}$

$$= \dfrac{-300}{400} = \dfrac{-3}{4} \, JK^{-1}$$

$$\Delta_{surr}S = \dfrac{-q_{sys}}{T_{surr}} = -\dfrac{300}{273 + 27}$$

$$= \dfrac{300}{300} = +1 \, JK^{-1}$$

$\Delta_{total}S$ or $\Delta_{universe}S = \Delta_{sys}S + \Delta_{surr}S$

$$= \dfrac{-3}{4} + 1 = \dfrac{1}{4} = 0.25 \, J \, K^{-1}$$

$$\therefore 0.05x = 0.25$$

$$x = 5$$

13. (4) $Fe_2O_3 \quad + \quad 2Al \quad \rightarrow 2Fe \quad + \quad Al_2O_3$

$2 \times 56 + 48 = 160 \quad 2 \times 27 = 54$

Heat of reaction $= 399 - 199 = 200 \, kcal$ [Al and Fe are in their standard states]

Total weight of reactants $= 160 + 54 = 214 \, g$

$$\therefore \text{Fuel value/gram} = \dfrac{200}{214} = 0.9346 \, kcal/g$$

Volume of Al $= \dfrac{54}{2.7} = 20 \, cc$

Volume of $Fe_2O_3 = \dfrac{160}{5.2} = 30.77 \, cc$

Total volume $= 20 + 30.77 = 50.77 \, cc$

$$\therefore \text{Fuel value per cc} = \dfrac{200}{50.77} = 3.94 \simeq 4 \, kcal/cc$$

14. (8) For adiabatic process, $W = P(V_2 - V_1)$

Here $P_1 = 1 \, bar, P_2 = 100 \, bar, V_1 = 100 \, mL, V_2 = 99 \, mL$;
For adiabatic process, $q = 0 \setminus \Delta U = w$

$$\Delta U = q + W$$

$$= q - P(V_2 - V_1) \text{ since } W = -P(V_2 - V_1)$$

$$= 0 - 100(99 - 100) = 100 \, bar \, mL$$

$$\Delta H = \Delta U + \Delta(PV) = \Delta U + (P_2 V_2 - P_1 V_1)$$

$$= 100 + [(100 \times 99) - (1 \times 100)]$$

$$= 100 + (9900 - 100) = 9900 \, bar \, mL$$

$$\Delta U + \Delta H = 100 + 9900 = 10000$$

$$\therefore \text{the value of } \dfrac{\Delta U + \Delta H}{1000} - 2 = \dfrac{10000}{1000} - 2 = 8$$

15. (b) Path A - reversible isothermal expansion.
According to first law of thermodynamics

$$\Delta U = q - w$$

$$q = w$$

Isothermal process $\Delta U = 0$

$$= \left(nRT_1, \ln \dfrac{V_2}{V_1} \right)$$

16. (d) Path B + C - reversible adiabatic expansion followed by reversible heating at constant volume $q = 0$

$$\Delta S = \dfrac{q_{rev}}{T}, \, q_{rev} = T \Delta S$$

$$\therefore \quad q_{rev} = nR \ln \dfrac{V_2}{V_1}$$

17. (c) D + E - Reversible expansion at constant pressure followed by a reversible cooling at constant volume.

$$w = q = P_1(V_2 - V_1)$$

18. (a) At constant volume,

$$\Delta S = nC_v \ln \dfrac{T_2}{T_1}$$

Given $n = 14 \, g$ of nitrogen

$$= \dfrac{14}{28} \text{ mole or } 0.5 \, mole$$

$$\therefore \quad \Delta S = 0.5 \times 4.94 \times 2.303 \log \dfrac{400}{300}$$

$$\left[\ln \dfrac{T_2}{T_1} = 2.303 \log \dfrac{T_2}{T_1} \right]$$

$= 0.70 \, \text{cal K}^{-1}$

At constant pressure

$$\Delta S = nC_p \, ln \frac{T_2}{T_1}$$

Since $C_p = C_v + R$

$\therefore \quad C_p = 4.94 + 2.0 = 6.94 \, \text{cal/mole}$

$$\therefore \quad \Delta S = \frac{1}{2} \times 6.94 \times 2.303 \, \log\frac{400}{300} \, [\because \, n = \frac{1}{2}]$$

$$= 0.99 \, \text{cal K}^{-1}$$

19. (c) Using the relation, $\Delta S = nC_p \, \ln \frac{T_2}{T_1}$

We get,

$$\Delta S = 2 \times \frac{5}{2} R ln \frac{600}{300} = 5 \, R ln 2$$

20. A-q; B-q, r, s; C-r; D-p, q, r

(A) For a reversible process, $\Delta S_{\text{system}} = - \Delta S_{\text{surr}}$.

or $\quad \Delta S_{\text{system}} + \Delta S_{\text{surr}} = \Delta S_{\text{Total}} = 0$

(B) From first law, $dE = \delta q_{\text{rev}} + W = \delta q_{\text{rev}} - PdV$

$\delta q_{\text{rev}} = TdS = dE + PdV = CvdT + PdV$

$$dS = C_v \frac{dT}{T} + \frac{PdV}{T} = C_v \frac{dT}{T} + R\frac{dV}{V} = R\frac{dV}{V}$$

(dT = 0 for isothermal process)

$$dS = \int_1^2 R \frac{dV}{T}$$

Integrating $\int_1^2 dS = S_2 - S_1 = \Delta S = \int_1^2 R\frac{dV}{V} = R \ln \frac{V_2}{V_1}$

(C) In perfect gas intermolecular forces do not exit.

Hence, $\left(\dfrac{dP}{dT}\right)_H = \mu_{\text{J.T.}} = 0$

(D) For adiabatic and reversible process,

$$\delta q_{\text{rev}} = 0 = dE + PdV = CvdT + RT \, \frac{dV}{V}$$

(for ideal gas)

$$\frac{dT}{T} = -\frac{R}{C_v} \times \frac{dV}{V} = -\frac{Cp - C_v}{C_v} \times \frac{dV}{V} = -(\gamma - 1)\frac{dV}{V}$$

Integrating, $\int_1^2 \dfrac{dT}{T} = \ln \dfrac{T_2}{T_1}$

$$= -\int_1^2 (\gamma - 1)\frac{dV}{V} = -(\gamma - 1)\ln \frac{V_2}{V_1} = (\gamma - 1)\ln \frac{V_1}{V_2}$$

$$= \ln \left(\frac{V_1}{V_2}\right)^{\gamma - 1}$$

$\dfrac{T_2}{T_1} = \left(\dfrac{V_1}{V_2}\right)^{\gamma - 1}$ for ideal gas $\dfrac{T_2}{T_1} = \dfrac{P_2 V_2}{P_1 V_1}$

Hence, $\dfrac{P_2 V_2}{P_1 V_1} = \left(\dfrac{V_1}{V_2}\right)^{\gamma - 1}$ $\quad P_1 V_1^{\gamma} = P_2 V_2^{\gamma} = \text{a constant}$

1. (a) $A^- + H_2O \rightleftharpoons HA + OH^-$

0.001 M	0	0	(At start)
$(0.001 - h)$	$(0.001 \times h)$	$(0.001 \times h)$	(At eq.)

$$K_h = \frac{(0.001 \times h)(0.001 \times h)}{(0.001 - h)}$$

or, $K_h = 0.001 \times h^2$ (as, $0.001 - h \approx 0.001$)

$$10^{-9} = 0.001 \times h^2 \qquad \left(K_h = \frac{K_w}{K_a} = \frac{10^{-14}}{10^{-5}} = 10^{-9} \right)$$

$h^2 = 10^{-6} \qquad \therefore \ h = 10^{-3}$

2. (a) Let the initial moles of X be 'a' and that of Z be 'b' then for the given reactions, we have

$$X \ \rightleftharpoons \ 2Y$$

Initial	a moles	0
At equi. (moles)	$a(1 - \alpha)$	$2a\alpha$

Total no. of moles $= a(1 - \alpha) + 2a\alpha$

$$= a - a\alpha + 2a\alpha$$
$$= a(1 + \alpha)$$

Now, $\quad K_{P_1} = \dfrac{(n_y)^2}{n_x} \times \left(\dfrac{P_{T_1}}{\Sigma n} \right)^{\Delta n}$

or, $\quad K_{P_1} = \dfrac{(2a\alpha)^2 . P_{T_1}}{[a(1 - \alpha)][a(1 + \alpha)]}$

$$Z \ \rightleftharpoons \ P \ + \ Q$$

Initial	b moles	0	0
At equi. (moles)	$b(1 - \alpha)$	$b\alpha$	$b\alpha$

Total no. of moles $= b(1 - \alpha) + b\alpha + b\alpha$

$$= b - b\alpha + b\alpha + b\alpha$$
$$= b(1 + \alpha)$$

Now $K_{P_2} = \dfrac{n_Q \times n_P}{n_z} \times \left[\dfrac{P_{T_2}}{\Sigma n} \right]^{\Delta n}$

or $\quad K_{P_2} = \dfrac{(b\alpha)(b\alpha).P_{T_2}}{[b(1 - \alpha)][b(1 + \alpha)]}$

or $\quad \dfrac{K_{P_1}}{K_{P_2}} = \dfrac{4\alpha^2 . P_{T_1}}{(1 - \alpha^2)} \times \dfrac{(1 - \alpha)^2}{P_{T_2} . \alpha^2} = \dfrac{4P_{T_1}}{P_{T_2}}$

or $\quad \dfrac{P_{T_1}}{P_{T_2}} = \dfrac{1}{9} \ \left[\because \dfrac{K_{P_1}}{K_{P_2}} = \dfrac{1}{9} \ \text{given} \right]$

or $\quad \dfrac{P_{T_1}}{P_{T_2}} = \dfrac{1}{36} \ $ or $\ 1 : 36$

i.e., (a) is the correct answer.

3. (b) (I) $N_2 + 2O_2 \xrightleftharpoons{K_1} 2NO_2$

$$K_1 = \frac{[NO_2]^2}{[N_2][O_2]^2} \qquad \ldots(i)$$

(II) $2NO_2 \xrightleftharpoons{K_2} N_2 + 2O_2$

$$K_2 = \frac{[N_2][O_2]^2}{[NO_2]^2} \qquad \ldots(ii)$$

(III) $NO_2 \xrightleftharpoons{K_3} \dfrac{1}{2}N_2 + O_2$

$$K_3 = \frac{[N_2]^{1/2}[O_2]}{[NO_2]}$$

$$\therefore \ (K_3)^2 = \frac{[N_2][O_2]^2}{[NO_2]^2} \qquad \ldots(ii)$$

$\therefore$ from equation (i), (ii) and (iii)

$$K_1 = \frac{1}{K_2} = \frac{1}{(K_3)^2}$$

4. (b) $Cr_2(SO_4)_3 \rightleftharpoons \underset{2s}{2Cr^{3+}} + \underset{3s}{3SO_4^{2-}}$

$$K_{sp} = (2s)^2 (3s)^3 = 4s^2 \times 27s^3 = 108s^5$$

$$s = \left(\frac{K_{sp}}{108} \right)^{1/5}$$

$$Hg_2Cl_2 \rightleftharpoons \underset{2s}{2Hg^{2+}} + \underset{2s}{2Cl^-}$$

$$K_{sp} = (2s)^2 \times (2s)^2 = 16s^4$$

$$s = \left(\frac{K_{sp}}{16}\right)^{1/4}$$

$$BaSO_4 \rightleftharpoons \underset{s}{Ba^{2+}} + \underset{s}{SO_4^{2-}}$$

$$K_{sp} = s^2$$

$$s = \sqrt{K_{sp}}$$

$$CrCl_3 \rightleftharpoons \underset{s}{Cr^{3+}} + \underset{3s}{3Cl^-}$$

$$K_{sp} = s \times (3s)^3 = 27s^4$$

$$s = \left(\frac{K_{sp}}{27}\right)^{1/4}$$

Hence the correct order of solubilities of salts is

$$\sqrt{K_{sp}} > \left(\frac{K_{sp}}{16}\right)^{1/4} > \left(\frac{K_{sp}}{27}\right)^{1/4} > \left(\frac{K_{sp}}{108}\right)^{1/5}$$

5. (b) $NH_2COONH_4(s) \rightleftharpoons 2NH_3(g) + CO_2(g)$

$$K_P = \frac{\left(P_{NH_3}\right)^2 \times \left(P_{CO_2}\right)}{P_{NH_2COONH_4}(s)} = \left(P_{NH_3}\right)^2 \times \left(P_{CO_2}\right)$$

As evident by the reaction, NH_3 and CO_2 are formed in molar ratio of $2 : 1$. Thus if P is the total pressure of the system at equilibrium, then

$$P_{NH_3} = \frac{2 \times P}{3} \qquad P_{CO_2} = \frac{1 \times P}{3}$$

$$K_P = \left(\frac{2P}{3}\right)^2 \times \frac{P}{3} = \frac{4P^3}{27}$$

Given $K_P = 2.9 \times 10^{-5}$

$$\therefore \quad 2.9 \times 10^{-5} = \frac{4P^3}{27}$$

$$P^3 = \frac{2.9 \times 10^{-5} \times 27}{4}$$

$$P = \left(\frac{2.9 \times 10^{-5} \times 27}{4}\right)^{1/3} = 5.82 \times 10^{-2} \, atm$$

6. (b,c)

(a) $50 \times 0.1 = 5$ m mole of CH_3COOH will neutralize completely $50 \times 0.1 = 5$ m mole of NaOH to form CH_3COONa and water. But acetate ion (being strong conjugate base of the weak acid CH_3COOH) of the salt hydrolyses to give basic solution.

$$CH_3COO^- + H_2O \rightleftharpoons$$

$$CH_3COOH + OH^- \qquad (pH > 7)$$

(b) $100 \times 0.1 = 10$ m mole of CH_3COOH and $50 \times 0.2 = 10$ m mole of NH_3 will neutralize each other completely to give CH_3COONH_4. Both anion and cation of the salt hydrolyse equally ($K_a = 1.8 \times 10^{-5}$; $K_b = 1.8 \times 10^{-5}$) to give neutral solution.

$$CH_3COO^- + NH_4^+ + H_2O \longrightarrow$$

$$CH_3COOH + NH_4OH \qquad (pH = 7)$$

(c) $100 \times 0.1 = 10$ m mole of HCl and $5.0 \times 0.2 = 10$ m mole of KOH neutralize each other completely to give KCl. Neither K^+ ion (weak acid) nor Cl^- ion (weak base) hydrolyse $(pH = 7)$

(d) $50 \times 0.1 = 5$ m mole of HCl and $50 \times 0.1 = 5$ m mole of NH_3 neutralize one another completely. However, the cation (NH_4^+ ion) of the salt hydrolyses to give acidic solution.

$$NH_4^+ + H_2O \longrightarrow NH_3 + H_3O^+ \quad (pH < 7)$$

7. (b,c,d)

(a) K_b permitts the calculation of $[OH^-]$. For $[H^+]$ and hence pH calculation K_w is also required.

(b) From K_b value, $[OH^-]$ can be calculated. Using $K_w = 1.0 \times 10^{-14}$, $[H^+]$ can be calculated. Hence the pH.

(c) pH (acid buffer)

$$= pK_a + \log\frac{[A^-]}{[HA]} \qquad (K_a \text{ suffices})$$

(d) The CH_3COO^- ion of the salt hydrolyses as

$$CH_3COO^- + H_2O \longrightarrow CH_3COOH + OH^-$$

$$pH = \frac{1}{2}pK_w + \frac{1}{2}pK_a + \frac{1}{2}\log[\text{Anion}]$$

Both K_a and K_w are needed.

8. **(b,d)**

(a) Addition of NH_2COONH_4 (solid) does not affect the position of the equilibrium.

(b) On addition of NH_3, equilibrium shifts in backward direction leading to decrease in partial pressure of CO_2. To maintain K_P, P_{NH_3} would now be larger.

(c) Addition of CO_2 causes the equilibrium to shift in reverse direction resulting the decrease of, P_{NH_3}.

(d) Dissociation of NH_2COONH_4 is endothermic, favoured by elevated temperature.

9. **(a,d)** $XY_2(g) \rightleftharpoons XY(g) + Y(g)$

$$1-\alpha \qquad\qquad \alpha \qquad \alpha$$

If P is the equilibrium pressure, then

$$P_{xy_2} = \frac{1-\alpha}{1+\alpha}.P$$

[Total moles : $1 - \alpha + \alpha + \alpha = 1 + \alpha$]

$$P_{xy} = P_y = \frac{\alpha}{1+\alpha}.P$$

Hence, $K_P = \dfrac{P_{xy} \times P_y}{P_{xy_2}} = \dfrac{\dfrac{\alpha}{1+\alpha}.P \times \dfrac{\alpha}{1+\alpha}.P}{\dfrac{1-\alpha}{1+\alpha}.P}$

$$= \frac{\alpha^2 P}{1-\alpha^2} = \alpha^2 P \qquad [\because \alpha \ll 1]$$

or $\alpha = \left(K_P/P\right)^{1/2}$ or $\alpha \propto \dfrac{1}{P^{1/2}}$

Hence, (d) is correct.

Since, V is inversely proportional to P

so $\alpha \propto V^{1/2}$; hence (a) is correct.

Alternatively, $[XY_2] = \dfrac{1-\alpha}{V}$; $[XY] = [Y] = \dfrac{\alpha}{V}$

Hence, $K_C = \dfrac{[XY][Y]}{[XY_2]} = \dfrac{\alpha/Y \times \alpha/V}{(1-\alpha)/V} = \dfrac{\alpha^2}{V}$

or $\alpha = (K_C V)^{1/2}$ or $\alpha \propto V^{1/2}$

10. **(3)** $K_p = \dfrac{(P_{H_2O})^2}{(P_{H_2})^2}$

Given H_2 is 45% by volume at constant temperature in closed vessel ($P \propto V$). So $P_{H_2O} = 0.55$ and $P_{H_2} = 0.45$

$$K_p = \left(\frac{0.55}{0.45}\right)^2 = 1.5$$

$\Rightarrow$ $2K_p = 1.5 \times 2 = 3$

11. **(4)** The given equilibrium is

$$N_2(g) + 3H_2(g) \rightleftharpoons 2NH_3(g)$$

At t = 0   4   16   0

At equilibrium $4-x$ $16-3x$ $2x$

Total gaseous moles initially $= 20$

Total gaseous moles at equilibrium

$$= 4-x+16-3x+2x = (20-2x)$$

Since, pressure has fallen to 9/10 of its original value, hence no. of moles will also fall up to the same extent.

$$\therefore (20-2x) = \frac{9}{10} \times 20 = 18 \Rightarrow x = 1$$

$$\therefore [N_2] = \frac{4-x}{1} = \frac{4-1}{1} = 3 \text{ mol/litre}$$

$$[H_2] = \frac{16-3x}{1} = 13 \text{ mol/litre}$$

$$[NH_3] = \frac{2x}{1} = 2 \text{ mol/litre}$$

$$K_C = \frac{[NH_3]^2}{[N_2][H_2]^3} = \frac{2^2}{(3)(13)^3} = 6.07 \times 10^{-4}$$

According to question

$y \times 10^{-z} = 6.07 \times 10^{-4}$

$-z = -4$

$z = 4$

12. **(9)** $HA + NaOH \longrightarrow NaA + H_2O$

At the end point, the solution contains only NaA whose concentration is $0.1/2 = 0.05$ M

Since the salt NaA is formed by strong alkali (NaOH) and weak acid HA (indicated by its low K_a value), its pH can be evaluated by the following relation.

$$pH = \frac{1}{2}(pK_w + pK_a + \log C)$$

$$= \frac{1}{2}(14 + 5.3010 + (-1.3010)] = 9$$

13. **(4)** Given $[OH^-] = 10^{-3}$

$\therefore$ pOH = 3

$\because$ pH + pOH = 14

$\therefore$ pH = 14 − 3 = 11

According to question,

$15 - x = 11$

$-x = 11 - 15$

$x = 15 - 11 = 4$

14. (4) Given $[H_3O^+] = 1 \times 10^{-10} M$

at 25° $[H_3O^+][OH^-] = 10^{-14}$

$$\therefore [OH^-] = \frac{10^{-14}}{10^{-10}} = 10^{-4}$$

Now, $[OH^-] = 10^{-4}$

$\therefore pOH = 4$

15. (c) Salts of strong acid and strong bases like Na_2SO_4 do not undergo hydrolysis. Hence the pH of the solution remains same.

16. (a) For salts of weak base and strong acids like NH_4Cl

$$K_h = \frac{K_w}{K_b} \text{ and } pH = 7 - \frac{1}{2}(pK_b + \log C)$$

17. (d) For the salts of weak acid and weak base like CH_3COONH_4

$$K_h = \frac{h^2}{(1-h)^2} \text{ and } pH = 7 + \frac{1}{2}(pK_a - pK_b)$$

18. (b)

	A +	B	$\rightleftharpoons$	C	+ D
Initial	a	b		0	0
Equi.	$(a-x)$	$(b-x)$		x	x

From the given information $a = 2b$ .....(i)

and $x = 3(b-x)$

or $4x = 3b$

$$\text{or } x = \frac{3}{4}b \qquad \qquad ...(ii)$$

Using law of mass action

$$K = \frac{x \times x}{(a-x)(b-x)}$$

$$= \frac{\left(\frac{3}{4}b\right)^2}{\left(2b - \frac{3}{4}b\right)\left(b - \frac{3}{4}b\right)} \quad [\because x = \frac{3}{4}b, a = 2b]$$

$$= \frac{9}{5} \text{ or } 1.8$$

19. (c)

	H_2	+	I_2	$\rightleftharpoons$	$2HI$
Initial :	a		b		0
Equi.	$(a-x)$		$(b-x)$		$2x$

$$a = \frac{0.02}{2} \text{ mole} = 0.01 \text{ mole}$$

$$b = \frac{2.54}{2.54} \text{ mole} = 0.01 \text{ mole}$$

Thus at equilibrium, we have

$H_2 = (0.01 - x)$ mole $\qquad\qquad I_2 = (0.01 - x)$ mole

$$\therefore K_c = \frac{[HI]^2}{[H_2][I_2]} = \frac{4x^2}{(0.01-x)^2}$$

But $(0.01 - x) = 0.0021$ mole [conc. of I_2 at equilibrium]

$x = 0.0079$

$$K_c = \frac{4 \times (0.0079)^2}{(0.01 - 0.0079)^2} \text{ or } \frac{4 \times (0.0079)^2}{(0.0021)^2}$$

or $K_c = 56.6$

20. A – q; B – r; C – p; D – p; s

(A) $KCN + H_2O \longrightarrow KOH + HCN$ (weak acid)

$$pH = \frac{1}{2}(pK_w + pK_a + \log[CN^-])$$

$$= \frac{1}{2}[14 + pK_a + \log 0.1] = 6.5 + \frac{1}{2}pK_a$$

(B) $C_6H_5NH_3Cl + H_2O \longrightarrow C_6H_5NH_3OH + HCl$

(Cataionic hydrolysis)

$$pH = \frac{1}{2}(pK_a - pK_b - \log[C_6H_5NH_3^+])$$

$$= \frac{1}{2}(14 - pK_b - \log 0.1] = 7.5 - \frac{1}{2}pK_b$$

(C) KCl – Salt of strong acid (HCl) and strong base (KOH), hence no salt hydrolysis; $pH = 7$

(D) $CH_3COO^- + NH_4^+ + H_2O \longrightarrow$

$$CH_3COOH + NH_4OH$$

$$pH = \frac{1}{2}(pK_w + pK_b - pK_b) = \frac{1}{2}[14 + pK_a - pK_b] = 7$$

$(pK_a = pK_b$ in this case$)$

1. (b) At first, $Bi(NO_3)_3$ undergoes hydrolysis. Nitric acid is formed which oxidises KI to iodine. The liberated iodine dissolves in KI to form yellow solution of KI_3.

$$Bi(NO_3)_3 + H_2O \longrightarrow [Bi(OH)(NO_3)_2] + HNO_3 \;;$$

$$2HNO_3 \longrightarrow H_2O + 2NO_2 + O$$

$$2KI + H_2O + O \longrightarrow 2KOH + \underset{\text{Dark brown}}{I_2} \;;$$

$$I_2 + KI \longrightarrow \underset{\text{Yellow solution}}{KI_3}$$

2. (d) Sodium sesquicarbonate $(Na_2CO_3.NaHCO_3.2H_2O)$ is neither deliquescent nor efflorescent and is used for wool washing.

3. (c) $$\underset{M}{3Mg} + N_2 \longrightarrow \underset{Y}{Mg_3N_2}$$

$$\underset{Y}{Mg_3N_2} + 6H_2O \longrightarrow 3Mg(OH)_2 + \underset{\text{colourless}}{2NH_3 \uparrow}$$

$$CuSO_4 + 4NH_3 \longrightarrow \underset{\text{Blue complex}}{[Cu(NH_3)_4]SO_4}$$

4. (b) $X = Na_2S_2O_3.5H_2O$

$$Na_2S_2O_3 + 2HCl \longrightarrow 2NaCl + H_2O + S + SO_2$$

$$KI_3 + 2Na_2S_2O_3 \longrightarrow KI + 2NaI + Na_2S_4O_6$$

$$2AgNO_3 + Na_2S_2O_3 \longrightarrow Ag_2S_2O_3 + 2NaNO_3$$

$$Ag_2S_2O_3 + H_2O \longrightarrow Ag_2S + H_2SO_4$$

5. (c) From the given information, we can see that the reaction proceeds via formation of H_2O_2 (which is dibasic conjugate acid of peroxide ion), H_2O_2 then disproportionates into water and oxygen.

$$Na_2O_2(s) + H_2O(l) \longrightarrow 2NaOH(aq) + H_2O_2(aq)$$

$$H_2O_2(aq) \longrightarrow H_2O(l) + \frac{1}{2}O_2(g)$$

Thus over all reaction is

$$Na_2O_2(s) + H_2O(l) \longrightarrow 2NaOH(aq) + \frac{1}{2}O_2(g)$$

6. (a) As we move down the group, the lattice energies of carbonates remain approximately the same. However the hydration energies of the metal cation decreases from Be^{++} to Ba^{++}, hence the solubilities of carbonates of the alkaline earth metal decrease down the group

mainly due to decreasing hydration energies of the cations from Be^{++} to Ba^{++}.

7. (a, b, c)

$$Na_2HPO_4 + NH_4Cl \longrightarrow Na(NH_4)HPO_4 + NaCl$$

Microcosmic salt is a white crystalline salt.

Use of microcosmic salt in qualitative inorganic analysis.

$$Na(NH_4)HPO_4 \longrightarrow NH_3 + H_2O + \underset{\substack{\text{(transparent}\\\text{glassy bead)}}}{NaPO_3}$$

$$CuSO_4 \xrightarrow{\Delta} CuO + SO_3$$

$$CuO + NaPO_3 \longrightarrow \underset{\text{(blue bead)}}{CuNaPO_4}$$

8. (b, c, d)

pOH $= 1$, strong basic medium

$$MnO_4^- \longrightarrow MnO_4^{2-} \qquad (\textit{n}\text{-factor} = 1)$$

$$2\overset{-}{O}H + H_2O_2 \longrightarrow O_2 + 2H_2O + 2e^-$$

mEq of $H_2O_2 =$ mEq of MnO_4^-

$$\frac{x}{34/2} \times 1000 = 100 \times \left[\frac{1}{5} \times 1\right]$$

$$x = 0.34\,g$$

9. (a, b, d)
i. mEq of $H_2O_2 =$ m Eq of $Cr_2O_7^{2-}$
$\quad (n = 2) \qquad\qquad (n = 2)$
$\quad 20\,mL \times N_1 = 40\,mL \times N_2$ ....(i)
a. mEq of $Cr_2O_7^{2-} \equiv$ mEq of $Cr_2O_7^{2-}$
$\qquad\qquad\qquad\qquad\qquad\qquad (n = 2)$

$$2.0 \times N_2 \equiv 5.0 \times 1.0 \times 2$$
$$N_2\,(Cr_2O_7^{2-}) = 5 \qquad\qquad ....(ii)$$

Substituting the value of N_2 from (ii) in (i)
$$20\,mL \times N_1 = 40\,mL \times 5$$

$$M_1\,(H_2O_2) = \frac{10}{2} = 5\,M$$

b. $1\,N\,H_2O_2 = 5.6\,V$
$\quad \therefore\ 10\,N\,H_2O_2 = 56\,V$

d. $N_1V_1 + N_2V_2 = N_3V_3\,(V_3 = 10 + 40 = 50\,mL)$

$$10 \times 10 + 40 \times \frac{5}{8} \times 2 = N_3 \times 50$$

$N_3\,(H_2O_2) = 3\,N$
The volume strength of $H_2O_2 = 5.6 \times 3 = 16.8\,V$

10. (a, b, d) The nitrates of Mg and Ba decompose as follows

$$2M(NO_3)_2 \xrightarrow{\text{heat}} 2MO + 4NO_2(g) + O_2(g)$$
$$[M = Mg \text{ or } Ba]$$

The option (c) is incorrect because of the fact that $Mg(NO_3)_2$ is more covalent than $Ba(NO_3)_2$. Due to this $Mg(NO_3)_2$ decomposes more readily.

11. **(5)** $[CuSO_4 + 2NaCN \longrightarrow Cu(CN)_2 + Na_2SO_4] \times 2$

$Cu(CN)_2 \longrightarrow 2CuCN + (CN)_2$

$[CuCN + 3NaCN \longrightarrow Na_3[Cu(CN)_4] \times 2$

$2CuSO_4 + 10NaCN \longrightarrow 2Na_3[Cu(CN)_4] + (CN)_2$
$\qquad\qquad\qquad\qquad\qquad\qquad\qquad + 2Na_2SO_4$

1 mole $CuSO_4 \equiv 5$ mole $NaCN$

12. **(5)** Hydration energy of $NaCl$ = Hydration energy of Na^+
+ Hydration energy of Cl^-

$= -389\ kJ\ mol^{-1} - 382\ kJ\ mol^{-1}$

$= -771\ kJ\ mol^{-1}$

Heat of solution (Δ soln H^-)

= Hydration energy – lattice energy

$= [-771 - (-776)]\ kJ\ mol^{-1}$

$= 5\ kJ\ mol^{-1}$

13. **(8)** On heating, only Li_2CO_3 decomposes.

$Li_2CO_3 \longrightarrow Li_2O + CO_2$

$\therefore$ On heating 8 moles of Li_2CO_3, 8 moles of CO_2 will be evolved.

14. **(8)** $CaC_2 + N_2 \longrightarrow CaCN_2 + C$
$\quad 40 + (12 \times 2) \qquad 40 + 12 + (14 \times 2)$
$\quad\quad = 64\ g \qquad\qquad = 80\ g$

$\Rightarrow \dfrac{80}{64} \times 6.4 = 8$

15. **(c)** (a) is false because it would support a lighted splint (*fire burns in the presence of oxygen*). (b) (molecular weight or MW of CO = 28 g/mol) is somewhat lighter that air which is mostly nitrogen (78%, MW = 28 g/mol) with oxygen (21%, MW = 32 g/mol). (d) is an anion (*carbonate*) not a gas. Thus we are left with carbon dioxide (MW = 44 g/mol) which is heavier than air and does not support a lighted splint.

16. **(a)** Using $K_b = \dfrac{[X^+][OH^-]}{[XOH]}$; X is most probably a Group I metal since no decomposition occurred which implies that the anion (OH^-) and cation (X^+) are of comparable size.

Assuming that $[X^+] = [OH^-]$ approximately.

$K_b = \dfrac{[OH^-]^2}{[XOH]}$, where $XOH \approx 1.0$ M at equilibrium,

thus : $1.0 \times 10^{-6} = [OH^-]^2/1$

or $\quad [OH^-]^2 = 1.0 \times 10^{-6}$

Hence, $[OH^-] = 1.0 \times 10^{-3}\ mol\ dm^{-3}$

$pOH = -\log[OH^-] = -\log(1.0 \times 10^{-3}) = -(-3) = 3$

Using $pH + pOH = 14$, we get : $pH = 14 - pOH = 14 - 3$
$= 11$

17. **(d)** Element 'A' is Barium (Ba).

$3'A' + N_2 \longrightarrow A_3N_2$
$\qquad\qquad\qquad\quad 'B'$

$A_3N_2 + 6H_2O \longrightarrow 3A(OH)_2 + 2NH_3$
$\;'B' \qquad\qquad\qquad\quad 'C' \qquad 'D'$

$A(OH)_2 + CO_2 \longrightarrow ACO_3 + H_2O$
$\quad 'C' \qquad\qquad\qquad\quad$ milkiness

Thus Element 'A' could be either Ca or Ba. However it is not magnesium because $Mg(OH)_2$ has a very low solubility. The element 'A' is Ba.

18. **(d)** Since element 'A' is Ba, thus

$3Ba + N_2 \longrightarrow Ba_3N_2$
$\;'A' \qquad\qquad\qquad\; 'B'$

$Ba_3N_2 + 6H_2O \longrightarrow 3Ba(OH)_2 + 2NH_3$
$\quad 'B' \qquad\qquad\qquad\qquad 'C'$

19. **A-p; B-p; C-p, q; D-r, s**

Alkaline earth metals readily liberate hydrogen from dilute acids, on account of their high oxidation potentials.

The reactivity of alkaline earths with acids increases on moving down the group. This is due to increase in electropositive character from Be to Ba. Thus beryllium reacts very slowly, Mg reacts very rapidly while Ca, Sr and Ba react explosively.

Complex formation is favoured by small size, highly charged ion and suitable empty orbitals; alkaline earth metal ions, not having these characteristics, do not have a significant tendency (although it is more than in the alkali metals by virtue of their double charge) to form complexes. However, beryllium, due to its small size, forms a number of stable complexes, e.g., $[BeF_2]^-$, $[BeF_4]^{2-}$, $[Be(H_2O_4)]^{2+}$ etc.

Beryllium and magnesium salts are generally very soluble. It is due to high energies of these much smaller ions.

Due to small size, beryllium has a high charge density and therefore, exhibits strong tendency to form covalent compounds.

20. **A-q; B-p, s; C-r; D-r**

Al_2O_3 is amphoteric in nature.

BeC_2 and Al_2C_3 liberate methane on reaction with water.

$BeCl_2$ is an electron deficient compound and behaves as lewis acid. It forms a polymeric chain in solid structure and contains three centred bonds.

1. **(a)** (X) is borax, $Na_2B_4O_7 \cdot 10H_2O$

(i) $Na_2B_4O_7 + 7H_2O \underset{\text{Base}}{\overset{\text{(Strong)}}{\rightleftharpoons}} 2NaOH + \underset{\text{acid}}{\overset{\text{(Weak)}}{4H_3BO_3}}$

Due to presence of NaOH, the aqueous solution is alkaline to litmus.

(ii) $Na_2B_4O_7 \cdot 10H_2O \xrightarrow[\text{(swells)}]{\text{Heat}} Na_2B_4O_7 + 10H_2O$

$\longrightarrow 2NaBO_2 + \underset{\text{Glassy bead}}{B_2O_3}$

(iii) $Na_2B_4O_7 + H_2SO_4 + 5H_2O \longrightarrow$

$Na_2SO_4 + \underset{\text{white crystals}}{4H_3BO_3}$

2. **(a)** The boron atom in boric acid, H_3BO_3 is electron deficient i.e., boric acid is a Lewis acid with one *p*-orbital vacant. There is no *d*-orbital of suitable energy in boron atom. So, it can accommodate only one additional electron pair in its outermost shell.

3. **(b)** Because they react with water to form methane gas

$\underset{\substack{\text{Aluminium}\\\text{carbide}}}{Al_4C_3} + 12H_2O \longrightarrow 4\,Al(OH)_3 + \underset{\text{Methane}}{3CH_4{\uparrow}}$

$\underset{\text{Beryllium carbide}}{Be_2C} + 4H_2O \longrightarrow 2Be(OH)_2 + \underset{\text{Methane}}{CH_4 \uparrow}$

4. **(c)** $SnCl_2 + 2NaOH \rightarrow Sn(OH)_2 + 2NaCl$

$Sn(OH)_2 + 2NaOH \rightarrow Na_2SnO_2 + 2H_2O$

5. **(c)** The cross linked polymers will be formed by $RSiCl_3$

$$nRSiCl_3 \xrightarrow[-3n\,HCl]{3n\,H_2O} nR - \underset{\underset{OH}{|}}{\overset{\overset{OH}{|}}{Si}} - OH \longrightarrow$$

$$\begin{array}{ccc} & | & | \\ & O & O \\ & | & | \\ R-&Si-O-Si&-R \\ & | & | \\ & O & O \\ & | & | \\ R-&Si-O-Si&-R \\ & | & | \\ & O & O \\ & | & | \end{array}$$

(Cross linked polymer)

6. **(b)** Aluminium oxide is amphoteric oxide because it shows the properties of the both acidic and basic oxides. It reacts with both acids and bases to form salt and water.

$Al_2O_3 \cdot xH_2O + 2NaOH \longrightarrow NaAlO_2 + H_2O$

$Al_2O_3 \cdot xH_2O + HCl \longrightarrow AlCl_3 + H_2O$

7. **(a, b, c)**

$B_2H_6 + 6H_2O \rightarrow 2H_3BO_3 + 6H_2$

$B_2H_6 + NH_3\,(\text{excess}) \xrightarrow{\text{low temp.}} B_2H_6 \cdot 2NH_3$

$B_2H_6 + NH_3\,(\text{excess}) \xrightarrow{\text{high temp.}} \text{Boron nitride}$

8. **(a, b, d)**

It is a bluish grey metal with bright metallic lustre when freshly cut and leaves a black mark on paper.

It is soft in nature and can be cut with knife

It is a heavy metal (sp. gr. $11.35 g/cm^3$) and melts at 327°C. Compound of lead are poisonous.

The dissolution of lead in water is known as Plumbo-Solvency. Plumbo-Solvency increases if the water contains nitrates, organic acids and ammonium salts and decreases in the presence of soluble sulphates, phosphates, carbonates etc., due to formation of a protective thin layer of insoluble lead salts.

9. **(a, b)** There is a high charge (+3) on aluminium ion (Al^{3+}) and the ratio, $\dfrac{\text{charge}}{\text{surface area}}$, is high (i.e., charge density is high) so it polarises the H_2O (ligand) and H^+ ions are removed. Due to this (i.e., polarisation of Al^{3-} ion) there occurs a drift of electron density towards Al^{3+} ion and thus the O – H bond weakens i.e., the O – H bond in $[Al(H_2O)_6]^{3+}$ is weaker than in water.

$(H_2O)_5Al^{3+} \leftarrow O{\overset{H}{\underset{H}{\Big\langle}}} \longrightarrow [(H_2O)_5\,Al(OH)_2]^{2+} + H^+$

10. **(a, b, c)**

(a) Because it burns in air and evolves a considerable amount of heat.

(b) It forms carboxyhaemoglobin with the haemoglobin of the blood.

(c) $HCOOH + H_2SO_4 \rightarrow CO + H_2O$

11. **(6)** In aqueous solution the probable aluminate species is $[Al(H_2O)_2(OH)_4]$, hence, co-ordination number of Al is 6

12. **(3)** CO_2, SiO_2 acidic CaO basic and SnO_2 amphoteric.

13. **(1)** $S_2O_8^{2-}$ does not have S–S linkage.

14. (0) $Na_2B_4O_7 + 2NH_4Cl \longrightarrow 2NaCl + 2BN + B_2O_3 + 4H_2O$
Nitrogen is not evolved.

15. (a) $SiMe_3Cl \xrightarrow{H_2O} SiMe_3OH$

$SiMe_2Cl_2 \xrightarrow{H_2O} SiMe_2(OH)_2$

16. (b) $Si\,Me\,Cl_3 \xrightarrow{H_2O} Si\,Me(OH)_3$

17. (d) Due to inert pair effect, lower oxidation state, i.e. +2, becomes more stable down the group ($\downarrow$). Hence, for Pb, +2 oxidation state will be more stable and PbO_2 will behave as a strong oxidant.
$PbO_2 \rightarrow PbO + O_2$

18. (d) Oxidation state of Ge in $GeCl_2$ is +2. Due to inert pair effect, down the group ($\downarrow$), +2 oxidation state is more stable than +4 oxidation state. Hence, Ge in +2 oxidation state is less stable than Sn (+2) and acts as strong reducing agent.

19. **A - s; B - r; C - p; D - q**

20. **A - q, s; B - r; C - q, s; D - t**

1. **(b)** For an E2 reaction, – H and –X must be oriented anti and coplanar (at a dihedral angle of $180°$) to one another

$$\underset{meso}{\overset{H\cdots\qquad\qquad\cdots H}{\underset{Br\qquad\qquad Br}{C_6H_5-C-C-C_6H_5}}} \xrightarrow[\substack{\text{carbon by }60° \\ \text{to bring }-H\text{ and} \\ -Br\text{ into required} \\ \text{conformation}}]{\text{rotate left}}$$

$$\underset{C_6H_5\qquad\qquad Br}{\overset{H\qquad\qquad H}{Br-C-C-C_6H_5}} \xrightarrow{\text{Base}} \underset{C_6H_5\qquad\qquad C_6H_5}{\overset{Br\qquad\qquad H}{C=C}}$$

(E)

$$\underset{Br\quad Racemic\quad Br}{\overset{C_6H_5\qquad\qquad H}{H-C-C-C_6H_5}} \xrightarrow[\text{C by }60°]{\text{rotate left}}$$

$$\underset{Br\qquad\qquad Br}{\overset{H\qquad\qquad H}{C_6H_5-C-C-C_6H_5}} \xrightarrow{\text{Base}} \underset{Br\qquad\qquad C_6H_5}{\overset{C_6H_5\qquad\qquad H}{C=C}}$$
(Z)

2. **(d)** The nature of hybridisation of a carbon can be ascertained by knowing the total number of electron pairs (ep) in the hybrid orbitals of that carbon atom :
$$ep = \sigma bp + lp$$

σbp is the number of bond pair in hybrid orbitals involved in σ bond formation, while lp is the number of lone pair in hybrid orbital. The nature of hybridisation is thus ascertained as sp^3 (when ep is 4), sp^2 (when ep is 3) and sp (when ep is 2).

(i) $CH_2=\overset{+}{C}H$ (ii) $CH_3\overset{-}{C}HCH_3$ (iii) $CH_2=\overset{-}{C}H$

σbp	3	2	4	3	3	2
lp	0	0	0	1	0	1
ep	3	2	4	4	3	3
Hybrid.	sp^2	sp	sp^3	sp^3	sp^2	sp^2

(iv) $CH\equiv\overset{-}{C}$ (v) $CH_3\overset{\bullet}{C}(CH_3)_2$

σbp	2	1	4	3
lp	0	1	0	0
ep	2	2	4	3
Hybrid.	sp	sp	sp^3	sp^2

3. **(c)** Halohydrin formation is an *anti*-addition reaction in which same cyclic chloronium ion is formed in *cis*-but-2-ene whether Cl_2 attacks from the top side or from the bottom side of the molecule. Nucleophile now adds on this chloronium ion from the opposite side forming *threo* halohydrin.

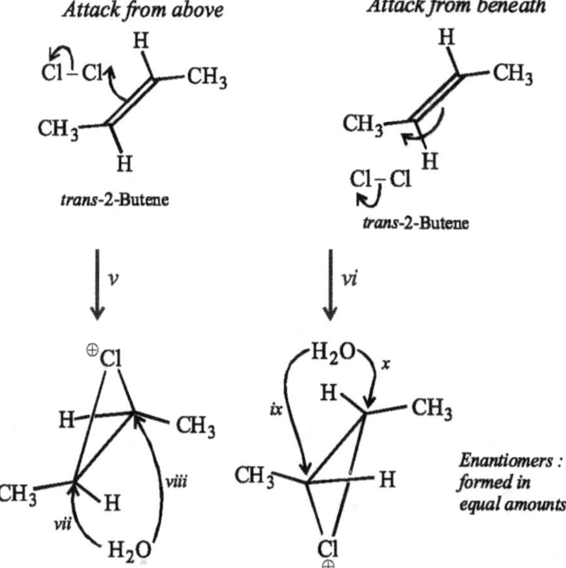

However in *trans*-2-butene two different (an enantiomeric pair) cyclic chloromium ions will be formed, one due to attack from above and another due to attack from below. However, each enantiomer gives only one chlorohydrin on reaction with nucleophile (H_2O) leading to two enantiomeric chlorohydrins.

Identical

Identical

or   or

CH₃
H——Cl
H——OH
CH₃

CH₃
Cl——H
HO——H
CH₃

Enantiomers

erythro-3-Chloro-2-butanol
Racemic modification

4. (a)

IUPAC name of the structure is 3-ethyl-2-hydroxy-4-methylhex-3-en-5-ynoic acid

5. (b) Carboxylic acids are stronger acids than $-NH_3^{\oplus}$ because the corresponding conjugate base ($-COO^-$) is more stable than $-NH_2$. Hence Y is the strongest acid. Since $-COOH$ has $-I$ effect which decreases with distance, therefore, effect is more pronounced in Z than in X. As a result, Z is more acidic than X. Hence the true option is Y > Z > X.

6. (b) Percentage of nitrogen by Kjeldahl's method

$$= \frac{14}{1000} \times \frac{\text{Normality of acid} \times \text{vol. of acid used}}{\text{wt. of organic compound}}$$

Mass of organic compound = 0.5 g
Unused acid required = 80 mL of 0.5 M NaOH
= 80 mL of 0.5 N NaOH
≡ 40 mL of 0.5 M or 1 N H_2SO_4
Acid used for absorption of ammonia
= (50 − 40) mL of 1 N H_2SO_4
= 10 mL of 1 N H_2SO_4

$$\% \text{ of nitrogen} = \frac{1.4 \times 1 \times 10}{0.5} = 28\%$$

7. (a,d) $CH_3 - \overset{*}{C}H - CH = CH - \overset{*}{C}H - CH_3$ with OH on each starred carbon.

Stereoisomer	Configuration		
I	d	cis	d
II	l	cis	l
III	d	cis	l
IV	d	trans	d
V	l	trans	l
VI	d	trans	l

Enantiomers : I and II; IV and V
                 cis   trans
Diastereomers : I (or II), III (or IV), V and VI
Meso : III and IV

8. (a,b,c) Lone pair of electrons on N_9 belongs to p orbital, hence involved in delocalisation, while the lone pair of electrons on other N's lies in sp^2 orbitals; which being static are available for protonation.

9. (a, c, d) On the basis of hybridisation, N (sp^3) of NH_2 with s less character should be more basic than N (sp^2) of the imino ($=NH$) group. However, N of imino group is more basic and it is this nitrogen which is protonated because its conjugate acid is resonance hybrid of three equivalent structures which accounts its unusual stability.

Guanidine

Conjugate acid of guanidine

Unusual stability of the conjugate acid of guanidine explains why guanidine is the strongest organic known base

10. (a,c) (a) has chiral N and also resolvable because it has a resolvable mirror image.

(b) has chiral N but not resolvable because of rapid N-inversion

(c) has chiral N and chiral C and also resolvable because of presence of bulky alkyl groups.

(d) $-COOH$ groups are small, hence do not provide sufficient steric hindrance to prevent rotation about C–C single bond, hence compound is non-resolvable.

11. (3) Alcohols give CAN test while phenol gives $FeCl_3$ test. So compounds containing both groups will give both coloured test. So the answer is:

V, VI, and VII.

12. (8)

$$CH_3CH_2\underset{\underset{CH_3}{|}}{C}H-CH_2CH_3 \xrightarrow[h\nu]{Cl_2} CH_3CH_2-\overset{H}{\underset{\underset{CH_3}{|}}{\overset{|}{C^*}}}-CH_2CH_2Cl$$

(1-chiral centre)
2-stereo-isomers
(*d* and *l*)

$$+ CH_3CH_2-\overset{H}{\underset{\underset{CH_3}{|}}{\overset{|}{C^*}}}-\overset{H}{\overset{|}{C^*}}H-CH_3 \quad (2\text{-chiral center})$$

4- stereo isomers (Two pairs of enantomers)

$$+ CH_3CH_2-\overset{H}{\underset{\underset{CH_2-Cl}{|}}{\overset{|}{C}}}-CH_2-CH_3 + C_2H_5-\overset{Cl}{\underset{\underset{CH_3}{|}}{\overset{|}{C}}}-C_2H_5$$

Therefore, total isomers = 8.

13. (3)

There are 3-α-H-atoms which are acidic due to EWG ($>C = O$) and they can be replaced by deuterium in basic medium as shown by circle.

14. (9)

15. (c) All amines have a lone pair of electrons on N which enables them to form a H bond. However, tertiary amines although can form H–bond with water or other hydroxylic solvents, it does not form H-bond with its second molecule because of absence of H on N. Only lower amines (1°, 2° as well as 3°) are quite soluble in water, solubility in water decreases with the increase in the size of the alkyl group.

16. (d) Although the mirror image of $R_1R_2R_3\ddot{N}$ type of amine is not superimposable on its object, yet the molecule is optically inactive because of rapid inversion of configuration between the two arrangements i.e. the two enantiomers are only hypothetical, these are not isolated.

17. (a) Acid weakening groups are electron donating and hence they activate the ring toward the attack by an electrophile.

18. (d) The H^- (in aldehydes) formed due to C – H cleavage and CH_3^- (in ketones, e.g. acetone) formed due to C – C cleavage are very poor leaving groups, hence can't be removed.

19. A-q, s; B-q, s; C-p, s; D-r

(A) $N_2CHCOOC_2H_5 \xrightarrow{\text{heat}} :CHCOOC_2H_5 + N_2$
Diazoacetic ester · Carbene (neutral)

(B) $CH_2N_2 \xrightarrow{\text{heat}} :CH_2$
Diazomethane · Carbene (neutral)

(C) $CH_3N = NCH_3 \xrightarrow{\text{heat}} \overset{\bullet}{C}H_3 + N_2$
Methyl radical (neutral)

(D) $C_6H_5 - N^+\!\equiv NCl^- \longrightarrow C_6H_5^+ + N_2$
Carbocation (although, unstable)

20. A-q; B-p, q, r; C-p, q, s; D-q

(A) Here although two products are possible, only one is formed, the reaction is 100% stereoselective.

(B) The reaction involves the addition of Br_2 on *trans*-alkene to form 100% *meso* product. It is **stereospecific** in the sense that it involves the addition on a stereoisomer (*trans*) and forms a stereoisomeric product (*meso*). Further every stereospecific reaction is **stereoselective**. Since here cyclic bromonium ion is formed as an intermediate, the two bromine atoms add in *anti*-manner.

(C) This reaction is just the reverse of the above one, i.e. it involves the conversion of an optical isomer to geometrical isomer through elimination reaction, it is stereospecific, stereoselective and involves *anti* elimination.

(D) Here one of the stereoisomeric product (95%) is formed from compound having no stereoisomerism, it is **highly stereoselective**.

1. **(c)**

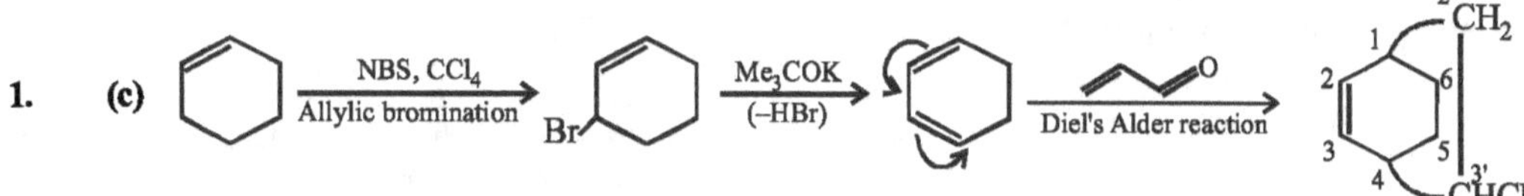

Numbering is done only for explaining the two six membered rings. The numbering is not in accordance with IUPAC rule

2. **(d)** Chlorination of methane is a free radical reaction and hence it can be initiated by any factor that can produce chlorine free radical.

(a) $Cl—Cl \xrightarrow{UV} Cl^{\cdot} + Cl^{\cdot}$
$CH_4 + Cl^{\cdot} \longrightarrow CH_3^{\cdot} + HCl$
$CH_3^{\cdot} + Cl—Cl \longrightarrow CH_3Cl + Cl^{\cdot}$

(b) $(C_2H_5)_4Pb \xrightarrow{heat} 4CH_3CH_2^{\cdot} + Pb^{\cdot}$
$CH_3CH_2^{\cdot} + Cl—Cl \longrightarrow CH_3CH_2Cl + Cl^{\cdot}$
$CH_4 + Cl^{\cdot} \longrightarrow CH_3^{\cdot} + HCl$
$CH_3^{\cdot} + Cl—Cl \longrightarrow CH_3Cl + Cl^{\cdot}$

(c) $(CH_3)_3COCl \xrightarrow{UV} (CH_3)_3CO^{\cdot} + Cl^{\cdot}$
$CH_4 + (CH_3)_3CO^{\cdot} \longrightarrow CH_3^{\cdot} + (CH_3)_3COH$
$CH_3^{\cdot} + (CH_3)_3COCl \longrightarrow CH_3Cl + (CH_3)_3CO^{\cdot}$

3. **(c)** Ethene is obtained by electrolysis of dipotassium succinate as follows

$$\underset{\text{Pot. Succinate}}{\overset{\displaystyle CH_2COOK}{\underset{\displaystyle CH_2COOK}{|}}} \xrightarrow{\text{ionization}} \overset{\displaystyle CH_2COO^-}{\underset{\displaystyle CH_2COO^-}{|}} + 2K^+$$

$$2H_2O \underset{\text{ionization}}{\rightleftharpoons} 2OH^- + 2H^+$$

At anode :

$$\overset{\displaystyle CH_2COO^-}{\underset{\displaystyle CH_2COO^-}{|}} \xrightarrow{-2e^-} \left[\overset{\displaystyle CH_2COO}{\underset{\displaystyle CH_2COO}{|}}\right] \longrightarrow \overset{\displaystyle CH_2}{\underset{\displaystyle CH_2}{\|}} + 2CO_2$$

Unstable

At cathode :

$$2H^+ + 2e^- \longrightarrow [2H] \longrightarrow H_2$$

4. **(b)**

$$\text{(cyclohexyl–C≡CH)} \xrightarrow[H_2O]{HgSO_4\ H_2SO_4} \left[\text{(cyclohexyl–C(OH)=CH}_2)\right]$$

$$\xrightarrow{\text{Tautomerisation}} \text{(cyclohexyl–CO–CH}_3)$$

5. **(c)** (i) and (ii) methods will form isopropylbenzene because n-propyl carbocation, being less stable, rearranges to the more stable (2°) isopropyl carbocation. Moreover, method (i) will lead to polyalkylation. Methods (iii) and (iv) can be used for preparing n-propylbenzene.

(benzene) $+ ClCH_2CH=CH_2 \xrightarrow{(i)\ AlCl_3}$

$CH_2–CH=CH_2$ (on benzene) $\xrightarrow{H_2/Pt}$ $CH_2CH_2CH_3$ (on benzene)

n-Propylbenzene

(benzene) $+ CH_3CH_2COCl \xrightarrow{(AlCl_3)}$

$COCH_2CH_3$ (on benzene) $\xrightarrow[HCl]{Zn/Hg}$ $CH_2CH_2CH_3$ (on benzene)

6. **(c)** $H_3CO—\langle O \rangle—CH=CHCH_3 \xrightarrow{H^+} H_3CO—\langle O \rangle—\overset{+}{C}HCH_2CH_3 \xrightarrow{Br^-}$

Benzylic carbocation

$2\ H_3CO—\langle O \rangle—\underset{\underset{\displaystyle Br}{|}}{C}HC_2H_5 \xrightarrow[\text{(ii) HBr (Demethylation)}]{\text{(i) Na (Fittig reaction)}} HO—\langle O \rangle—\underset{\underset{\displaystyle C_2H_5}{|}}{C}H—\underset{\underset{\displaystyle C_2H_5}{|}}{C}H—\langle O \rangle—OH$

7. **(a, b, c).** $C_2H_6 + Cl_2 \xrightarrow{h\nu} C_2H_5Cl + HCl$

$C_2H_5Cl + Cl_2 \xrightarrow{h\nu} CH_3CHCl_2 + CH_2Cl.CH_2Cl$

The attack of chlorine atom on the hydrocarbon is selective, that is, a tertiary C – H hydrogen atom is abstracted more easily than a secondary or a primary hydrogen. Thus rate of abstraction of hydrogen atom follows the order $3° > 2° > 1°$.

$$CH_3CHCH_3 + Cl_2 \xrightarrow{h\nu} CH_3-\underset{\underset{CH_3}{|}}{\overset{\overset{CH_3}{|}}{C}}-Cl(67\%) + CH_3CHCH_2Cl(33\%)$$

with CH_3 substituent.

It is likely that the activation energy required to form a 3° free radical is much less than that for the formation of 2° or 1° free radical. The ease of formation of free radicals thus parallels their stability, i.e. $3° > 2° > 1°$. Thus more stable a free radical, the more easily it is formed.

8. **(c, d)** (a) $CH_3-Cl \xrightarrow{Zn/dust} CH_3-CH_3$

(b) $CH_3-CH_2Cl \xrightarrow{LiAlH_4} CH_3-CH_3$

(c) $Al_4C_3 \xrightarrow{H_2O/HCl} CH_4$

(d) $CaC_2 \xrightarrow{H_2O/H^+} C_2H_2$

9. **(b, c)**

$$CH_2 = \underset{\underset{CH_3}{|}}{C} - CH_3(\text{II}) > CH_2 = CH - CH_3(\text{I}) > $$

$$CH_2 = CH_2(\text{III})$$

Intermediate $CH_3 - \underset{\underset{CH_3}{|}}{\overset{+}{C}} - CH_3 > CH_3 - \overset{+}{CH} - CH_3$

          3° carbocation   2° carbocation

               (II)   (I)

$$> CH_3 - \overset{+}{CH_2}$$

        1° carbocation

            (III)

10. **(a, b, c)**

$$\text{CH}_2=\text{CH-CH}_2\text{-CH}_2\text{-CH}_2\text{-CH}_3 \xrightarrow{NBS} \left[\text{allylic radical} \leftrightarrow \overset{\cdot}{C}H_2 \text{ resonance} \right]$$

gives the allylic bromides (with Br) *cis-* and *trans-*

11. **(1)**

$n_1 = $ (chlorocyclopentane); $n_2 = $ (two dichlorocyclopentane isomers, with Cl substituents)

and (four structures with Cl substituents: n_3)

Hence $\dfrac{n_1 + n_2}{n_3} = \dfrac{4}{4} = 1$

12. **(5)** 1, 3-Dichlorocyclobutane can exist in *cis* and *trans* forms. *trans*-1, 2-Dichlorocyclobutane can exist in $(+)-$ and $(-)-$forms. However, *cis*-1, 2 Dichlorocyclobutane has a plane of symmetry and hence it can exist as *meso* isomer.

13. **(4)** All alkyl bromides having carbon skeleton of isopentane (2-methylbutane $(CH_3)_2CHCH_2CH_3$) will give isopentane via Grignard reagent.

$$\underset{\underset{CH_3}{|}}{BrCH_2CHCH_2CH_3} \qquad \underset{\underset{CH_3}{|}}{CH_3CBrCH_2CH_3}$$

$$\underset{CH_3CH\ CHCH_3}{\overset{CH_3\ Br}{|\quad |}} \qquad \underset{\underset{CH_3}{|}}{CH_3CHCH_2CH_2Br}$$

14. **(3)**

$$CH_3 - CH_2 - CH_2 - \underset{\underset{CH_3}{|}}{CH} - \underset{\underset{CH_2-CH_3}{|}}{CH} - CH_2 - CH_3$$

3-Ethyl-4-methylheptane

$$CH \equiv C - CH_2 - \underset{\underset{CH_3}{|}}{CH} - \underset{\underset{CH_2CH_3}{|}}{CH} - CH_2 - CH_3$$

$$CH_3 - CH_2 - CH_2 - \underset{\underset{CH_3}{|}}{CH} - \underset{\underset{C \equiv CH}{|}}{CH} - CH_2CH_3$$

$$CH_3 - C \equiv C - \underset{\underset{CH_3}{|}}{CH} - \underset{\underset{CH_2CH_3}{|}}{CH} - CH_2CH_3$$

15. **(b)**   **16.** **(a)**

(X) methylcyclopentane $\xrightarrow[h\nu]{Br_2}$ (Y) 1-bromo-1-methylcyclopentane

(Y) $\xrightarrow{alc.\ KOH}$ (Z) 1-methylcyclopentene $\xrightarrow[Zn]{O_3, H_2O}$ (T) keto-aldehyde ($CH_3CO-...-CH=O$)

(T) $\xrightarrow{AgNO_3/NH_4OH}$ (W) ($-COCH_3$, $-COOH$)

(W) $\xrightarrow{I_2/NaOH}$ (U) $HOOC-(CH_2)_3-COOH$ $\xrightarrow[\Delta]{P_2O_5}$ (V) cyclic anhydride

17. **(c)** The chain-initiating step $(Cl - Cl \longrightarrow 2\,^{\bullet}Cl)$ is highly endothermic $(\Delta H = +58$ kcal/mol$)$ and therefore requires high temperatures.

18. **(b)** Oxygen reacts with the methyl radical to form new radical $(CH_3OO^{\bullet})$ which is *markedly less reactive*

$$^{\bullet}CH_3 + O - O \longrightarrow CH_3 - O - O^{\bullet}$$

than $^{\bullet}CH_3$ and therefore drastically slows down the chain reaction.

19. **A-q, r; B-s; C-s; D-p, s**

(A) $CH_3CH_2CH_2\overset{+}{C}HCH_3 \xleftarrow{\;H^+\;} CH_3CH_2CH = CHCH_3 \xrightarrow{\;H^+\;} CH_3CH_2\overset{+}{C}HCH_2CH_3$

    (Five hyperconjugative structures)   Highly favoured due to inductive of ethyl group (4 hyperconjugative structures)

$\downarrow Cl^-$ $\downarrow Cl^-$

        $\overset{\textstyle Cl}{\underset{\textstyle |}{}}$ $CH_3CH_2CHCH_2CH_3$

$CH_3CH_2CH_2CHCH_3$ $\underset{\textstyle Cl}{\overset{\textstyle |}{}}$

(B) $CH_2 = CH - CH = CH_2 \xrightarrow{\;H^+\;} \left[CH_3\overset{+}{C}HCH = CH_2 \longleftrightarrow CH_3CH = CH\overset{+}{C}H_2 \right]$

         $2°$Carbocation, stable due to resonance

$\xrightarrow{\;Cl^-\;} \underset{(1,2-\text{addition})}{CH_3\overset{|\;\;Cl}{C}HCH = CH_2} + \underset{(1,4-\text{addition})}{CH_3CH = CH\overset{|\;\;Cl}{C}H_2}$

(C) $\bigcirc\!\!\!-CH = CHCH_3 + H^+ \longrightarrow \bigcirc\!\!\!-\overset{+}{C}HCH_2CH_3 \xrightarrow{\;Br^-\;} \bigcirc\!\!\!-\overset{|\;\;Br}{C}HCH_2CH_3$

         Highly stable benzyl carbocation

(D) $\bigcirc\!\!\!-CH_2CH = CH_2 + H^+ \longrightarrow \bigcirc\!\!\!-CH_2\overset{+}{C}HCH_3 \xrightarrow[\text{hydride shift}]{1,2-}$

         $2°$ carbocation

$\bigcirc\!\!\!-\overset{+}{C}HCH_2CH_3 \xrightarrow{\;Br^-\;} \bigcirc\!\!\!-\overset{|\;\;Br}{C}HCH_2CH_3$

         More stable benzyl carbocation

20. **A-r; B-s; C-q; D-p, q, r**

(A) The electron-withdrawing group $(-C \equiv N)$ is in conjugation with the carbon-carbon double bond, hence the intermediate carbanion, formed by the attack of nucleophile, stabilizes due to resonance. Hence such alkenes undergo nucleophilic addition reactions.

(B) Vinyl monomers when heated in presence of catalyst undergo free radical polymerisation.

(C) Acyl halides, typically, undergo nucleophilic substitution. This is due to the fact that $-Cl$ is a good leaving group.

(D) The given compound has $1°$ alkyl halide, hence undergoes $S_{N}2$ reaction involving transition state with pentavalent carbon. Further the presence of $-CH_2CH = CN$ grouping causes the compound to undergo nucleophilic addition.

1. **(a)** Fraction of unoccupied sites in NaCl crystal

$$= 1 - \frac{2.165 \times 10^3}{2.178 \times 10^3}$$

$$= \frac{2.178 \times 10^3 - 2.165 \times 10^3}{2.178 \times 10^3} = \frac{0.13 \times 10^3}{2.178 \times 10^3}$$

$$= \frac{130}{2178} = 5.96 \times 10^{-3}$$

2. **(d)** $M = \dfrac{\rho \times a^3 \times N_A \times 10^{-30}}{z}$

$$= \frac{10 \times (100)^3 \times 6.02 \times 10^{23} \times 10^{-30}}{4} = 15.05$$

$\therefore$ Number of atoms in 100 g $= \dfrac{6.02 \times 10^{23}}{15.05} \times 100$

$$= 4 \times 10^{25}$$

3. **(a)** $\dfrac{r_{Na^+}}{r_{Cl^-}} = 0.55$ and $\dfrac{r_{K^+}}{r_{Cl^-}} = 0.74$

$$\frac{r_{Na^+}}{r_{Cl^-}} + 1 = 0.55 + 1 \text{ and } \frac{r_{K^+}}{r_{Cl^-}} + 1 = 0.74 + 1$$

$$\frac{r_{Na^+} + r_{Cl^-}}{r_{Cl^-}} = 1.55 \text{ and } \frac{r_{K^+} + r_{Cl^-}}{r_{Cl^-}} = 1.74$$

Now edge length ratio of KCl and NaCl is

$$\frac{1.74}{1.55} = \frac{r_{K^+} + r_{Cl^-}}{r_{Cl^-}} \times \frac{r_{Cl^-}}{r_{Na^+} + r_{Cl^-}} = 1.123.$$

4. **(c)** For bcc structure

$$d = \frac{\sqrt{3}\,a}{2}$$

where d = distance between two atoms
a = edge length

$$1.73 = \frac{\sqrt{3}}{2}a$$

$$a = \frac{2 \times 1.73}{\sqrt{3}} = 2\text{Å} = 200 \text{ pm}$$

5. **(b)** For bcc structure

Interionic distance $= r^+ + r^- = \dfrac{\sqrt{3}}{2}a$

$\qquad\qquad\qquad\qquad\qquad$ (a = edge length)

$$r^+_{NH_4^+} + r^-_{Cl^-} = \frac{\sqrt{3}}{2}a$$

$$r^+_{NH_4^+} + 180 = \frac{\sqrt{3}}{2} \times 390$$

$$r^+_{NH_4^+} = 338\text{pm} - 180\text{pm} = 158 \text{ pm}$$

6. **(b)** The closed packed structure have both octahedral and tetrahedral voids. In a ccp structure, there is one octahedral void on the edge. Each one of which is common to four other unit cells. Thus, in cubic close packed structure,

Octahedral voids in the centre of the cube $= 1$

Effective number of octahedral voids located at the

12 edge of cube $= 12 \times \dfrac{1}{4} = 3$

$\therefore$ Total number of octahedral voids $= 4$

7. **(a, b)** Ionic solids are soluble in water as also in other polar solvents.

8. **(a, b)** In case of monotropy (i.e. only one form of solid is stable at all temperatures) the transition point lies above the m.p. whereas in case of enantiotropy the transition point lies below m.p.

9. **(a, b)** Diamond and graphite are covalent crystals.

10. **(a, b, c, d)**

(a) Vacancy defects lower the density of the substance

(b) Interstitial defects increase the density of the substance

(c) Schottky defects, preserve the electrical neutrality of the crystal.

(d) Frenkel defects do not affect the density of the crystal.

Hence all statements are correct.

11. **(8)** Diameter of Cs $= 2 \times 2.6 = 5.2\,\text{Å} = 5.2 \times 10^{-8}$ cm

Number of atoms of 2.50 cm row $= \dfrac{2.50}{5.2 \times 10^{-8}}$

$$= 0.48 \times 10^8$$

$$= 4.8 \times 10^7 \text{ Cs atoms}$$

$\therefore$ Moles of Cs atoms $= \dfrac{4.8 \times 10^7}{6 \times 10^{23}} = 0.8 \times 10^{-16}$

$$= 8 \times 10^{-17}$$

$\therefore x \times 10^{-17} = 8 \times 10^{-17} \Rightarrow x = 8$

12. (4) a. Number of X atoms $= 8 \times \dfrac{1}{8} = 1$ /unit cell.

Number of Y atoms $= 1$/unit cell

Number of O atoms $= 12 \times \dfrac{1}{4} = 3$ /unit cell.

Formula is : $XYO_3 \Rightarrow X_a Y_b O_c$

b. Number of O atoms missing from two edge centres

per unit cell $= 2 \times \dfrac{1}{4} = \dfrac{1}{2}$ /unit cell

Number of O atoms left $= 3 - \dfrac{1}{2} = 2.5$ /unit cell

Formula is $XYO_{2.5} \Rightarrow X_2 Y_2 O_5 \Rightarrow X_x Y_y O_z$

$\therefore$ The value of

$(x+y+z)-(a+b+c)=(2+2+5)-(1+1+3)=4$

13. (1) Atomic radius of the metal has been assumed to be the same in the two modifications. In *'bcc'* lattice number of atoms (z) per unit cell is 2 and two spherical units with their centres at the extrimities of the diagonal of the cube touch the spherical unit at the centre of the cube.

Hence $z = 2$; $4r = \sqrt{3}a$, $a = \dfrac{4}{\sqrt{3}}r$

$$d\,(\alpha\text{-form}) = \dfrac{Mz}{N_A a^3} = \dfrac{M \times 2}{N_A \times \left(\dfrac{4}{\sqrt{3}}r\right)^3} \qquad ......(i)$$

In *fcc*, $z = 4$ and $4r = \sqrt{2}a$ (diagonal of face)

$a = 2\sqrt{2}r$

(Two spherical units with their centres at the extrimities of the diagonal of the face are in the touch with a sphere at the centre of the face.)

$$d\,(\gamma\text{-form}) = \dfrac{Mz}{N_A a^3} = \dfrac{M \times 4}{N_A (2\sqrt{2}r)^3} \qquad .....(ii)$$

From equation (i) and (ii),

$$\dfrac{d(\gamma\text{-form})}{d(\alpha\text{-form})} = \dfrac{4}{(2\sqrt{2}r)^3} \bigg/ \dfrac{2}{\left(\dfrac{4}{\sqrt{3}}r\right)^3} = 1.0887 \approx 1$$

14. (1) NaCl and KCl crystallize in fcc cubic lattice. As shown in the figure, two Cl^- ions with their centres at the adjacent corners of the cube are in touch with Na^+ ion at the centre of edge length.

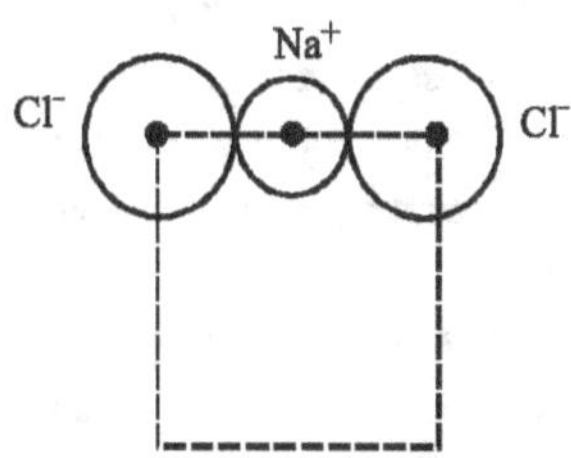

Hence, $2r_{Cl^-} + 2r_{Na^+} = a$ (edge length)

$r_{Cl^-} + r_{Na^+} = \dfrac{a}{2}$

$\dfrac{r_{Cl^-}}{r_{Na^+}} + 1 = \dfrac{a}{2r_{Na^+}}$

$\dfrac{1}{0.5} + 1 = \dfrac{a}{2r_{Na^+}} \Rightarrow a = 6r_{Na^+} \qquad ......(i)$

$\dfrac{r_{Na^+}}{r_{Cl^-}} = 0.5$ and $\dfrac{r_{Na^+}}{r_{K^+}} = 0.7$

Hence, $\dfrac{r_{Cl^-}}{r_{K^+}} = 1.4$

$1 + \dfrac{r_{Cl^-}}{r_{K^+}} = \dfrac{a'}{2r_{K^+}}$

$1 + 1.4 = \dfrac{a'}{2r_{K^+}} \Rightarrow a' = 4.8r_{K^+} \qquad ......(ii)$

From (i) and (ii), $\dfrac{a'}{a} = \dfrac{4.8r_{K^+}}{6r_{Na^+}} = \dfrac{4.8}{6 \times 0.7} = 1.143$

15. (b) Given: Edge length $= 200\,\text{pm} = 200 \times 10^{-10}\,\text{cm}$

$\therefore$ Volume of unit cell $= (200 \times 10^{-10})^3\,\text{cm}^3 = 8 \times 10^{-24}\,\text{cm}^3$

For fcc, $n = 4$

$\therefore$ Mass of unit cell $= n \times A = \dfrac{4 \times 200}{24 \times 10^{23}}$

$= 33.3 \times 10^{-23}\,\text{g}$

$\text{Density} = \dfrac{\text{mass of unit cell}}{\text{Volume of unit cell}}$

$= \dfrac{33.3 \times 10^{-23}}{8 \times 10^{-24}} = 41.6\,\text{g cm}^{-3}$

16. (d) For a fcc crystal

face diagonal $= 4 \times$ radius of atom

$\therefore$ face diagonal of copper crystal $= 4 \times 128\,\text{pm} = 512\,\text{pm}$

Again face diagonal $= \sqrt{2} \times$ edge length

$\therefore$ Edge length $= \dfrac{512}{\sqrt{2}} = 362\,\text{pm} = 362 \times 10^{-10}\,\text{cm}$

17. **(d)** The angle of intersection between corresponding faces in crystals "*A*" and "*B*" will be same. Thus it will be constant and it will be equal as both "*A*" and "*B*" represent crystal structure of the same substance.

18. **(a)** The law is still valid because the external form depends upon rate of deposition of atoms or ions on different faces.

19. **A-r; B-s; C-p; D-q**

The unit cell of CsCl consists of Cl^- on the corners of the cube and Cs^+ at its centre.

(A) An additional lattice plane (100) can be drawn passing through the centre of the cube in between two (100) planes. Hence, $d_{100} = a/2$.

(B) (110) plane includes both Cs^+ and Cl^- ions and no additional plane of this type can be drawn between two (110) planes.

Hence, $d_{110} = \dfrac{\text{Diagonal of the face}}{2} = \dfrac{a\sqrt{2}}{2}$

(C) (100) planes consist of either Cl^- ions or Cs^+ ions alternately.

(D) (110) planes consist of both Cs^+ and Cl^- ions.

20. **A-p, q; B-r, s; C-p; D-q**

$A \to p, q$: Schottky defect is observed in case of both NaCl and KCl.

$B \to r, s$: Frenkel defect is shown by silver halides. Due to this defect the density remains unaffected but dielectric constant increases.

$C \to p$: The yellow colour of non-stoichiometric NaCl is due to **metal excess defect**, a non-stoichiometric defect.

$D \to q$: The blue-lilac colour of non-stoichiometric KCl is due to metal excess defect, a non-Stoichiometric defect. Non-stoichiometric defects are also known as **Berthollide defects**.

1. **(b)** $P_{total} = P_A^\circ X_A + P_B^\circ X_B$

$$550 = P_A^\circ \times \frac{1}{4} + P_B^\circ \times \frac{3}{4}$$

$$P_A^\circ + 3P_B^\circ = 550 \times 4 \qquad \text{...(i)}$$

In second case

$$P_{total} = P_A^\circ \times \frac{1}{5} + P_B^\circ \times \frac{4}{5}$$

$$P_A^\circ + 4P_B^\circ = 560 \times 5 \qquad \text{...(ii)}$$

Subtract (i) from (ii)

$$\therefore P_B^\circ = 560 \times 5 - 550 \times 4 = 600$$

$$\because P_A^\circ = 400$$

2. **(c)** Let vapour pressure of $A = P_A^o$

Vapour pressure of $B = P_B^o$

In first solution,

Mole fraction of $A(x_A) = \dfrac{1}{1+2} = \dfrac{1}{3}$

Mole fraction of $B(x_B) = \dfrac{2}{1+2} = \dfrac{2}{3}$

According to Raoult's law,

Total vapour pressure

$$= 250 = P_A^o x_A + P_B^o x_B$$

$$250 = \frac{1}{3} P_A^o + \frac{2}{3} P_B^o \qquad \text{...(i)}$$

In second solution

Mole fraction of $A(x_A) = \dfrac{2}{2+2} = \dfrac{2}{4} = \dfrac{1}{2}$

Mole fraction of $B(x_B) = \dfrac{2}{4} = \dfrac{1}{2}$

$\therefore$ Total vapour pressure

$$= 300 = P_A^o x_A + P_B^o x_B$$

$$300 = \frac{1}{2} P_A^o + \frac{1}{2} P_B^o \qquad \text{...(ii)}$$

Multiplying equation (i) by $\dfrac{1}{2}$ and equation (ii) by $\dfrac{1}{3}$

$$\frac{1}{6} P_A^o + \frac{2}{6} P_B^o = 125$$

$$\frac{1}{6} P_A^o + \frac{1}{6} P_B^o = 100$$
$$\overline{\qquad\qquad\qquad\qquad}$$
$$\frac{1}{6} P_B^o = 25$$

$$P_B^o = 25 \times 6 = 150 \text{ mm Hg}$$

On substituting value of P_B^o in equation (ii) we get

$$300 = P_A^o \times \frac{1}{2} + 150 \times \frac{1}{2}$$

$$P_A^o = 450 \text{ mm Hg}$$

3. **(c)** van't Hoff factor (i) and the degree of association are related as below :

$$i = 1 - \alpha\left(1 - \frac{1}{n}\right)$$

$$0.9 = 1 - 0.2\left(1 - \frac{1}{n}\right)$$

On solving,

$$\left(1 - \frac{1}{n}\right) = \frac{1}{2}$$

$$\frac{1}{n} = 1 - \frac{1}{2} = \frac{1}{2}$$

$$\therefore \ n = 2$$

4. **(a)** Molarity $= \dfrac{\% \times 10 \times d}{\text{GMM}} = \dfrac{22 \times 10 \times 1.253}{342} = 0.805 \text{M}.$

Normality $= \dfrac{\% \times 10 \times d}{\text{GEM}} = \dfrac{22 \times 10 \times 1.253}{342/6} = 4.83 \text{N}$

Molality $= \dfrac{22 \times 1000}{342(100 - 22)} = 0.825 \text{m}$

5. **(a)** $K_H = 100 \text{ kbar} = 10^5 \text{ bar}, P = 1 \text{ bar}$
$P = K_H \times x_A$

$$x_A = \frac{P}{K_H} = \frac{1}{100 \times 10^3} = 10^{-5}$$

Moles of water $= \dfrac{1000}{18} = 55.5$

Weight of water $= 1000 \text{ g}$ $(\because 1000 \text{ mL} = 1000 \text{ g})$

Mole fraction $= 10^{-5} = \dfrac{x}{55.5 + x}$

As $55.5 >>> x$, thus neglecting x from denominator

$$10^{-5} = \frac{x}{55.5} \Rightarrow x = 55.5 \times 10^{-5} \text{ moles}$$

or 0.555 millimoles.

6. **(c)** For dilute solution, $\dfrac{\Delta P}{P^\circ} \Rightarrow \dfrac{n_{solute}}{n_{solvent}}$

For solution in A, $\dfrac{\Delta P_A}{P^c_A} = \dfrac{W/M}{W_A/M_A} = \dfrac{W}{M} \times \dfrac{M_A}{W_A}$

$$.........(i)$$

For solution in B, $\dfrac{\Delta P_B}{P^\circ_A} = \dfrac{W}{M} \times \dfrac{M_B}{W_B}$ $.........(ii)$

From (i) and (ii), $\dfrac{\Delta P_A/P^\circ_A}{\Delta P_B/P^\circ_B} = 2 = \dfrac{M_A W_B}{M_B W_A} = \dfrac{M_A}{M_B}$

$(W_A = W_B)$

7. **(a, b, c)** when $n_A = n_B$, we have $x_A = \dfrac{n_A}{n_A + n_B} = \dfrac{1}{2}$

and $x_B = \dfrac{n_B}{n_A + n_B} = \dfrac{1}{2}$

Using the given relation, we have

$P_S = (110 \times \dfrac{1}{2} + 125 \times \dfrac{1}{2})$ mm of Hg

$= 117.5$ mm of Hg

In case of pure A or pure B the mole fraction of other component will be zero, then

For pure A; $x_A = 1, x_B = 0$

$\therefore P_A = (110 \times 1 + 125 \times 0)$ mm of Hg

$= (110 + 0)$ mm of Hg

$= 110$ mm of Hg

Similarly, $P^\circ_B = 125$ mm of Hg $[x_B = 1, x_A = 0]$

From the above calculations it is clear that

when $n_A = n_B : P_s < P^\circ_B$ $[P_S = 117.5$ mm and

$P^\circ_B = 125$ mm$]$

$n_A = n_B : P_S > P^\circ_A$ $[P_S = 117.5$ mm

and $P^\circ_A = 110$ mm$]$

Also $P^\circ_A = 110$ mm of Hg and $P^\circ_B = 125$ mm of Hg

Statement (d) is incorrect.

8. **(a, b, c)**

Since the solute X behaves as univalent electrolyte in solution, so for this solute, $i = 2$

Since the solute Y dimerises in solution, so for this

solute $i = \dfrac{1}{2}$

We know that

b.p. $\propto i$, $\therefore$ b.p. of X will be greater than that of Y

Osmotic pressure $\propto i$, $\therefore$ O.P. of $X >$ O.P. of Y

Freezing point $\propto \dfrac{1}{i}$; $\therefore$ f.p. of $X <$ f.p. of Y

and relative lowering of V.P. i.e. $\dfrac{\Delta P}{P^\circ} \propto i$

$\therefore \left(\dfrac{\Delta P}{P^\circ}\right)_X > \left(\dfrac{\Delta P}{P^\circ}\right)_Y$

Thus statement (d) is incorrect. All other statements are correct.

9. **(b, c)** Vapour pressure of solution containing non-volatile solute is always smaller than that of solvent. Points a and b represent the boiling points of solvent and solution respectively (temperatures at which their V.P. = 1 atm each). Hence gap $ab = K_b m =$ elevation of boiling point.

10. **(b)** $P_{Total} = X_A p^\circ_A + X_B p^\circ_B = X_A p^\circ_A + (1 - X_A) p^\circ_B$

$= p^\circ_B + (p^\circ_A - p^\circ_B) X_A$

11. **(2)** Let x g be the mass of element in 51.0 g of saturated solution.

Mass of benzene in 51.0 g of saturated solution
$= 51.0 - x$ g

Total mass of benzene containing x g of solute $= 50 + 51 - x = (101 - x)$ g

$\Delta T_f = \dfrac{1000 K_f W_B}{M_B W_A} = \dfrac{1000 \times 5.5 \times x}{4 \times 25 \times (101 - x)} = 0.55$ (given)

$\Rightarrow x = 1.0$g

Hence, solubility $= \dfrac{W_B \times 100}{W_A} = \dfrac{1}{(51-1)} \times 100 = 2.0$ g

12. **(2)** $\Delta T = i K_f m$

$(273 - 269.28) = i \times 1.86 \times 1$

$3.72 = i \times 1.86$

$i = 2$

$\alpha = \dfrac{i-1}{n-1} ; (\alpha = 100\% = 1)$

$1 = \dfrac{2-1}{n-1} \Rightarrow n = 2$

13. **(2)** Let $\pi_1 = 200$ mm; $T_1 = 283$

$\pi_2 = 105.3$; $T_2 = 298$

Now, $\pi = \dfrac{n}{V} RT$

At $T_1, 200 = \dfrac{n}{V_1} R \times 283$

At $T_2, 105.3 = \dfrac{n}{V_2} \times R \times 298$

Dividing Eq. (i) by Eq. (ii), we get

$\dfrac{200}{105.3} = \dfrac{V_2}{V_1} \times \dfrac{283}{298} \Rightarrow V_2 = 2V_1$

14. **(4)** $\pi = CRT = \dfrac{\left(\dfrac{W_2}{Mw_2}\right) RT}{V}$

Given $W_2 = 40$ g

$Mw_2 = 246$

$T = 27°C = 300\,K$

$V = 1\,L$

Substituting all the values, we get

$$\pi = \frac{40}{246} \times 0.082 \times 300 = 4\ \text{atm}$$

15. (d) Molality of water in ethanol $= \dfrac{0.1 \times 1000}{0.9 \times 46} = 2.41$

$\Delta T_f = K_f m = 2.0 \times 2.41 = 4.82\,K;$

Hence, freezing point $= 150.7 - 4.82 = 150.9\,K$

16. (a) Vapour pressure of solution $= X_A P^o_A + X_B P^o_B$

$= 0.9 \times 40 + 0.1 \times 32.8 = 39.3\ \text{torr}$

17. (b) From the given data, we have

$w = 0.5 \times 10^{-3}\,kg$ [0.5 % solution]

$W = 100 \times 10^{-3}\,kg$

           [solvent in water, density $= 1\ g/km^3$]

$\Delta T_f = 273 - 272.76 = 0.24$

$K_f = 1.86\,K\,kg\,mol^{-1}$

$$\therefore M = \frac{1000 \times K_f \times w}{\Delta T_f \times W}$$

$$= \frac{1000 \times 1.86 \times 0.5 \times 10^{-3}}{0.24 \times 100 \times 10^{-3}} = 38.76$$

$\therefore$ The apparent molecular weight of KCl $= 38.76$

The molar mass of KCl $= 39 + 35.5 = 74.5$

$$\therefore i = \frac{\text{Normal molecular weight}}{\text{Apparent molecular weight}}$$

$$= \frac{74.5}{38.76} = 1.92 \approx 2$$

18. (c) In solution KCl dissociates as follows

$$KCl \rightleftharpoons K^+ + Cl^-$$

If α is degree of dissociation, then

$$KCl \rightleftharpoons K^+ + Cl^-$$

$(1-\alpha)$ α α

The number of effective particles is $1 - \alpha + \alpha + \alpha$

$= (1 + \alpha)$

$$\therefore i = \frac{1+\alpha}{1}$$

or $\alpha = i - 1$

$= 1.92 - 1$ $[i = 1.92]$

$= 0.92$ or 92.0%

19. A-s; B-p; C-q; D-r

(A) All gases dissolve in water exothermically with decrease in randomness. Hence $\Delta H < 0$, $\Delta S < 0$.

(B) Since solubility of the given solid in water increases on raising temperature, dissolution is endothermic. Hence $\Delta H > 0$ and $\Delta S > 0$ (Increase in disorder on dissolution).

(C) In a saturated solution, there is no further dissolution of solid. Hence $\Delta H = 0$ and $\Delta m = 0$.

(D) On adding solid to super saturated solution, excess of solid dissolved separates out with the evolution of heat. Hence $\Delta H < 0$ and $\Delta m < 0$.

20. A-r, s; B-p, q; C-r, s; D-p, q

(A) $K_f = \dfrac{RT_f^{o2}}{1000\,L_f} = \dfrac{RT_f^{o2}\,M}{1000\ \Delta H_f}$;

$T_f^{o}(\text{water}) = 273K,\ M = 18$

(B) $K_b = \dfrac{RT_b^{o2}}{1000\,L_v} = \dfrac{RT_b^{o2}\,M}{1000\ \Delta H_f}$

$T_b^{o}\ (\text{water}) = 373\,K,\ M = 18$

(C) $\Delta T_f = K_f \times m = K_f \times \dfrac{9 \times 1000}{180 \times 50} = K_f$

(D) $\Delta T_b = K_b \times m = K_b \times \dfrac{3 \times 1000}{60 \times 50} = K_b$

1. **(c)** $CH_3OH\,(l) + \dfrac{3}{2}O_2\,(g) \rightarrow CO_2\,(g) + 2H_2O\,(l)$

$\Delta G_r = \Delta G_f(CO_2,(g)) + 2\Delta G_f(H_2O,(l)) -$

$$\Delta G_f(CH_3OH,(l)) - \dfrac{3}{2}\Delta G_f(O_2,(g))$$

$= -394.4 + 2(-237.2) - (-166.2) - 0$

$= -394.4 - 474.4 + 166.2 = -702.6\,kJ$

$\%\text{ efficiency} = \dfrac{702.6}{726} \times 100 = 97\%$

2. **(a)** Given for 0.2 M solution

$R = 50\,\Omega$

$\kappa = 1.4\,S\,m^{-1} = 1.4 \times 10^{-2}\,S\,cm^{-1}$

Now, $R = \rho\dfrac{1}{a} = \dfrac{1}{\kappa} \times \dfrac{1}{a}$

$\Rightarrow \dfrac{1}{a} = R \times \kappa = 50 \times 1.4 \times 10^{-2}$

For 0.5 M solution

$R = 280\,\Omega$

$\kappa = ?$

$\dfrac{1}{a} = 50 \times 1.4 \times 10^{-2}$

$\Rightarrow R = \rho\dfrac{1}{a} = \dfrac{1}{\kappa} \times \dfrac{1}{a}$

$\Rightarrow \kappa = \dfrac{1}{280} \times 50 \times 1.4 \times 10^{-2}$

$\qquad = \dfrac{1}{280} \times 70 \times 10^{-2}$

$\qquad = 2.5 \times 10^{-3}\,S\,cm^{-1}$

Now, $\Lambda_m = \dfrac{\kappa \times 1000}{M} = \dfrac{2.5 \times 10^{-3} \times 1000}{0.5}$

$= 5\,S\,cm^2\,mol^{-1} = 5 \times 10^{-4}\,S\,m^2\,mol^{-1}$

3. **(b)** Given

$Fe^{3+} + 3e^- \rightarrow Fe,$

$E^\circ_{Fe^{3+}/Fe} = -0.036\,V \qquad\qquad ...(i)$

$Fe^{2+} + 2e^- \rightarrow Fe,$

$E^\circ_{Fe^{2+}/Fe} = -0.439\,V \qquad\qquad ...(ii)$

we have to calculate

$Fe^{3+} + e^- \rightarrow Fe^{2+},\ \Delta G = ?$

To obtain this equation subtract equ (ii) from (i) we get

$Fe^{3+} + e^- \rightarrow Fe^{2+} \qquad\qquad ...(iii)$

As we know that $\Delta G = -nFE$

Thus for reaction (iii)

$\Delta G = \Delta G_1 - \Delta G_2$

$-nFE^\circ = -nFE_1 - (-nFE_2)$

$-nFE^\circ = nFE_2 - nFE_1$

$-1FE^\circ = 2 \times 0.439\,F - 3 \times 0.036\,F$

$-1\,FE^\circ = 0.770\,F$

$\therefore\ E^\circ = -0.770\,V$

4. **(a)** (i) $Mn^{n+} + ne^- \rightleftharpoons M$, for this reaction, high negative value of E° indicates lower reduction potential, that means M will be a good reducing agent.

> Stronger reducing agent $\Rightarrow$ Easy to oxidise
>
> $\Downarrow$
>
> Lower reduction potential $\Leftarrow$ higher oxidation potential

(ii)

Element	F	Cl	Br	I
Reduction potential (E° volt)	+2.87	+1.36	+1.06	+0.54

As reduction potential decreases from fluorine to iodine, oxidising nature also decreases from fluorine to iodine.

(iii) The size of halide ions increases from F^- to I^-. The bigger ion can loose electron easily. Hence the reducing nature increases from HF to HI.

5. **(c)** According to Faraday's first law of electrolysis

$$W = \dfrac{E \times i \times t}{96500}$$

Where E = equivalent weight

$$= \dfrac{\text{mol. mass of metal}\,(M)}{\text{oxidation state of metal}\,(x)}$$

Substituting the value in the formula

$$W = \dfrac{M}{x} \times \dfrac{i \times t}{96500}$$

or $x = \dfrac{M}{W} \times \dfrac{i \times t}{96500} = \dfrac{10 \times 2 \times 60 \times 60}{96500 \times 0.250} = 3$

$$\left[\text{Given : no. of moles} = \dfrac{M}{W} = 0.250\right]$$

Hence oxidation state of metal is (+3)

6. **(b,c)** Cathode : $Cu^{2+}_{(aq)} + 2e^- \longrightarrow Cu_{(s)}$

1 mole of Cu deposited $\equiv$ 2 mole of electrons

$Hg^{2+}_{2(aq)} + 2e^- \longrightarrow 2Hg_{(l)}$

1 mole of $Hg_{(l)}$ deposited $\equiv$ 1 mole of electrons

Anode (each cell) :

$2H_2O_{(l)} \longrightarrow 4H^+_{(aq)} + O_{2(g)} + 4e^-;$

1 mole of $O_2 \equiv 4$ mole of electrons

7. **(a,c)**

(a) The MnO_4^{2-} is reduced to Mn^{2+}, so it must also be oxidised to Mn^{7+} MnO_4^- since H^+ is already in its maximum oxidation state.

$$5MnO_4^{2-} + 8H^+ \longrightarrow Mn^{2+} + 4MnO_4^- + 4H_2O$$

(c) NO_2 disproportionates to NO and NO_2^+. (Oxidation state of N is +5)

$$3NO_2 + H_2O \longrightarrow NO + 2NO_3^- + 2H^+$$

8. **(a, b, c)** (a) Cell reaction :

$$2H^+(aq) + Zn(s) \longrightarrow H_2(g) + Zn^{2+}(aq)$$

Reaction quotient,

$$Q = \frac{P_{H_2} \times [Zn^{2+}]}{[H^+]^2} = \frac{1 \times 0.01}{(0.1)^2} = 1,\ \log Q = 0$$

(b) Cell reaction :

$$2Ag^+(aq) + Cu(s) \longrightarrow Cu^{2+}(aq) + 2Ag(s)$$

$$Q = \frac{[Cu^{2+}]}{[Ag^+]^2} = \frac{0.25}{(0.5)^2} = 1$$

(c) Cell reaction :

$$2H^+(aq) + Cd(s) \longrightarrow H_2 + Cd^{2+}(aq)$$

$$Q = \frac{P_{H_2} \times [Cd^{2+}]}{[H^+]^2} = \frac{1 \times 0.01}{(0.1)^2} = 1$$

(d) Cell reaction :

$$2H^+(aq) + Zn(s) \longrightarrow H_2 + Zn^{2+}(aq)$$

$$Q = \frac{P_{H_2} \times [Zn^{2+}]}{[H^+]^2} = \frac{1 \times 0.1}{(0.1)^2} = 10$$

9. **(b,d)** It is the concentration cell in respect to Ag^+ ions.

Hence, $E_{cell} = 0.0592 \log \dfrac{[Ag^+]_2}{[Ag^+]_1}$

$$K_{sp}(Ag_2C_2O_4) = [Ag^+]_2^2 [C_2O_4^{2-}]$$

$$= [Ag^-]_2^2 \times \frac{[Ag^+]_2}{2}$$

or $\quad [Ag^+]_2 = \left[2K_{sp}(Ag_2C_2O_4)\right]^{1/3}$

$$K_{sp}(AgI) = [Ag^+]_1 [I^-]$$

$$= [Ag^+]_1^2$$

or $\quad [Ag^+]_1 = [K_{sp}(AgI)]^{1/2}$

10. **(5)** Let x mole of O_2 is liberated and $3x$ mole of $H_2S_2O_8$ is formed. Reactions at cathode (reduction):

$$2H_2O + 2e^- \rightarrow H_2 + 2\overset{\ominus}{O}H$$

Reactions at anode (oxidation):

i. $2H_2O \rightarrow O_2 + 4H^\oplus + 4e^- \begin{bmatrix} 1\ \text{mole}\ O_2 \equiv 4F \\ x\ \text{mole}\ O_2 = 4xF \end{bmatrix}$

ii. $2SO_4^{2-} \rightarrow S_2O_8^{2-} + 2e^- \begin{bmatrix} 1\ \text{mole}\ S_2O_8^{2-} = 2F \\ 3x\ \text{mole}\ S_2O_8^{2-} = 6xF \end{bmatrix}$

Total Faradays at anode $= (4x + 6x)\,F = 10x\,F$.

Total Faradays at cathode $= 2F \equiv 1$ mole H_2.

$10x\,F \equiv$ Total Faradays at cathode $=$ Total Faradays at anode

$\because$ 2 F at cathode $\equiv 1$ mole of H_2.

$$10xF \text{ at cathode } \equiv \frac{1}{2F} \times 10xF = 5x \text{ mole of } H_2 .$$

$$\text{Ratio} = \frac{\text{Moles of } H_2 \text{ at cathode}}{\text{Moles of } H_2S_2O_8 \text{ at anode}} = \frac{5x}{3x} = \frac{5}{3}$$

Number of moles of $H_2 = 3 \times \dfrac{5}{3} = 5$

Alternatively

Molar ratio of $H_2S_2O_8\quad :\quad O_2$
$\qquad\quad$ (n factor = 2)$\qquad$ (n factor = 4)
$\qquad\qquad\qquad = 3 : 1$

Equivalent ratio $= 3 \times 2 : 1 \times 4 = 6 : 4$

Total equivalent of $H_2S_2O_8$ and O_2 at anode $= 6 + 4$
$\qquad\qquad\qquad\qquad\qquad\qquad\qquad = 10$ Eq.

So total equivalent of H_2 at cathode $= 10$

$\therefore$ moles of H_2 (n factor = 2) $= \dfrac{10}{2} = 5$ moles

11. **(3)** Balance the equation.

$$15H_2O + 3CN^- \longrightarrow 3CO_2 + 3NO_3^- + 3OH^+ + 30e^-$$

$\therefore$ Number of e^-s $= \dfrac{30}{10} = 3$

12. **(3)** Discharging reaction:

$$PbO_2 + 4H^+ + SO_4^{2-} + 2e^- \rightleftharpoons PbSO_4 + 2H_2O$$

$$M_1 = \frac{\% \text{ by weight} \times 10 \times d}{Mw_2} = \frac{40 \times 1.225 \times 10}{98} = 5\ M$$

$$M_2 = \frac{\% \text{ by weight} \times 10 \times d}{Mw_2} = \frac{20 \times 10 \times 0.98}{98} = 2\ M$$

Change is molarities $= M_1 - M_2 = 5 - 2 = 3\ M$

13. **(6)** Let $x\,\%$ is the current efficiency of $KClO_3 = $ Number of Faradays.

$$\frac{10g}{122.5/6} = \frac{2 \times x \times 10.941 \times 3600}{100 \times 96500}$$

$\therefore x = 60\%$

$\therefore\quad \dfrac{\text{Percentage current efficiency}}{10} = \dfrac{60}{10} = 6$

14. (6) Statement (a), (b) and (c) are correct.

Hence, total score $= 1 + 2 + 3 = 6$.

Statement (a) : pH $= 0$, means $[H^+] = 1$ M

E°_{red} of $MnO_4^- \mid Mn^{2+} > E^-_{red}$ of $Fe^{3+} \mid Fe^{2+}$

So MnO_4^- will undergo reduction and acts as strong oxidant whereas Fe^{2+} undergoes oxidation. Statement (a) is correct.

Statement (b): MnO_4^- titrations in the presence of HCl are unsatisfactory since Cl^- is oxidized to Cl_2. Statement (b) is correct.

Statement (c):

Since $E^{\circ}_{red\ Ce^{4+} \mid Ce^{3+}} > E^{\circ}_{red\ MnO_4^- \mid Mn^{2+}}$. So Ce^{4+} will reduce to Ce^{3+} . So MnO_4^- cannot oxidize Ce^{3+} to Ce^{4+}. Statement (c) is correct.

Statement (d): Fe^{2+} can be titrated against $KMnO_4$ in acid medium ($[H^+] = 1$ M).

Since $E^{\circ}_{red\ MnO_4^- \mid Mn^{2+}} > E^{\circ}_{red\ Fe^{3+} \mid Fe^{2+}}$

So Fe^{2+} can be oxidized to Fe^{3+} by MnO_4^- .

But Ce^{3+} will not be oxidized to Ce^{4+}.

Since $E^{\circ}_{red\ Ce^{4+} \mid Ce^{3+}} > E^{\circ}_{red\ MnO_4^- \mid Mn^{2+}}$

So, statement (d) is wrong.

15. (b) $E_{cell} = -\dfrac{0.059}{1} \log \dfrac{\left[H^+\right]_a}{\left[H^+\right]_c}$

$\qquad = -0.059(pH_c - pH_a)$

$\qquad = -0.059(6-3) = -0.177$ V

$\because E_{cell}$ is $-$ve, so reaction is Non-spontaneous.

16. (a) $E_{cell} = E_{(Q,2H^+ \mid H_2O)} - E_{SCE}$

Where,

$E_{(Q,2H^+/H_2O)} = E^{\circ}_{(Q,2H^+/H_2O)} - 0.059$ pH

$\therefore\ E_{cell} = \left[(E^{\circ}_{(Q,2H^+/H_2O)} - 0.059\ \text{pH}) - E_{SCE} \right]$

$\qquad = (0.7 - 0.059\,\text{pH}) - (0.24\,\text{V})$

$\qquad = (0.7 - 0.059 \times 10) - (0.24\,\text{V}) = -0.13$ V

$\because\ E_{cell}$ is $-$ve, so reaction is endergonic (i.e $\Delta G = +$ve)

17. (b) $E_{cell} = E^{\circ} - 0.059\,\text{pH}$

$\qquad = 0.7 - 0.059 \times 2 = 0.582$ V

Since E_{cell} is $+$ve, so reaction is exergonic (i.e. $\Delta G = -$Ve)

18. (c) The cell reactions for the passage of 2 Faradays, are

(1) $Pb(s) + 2AgCl(s) \rightarrow PbCl_2(s) + 2Ag(s)$; $\Delta H_1 = ?$

(2) $Pb(s) + 2AgI(s) \rightarrow PbI_2(s) + 2Ag(s)$; $\Delta H_2 = ?$

(1) $-$ (2) gives

$\qquad PbI_2(s) + 2AgCl(s) \rightarrow PbCl_2(s) + 2AgI(s)$

$\qquad \Delta H = \Delta H_1 - \Delta H_2$

$\Delta H_1 = nF\left[T\left(\dfrac{\partial E_1}{\partial T}\right) - E_1 \right]$

$\qquad = \dfrac{2 \times 96500 \left[298 \times (-0.000186) - 0.4902 \right]}{4.18}$

$\qquad = -25183$ cal

$\Delta H_2 = nF\left[T\left(\dfrac{\partial E_2}{\partial T}\right) - E_2 \right]$

$\qquad = \dfrac{2 \times 96500 \left[298(-0.000127) - 0.2111 \right]}{4.18}$

$\qquad = -11489$ cal

Hence, $\Delta H = \Delta H_1 - \Delta H_2 = -25183 - (-11489)$ cal

$\qquad = -13694$ cal.

19. (a) The reaction in Daniel's cell is

$Cu^{2+}(aq) + Zn(s) \rightarrow Cu(s) + Zn^{2+}(aq)$ $(n = 2)$

Heat of the reaction may be expressed as

$\Delta H = nF\left[T\left(\dfrac{\partial E}{\partial T}\right)_P - E \right]$

$\qquad = 2 \times 96500 \left[\dfrac{288 \times \left(-4.28 \times 10^{-4}\right) - 1.0934}{4.18} \right]$

$\qquad = -56187$ cal

20. **A-s; B-r; C-p; D-q**

(A) $2H^+ + 2e^- \longrightarrow H_2$

$E_{H^+/H_2} = E^{\circ} - \dfrac{0.0591}{2} \log \dfrac{P_{H_2}}{[H^+]^2}$

$\qquad = 0 - \dfrac{0.0591}{2} \log \dfrac{1}{[H^+]^2} = 0.0591 \log[H^+]$

Since maximum activity of $H^+ = 1$, So $E_{H^+/H_2} = 0$

(B) $[H^+]_{minimum} = 10^{-14}$ M ;

$E_{minimum} = 0.0591 \log 10^{-14} = -0.0591 \times (-14)$

$\qquad = -0.827$ V

(C) For KCl(aq) $[1M]$, pH $= 7$ $[H^+] = 10^{-7}$ M

Hence, $E = 0.0591 \log 10^{-7} = 0.0591 \times (-7)$

$\qquad = -0.414$ V

(D) $E = -\dfrac{0.0591}{2} \log \dfrac{P_{H_2}}{[H^+]^2}$

$\qquad = \dfrac{-0.0591}{2} \log \dfrac{4}{1^2} = -0.0591 \log 2$

$\qquad = -0.0591 \times 0.301 = -0.018$ V

1. (d) $\text{Rate}_1 = k[A]^n [B]^m$

$$\text{Rate}_2 = k[2A]^n \left[\frac{1}{2}B\right]^m$$

$$\therefore \frac{\text{Rate}_2}{\text{Rate}_1} = \frac{k[2A]^n \left[\frac{1}{2}B\right]^m}{k[A]^n [B]^m} = (2)^n \left(\frac{1}{2}\right)^m$$

$$= 2^n \cdot (2)^{-m} = 2^{n-m}$$

2. (b) According to Arrhenius equation

$$\log \frac{k_2}{k_1} = \frac{E_a}{2.303R} \left(\frac{1}{T_1} - \frac{1}{T_2}\right)$$

$$\log \frac{1.3 \times 10^{-3}}{1.3 \times 10^{-4}} = \frac{E_a}{2.303 \times 8.314} \left[\frac{1}{373} - \frac{1}{423}\right]$$

$$1 = \frac{E_a}{2.303 \times 8.314} \left[\frac{1}{373} - \frac{1}{423}\right]$$

$$E_a = 60 \text{ kJ/mol}$$

3. (b) $T_2 = T$(say), $T_1 = 25°C = 298K$,
$E_a = 104.4 \text{ kJ mol}^{-1} = 104.4 \times 10^3 \text{ J mol}^{-1}$
$k_1 = 3 \times 10^{-4}, k_2 = ?,$

$$\log \frac{k_2}{k_1} = \frac{E_a}{2.303R} \left[\frac{1}{T_1} - \frac{1}{T_2}\right]$$

$$\log \frac{k_2}{3 \times 10^{-4}} = \frac{104.4 \times 10^3 \text{ J mol}^{-1}}{2.303 \times (8.314 \text{ J K}^{-1}\text{mol}^{-1})} \left[\frac{1}{298} - \frac{1}{T}\right]$$

As $T \to \infty, \dfrac{1}{T} \to 0$

$$\therefore \log \frac{k_2}{3 \times 10^{-4}} = \frac{104.4 \times 10^3 \text{ J mol}^{-1}}{2.303 \times 8.314 \times 298}$$

$$\log \frac{k_2}{3 \times 10^{-4}} = 18.297, \frac{k_2}{3 \times 10^{-4}} = 1.98 \times 10^{18}$$

$$k_2 = (1.98 \times 10^{18}) \times (3 \times 10^{-4}) = 6 \times 10^{14} \text{s}^{-1}$$

4. (d) Let rate of reaction $= \dfrac{d[C]}{dt} = k[A]^x [B]^y$

Now from the given data
$1.2 \times 10^{-3} = k[0.1]^x[0.1]^y$ .....(i)
$1.2 \times 10^{-3} = k[0.1]^x[0.2]^y$ .....(ii)
$2.4 \times 10^{-3} = k[0.2]^x[0.1]^y$ .....(iii)
Dividing equation (i) by (ii)

$$\Rightarrow \frac{1.2 \times 10^{-3}}{1.2 \times 10^{-3}} = \frac{k[0.1]^x[0.1]^y}{k[0.1]^x[0.2]^y}$$

We find, $y = 0$
Now dividing equation (i) by (iii)

$$\Rightarrow \frac{1.2 \times 10^{-3}}{2.4 \times 10^{-3}} = \frac{k[0.1]^x[0.1]^y}{k[0.2]^x[0.1]^y}$$

We find, $x = 1$

Hence $\dfrac{d[C]}{dt} = k[A]^1[B]^0$

5. (d) From 1st and 2nd sets of data - no change in rate is observed with the change in concentration of 'C'. So the order with respect to 'C' is zero.
From 1st and 4th sets of data
Dividing eq. (4) by eq. (1)

$$\frac{1.25 \times 10^{-3}}{5.0 \times 10^{-3}} = \left[\frac{0.005}{0.010}\right]^x$$

or $0.25 = (0.5)^x$ or $(0.5)^2 = (0.5)^x$
$\therefore x = 2$
The order with respect to 'A' is 2 from the 1st and 3rd sets of data Dividing eq. (1) by eq. (3)

$$\frac{5.0 \times 10^{-3}}{1.0 \times 10^{-2}} = \left[\frac{0.005}{0.010}\right]^y$$

or $(0.5)^1 = (0.5)^y \Rightarrow y = 1$
The order with respect to 'B' is 1
So the order with respective the reactants A, B and C is 2, 1 and 0.

6. (a,c) In acid catalysed reaction, the rate constant is directly proportional to the extent of ionization of the acid and hence the strength of the acid.
Relative strength of (I)HX and (II)HY

$$= \frac{\alpha_I}{\alpha_{II}} = \frac{k_I}{k_{II}} = \frac{3 \times 10^{-3}}{5 \times 10^{-3}} = 0.6$$

7. (a,b,c) Since $t_{1/2}$ is independent of initial concentration of sugar, the reaction is first order w.r.t. sugar. The rate increases ten fold on increasing H^+ ion concentration 10 times (decreasing pH by unity), the reaction is also first order in H^+ ion.
Since $[H^+]$ in a particular run remains constant (H^+ ion being catalyst), the rate is independent of $[H^+]$.
Hence, rate $= k[\text{sugar}]$ (Pseudo first order reaction).

8. (b,c,d) On doubling the volume of the vessel, all the concentrations are halved at that moment.

$$\frac{(\text{Rate})_2}{(\text{Rate})_1} = \frac{k\left(\frac{[A]}{2}\right)^2 \left(\frac{[B]}{2}\right)}{k[A]^2[B]} = \frac{1}{8}$$

9. (b) In more than one reactant system, the half-life time $(t_{1/2})$ is the time for half of the reactant present in small amount.

For set (1) and (2), B is in small amount and according to rate law, the reaction is of first order w.r.t B. So in these sets the half-life is independent of initial concentration and so the $t_{1/2}$ for set (2) will be same as that for set (1) i.e. 62.6 sec.

In set (3) and (4), A is present in small quantity and $t_{1/2}$ will depend on $[A]$. According to rate law expression the order w.r.t. A is 2.

$$\therefore t_{1/2} = \frac{1}{k.a} = \frac{1}{k[A]_0} \quad \text{or} \quad \frac{(t_{1/2})_3}{(t_{1/2})_4} = \frac{[A_0]_4}{[A_0]_3}$$

$$\text{or} \quad \frac{625}{(t_{1/2})_4} = \frac{10}{5} \text{ or } 2$$

$$\therefore (t_{1/2})_4 = \frac{625}{2} = 312.5 \text{ sec.}$$

i.e. $y = 312.5$ sec.

10. (9) $k = \dfrac{0.693}{15 \text{ hr}} = 0.0462 \text{ hr}^{-1}$

$$k = \frac{2.3}{14 \times 24 \text{ hr}} \log \frac{c_0}{c_t}$$

$$0.0462 \text{ hr}^{-1} = \frac{2.3}{14 \times 24 \text{ hr}} \log \frac{1\text{Ci}}{c_t}$$

Solve for c_t:

$\therefore c_t = 1.82 \times 10^{-7} \text{ Ci} \approx 0.18 \,\mu\text{Ci} = 0.02x \,\mu\text{Ci}$

$\therefore x = 9$

11. (5) $\dfrac{-d[RX]}{dt} = k_2[RX][\overset{\ominus}{OH}]$ (by S_N2 path way)

k_2 = rate constant of S_N2 reaction

$\dfrac{-d[RX]}{dt} = k_1[RX]$ (by S_N1 path way)

k_1 = rate constant of S_N1 reaction

$$\frac{-d[RX]}{dt} = k_2[RX][\overset{\ominus}{OH}] + k_1[RX]$$

$$-\frac{1}{[RX]}\frac{d[RX]}{dt} = k_2[\overset{\ominus}{OH}] + k_1$$

This is the equation of a straight line for $-\dfrac{1}{[RX]}\dfrac{d[RX]}{dt}$

vs $[\overset{\ominus}{OH}]$ plot with slope equal to k_2 and inercept equal to k_1.

From questions:

$k_2 = 2 \times 10^3 \text{ mol}^{-1} \text{ L hr}^{-1}, k_1 = 1 \times 10^2 \text{ hr}^{-1}$

$[RX] = 1.0 \text{ M and } [\overset{\ominus}{OH}] = 0.1 \text{ M}$

Hence,

$$\frac{d[RX]}{dt} = 2 \times 10^3 \times 1 \times 0.1 + 1 \times 10^2 \times 1$$

$$= 300 \text{ mol L}^{-1} \text{ hr}^{-1}$$
$$= 5 \text{ mol L}^{-1} \text{ min}^{-1}$$

12. (4) $t_{1/2} = \dfrac{0.0693}{k_1}$

Also, $t_{93.75} = \dfrac{2.303}{k_1} \log \dfrac{100}{100 - 93.75}$

$$= \frac{2.303}{k_1} \log \frac{100}{6.25}$$

$$= \frac{2.303}{k_1} \log 2^4$$

$$= \frac{4 \times 2.303 \times \log 2}{k_1} = \frac{4 \times 0.693}{k_1} = 4t_{1/2}$$

13. (5) For second order reaction:

$[R]_{initial} = 0.08, \text{M}; [R]_{final} = 0.01 \text{ M}$

$x = 0.08 - 0.01 = 0.07 \text{ M}$

$\therefore (a - x) = 0.08 - 0.07 = 0.01 \text{ M}$

$$k_2 = \frac{1}{t}.\frac{x}{a(a-x)}$$

$$k_2 = \frac{1}{70 \text{ min}} \times \frac{0.07 \text{ M}}{0.08 \text{M} \times 0.01 \text{M}} \qquad \text{...(i)}$$

Now, time required to become concentration = 0.04 M. i.e., $x = 0.04 \text{ M}$

$$k_2 = \frac{1}{t} \times \frac{0.04 \text{ M}}{0.08 \text{M} \times (0.08 - 0.04)\text{M}} \qquad \text{...(ii)}$$

From Eqs. (i) and (ii)

$$\frac{0.07}{70 \times 0.08 \times 0.01} = \frac{0.04}{t \times 0.08 \times 0.04}$$

$t = 10 \text{ min} = 2x \text{ min}$

$\therefore x = 5 \text{ min}$

14. (1) Rate $= k[a]^n$

Case I: $r_1 = k\left[\dfrac{a}{V}\right]^n$ ... (i)

Case II: $\dfrac{r_1}{2} = k\left[\dfrac{a}{2V}\right]^n$ ... (ii)

By Eqs. (i) and (ii),

$(2)^1 = (2)^n$

$\therefore n = 1$

15. (c)   **16. (a)**   **17. (c)**

18. (c) The concentration of A falls exponentially, whereas the amount of C will rise until it approaches that of A (not of B), thus (a) is incorrect.

The concentration of B will first increase and then it will decrease showing a maxima. (see figure below).

Thus (b) is incorrect and (c) is correct.

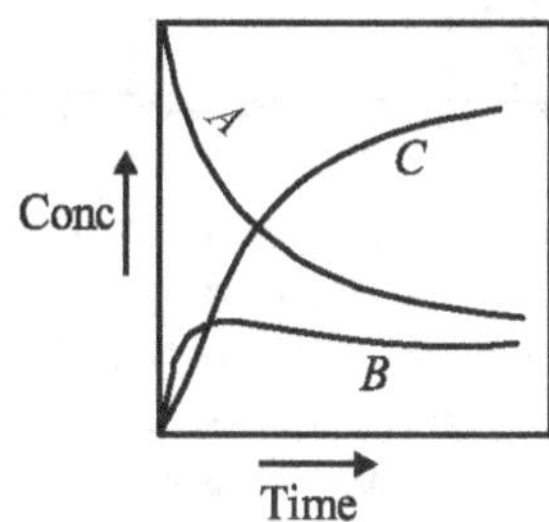

19. (a) We have
$$C_0 = C_1 + C_2 + C_3$$
The rate of disappearance of A is

$$-\frac{dC_1}{dt} = k_1 C_1 \qquad \qquad ...(i)$$

Rearranging and integrating the above equation

$$C_1 = C_0 e^{-k_1 t}$$

Since rate of formation of B is given by $k_1.C_1$ and the rate of decomposition of B into C is given by $k_2.C_2$, the rate at which B accumulates in the system is given by

$$\frac{dC_2}{dt} = k_1 C_1 - k_2 C_2$$

or $\qquad \dfrac{dC_2}{dt} + k_2 C_1 = k_1 C_1$

Putting the values of C_1 from equation (i)

$$\frac{dC_2}{dt} + k_2 C_2 = k_1.C_0.e^{-k_1 t}$$

Multiplying both sides by $e^{k_2 t}$, we get

$$e^{k_2 t}.\frac{dC_2}{dt} + e^{k_2 t} k_2 C_2 = k_1.C_0.e^{(k_2 - k_1)t}$$

On integration under the condition, $t = 0$ at $C_2 = 0$

$$C_2 = \frac{k_1 C_0}{k_2 - k_1}[e^{-k_1 t} - e^{-k_2 t}]$$

From this equation values of k_1 and k_2 can be determined.

20. A - s; B - r; C - q; D - p

(A) 2 moles of gaseous reactant gives 5 moles of gaseous products. Hence, pressure of the reaction system at constant volume and temperature will increase with the progress of the reaction.

(B) With the progress of the reaction, more and more CH_3COOH will be formed and total acid concentration would increase as the reaction proceeds. Hence, kinetics can be followed by titrimetric method.

(C) Volume of N_2 gas (at constant temperature and pressure) will increase with the progress of the reaction.

(D) Dextro rotatory sucrose on hydrolysis gives laevo rotatory equimolar mixture of glucose and fructose. Hence, measurement of optical rotation of the reaction mixture can be used to study the kinetics of the reaction. Optical rotation would decrease with time.

1. **(d)** A negative ion causes the precipitation of positively charged sol and *vice-versa*. Since As_2S_3 is a negative sol so more will be the positive charge on cation more effective it will be in causing coagulation of As_2S_3 sol. Among the given ions, Al^{3+} has the greatest valency and thus is the most effective coagulating agent.

2. **(d)** $FeCl_3 + 3NaOH \longrightarrow Fe(OH)_3(s) + 3NaCl$

$Fe(OH)_3 + OH^-$ (from excess of NaOH)

$\longrightarrow [Fe(OH)_3]OH^-$

The sol is negatively charged and would be coagulated most effectively by Al^{3+}.

3. **(d)** Gold number $= \dfrac{6.0 \times 10^{-5} \times 10^3 \,(mg) \times 10}{20} = 0.03$

4. **(c)** Sols of Al_2O_3 and even inorganic lyophilic sols e.g. silica, stannic oxide show no difference in surface tension as compared to water.

If protein is dissolved in water it will lower the surface tension to some extent.

5. **(a)** Particle size of colloidal particle $= 1m\mu$ to $100\,m\mu$

(suppose $10\,m\mu$)

$$V_C = \frac{4}{3}\pi r^3 = V_C = \frac{4}{3}\pi(10)^3$$

Particle size of true solution particle $= 1m\mu$

$$V_S = \frac{4}{3}\pi(1)^3$$

Hence $\dfrac{V_C}{V_S} = 10^3$

6. **(c)** Freundlich adsorption isotherm gives straight line on plotting log x/m vs log p as show below.

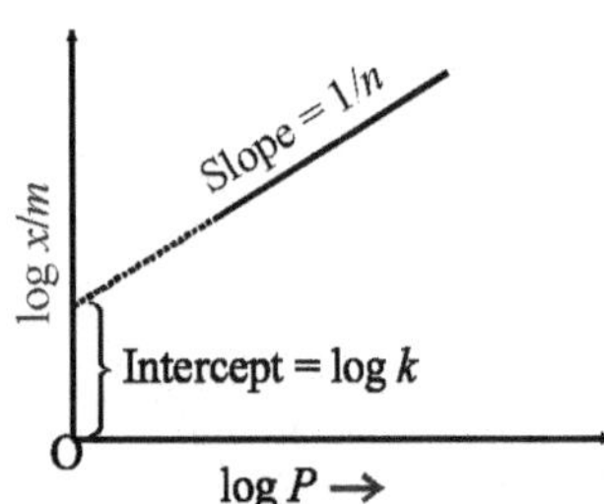

7. **(a, b, d)** At pH < isoelectric pH, $-NH_2$ group is protonated to $-\overset{+}{N}H_3$ and the sol is positively charged. At pH > isoelectric pH, $-COOH$ is deprotonated to $-COO^-$ and the sol is negatively charged. At isoelectric pH both groups are equally ionised, the sol particles carry no net charge.

8. **(a, d)** If a univalent ion is used for coagulating a hydrophilic sol, the coagulating power increases with increasing dilution of the sol. But if a polyvalent ion is used, the coagulating power decreases with increasing dilution of the sol.

9. **(a, b)** The solutions of colloidal electrolytes have lower osmotic pressure than expected because the number of particles decreases due to association or aggregation of several ions to form micelles. Colloidal electrolytes can not be regarded as macro-molecules, as they are individual molecules of very big size in solution.

10. **(a, c)**

(a) $\Delta G = \Delta H - T\Delta S < 0$ as $\Delta S < 0$, so ΔH has to be negative

(b) micelles formation will take place above T_k and above CMC

(c) this solution will be negatively charged.

(d) Fe^{3+} ions will have greater flocculatibility power so smaller flocculating value.

11. **(4)** 2 mL of 1 M NaCl contains $NaCl = \dfrac{2}{1000} = 2$ m mole

Thus 500 mL of As_2S_3 sol require NaCl for complete coagulation = 2 m mole

Hence 1 L, i.e., 1000 mL of the sol require NaCl for complete coagulation = 4 m mole

Therefore, flocculation value of NaCl = 4.

12. **(1)** Gold number of gelatin = 0.01

or 0.01 mg gelatin required to be added to 10 mL of gold sol to completely prevent coagulation of 1 mL of 10% NaCl solution.

Therefore, gelatin added to 1000 mL of gold sol to prevent coagulation $= \dfrac{0.01 \times 1000}{10} = 1$ mg

13. **(4)** Mass of HCl acid adsorbed by 10 g charcoal

$= 526.3 \times 10^{-3}\,(0.5 - 0.4) \times 38 \approx 2$

(Mw of HCl = 38 g mol^{-1})

The amount of adsorption

$$\frac{x}{m} = \frac{2}{0.5} = 4$$

14. **(6)** $\log\dfrac{x}{m} = \log K + \dfrac{1}{n}\log P$

$\therefore$ Plot of $\log\dfrac{x}{m}$ versus log P is linear with slope

$= \dfrac{1}{n}$ and intercept $= \log K$

Thus $\dfrac{1}{n} = \tan\theta = \tan 45° = 1$ or $n = 1$

$\log K = 0.301$ or $K = $ antilog $0.301 = 2$

At $P = 3$ atm

$$\dfrac{x}{m} = KP^{1/n} = 2 \times (3)^1 = 6$$

15. **(c)** As_2S_3 sol is negatively charged due to preferential adsorption of S^{2-} ions by As_2S_3 particles. Hence, cation of largest valence would be most effective in causing coagulation of the sol.

   Coagulating value of Ba^{2+} ion $= \dfrac{1.0 \times 10^{-4} \times 10^3}{9+1}$

   $= 1.0 \times 10^{-2}$ mol $L^{-1} = 10.0$ m mol L^{-1}

16. **(c)** Both KCl and RCOOK (Potassium oleate) are 1 : 1 electrolytes (salts) and are expected to have a van't Hoff factor $i = 2$. But in potassium oleate solution, the oleate ions, being ampiphilic in nature, associate to give much bigger particles (micelles). As a result the concentration of particles in this solution is very much decreased and so also the colligative properties.

17. **(d)** $SnO_2 + 2NaOH \rightarrow Na_2SnO_3$

   SnO_2 particles adsorb SnO_3^{2-} ions preferrentially, and acquire negative charge. Hence cation of maximum valence would be most effective in bringing about coagulation.

18. **(c)** Sodium oleate (soap) is a hydrophilic sol. Sol particles are heavily hydrated. For coagulation, both removal of charge and solvation have to be effected.

19. **A $\rightarrow$ q ; B $\rightarrow$ r; C $\rightarrow$ s; D $\rightarrow$ p**
   $FeCl_3 + NaOH$ forms $Fe(OH)_3 : OH^-$
   colloidal particles in the sol.

20. **A $\rightarrow$ s ; B $\rightarrow$ r; C $\rightarrow$ p; D $\rightarrow$ q**
   Dialysis is used for purification, peptisation is used for colloidal sol formation, emulsification helps in cleansing action of soap and electrophoresis leads to coagulation of sol.

1. **(c)** The reduction of metal sulphides by carbon reduction process is not spontaneous because ΔG for such a process is positive. The reduction of metal oxide by carbon reduction process is spontaneous as ΔG for such a process is negative.

On thermodynamic considerations, CO_2 is more stable than CS_2 and the metal sulphides are more stable than corresponding oxides.

In view of above the factor listed in choice (c) is incorrect and so is of no significance.

2. **(a)** Fused alumina (Al_2O_3) is a bad conductor of electricity. Therefore, cryolite (Na_3AlF_6) and fluorspar (CaF_2) are added to purified alumina which not only make alumina a good conductor of electricity but also reduce the melting point of the mixture to around 1140 K.

3. **(d)** Calcination is a process of heating a substance to a high temperature but below the melting or fusion point, causing loss of moisture, reduction or oxidation and dissociation into simpler substances.

4. **(a)** The conversion of metal sulphide to metal oxide involves the process of **roasting** (i.e., x is roasting). The metal oxides can then be converted to impure metal by reduction. Of the given choices in (a) and (b) the reduction process is that of **smelting**. (i.e., 'y' is smelting)

The conversion of impure metal to pure metal involves a process of purification. Thus it is electrolysis (z).

5. **(d)** (A) $Cr_2O_3 + 2Al \xrightarrow{-3} Al_2O_3 + 2Cr$

(B) $2FeS + 3O_2 \rightarrow 2FeO + 2SO_2 \uparrow$

$FeO + SiO_2 \rightarrow \underset{\text{(Slag)}}{FeSiO_3}$

(C) Statement is true

(D) $Ag_2S + 4NaCN \xrightarrow{O_2} 2Na[Ag(CN)_2] + Na_2S$

$2Na[Ag(CN)_2] + Zn \longrightarrow Na_2[Zn(CN)_4] + 2Ag$

6. **(a, b)** $2Au + 4CN^- + H_2O + \dfrac{1}{2}O_2 \longrightarrow$

$\qquad\qquad\qquad 2[Au(CN)_2]^- + 2OH^-$

$2[Au(CN)_2]^- + Zn \longrightarrow [Zn(CN)_4]^{2-} + 2Au$

7. **(a, c, d)** Mercury does not form amalgam with iron and therefore, it is transported in iron containers.

Free state occurence of metals is called native ore. All minerals are not ores. Combined state occurence of metals is called mineral.

Calcination is done in absence of air. Cassiterite is SnO_2.

8. **(a,b)** Mg and aluminium can be extracted by electrolysis of their fused salts (both are reactive metals). Mg is obtained from fused $MgCl_2$ and aluminium from alumina (Al_2O_3).

9. **(a,b,c)** Reduction during smelting may be carried out by using carbon, aluminium or hydrogen.

10. **(8)** $4Au + 8CN^{\ominus} + 2H_2O + O_2 \rightarrow 4[Au(CN)_2]^- + 4OH^-$

11. **(3)** Galena (PbS), sphalerite (Zn, Fe)S, chalcocite (Cu_2S). Although argentite (Ag_2S) is a sulphide ore, it is not concentrated by froth flotation process since its silver content is low. It is better concentrated by leaching with NaCN.

12. **(6)** Cuprite (Cu_2O), zincite (ZnO_2), haematite (Fe_2O_3), bauxite $(Al_2O_3.2H_2O)$, magnetite (Fe_3O_4) and cassiterite (SnO_2).

13. **(4)** Roasting is heating the ore in presence of O_2. Reactions (i), (ii), (iii) and (iv) can be termed roasting.

14. **(4)** Cassiterite (SnO_2), rutile (TiO_2), magnetite (Fe_3O_4), cinnabar (PbS)

15. **(c)** Glauber's salt - $Na_2SO_4.10H_2O$ - Deliquescent. The Glauber's salt was historically used as laxative. It is effective for the removal of certain drugs such as paracetamol from the body.

16. **(d)** Washing soda - $Na_2CO_3.10H_2O$, efflorescent. Efflorescent is the property of material which means spontaneous loss of water by a hydrated salt.

17. **(b)** Mohr's salt $(FeSO_4.(NH_4)_2SO_4.6H_2O$ is commonly used in iron plating

18. **(b)** Ionisation potential or energy (IE) increases across a period but with certain breaks. IE_1 of Al $(3s^2 p^1)$ is less than IE_1 of Mg $(3s^2)$ as electron is to be removed from 3p which is easy as compared to 3s. Further IE_3 shows the reverse trend because now for Al^{2+} $(3s^1)$ electron is to be removed from 3s as compared to the completely filled 2p orbitals in Mg^{2+}. The same becomes true for IE_2 of Na, hence option (b) is correct. i.e. incorrect statement.

19. (c) Being strong reducing agent, they can not be extracted by reduction of their oxides. Being highly electropositive in nature they can not be displaced from their salt solutions.

Further, on electrolysis of aqueous solution of alkali metal salts (containing metal cation, H^+, OH^- and other anion) the alkali metal cations having higher discharge potential than H^+ and thus do not discharge at cathode. On the contrary it is the H^+ ion which is discharged at cathode to give H_2.

However, electrolysis of fused metal salt, liberates metal at cathode due to discharge of metal cation at cathode.

20. **A-p,r,s; B-s, ; C-q ; D-p,q**

Liquation process : This process is used when the impurity is less fusible than the metal itself (e.g. Pb, Sn etc.)

Cupellation is the oxidation process used for Ag.

Hydrometallurgy : This method is based on the fact that more electropositive metals displace less electropositive metals from their salt solution.

$$4Ag + 8NaCN + O_2(air) + 2H_2O \longrightarrow$$
$$4Na[Ag(CN)_2] + 4NaOH$$

$$AgCl + 2NaCN \longrightarrow Na[Ag(CN)_2] + NaCl ;$$

$$2Na[Ag(CN)_2] + Zn \longrightarrow Na_2[Zn(CN)_4] + 2Ag \downarrow$$

Similarly, copper is precipitated from copper sulphate solution by adding iron.

$$CuSO_4 + Fe \longrightarrow FeSO_4 + Cu \downarrow$$ This method is also called **wet process**.

Ni is purified using CO gas (***Mond's process***). Further, Carbon monoxide reduces the metallic oxides of Pb and Cu to free metals.

$$PbO + CO \longrightarrow Pb + CO_2 ;$$

$$CuO + CO \longrightarrow Cu + CO_2$$

1. **(b)** $\overset{-1}{4KI} + 2CuSO_4 \rightarrow \overset{0}{I_2} + Cu_2I_2 + 2K_2SO_4$

$\overset{0}{I_2} + 2Na_2\overset{2+}{S_2}O_3 \rightarrow Na_2\overset{+2.5}{S_4}O_6 + 2\overset{-1}{NaI}$

Thus, CuI_2 is not formed.

2. **(d)** $XeF_6 + H_2O \xrightarrow{\text{Partial}} XeOF_4 + 2HF$

$XeF_6 + 2H_2O \xrightarrow{\text{Partial}} XeO_2F_2 + 4HF$

$XeF_6 + 3H_2O \xrightarrow{\text{Complete}} XeO_3 + 6HF$

3. **(c)** $\underset{\text{(Yellow powder)}}{S} + 3F_2 \xrightarrow{\text{heat}} \underset{\text{'X'}}{SF_6}$

$3SCl_2 + 4NaF \xrightarrow{\text{heat}} \underset{\text{'Y'}}{SF_4} + S_2Cl_2 + 4NaCl$

[Note : SF_6 and SF_4 consist of sulphur and fluorine]

4. **(b)** $2KI + Cl_2 \rightarrow 2KCl + I_2$

$I_2 + CCl_4 \rightarrow$ Violet Colour

Note: The excess of Cl_2 should be avoided. The layer may become colourless due to conversion of I_2 to HIO_3

$I_2 + 5Cl_2 + 6H_2O \rightarrow 2HIO_3 + 10HCl$

In case of Br_2 : $Br_2 + 2H_2O + Cl_2 \rightarrow 2HBrO + 2HCl$

The layer test is based upon distribution law

5. **(d)** (i) The first ionization energy of xenon $(1,170\,kJ\,mol^{-1})$ is quite close to that of dioxygen $(1,180\,kJ\,mol^{-1})$.
(ii) The molecular diameters of xenon and dioxygen are almost identical.
Based on the above similarities Barlett (who prepared $O_2^+[PtF_6]^-$ compound) suggested that since oxygen combines with PtF_6, so xenon should also form similar compound with PtF_6.

6. **(a, b, c)** Being a basic gas, ammonia will not get dehydrated by conc. H_2SO_4, anhydrous $CaCl_2$ and P_4O_{10} whereas it can directly react with them.

$H_2SO_4 + 2NH_3 \longrightarrow (NH_4)_2SO_4$;

$CaCl_2 + 8NH_3 \longrightarrow CaCl_2.8NH_3$;

$P_4O_{10} + 12NH_3 + 6H_2O \longrightarrow 4(NH_4)_3PO_4$

7. **(a, b, d)** Sodium nitrate on decomposition upto 500°C gives $NaNO_2$ and oxygen.

$2NaNO_3 \xrightarrow{\Delta} 2NaNO_2 + O_2 \uparrow$

While at higher temperature (i.e. above to 800°C), $NaNO_2$ further decomposes into Na_2O, N_2 and O_2.

$2NaNO_2 \xrightarrow{800°C} Na_2O + 3/2O_2 \uparrow + N_2 \uparrow$

8. **(b, d)**

In case of oxy-acids of halogens, acidic strength increases with increase in number of oxygen atom. Thus the correct acidic strength is $HClO < HClO_2 < HClO_3 < HClO_4$.
For the given ions the correct order of oxidising power is $ClO_4^- < BrO_4^- < IO_4^-$

9. **(a, b, c)**

I^- is a strong reducing agent so it gets oxidised by H_2SO_4 (conc.) to I_2.
The products obtained by reduction of H_2SO_4 are SO_2, S and H_2S (compounds of sulphur) and so they act as contaminants for the product.

10. **(6)** There are 6 P–O–P bonds in P_4O_8.

11. **(3)** CrO_3, Mn_2O_7 and SO_2 are acidic oxides.

12. **(2)**

sp^3d with 2 lp

13. **(4)** XeO_4 is sp^3 hybridised.

14. **(3)** In XeF_2

Hence, there are 3 lps in Xe in XeF_2.

15. **(c)** Persulfuric acid (H_2SO_5) is also known as caro's acid

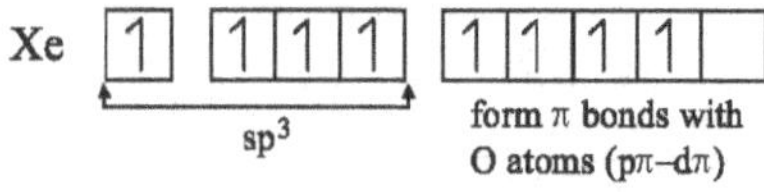

16. **(d)** Peroxydisulfuric acid ($H_2S_2O_8$) is also known as Marshall's acid

$$H-O-\overset{\overset{O}{\underset{\|}{\pi\|\sigma}}}{\underset{\underset{O}{\pi\|\sigma}}{S}}-O-O-\overset{\overset{O}{\underset{\|}{\pi\|\sigma}}}{\underset{\underset{O}{\pi\|\sigma}}{S}}-O-H \quad (11\sigma, 4\pi)$$

17. **(c)** Dithionic acid ($H_2S_2O_6$)

$$H-O-\overset{\overset{O}{\pi\|\sigma}}{\underset{\underset{O}{\pi\|\sigma}}{S}}-\overset{\overset{O}{\pi\|\sigma}}{\underset{\underset{O}{\pi\|\sigma}}{S}}-O-H \quad (9\sigma, 4\pi)$$

18. **(c)** The basicity is determined by the number of OH groups attached to the P atom.

19. **(a)** $\quad H_3PO_4 \xrightarrow{\Delta} HPO_3 + H_2O$;
(D) ortho–   meta–

$$H_4P_2O_7 \xrightarrow{\Delta} 2HPO_3 + H_2O$$
(F) pyro–   meta–

20. **A-p, s; B-p, q, r, s; C-p, s; D-p, s**

A → H_2S decolourises acidified solution of $KMnO_4$

$$2KMnO_4 + 3H_2SO_4 + 5H_2S \longrightarrow$$
$$K_2SO_4 + 2MnSO_4 + 8H_2O + 5S$$

The shape of the H_2S molecule is similar to that of the water molecule i.e. V-shaped structure with bond length (H–S) 1.35Å and bond angle (H–S–H) 92.5° involving sp^3 hybridization of S atom.

B → SO_2 undergoes disproportionation (oxidation of two molecules of the same compound at the expense of the third which is reduced) reaction.

$$3SO_2 \xrightarrow{\text{Heat}} 2SO_3 + S$$

Decolourises $KMnO_4$

$$5SO_2 + 2KMnO_4 + 2H_2O \longrightarrow$$
$$K_2SO_4 + 2MnSO_4 + 2H_2SO_4$$

Sulphur dioxide acts as bleaching agent in the following way :

In the presence of water, it is oxidised with the liberation of nascent hydrogen which reduces the colouring matter to colourless.

$$SO_2 + 2H_2O \longrightarrow H_2SO_4 + 2[H]$$

$$\text{Colouring matter} + 2[H] \underset{\xrightarrow{\text{air}}}{\rightleftharpoons} \text{Colourless compound}$$

Sulphur dioxide has a planar triangular (V-shaped) structure involving sp^2 hybridisation of the sulphur atom (sp^2 hybridisation occurs between $3s^2 3p_x^{\ 1}$ and $3p_y^{\ 1}$ electrons).

C → NO_2 undergoes decolourisation of $KMnO_4$

$$2KMnO_4 + 3H_2SO_4 + 10NO_2 + 2H_2O \longrightarrow$$
$$K_2SO_4 + 2MnSO_4 + 10HNO_3$$

NO_2 molecule has angular structure (V-shape) with O–N–O bond angle of about 132° and N–O distance of about 1.19Å which is intermediate between a single and a double bond.

D → HNO_2 decolourises $KMnO_4$:

$$2KMnO_4 + 3H_2SO_4 + 5HNO_2 \longrightarrow$$
$$K_2SO_4 + 2MnSO_4 + 3H_2O + 5HNO_3$$

X-ray and Raman spectral studies indicate an angular structure for nitrite ion (NO_2^-) with O–N–O angle of 132° and bond length (N–O) of 1.13 Å.

1. **(d)** $Hg_2Cl_2 + 2NH_4OH \longrightarrow$
$$HgNH_2Cl + NH_4Cl + 2H_2O$$

2. **(a)**

(a) $V = 3d^3 4s^2 ; V^{2+} = 3d^3 = 3$ unpaired electrons
$Cr = 3d^5 4s^1 ; Cr^{2+} = 3d^4 = 4$ unpaired electrons
$Mn = 3d^5 4s^2 ; Mn^{2+} = 3d^5 = 5$ unpaired electrons
$Fe = 3d^6 4s^2 ; Fe^{2+} = 3d^6 = 4$ unpaired electrons
Hence the correct order of paramagnetic behaviour
$V^{2+} < Cr^{2+} = Fe^{2+} < Mn^{2+}$

(b) For the same oxidation state, the ionic radii generally decreases as the atomic number increases in a particular transition series. hence the order is
$Mn^{++} > Fe^{++} > Co^{++} > Ni^{++}$

(c) In solution, the stability of the compound depends upon electrode potentials, SEP of the transitions metal ions are given as
$Co^{3+}/Co = +1.97, Fe^{3+}/Fe = +0.77 ;$
$Cr^{3+}/Cr^{2+} = -0.41, Sc^{3+}$ is highly stable as it does not show $+2$ O.S.

(d) $Sc - (+2), (+3)$
$Ti - (+2), (+3), (+4)$
$Cr - (+1), (+2), (+3), (+4), (+5), (+6)$
$Mn - (+2), (+3), (+4), (+5), (+6), (+7)$
i.e. $Sc < Ti < Cr = Mn$

3. **(c)** In equation (i) $Fe_2(SO_4)_3$ and in equation (ii) $Fe_2(SO_4)_3$ on decomposing will form oxide instead of Fe.
The correct sequence of reactions is

$$Fe \xrightarrow{O_2, heat} Fe_3O_4 \xrightarrow{CO, 600°C}$$

$$Fe_2(SO_4)_3 \xrightarrow{\Delta} Fe$$

4. **(a)** $K_2Cr_2O_7 + 4H_2SO_4 + 3H_2S \longrightarrow$
$$K_2SO_4 + Cr_2(SO_4)_3 + 7H_2O + 3S$$

5. **(d)** $CuSO_4 + Na_2S_2O_3 \longrightarrow CuS_2O_3 + Na_2SO_4$

$$2CuS_2O_3 + Na_2S_2O_3 \longrightarrow Cu_2S_2O_3 + Na_2S_4O_6$$

$$3Cu_2S_2O_3 + 2Na_2S_2O_3 \longrightarrow Na_4[Cu_6(S_2O_3)_5]$$

6. **(c)** $Sm^{2+}(Z=62)[Xe]4f^6 6s^2 - 6$ unpaired e^-
$Eu^{2+}(Z=63)[Xe]4f^7 6s^2 - 7$ unpaired e^-
$Yb^{2+}(Z=70)[Xe]4f^{14} 6s^2 - 0$ unpaired e^-
$Ce^{2+}(Z=58)[Xe]4f^1 5d^1 6s^2 - 2$ unpaired e^-
Only Yb^{2+} is diamagnetic.

7. **(b,c,d)** (a) Hydrated ferric chloride ($FeCl_3.6H_2O$) upon heating gets hydrolysed by its own molecules of water of crystallisation to give $Fe(OH)_3$, which changes to Fe_2O_3 on further heating. Hence, (a) is not true.

$$FeCl_3.6H_2O \longrightarrow Fe(OH)_3 + 3HCl + 3H_2O$$

$$2Fe(OH)_3 \longrightarrow Fe_2O_3 + 3H_2O$$

(b) $C_2O_4^{2-}$ ion gets oxidized by acidified $KMnO_4$ resulting in decolorization of the latter.

$$C_2O_4^{2-} \rightarrow 2CO_2 + 2e^-$$

$$MnO_4^- + 8H^+ + 5e^- \rightarrow Mn^{2-} + 4H_2O$$

Thus (b) is true.

(c) Fe^{3+} salts are more stable than ferrous salts because Fe^{2+} easily oxidised by air.

(d) Mohr's salt is resistant to aerial oxidation.

8. **(b,c)** (b) $FeCl_3$ hydrolyses on standing.

$$FeCl_3 + 3H_2O \longrightarrow Fe(OH)_{3(s)} + 3HCl$$

(c) $2FeCl_3 + H_2S \longrightarrow 2FeCl_2 + 2HCl + S$

9. **(a,b)** (a) $^+Hg - Hg^+$ is also a divalent ion.

(b) Except Hg, oxidation potentials of zinc and cadmium are positive and hence are more reactive than coinage metals (negative oxidation potentials).

10. **(b,d)** (a) $HgCl_{2(aq)} + 2KI_{(aq)}$ (not in excess) $\rightarrow$
$$2KCl_{(aq)} + Hg I_{2(s)} \text{ (red ppt.)}$$

(b) No reaction of $SnCl_4$ with $HgCl_2$.

(c) $HgCl_2 + SnCl_2 \rightarrow Hg_2Cl_2 + SnCl_4 ;$
$Hg_2Cl_2 + SnCl_2 \rightarrow 2Hg + SnCl_4 ;$
$Hg_2Cl_2 + Hg_{(\ell)}$ appears grey.

(d) $HgCl_2$ is thermally stable.

11. **(6)** Butterfly structure (CrO_5) is:

$$\overset{-1}{O} \diagdown \underset{\overset{|}{\underset{+6}{Cr}}}{\overset{\overset{-2}{O}}{|}} \diagup \overset{-1}{O}$$

There are two peroxide ($-O-O-$) bond in CrO_5 in which O.S. of each O-atom is -1.
Hence O.S. of $Cr = +6$.

12. **(3)** Lower O.S. compounds are basic and higher O.S. compounds are acidic.

$$\underbrace{\overset{+2}{Mn}O, \overset{+3}{Mn_2}O_3}_{\text{Neutral}} \quad \underbrace{\overset{+4}{Mn}O_2, \overset{+6}{Mn}O_3, \overset{+7}{Mn_2}O_7}_{\text{Acidic}}$$

13. **(3)** $[RhCl(Ph_3P)_3]$

14. **(6)** Second and third triad of $4d$ and $5d$ series of group VIII or group, 8, 9 and 10 are collectively called platinum metals. These are:

4d series:	Ru	Rh	Pd
5d series:	Os	Ir	Pt

15. **(a)** ZnO shows yellow colour on heating and becomes white on cooling.

16. **(a)** $ZnO + 2HCl(aq) \longrightarrow \underset{\text{(Soluble)}}{ZnCl_2(aq)} + H_2O$

17. **(a)** The green colour is due to presence of MnO_4^{2-} which changes to MnO_4^- which has a purple colour.

$$\underset{\underset{Mn^{+6}}{\text{(green)}}}{3K_2MnO_4} + 2H_2O + 4CO_2 \longrightarrow$$

$$\underset{\underset{Mn^{+7}}{\text{(purple)}}}{2KMnO_4} + \underset{Mn^{+4}}{MnO_2} + 4KHCO_3$$

18. **(a)** Its function is to make solution acidic.

19. **A-q; B-p, q, r, s; C-p, q; D-r**

The substance left behind as waste in Kipp's apparatus is $FeSO_4.7H_2O$ which is known as green vitriol.

Both green vitriol ($FeSO_4.7H_2O$) and Mohr's salt $[FeSO_4(NH_4)_2SO_4.6H_2O]$ are green in colour and on heating they leave a brown residue.

Basic copper carbonate and hydrated cupric chloride are also green in colour.

Basic copper carbonate on heating leaves a black residue.

20. **A → p, s ; B → q, s ; C → r, t ; D → q, t**

A. $3Cu + 8\,HNO_3(\text{dil.})$

$$\longrightarrow 2\underset{p}{NO} + \underset{s}{Cu(NO_3)_2} + 4H_2O$$

B. $Cu + 4HNO_3(\text{conc.})$

$$\longrightarrow 2\underset{q}{NO_2} + \underset{s}{Cu(NO_3)_2} + 2H_2O$$

C. $4Zn + 10HNO_3(\text{dil.})$

$$\longrightarrow 4\underset{t}{Zn(NO_3)_2} + \underset{r}{N_2O} + 5H_2O$$

D. $Zn + 4HNO_3(\text{conc.})$

$$\longrightarrow \underset{t}{Zn(NO_3)_2} + 2\underset{q}{NO_2} + 2H_2O$$

1. **(a)** $CoCl_3.6NH_3 \longrightarrow xCl^-$
    2.675g

$xCl^- + AgNO_3 \longrightarrow x\,AgCl\downarrow$
                4.78g

Number of moles of the complex

$$= \frac{2.675}{267.5} = 0.01 \text{ moles}$$

Number of moles of AgCl obtained

$$= \frac{4.78}{143.5} = 0.03 \text{ moles}$$

$\therefore$ No. of moles of AgCl obtained
$= x \times$ No. of moles of complex

$$\therefore x = \frac{0.03}{0.01} = 3$$

Hence, the formula of complex is $[Co(NH_3)_6]Cl_3$

2. **(a)**

	Electronic configuration		No. of unpaired electrons
Co^{2+}	d^7	$\uparrow\downarrow\ \uparrow\downarrow\ \uparrow\ \uparrow\ \uparrow$	3
Cr^{2+}	d^4	$\uparrow\ \uparrow\ \uparrow\ \uparrow$	4
Mn^{2+}	d^5	$\uparrow\ \uparrow\ \uparrow\ \uparrow\ \uparrow$	5
Fe^{2+}	d^6	$\uparrow\downarrow\ \uparrow\ \uparrow\ \uparrow\ \uparrow$	4

$\therefore$ Since Co^{2+} has lowest no. of unpaired electrons hence lowest paramagnetic behaviour is shown by $[Co(H_2O)_6]^{2+}$

3. **(b)** Complexes of the type Mabcd may exist in three isomeric form. Similarily $[Pt(NO_2)(Py)(NH_3)(NH_2OH)^+]$ may exist in three isomeric form.

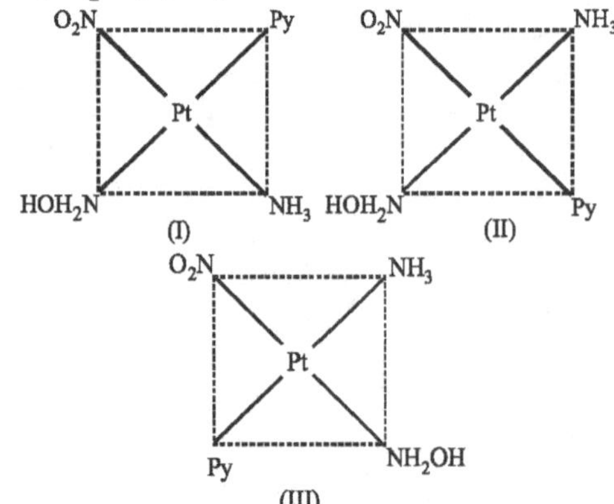

4. **(c)** Octahedral coordination entities of the type Ma_3b_3 exhibit geometrical isomerism. The compound exists both as facial and meridional isomers, both contain plane of symmetry

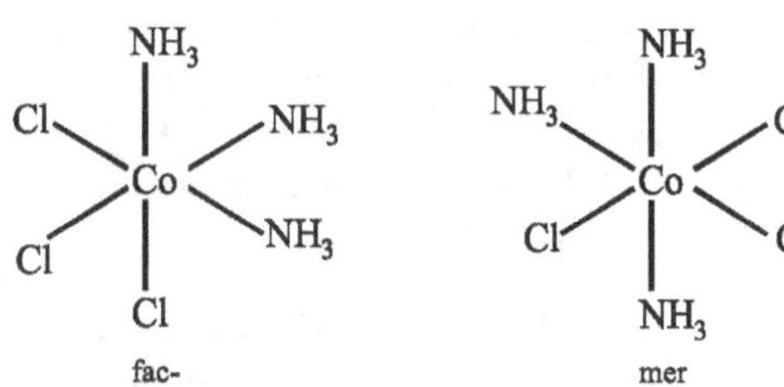

5. **(a)** $[NiL_4]^{2-}$

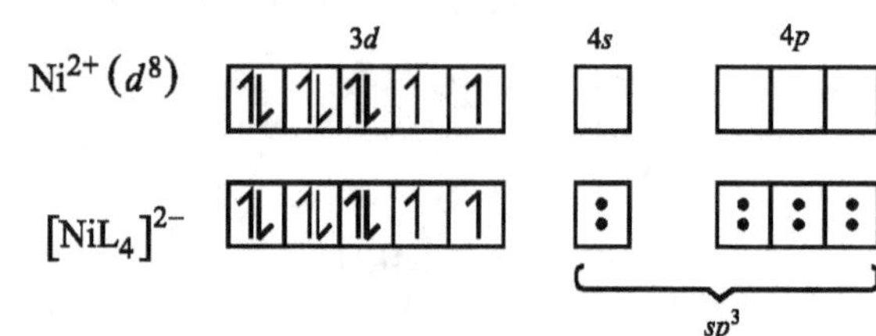

i.e, no. of unpaired electron = 2
hybridization $-sp^3$.

6. **(c, d)** **(a)** In $[Fe(C_5H_5)_2]$, EAN of $Fe = 26$, electron of

$Fe + 10$ electron from two $C_5H_5^-$ ions

(b) $[Fe(H_2O)_6]^{2+}$:

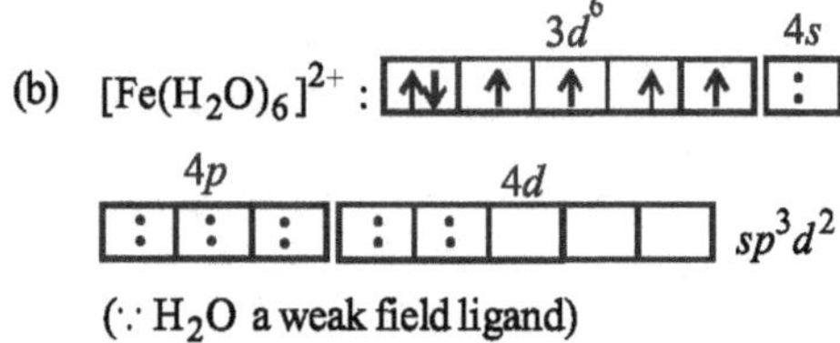

($\because H_2O$ a weak field ligand)

(c) $[Cr(NH_3)_6]^{3+}$:

d^2sp^3 (3 unpaired electrons)

(d) $[CoI_4]^{2-}$:

sp^3 (tetrahedral)

7. **(a, c)**

$[Cu(CN)_4]^{3-}$:

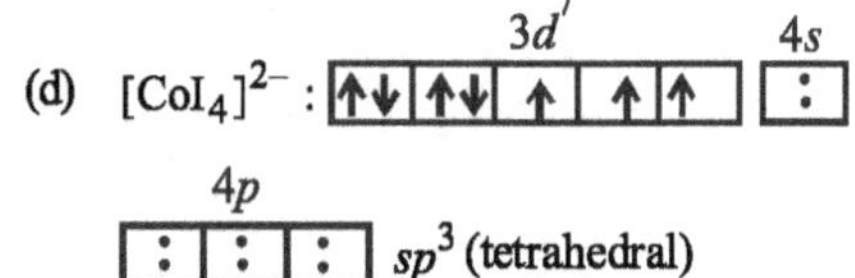

$4p$

$\boxed{:\ :\ \uparrow}$ dsp^2 hybridization

$[Ni(CN)_6]^{2-}$: $\boxed{\uparrow\downarrow\ \uparrow\downarrow\ \uparrow\downarrow\ \uparrow\ \uparrow}\ \boxed{:\ :\ :\ :}$

$\boxed{:\ :\ \quad\ \quad}$ sp^3d^2 hybridization

$[ZnBr_4]^{2-}$:

$\boxed{\uparrow\downarrow\ \uparrow\downarrow\ \uparrow\downarrow\ \uparrow\downarrow\ \uparrow\downarrow}\ \boxed{:\ :\ :\ :}$ sp^3
hybridization

$[Cr(NH_3)_6]^{3+}$: $\boxed{\uparrow\ \uparrow\ \uparrow\ :\ :}$

$\boxed{:\ \ :\ :\ :}$ d^2sp^3 hybridization

8. **(b,d)**

   (a) $AgCl + 2NH_3 \longrightarrow [Ag(NH_3)_2]^+ Cl^-$;
   cation is the complex ion.

   (b) $FeSO_4 + 6KCN \longrightarrow K_4[Fe(CN)_6] + K_2SO_4$;
   anion is complex ion.

   (c) $CuSO_4 + 4NH_3 \longrightarrow [Cu(NH_3)_4]SO_4$; cation is
   the complex ion.

   (d) $PtCl_4 + 2KCl \longrightarrow K_2[PtCl_6]$;
   anion is the complex ion.

9. **(b,c)**

   The chelates having five membered rings are more
   stable in the absence of double bonds in them. The
   chelates having six membered rings are more stable if
   they contain double bond. Thus (a) and (d) are incorrect.

10. **(3)** 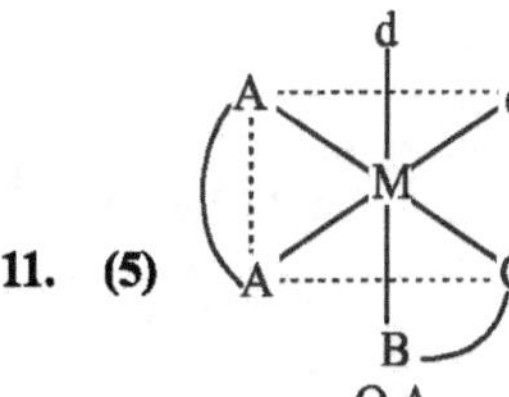

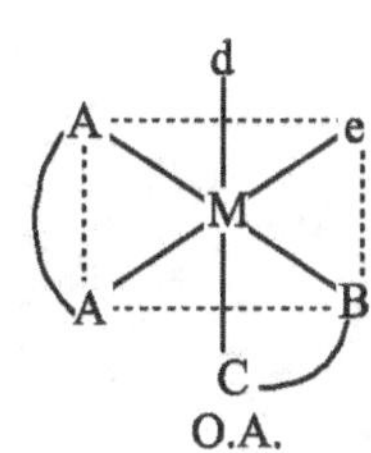

   are negative as well as flexidentate ligand.

11. **(5)** 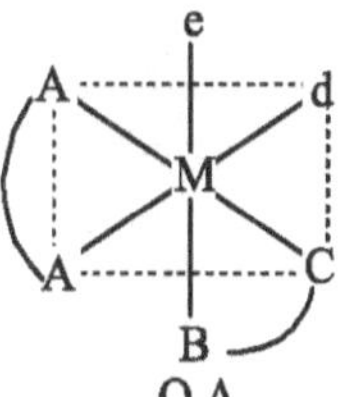 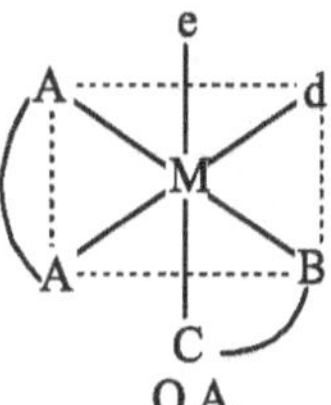

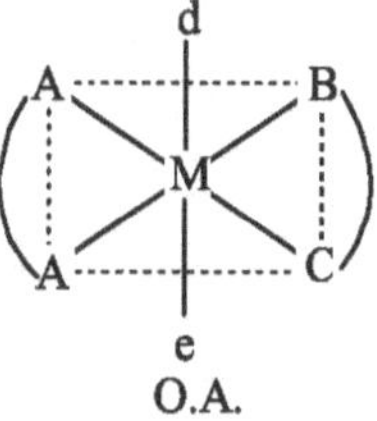

Five pairs of enantiomers are possible.

12. **(2)** Trans-isomer in A = 2
   Trans-isomer in B = 1

   $$\text{Ratio} = \frac{2}{1} = 2$$

   Hybridisation, VBT and CFT

13. **(0)** $[Co^{II}(SCN)_4]^{2-}$; $Co^{2+} = 3d^7$, C.N. = 4, TH complex.

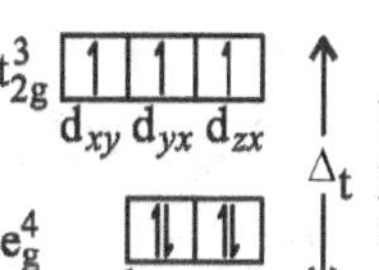

   Number of unpaired electron
   present in d-orbitals whose lobes
   are present along axis = 0.

14. **(9)** 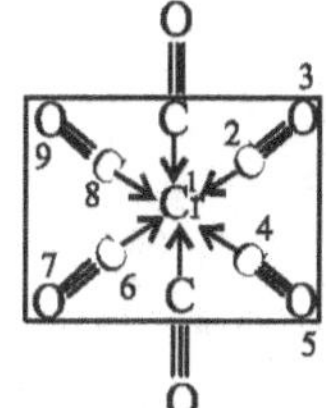

   9 atoms (as marked) are
   present in same plane.

15. **(c)** d^6 (high spin)

   $\underline{11}\ e_g^2$ $\text{CFSE} = -0.4 \times 4 + 0.6 \times 2$
   $\underline{111}\ t_{2g}^4$ $\qquad\qquad = 0.4$
   (n = 4)

   $$\mu\ \text{spin} = \sqrt{n(n+2)}\ \text{B.M}$$

   $$= \sqrt{4(4+2)} = \sqrt{24} = 4.90\ \text{B.M}$$

16. (d) d^3 = high spin

$$--e_g^0$$
$$\underline{1\;1\;1}\;t_{2g}^3$$
$$(n=3)$$

CFSE $= -0.4 \times 3$
$$= -1.2$$

μ spin $= \sqrt{n(n+2)}$ B.M

$$\sqrt{3(3+2)}$$
$$\sqrt{15}$$
$$= 3.87\,B.M$$

17. (c) d^7 (low spin) $\dfrac{1}{}-e_g^1$ CFSE $= -0.4 \times 6 + 0.6 \times 1$
$$= -1.8$$

$$\underline{1\!\!1\;1\!\!1\;1\!\!1}\;t_{2g}^6$$
$$n=1$$

μ spin $= \sqrt{n(n+2)}$ B.M
$$= \sqrt{1(1+2)}$$
$$= \sqrt{3}$$
$$= 1.73\,B.M$$

18. (c) Number of moles of Na_2O added

$$= \frac{\text{Mass of } Na_2O\ (g)}{\text{Molar mass}} = \frac{0.0307}{62} = 0.5 \times 10^{-3}$$

Moles of OH^- added $= 2 \times 0.5 \times 10^{-3} = 1 \times 10^{-3}$

Hence, $[OH^-]_{final} = 1.0 \times 10^{-5}$ (initial) $+ 1 \times 10^{-3}$

(added) $= 1.01 \times 10^{-3}\, mol L^{-1}$

$(pOH)_{final} = -\log 1.01 \times 10^{-3} \approx 3$, pH $= 14 - 3 = 11$

According to the Fig-1, the relative rate corresponding to pH 11 is 10 whereas for initial pH it is 5, i.e., the relative rate increases by a factor of 2.

19. (b) Molality of $[Co(NH_3)_6]Cl_3 = \dfrac{\text{Moles}}{\text{Mass of water (kg)}}$

$$= \frac{27/268}{\text{volume(L)}} = \frac{27}{268 \times 1} = 0.1$$

$$Co(NH_3)_6Cl_2 = \frac{23}{232 \times 1} = 0.1$$

$$[Co(NH_3)_6]Cl_3(aq) \longrightarrow [Co(NH_3)_6(aq)]^{3+} + 3Cl^-(aq)\ ;$$

$$[Co(NH_3)_6]Cl_2(aq) \longrightarrow [Co(NH_3)_6(aq)]^{2+} + 2Cl^-(aq)$$

Hence, total molality of all the species
$$= 0.1 \times (1+3) + 0.1\,(1+2) = 0.7$$

20. A-r; B-s; C-p; D-q

(A) $3d^3$ (Octahedral) : d^2sp^3 hybridization; 3 unpaired elecrtons

(B) d^5 (Octahedral, low spin) : d^2sp^3 hybridization ; 1 unpaired electron

(C) d^6 (Octahedral, low spin) : d^2sp^3 ; no unpaired electron

(D) d^6 (Octahedral, outer orbital) : sp^3d^2 ; 4 unpaired electrons

Magnetic moment $\sqrt{n(n+2)}$ B.M. (n unpaired electrons)

1. (b)

$$CH_3CH_2CH_2Br \xrightarrow{\text{aq. KOH}} CH_3CH_2CH_2OH \xrightarrow[\text{heat}]{Al_2O_3}$$

$$CH_3CH=CH_2 \xrightarrow{Cl_2/H_2O} CH_3CHOHCH_2Cl$$

2. (b)

Toluene (CH_3) $\xrightarrow[\text{heat}]{3Cl_2}$ CCl_3-benzene $\xrightarrow{Br_2/Fe}$

CCl_3-benzene with Br $\xrightarrow{Zn/HCl}$ CH_3-benzene with Br

3. (b)

2-methyl chlorobenzene $\xrightarrow[-33°C]{NaNH_2/NH_3}$ Benzyne derivative $\xrightarrow{\bar{N}H_2}$

CH_3 benzene with NH_2 (ortho) $+$ CH_3 benzene with NH_2 (meta)

4. (c) $(CH_3)_2CH-CH_2Cl \xrightarrow[\text{anhy.}]{AlCl_3} (CH_3)_2CH-\overset{\ominus}{CH_2}$

$$\xrightarrow{\text{Rearrangement}} (CH_3)\underset{3°}{\overset{+}{C}}$$

Benzene $+ (CH_3)_3\overset{+}{C} \longrightarrow$ $C(CH_3)_3$-benzene $+ H^+$

(A)

$(CH_3)_2CH-Cl \xrightarrow[\text{anhy.}]{AlCl_3} (CH_3)_2\underset{2°}{\overset{+}{CH}}$

Benzene $+ (CH_3)_2\overset{+}{CH} \longrightarrow$ $CH(CH_3)_2$-benzene $+ H^+$

(B)

5. (d)

$$CH_3-CH-CH-CH_2-CH_3$$
$$\quad\quad\; | \quad\;\; |$$
$$\quad\quad CH_3 \;\; Br$$

3-bromo-2-methyl Pentane

$\downarrow$ dehydrohalogenation

$H_3C-C=CH-CH_2CH_3 + H_3C-CH-CH=CHCH_3$
with CH_3 (X) and CH_3 (Y)

(X) $\downarrow$ ozonolysis

$$\begin{matrix} H_3C \\ H_3C \end{matrix}C=O$$
$+$
CH_3CH_2-CHO

(Y) $\downarrow$ ozonolysis

$(CH_3)_2CHCHO$
$+$
CH_3CHO

6. (a, b, d) Recall that the —Cl group present in the *o*- and *p*- positions to the electron-withdrawing group is activated toward nucleophilic substitution, hence only —Cl present on the *o*- and/or *p*-position to the —NO_2 group will be replaced.

7. (b, d) Aryl halides are stable due to resonance stabilization. The resonating structures

$\overset{+}{Cl}$ structures $\longleftrightarrow \longleftrightarrow$

stabilise the aryl halide. These structures include a double bond between C and Cl which is shorter and thus stronger than the usual C – Cl single bond. The sp^2 hybridised carbon, being electronegative, makes the C – Cl bond shorter and stronger.

8. (a, b) The lithium enolate bases from cyclohexanone react with alkyl halides in different ways.

Enolate $\longleftrightarrow$ $+$ Me$-$I $\xrightarrow{S_N1}$ Me-cyclohexanone $+$ LiI
(Acts as nucleophile)

(I)

Enolate $+ H-\overset{\beta}{CH_2}\overset{\alpha}{C}-Cl \xrightarrow{E1}$ $[$ OH-form $]$ $\xrightarrow{\text{Taut.}}$ cyclohexanone
Acts as base, Me, 3° RX

$+CH_2=C-Me$

(II)

9. **(a, b, c)**

Product (II) is cine substitution and product (III) is direct substitution. Reaction is ArSN (elimination–addition) reaction.

10. **(2)** For Anti elimination H and Cl must be in anti-position, only two moles of HCl are in anti position.

11. **(1)** **Only (b) diastereomers**

(a) $\xrightarrow{\text{NaNH}_3}$ (No G.I.)

(b) $\longrightarrow$ (Shows G.I.)

(c) $\longrightarrow$ (No G.I.)

(d) $\longrightarrow$ (No G.I.)

12. **(5)**

$\xrightarrow[\text{(a)}]{2PCl_5}$ $\xrightarrow[\text{(b)}]{\text{NaNH}_2}$ $\xrightarrow{\text{CH}_3\text{I}}$

$a = 2$, $b = 3$

$$\therefore a + b = 5$$

13. **(4)**

$\xrightarrow{\text{CH}_3\text{OH}}$

① ② substitution products

③ ④ Elimination products

14. **(3)**

$$\text{Me}-\overset{\text{Br}}{\underset{}{\text{CH}}}-\text{CH}_2\text{Br} + 2\text{NaNH}_2 \xrightarrow{-\text{HBr}}$$

$$\xrightarrow{\text{NaNH}_2} \text{Me}-\text{C}\equiv\text{CH} + 2\text{NaBr} + 2\text{NH}_3$$

$$\text{Me}-\text{C}\equiv\text{C}^{\ominus}\text{Na}^{\oplus} + \text{NH}_3 \xrightarrow{\text{C}_2\text{H}_5\text{Br}}$$

$$\text{Me}-\text{C}\equiv\text{C}-\text{C}_2\text{H}_5 + \text{NaBr}$$
Pent-2-yne

Hence, 3 mole NaNH_2 is used.

15. **(c)** Reaction II proceeds via carbene intermediate in presence of $\text{CHBrCl}_2 / \longrightarrow \text{ONa}$

$$\xrightarrow{\text{C-I break}} {}^{\ominus}:\text{CBrCl (Bromochlorocarbene)} + \text{I}^{\ominus}$$

$$\text{Ph}-\text{CH}=\text{CH}-\text{Ph} + :\text{CBrCl} \longrightarrow$$

16. **(b)**

$\xrightarrow{\text{NBS} + h\nu}$

Mechanism:

$$\text{N}-\text{Br} + \text{HBr} \overset{h\nu}{\rightleftharpoons} \text{Br}-\text{Br} + \text{N}-\text{H}$$

The resulting Br_2 can be fragmented homolytically:-

$$\text{Br}-\text{Br} \xrightarrow{h\nu} \text{Br}\overset{\frown}{}\text{Br} \longrightarrow 2\text{Br}^{\bullet} \text{ initiation}$$

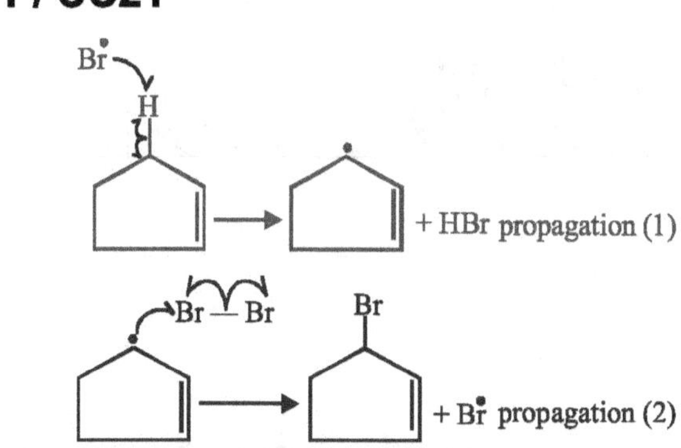

17. (a) HCl with peroxide does not undergo anti-Markovnikov's addition unlike HBr/peroxide, so reaction does not proceed by free-radical mechanism but by carbocation.

+ HBr propagation (1)

+ Br$\overset{\bullet}{}$ propagation (2)

The process repeats itself until the NBS is consumed.

18. (d) Isopropyl bromide, a 2° bromide, undergoes ionization to form 2° carbocation, a stable species which reacts with $C_2H_5O^-$ (a relatively small nucleophile) to form ether. (S_N1)

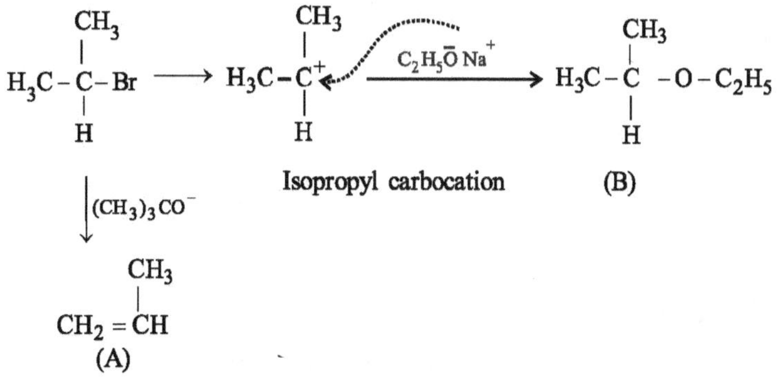

Isopropyl carbocation   (B)

(A)

However, the *tert*-butoxide ion, being large in size faces difficulty in attacking the carbon atom of isopropyl cation, which thus loses proton to form propene (A), E_2 reaction.

19. (d) (b) is the intermediate in S_N1, while (c) is an intermediate in S_N2 reaction, (a) species is ambiguous.

20. A-p; B-q; C-s; D-r

Although most of the dehydrohalogenation reactions follow **Saytzeff rule,** i.e. more substituted alkene is the major product, least substituted alkene is the major product **(Hoffmann rule)** under following conditions.

(i)   When the base is bulky.

(ii)   When there is steric hindrance at the γ-carbon.

(iii)   When the leaving group is poor viz. F, $\overset{+}{N}R_3$ and $\overset{+}{S}R_2$.

(iv)   When the parent compound contains a double bond at β-carbon.

(A) $Me_2\overset{\overset{\displaystyle Br}{|}}{C}CH_2CH_3 + OC_2H_5^- \longrightarrow Me_2C = CHCH_3$ (Saytzeff product)

(B) $Me_2\overset{\overset{\displaystyle Br}{|}}{C}CH_2CH_3 + Me_3CO^- \longrightarrow Me - \overset{\overset{\displaystyle CH_2}{||}}{C}CH_2CH_3$ (Hoffmann product)

             Bulky base

(C) $CH_3CH_2\overset{\overset{\displaystyle F}{|}}{C}HCH_3 + OCH_3^- \longrightarrow CH_3CH_2CH = CH_2$ (Hoffmann product)

    (F is poor leaving group)   (Major)

(D) $CH_3CH_2\overset{\overset{\displaystyle Cl}{|}}{C}HCH_3 + OCH_3^- \longrightarrow CH_3CH = CHCH_3$ (Saytzeff product)

                       (Major)

1. (c)

Toluene (with OH) $\xrightarrow[\text{Reimer Tiemann reaction}]{\text{CHCl}_3 + \text{NaOH}}$ → aldehyde (CHO) $\xrightarrow{\text{HCN}}$

Cyanohydrin $\xrightarrow{\text{HOH}}$ → $-\text{CH(OH)COOH}$

2. (b) *Victor Meyer's test:* The various steps involved are

(i) $RCH_2OH \xrightarrow{HI} RCH_2I \xrightarrow{AgNO_2} RCH_2NO_2 \xrightarrow{HNO_2}$

$$R - \underset{\underset{\text{NOH}}{\|}}{C} - NO_2 \xrightarrow{KOH} \text{Blood red colour}$$

Nitrolic acid

(ii) $RCHOHR \xrightarrow{HI} \overset{R}{\underset{R}{>}}CHI \xrightarrow{AgNO_2} \overset{R}{\underset{R}{>}}CHNO_2$

$\xrightarrow[\text{H}_2\text{O}]{\text{H}^+ \text{ } \bar{\text{O}}\text{NO}}$ ... $\xrightarrow{KOH}$ blue colour

(iii) $R_3COH \xrightarrow{HI} R_3CI \xrightarrow{AgNO_2} R_3CNO_2$

$\xrightarrow{HNO_2}$ No reaction $\xrightarrow{KOH}$ Colourless

3. (a) Whenever dehydration can produce two different alkenes, major product is formed according to **Saytzeff rule** *i.e.* more substituted alkene (alkene having lesser number of hydrogen atoms on the two doubly bonded carbon atoms) is the major product.

Such reactions which can produce two or more structural isomers but one of them in greater amounts than the other are called **regioselective** *; in case a reaction is 100% regioselective, it is termed as* **regiospecific.**

In addition to being regioselective, alcohol dehydrations are **stereoselective** (*a reaction in which a single starting material can yield two or more stereoisomeric products, but gives one of them in greater amount than any other*).

$$C_6H_5 - CH_2 - \underset{\underset{OH}{|}}{CH} - \underset{\underset{CH_3}{|}}{CH} - CH_3 \xrightarrow{\text{Conc. H}_2\text{SO}_4}$$

cis (minor): C_6H_5, H on one side, CH(CH$_3$)$_2$

trans (major): C_6H_5, H / H, CH(CH$_3$)$_2$

4. (a) $CH_3CH_2OCH(CH_3)_2$ (A) $\xrightarrow{\text{Conc. HI}}$

CH_3CH_2I + $(CH_3)_2CHI$

$CH_3CH_2I \xrightarrow{NaOH} CH_3CH_2OH$ (B) $\xrightarrow{[O]} CH_3COOH$

$(CH_3)_2CHI \xrightarrow{NaOH} (CH_3)_2CHOH$ (C) $\xrightarrow{[O]} (CH_3)_2CO$

hence the IUPAC name of ether is

$$\overset{}{CH_3} - CH_2 - O - \underset{\underset{3\,CH_3}{|}}{\overset{2}{CH}} - \overset{1}{CH_3}$$

2–ethoxypropane

5. (a)

Sodium Phenoxide (ONa) $+ CO_2 \xrightarrow[\text{5 atm}]{125°}$

(B) with OH and COONa $\xrightarrow{H_2SO_4}$

Salicylic acid (OH and COOH) $\xdownarrow{(CH_3CO)_2O}$

Aspirin (Acetyl Salicylate) (C): ring with $O-\overset{\overset{O}{\|}}{C}-CH_3$ and COOH $+ CH_3COOH$

6. (c) The C – O bond length in alcohols is 142 pm and in Phenol it is 136 pm. The C – O bond length in phenol is shorter than that in methanol due to the conjugation of unshared pair of electrons on oxygen with the ring, which imparts double bond character to the C – O bond.

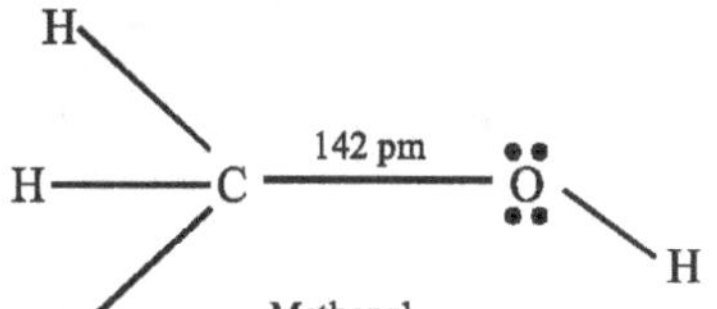

Methanol

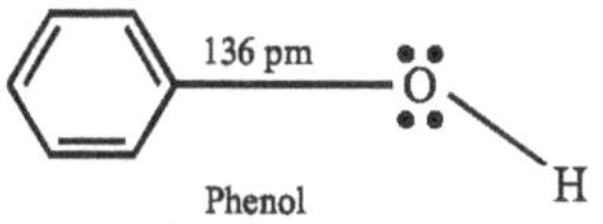

Phenol

7. (b, d)

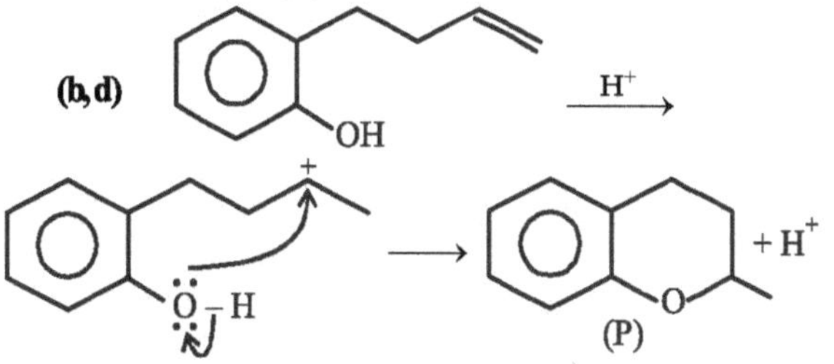

(P)

8. (b, c, d)

$\xrightarrow{\text{(i) } H^+}$ $\xrightarrow{\text{(ii)} -H_2O}$

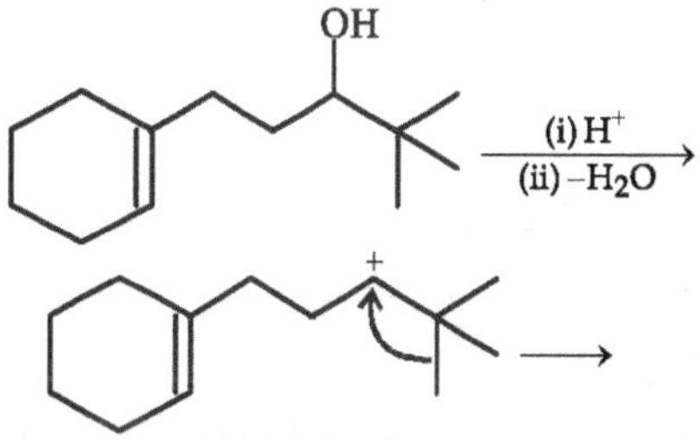

2° carbocation

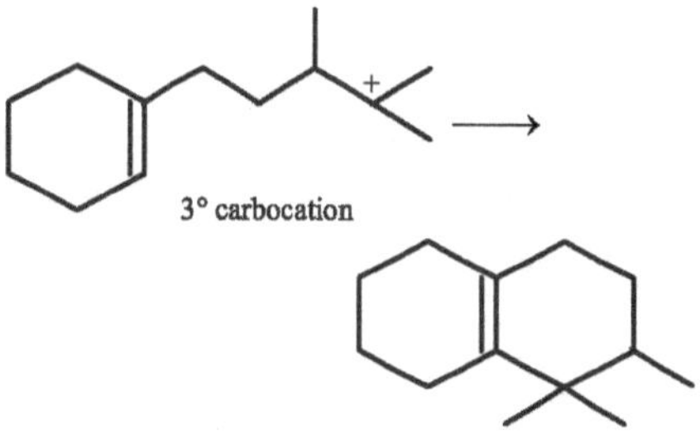

3° carbocation

9. (b, d) The combination $C_6H_5Br + CH_3CH_2OH$ has non-reactive C_6H_5Br, while in the combination $C_6H_5OH + Me_3CBr$, Me_3CBr being *tert*-halide will undergo elimination reaction rather than substitution. Hence, only combinations (*a*) and (*c*) can be used for preparing ether.

$$C_6H_5OH + (CH_3)_2SO_4 \xrightarrow{S_N} C_6H_5OCH_3 \;;$$

$$p\text{-}NO_2C_6H_4Br + CH_3CH_2OH \xrightarrow{Ar\,S_N}$$
$$p\text{-}NO_2C_6H_4OCH_2CH_3$$

10. (a, b, c) *tert*- and *sec*-carbocations are liable to undergo elimination reaction in presence of strong alkoxide bases. Aryl and vinyl halides do not undergo nucleophilic substitution.

11. (8)

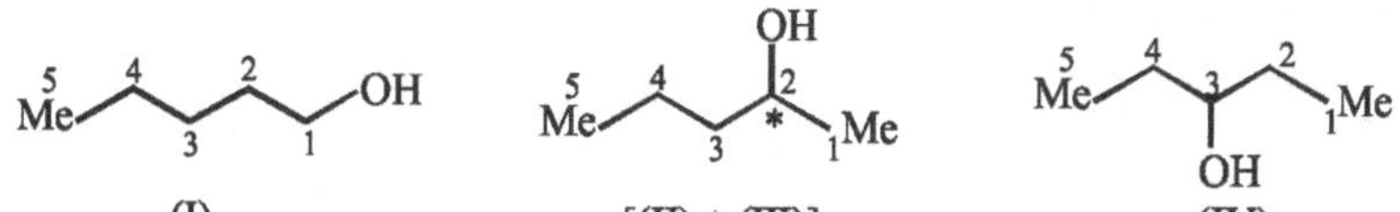

(I)

Pentan-1-ol

[(II) + (III)]

(±)-Pentan-2-ol (optically active)

(IV)

Pentan-3-ol

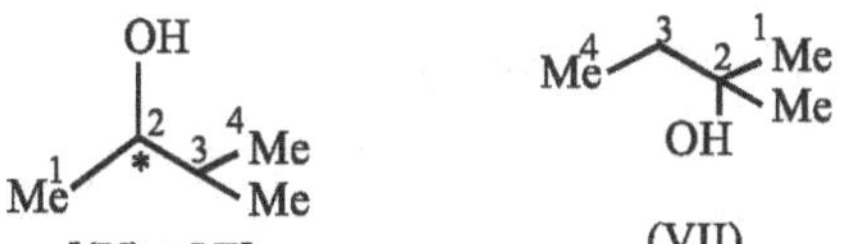

[(V) + VI]

(±)-3-Methyl butan-2-ol
(optically active)

(VII)

2-Methyl butan-2-ol

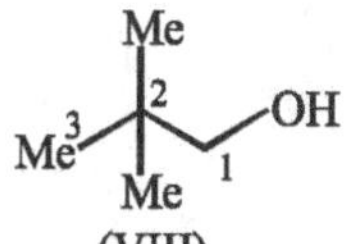

(VIII)

2, 2-Dimethyl propan-1-ol

Hence, total possible isomers including stereoisomers of $C_5H_{12}O$ are 8.

12. (7)

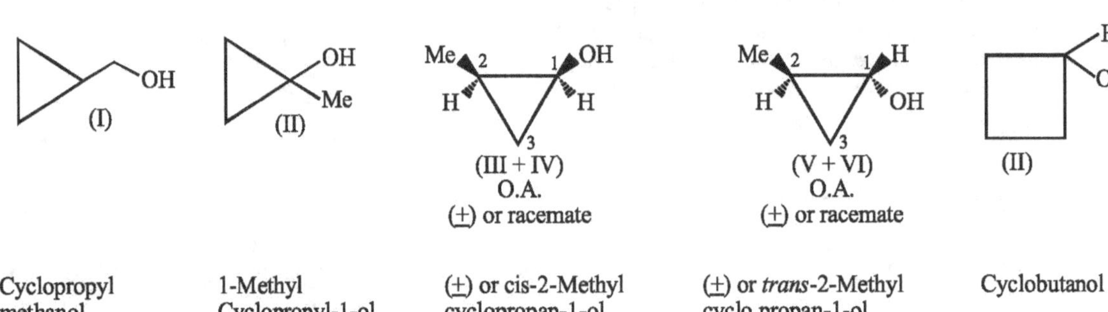

| Cyclopropyl methanol | 1-Methyl Cyclopropyl-1-ol | (±) or cis-2-Methyl cyclopropan-1-ol | (±) or *trans*-2-Methyl cyclo propan-1-ol | Cyclobutanol |

Hence, total possible isomers including stereoisomers of C_4H_7OH are 7.

13. (3) 2.68 gm of (A) gives 14.08 gm of AgI

$$134 \text{ gm of (A) gives } \frac{14.08 \times 134}{2.68}$$

$$= 704 \text{ gm of AgI}$$

$$= \frac{704}{235} = \text{mol of AgI}$$

$$= 3 \text{ (OMe) groups}$$

14. (4) (dℓ) 2-methyl butanoic acid and (dℓ) 2-butanol

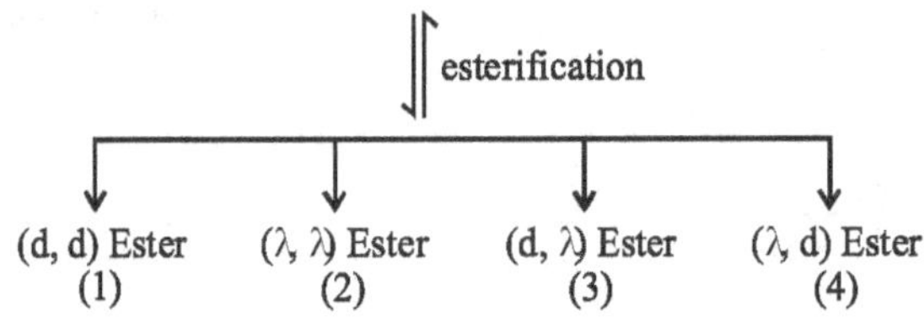

Ester consists of two stereocentres. Chiral center during whole reaction are not effected, that's why all esters are optical active.

15. (d) Primary alcohols, can form carbocations which may also undergo rearrangement, if structure permits. However, primary alcohols usually undergo S_N2 mechanism because of easy approach of the nucleophile on the less sterically hindered alkyl group and also because of relatively less stability of the 1° carbocation.

16. (a) Neopentyl alcohol is, although, a 1° alcohol, it undergoes S_N1 mechanism because of steric hindrance due to bulky alkyl group.

$$CH_3 - \underset{\underset{CH_3}{|}}{\overset{\overset{CH_3}{|}}{C}} - CH_2OH \xrightarrow[(-H_2O)]{H^+} CH_3 - \underset{\underset{CH_3}{|}}{\overset{\overset{CH_3}{|}}{\overset{+}{C}}} - CH_2$$

1° carbocation

$$\longrightarrow CH_3 - \underset{\underset{CH_3}{|}}{\overset{+}{C}} - CH_2CH_3$$

3° carbocation

17. (a) $CH_3CH_2CH_2CH_2OH \xrightarrow[350°C]{Al_2O_3}$
[A]

$$CH_3CH_2CH = CH_2 \longrightarrow CH_3CH_2\underset{\underset{[B]}{}}{\overset{\overset{OH}{|}}{C}}HCH_3$$

18. (c)

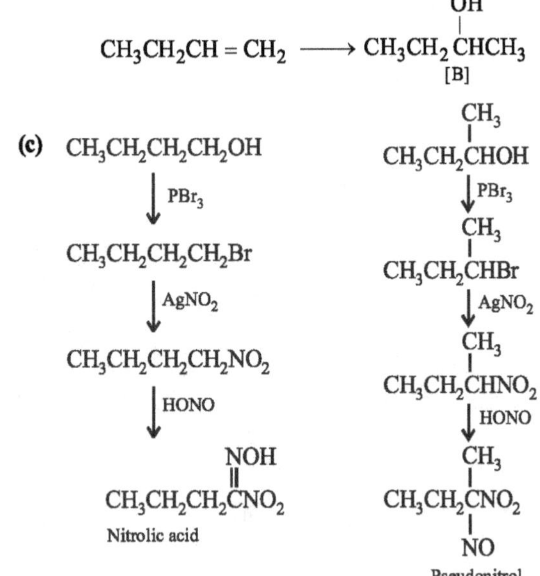

19. A-q; B-p; C-p, r; D-p, s

Hemiacetals are resistant to acids but can be hydrolysed by alkalies. On the other hand, acetals and ethers are hydrolysed by acids but not by alkalies. Glycosides are hemiacetals or acetals having carbohydrate moiety as one of the constituent. Ethers when heated with HI gives CH_3I which on treatment with $AgNO_3$ gives AgI (Ziesel method).

20. A-r; B-q; C-s; D-p

(A) We know that S_N1 reactions involve racemization as well as inversion, while S_N2 reactions involve inversion of configuration. However, here configuration is completely retained. This is because of the formation of a true intermediate in which carbocation and the anion $^-$OSOCl (ion pair) is present in a solvent cage and hence attack by Cl^- ion is likely to occur only on the same side of the R^+ from which OSOCl is departed. Such reactions in which entering and leaving groups are present in the same side of the molecule are known as intramolecular or internal nucleophilic substitution, S_Ni.

$$R - OH + ClSOCl \longrightarrow R - OSOCl + HCl$$

(B) When reaction between ROH and $SOCl_2$ is carried out in presence of a basic solvent like pyridine, the product RCl is found to have inverted configuration. This is so because the HCl formed in the first step is taken up by pyridine to form $C_5H_5NH^+Cl^-$ and now Cl^- being an effective nucleophile attacks the alkyl chlorosulphite 'from the back' as in a normal S_N2 reaction.

(C) This is an example of intramolecular nucleophilic substitution (S_Ni) involving allylic system which has also undergone allylic rearrangement. Such reaction is designated as S_Ni (intramolecular nucleophilic substitution with allylic inversion).

(D) This is an example of usual S_N1 reaction.

1. (a) Aldehydes and ketones can be reduced to hydrocarbons by the action (i) of amalgamated zinc and concentrated hydrochloric acid (Clemmensen reduction), or (b) of hydrazine (NH_2NH_2) and a strong base like NaOH, KOH or potassium *tert*-butoxide in a high-boiling alcohol like ethylene glycol or triethylene glycol (Wolf-Kishner reduction)

$$\text{(cyclohexyl) } CH{=}CH{-}COCH_3, \ HO-$$

$$\xrightarrow[\text{Reduction}]{NH_2NH_2/OH^-} \text{Wolf-kishner}$$

$$\text{(cyclohexyl) } CH{=}CH{-}CH_2{-}CH_3, \ HO-$$

–OH group and alkene are acid-sensitive groups so clemmensen reduction can not be used. Acid sensitive substrate should be reacted in the Wolf-Kishner reduction which utilise strongly basic conditions.

2. (d) $A \xrightarrow[(I)]{NH_3} B \xrightarrow{\Delta}_{II} C \xrightarrow[KOH,(III)]{Br_2} CH_3CH_2NH_2$

Reaction (III) is a Hofmann bromamide reaction. Now formation of $CH_3CH_2NH_2$ is possible only from a compound $CH_3CH_2CONH_2(C)$ which can be obtained from the compound $CH_3CH_2COO^-NH_4^+(B)$.

Thus (A) should be CH_3CH_2COOH

$$CH_3CH_2 - \overset{O}{\overset{\|}{C}} - OH \xrightarrow{NH_3} CH_3CH_2COO^-NH_4^+$$
$$\text{(A)} \qquad\qquad\qquad \text{(B)}$$

$$\xrightarrow{\Delta} CH_3CH_2CONH_2$$
$$\text{(C)}$$

$$\overset{KOH}{\underset{CH_3CH_2NH_2}{\Big\downarrow}} Br_2$$

3. (c) Given compound A is $CH_3 - CH_2 - \underset{CH_3}{\overset{}{C}} = C = O$

Reactions given are as following :

$$CH_3 - CH_2 - \underset{CH_3}{\overset{}{C}} = C = O \xrightarrow{NH_3}$$

$$\left[CH_3 - CH_2 - \underset{\overset{|}{CH_3}}{\overset{}{C}} = \underset{\overset{+}{NH_3}}{\overset{}{C}} - O^- \right]$$

$$\Big\downarrow$$

$$\left[CH_3 - CH_2 - \underset{\overset{|}{CH_3}}{\overset{}{C}} = \underset{\overset{|}{NH_2}}{\overset{}{C}} - OH \right]$$

$$\Big\uparrow \text{Tautomerisation}$$

$$CH_3 - CH_2 - \underset{\overset{|}{CH_3}}{\overset{}{CH}} = \overset{\overset{O}{\|}}{C} - NH_2$$

$$CH_3 - CH_2 - \underset{\overset{|}{CH_3}}{\overset{}{C}} = C = O \xrightarrow{H_2O}$$

$$CH_3 - CH_2 - \underset{\overset{|}{CH_3}}{\overset{}{CH}} - COOH$$

$$CH_3 - CH_2 - \underset{\overset{|}{CH_3}}{\overset{}{C}} = C = O \xrightarrow{CH_3COOH}$$

$$CH_3 - CH_2 - \underset{\overset{|}{CH_3}}{\overset{}{CH}} - \overset{\overset{O}{\|}}{C} - O - \overset{\overset{O}{\|}}{C} - CH_3$$

4. (a) $C_6H_5COOC_2H_5 \xrightarrow{CH_3MgBr} C_6H_5 - \underset{\overset{|}{CH_3}}{\overset{\overset{OMgBr}{|}}{C}} - OC_2H_5$
$\qquad\qquad$ 'A'

$$\xrightarrow{-Mg(OC_2H_5)Br} C_6H_5 - \overset{\overset{O}{\|}}{C} - CH_3 \xrightarrow[CH_3MgBr]{Excess}$$

$$C_6H_5 - \underset{\overset{|}{CH_3}}{\overset{\overset{OMgBr}{|}}{C}} - CH_3 \xrightarrow{H_2O} C_6H_5 - \underset{\overset{|}{OH}}{\overset{\overset{CH_3}{|}}{C}} - CH_3$$

$$\xrightarrow[\Delta]{\text{Conc. H}_2\text{SO}_4} \text{C}_6\text{H}_5 - \overset{\overset{\displaystyle CH_3}{|}}{C} = CH_2 \xrightarrow{\text{Ozonolysis}}$$

'B'

$$C_6H_5COCH_3 + HCHO$$

$$C_6H_5COCH_3 \xrightarrow{3I_2 + 4NaOH} CHI_3 + C_6H_5COO^-Na^+$$

5. **(a)**

6. **(a, d)** The hydrogen atom that is added to the carbonyl carbon of the aldehyde in the reduction is derived directly from the other aldehyde molecule as a hydride ion. The second hydrogen that is added to the negatively charged oxygen is coming from the solvent (consult mechanism of Cannizzaro reaction). Oxidation of one molecule of the compound at the expense of other molecule of the same compound is known as disproportionation.

7. **(a, c, d)**

8. **(c,d)** Substitution by one Br gives $C_6H_5COCHBrCH_3$, the electron-withdrawing Br increases the acidity of the remaining α hydrogen which reacts more rapidly than the hydrogens on the unsubstituted ketones.

$$\underset{\underset{\text{0.5 mole}}{}}{\overset{\overset{\text{Less acidic}}{\downarrow}}{C_6H_5COCH_2CH_3}} \xrightarrow[\text{OH}^-]{\text{0.5 mole Br}_2} \underset{\text{(0.5 mole, but not isolated)}}{[\overset{\overset{\text{More acidic}}{\downarrow}}{C_6H_5COCHBrCH_3}]} \xrightarrow[\text{OH}^-]{\text{0.5 mole Br}_2} \underset{\text{0.5 mole}}{C_6H_5COCBr_2CH_3}$$

9. **(a,c)**

$$R-\overset{O}{\overset{||}{C}} + \overset{-}{C}H_2-\overset{+}{N}=N \longrightarrow R-\overset{\overset{O^-}{|}}{\underset{R}{C}}-CH_2-\overset{+}{N}=N$$

$$\downarrow {-N_2}$$

$$R-\overset{O}{\overset{||}{C}}-CH_2R \longleftarrow R-\overset{\overset{O^-}{|}}{\underset{R}{C}}-\overset{+}{C}H_2 \longrightarrow R-\overset{O}{\overset{/\backslash}{C}-CH_2}$$

10. **(9)**

(E and Z isomer)

(E and Z isomer)

(Ans. = 7)

11. One product (Z).

(Y)

(Z)

$$\xrightarrow[\text{2. Zn, H}_2\text{O}]{1. \text{O}_3}$$

$$\xrightarrow[\text{2. Heat}]{1. \text{NaOH (aq.)}}$$

12. (3) $CH_3MgBr + CH_3CH_2-\overset{\overset{O}{||}}{C}-Cl \rightarrow$

$CH_3-\overset{\overset{O}{||}}{C}-CH_2CH_3 + Mg\begin{matrix}Br\\Br\end{matrix}$

2-Butanone

2-Butanone will show tautomerism.

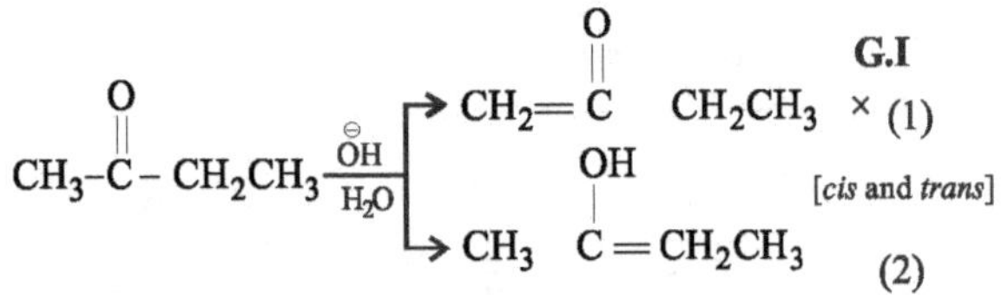

Total enol products = 1 + 2 = 3.

13. (2)

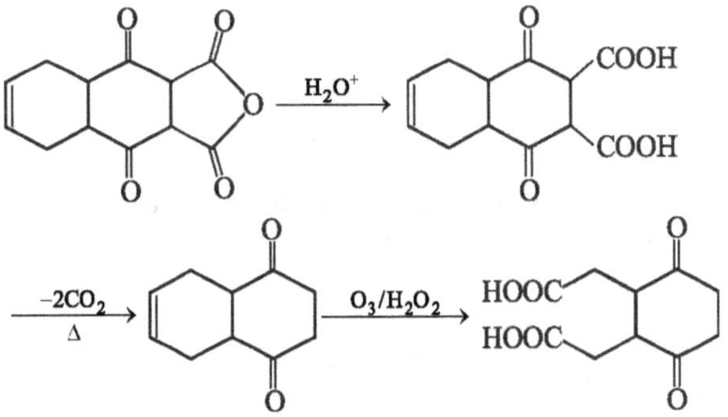

14. (4) I. Benzene $\xrightarrow[\text{Anhydrons } AlCl_3/CuCl]{CO+HCl}$ PhCHO (Benzaldehyde)

(Gattermann KOCH Aldehyde reaction)

II.

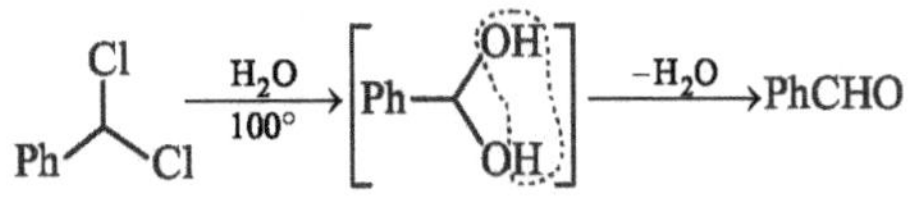

III.

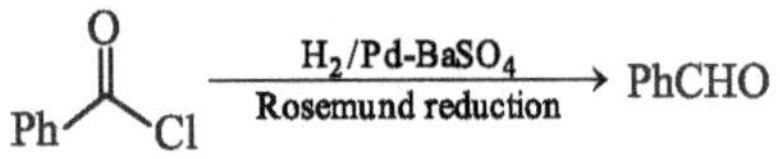

IV.

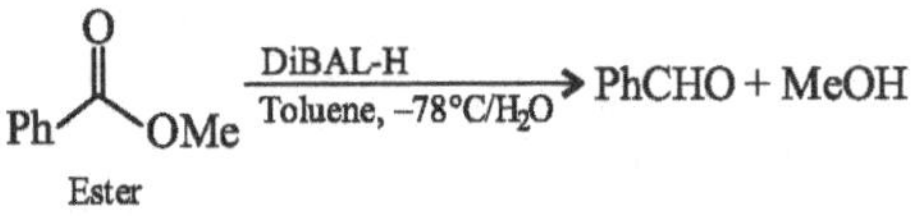

15. (c)

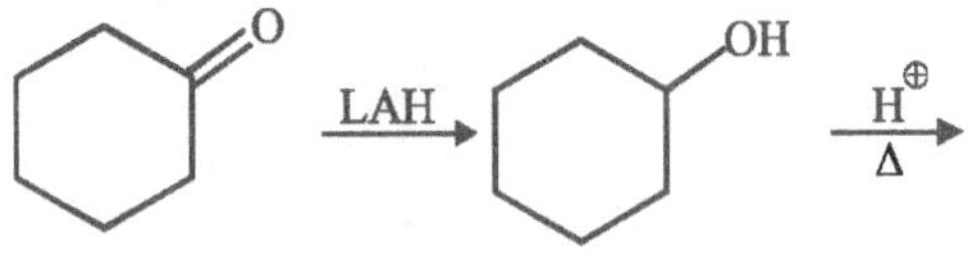

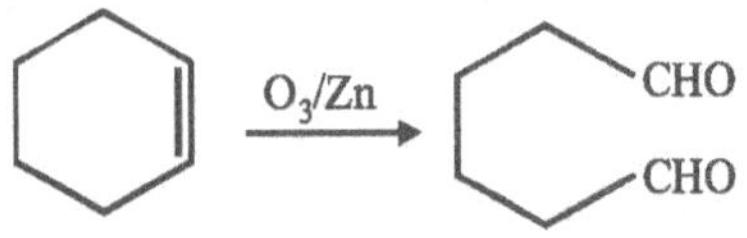

16. (d)

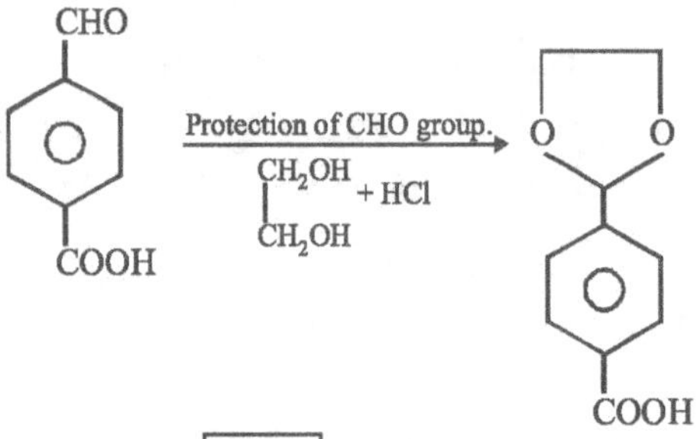

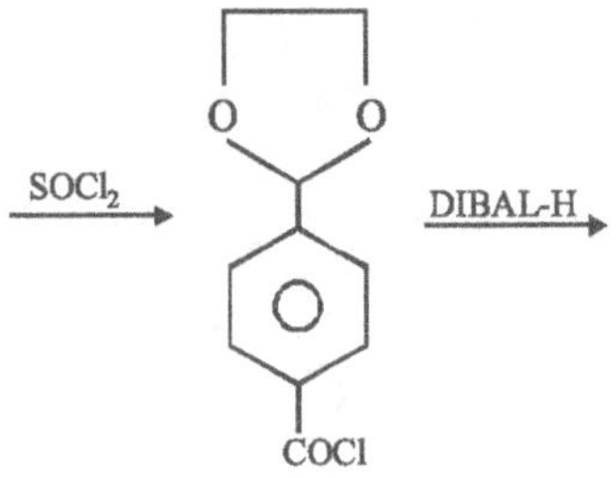

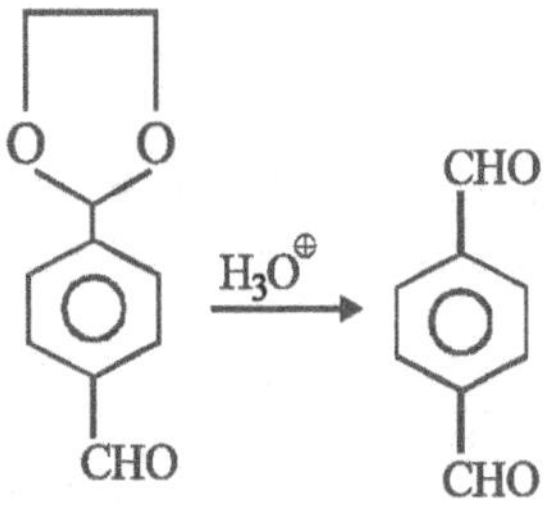

17. (c)

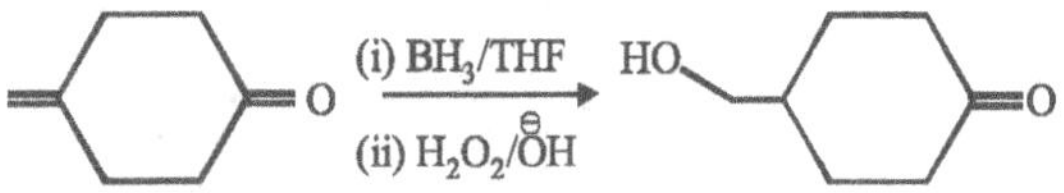

Preferentially oxidises (C = C) bond.

18. (d)

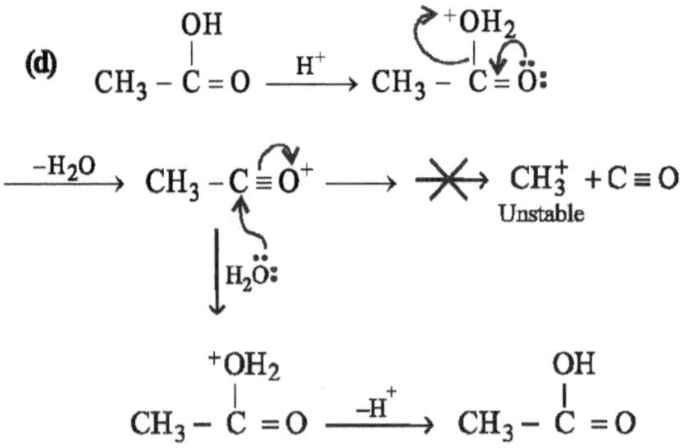

Thus acetic acid will be regenerated, i.e. there is no reaction.

19. **(c)** $C_6H_5 - \overset{\overset{O}{\|}}{C} - \overset{\overset{OH}{|}}{C} = O \xrightarrow[(-H_2O)]{H^+} C_6H_5 - \overset{\overset{\ddot{O}:}{\|}}{C} - C \equiv O^+$

$\longrightarrow C_6H_5 - C \equiv O^+ + CO$

$C_6H_5C \equiv \overset{+}{O}^+ \longleftrightarrow C_6H_5 - \overset{+}{C} = O$

$\xrightarrow{H_2O} C_6H_5 - \overset{\overset{OH}{|}}{C} = O$

20. $(A) \rightarrow r, s \,; (B) \rightarrow p, s \,; (C) \rightarrow r, s; (D) \rightarrow q, r$

(A) aq/NaOH (Carbanion)

H_2O (Nucleophilic addition)

$\overset{\ominus}{OH}/\Delta$ dehydration

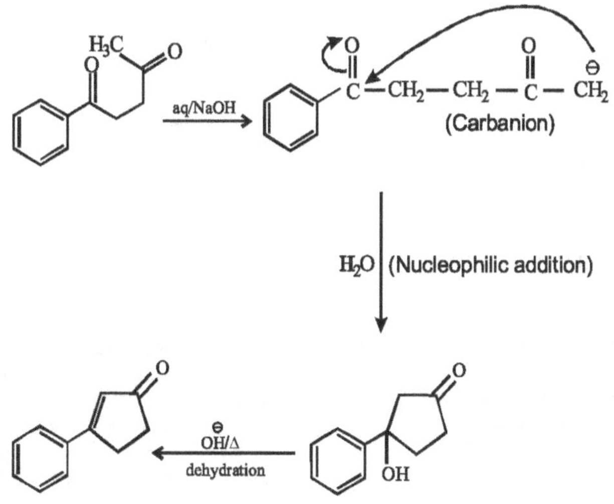

(B) $\xrightarrow[\text{addition}]{\underset{\text{Nucleophilic}}{CH_3MgI}}$

$\xrightarrow[\text{substitution)}]{H_2O \text{ (Nucleophilic}}$

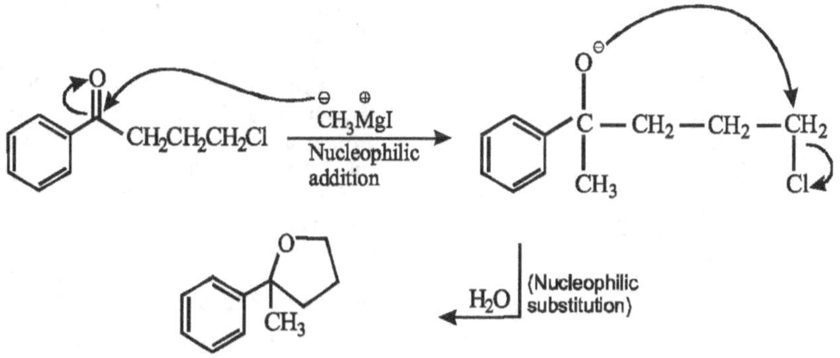

(C) $\xrightarrow{H_2SO_4}$

(Nucleophilic addition)

$\xleftarrow[\text{dehydration}]{H_2SO_4}$

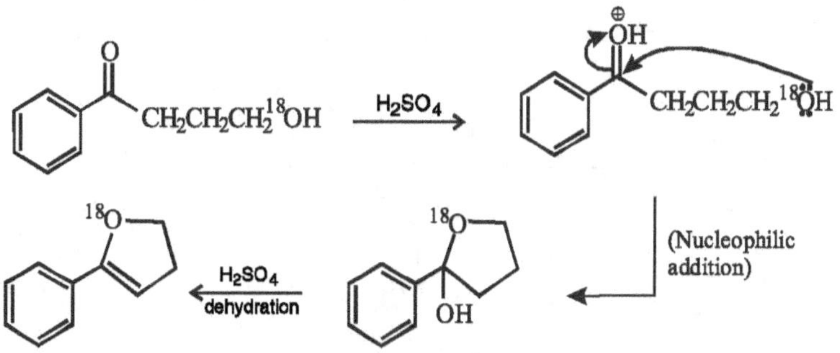

(D) $\xrightarrow[\text{dehydration}]{H_2SO_4}$ $\xrightarrow[\text{substitution}]{\text{Electrophilic}}$

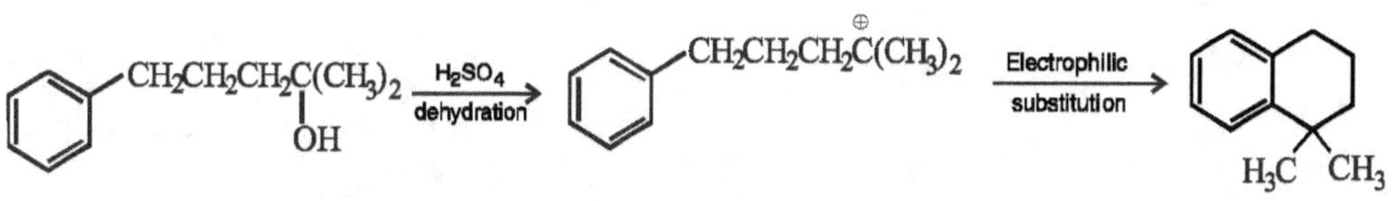

1. (c)

Nitrobenzene (A) $\xrightarrow[\text{reduction}]{\text{Sn+HCl}}$ (B) $\xrightarrow{\text{CHCl}_3+\text{KOH}}$ (C)

(C) $\xrightarrow[\text{Na/C}_2\text{H}_5\text{OH}]{\text{Reduction}}$ N-methylaniline

2. (b) Reduction reactions of given amines are following

$$\underset{\text{Ethanamide}}{\text{CH}_3\text{CONH}_2} \xrightarrow{\text{LiAlH}_4} \underset{\text{ethanamine (1° amine)}}{\text{CH}_3\text{CH}_2\text{NH}_2}$$

$$\underset{\text{N,N–dimethylethanamide}}{\text{CH}_3\text{CON(CH}_3)_2} \xrightarrow{\text{LiAlH}_4} \underset{\substack{\text{N,N–dimethylethanamine}\\(3°\text{amine})}}{\text{CH}_3\text{CH}_2\text{N(CH}_3)_2}$$

$$\underset{\text{Phenylmethanamide}}{\text{C}_6\text{H}_5\text{CONH}_2} \xrightarrow{\text{LiAlH}_4} \underset{\text{Phenylmethanamine (1° amine)}}{\text{C}_6\text{H}_5\text{CH}_2\text{NH}_2}$$

$$\underset{\text{N–methylethanamide}}{\text{CH}_3\text{CONH–CH}_3} \xrightarrow{\text{LiAlH}_4} \underset{\text{N–methylethanamine (2° amine)}}{\text{CH}_3\text{CH}_2\text{NHCH}_3}$$

3. (d)

Aniline $+3\text{Br}_2 \xrightarrow{\text{H}_2\text{O}}$ (2, 4, 6-tribromoaniline) $\xrightarrow[\text{and dil. HCl}]{\text{NaNO}_2}$

Diazonium salt $\xrightarrow[(-\text{NaCl})]{\text{NaBF}_4}$ Diazonium tetrafluoroborate $\xrightarrow[\substack{-\text{N}_2\\-\text{BF}_3}]{\Delta}$ 2,4,6-tribromofluorobenzene

4. (b) The order of basicity is I > III > II > IV
The lone pair of electrons on N is more readily available for protonation in I and III then in II. III contains an oxygen atom which has – I effect due to which it is less basic than I. In compound IV lone pair of e⁻s on N-atom is contributed towards the aromatic sextet formation and hence is not at all available for protonation. Hence option (b) is correct.

5. (a) Arylamines are less basic than alkyl amines and even ammonia. This is due to resonance. In aryl amines the lone pair of electrons on N is partly shared with the ring and is thus less available for sharing with a proton. In alkylamines, the electron releasing alkyl group increases the electron density on nitrogen atom and thus also increases the ability of amine for protonation. Hence more the no. of alkyl groups higher should be the basicity of amine. But a slight discrepancy occurs in case of trimethyl amines due to steric effect. Hence the correct order of basicity will be :

$$(\text{CH}_3)_2\text{NH} > \text{CH}_3\text{NH}_2 > (\text{CH}_3)_3\text{N} > \text{C}_6\text{H}_5\text{NH}_2$$
Hence, $(\text{CH}_3)_2\text{NH}$ will have the smallest pK_b value.

6. (b)

(A) $\xrightarrow[\text{FeBr}_3]{\text{Br}_2}$ (B) $\xrightarrow{\text{Sn/HCl}}$ (C) $\xrightarrow[\text{HCl}]{\text{NaNO}_2}$ (D) $\xrightarrow[\text{CuBr}]{\text{HBr}}$ (E)

7. **(b, c, d)** Vinyl and aryl halides do not undergo S_N2 reactions, unless activated by electron withdrawing group (in the *o-* and *p*-position in case of aryl halides). 3° Halides form alkenes on elimination.

8. **(a, b, d)** *tert*-Nitro compounds (Me_3CNO_2) do not react with HONO because they do not have any α-H. The three others react with HONO as usual.

$$CH_3-\underset{\underset{\text{2-Nitrobutane}}{}}{\overset{\overset{\displaystyle NO_2}{|}}{C}H}CH_2CH_3 \xrightarrow{\text{HONO}} CH_3-\underset{\underset{NO}{|}}{\overset{\overset{\displaystyle NO_2}{|}}{C}}-CH_2CH_3$$

Pseudonitrol (blue)

9. **(a, b, d)** Isonitriles (C_6H_5NC) on reduction give 2° amines ($C_6H_5NHCH_3$). All other three methods give aniline.

10. **(a, b, c)** $C_6H_5 \overset{..}{N}H_2 + AlCl_3 \longrightarrow \underset{\underset{\text{a meta director}}{\text{Substituent} (-NH_2AlCl_3^-)}}{C_6H_5 \overset{\overset{\displaystyle AlCl_3}{\overset{\displaystyle |}{|_+}}}{N}H_2} \xrightarrow{CH_3Cl}$ No reaction

11. **(2)** $LiAlH_4$ does not reduce $-NO_2$ group to $-NH_2$ group.

12. **(2)** Cope elimination is used for removing a nitrogen present outside the ring, while Hofmann elimination is used for removing nitrogen present inside as well as outside the ring.

13. **(2)** There are two structural isomers of a grignard reagent are possible for the formation of *n*-butane by reaction with ethyl amine:

$$\underset{}{\overset{\overset{\displaystyle CH_3}{|}}{}}$$
$CH_3CH_2CHMgBr$ and $CH_3CH_2CH_2CH_2MgBr$

$$CH_3CH_2\overset{\overset{\displaystyle CH_3}{|}}{\overset{-}{C}}\overset{+}{H}MgBr + C_2H_5\underset{\underset{H}{|}}{N}H \longrightarrow (C_2H_5\overset{-}{N}\overset{+}{H})MgBr + \underset{\text{(n-butane)}}{CH_3CH_2CH_2-CH_3}$$

$$CH_3CH_2CH_2\overset{-}{C}\overset{+}{H_2}MgBr + C_2H_5\underset{\underset{H}{|}}{N}H \longrightarrow (C_2H_5\overset{-}{N}\overset{+}{H})MgBr + \underset{\text{(n-butane)}}{CH_3CH_2CH_2CH_3}$$

14. **(3)** Diazomethane is used for methylating acidic groups, compound IV has enolic —OH group, hence it can also be methylated by CH_2N_2.

15. **(d) Reaction (i)**

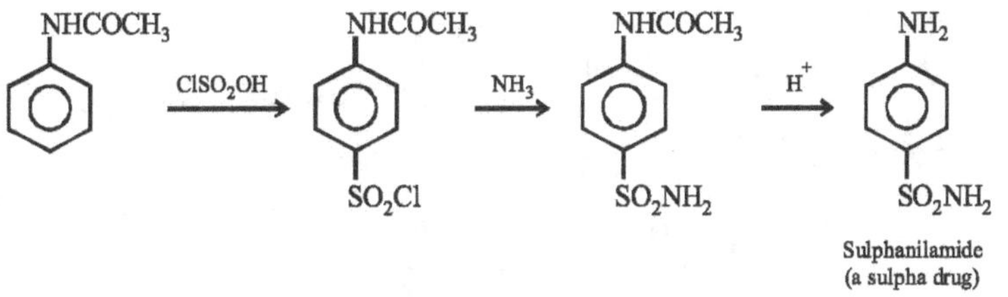

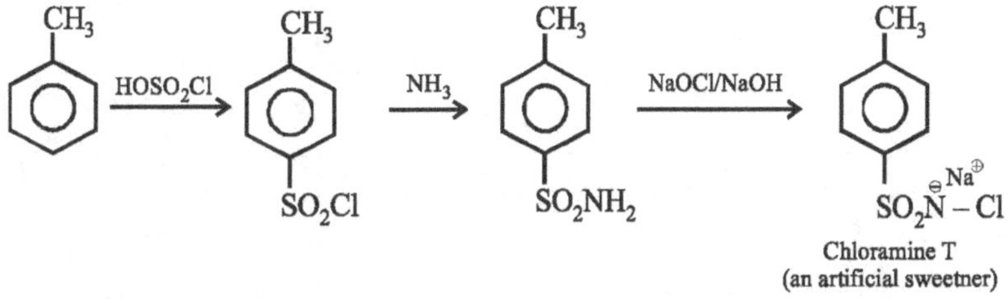

16. (a) Going backward, we can obtain answer :

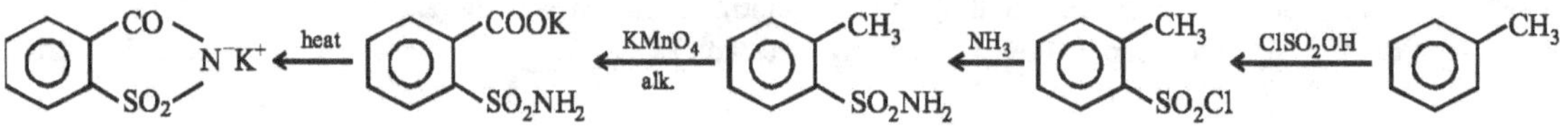

[chemical reaction scheme: toluene → (ClSO$_2$OH) o-toluenesulfonyl chloride (CH$_3$, SO$_2$Cl) → (NH$_3$) (CH$_3$, SO$_2$NH$_2$) → (KMnO$_4$ alk.) (CH$_3$, SO$_2$NH$_2$) → (with COOK, SO$_2$NH$_2$) → (heat) cyclic imide potassium salt (CO–N$^-$K$^+$, SO$_2$)]

17. (d)

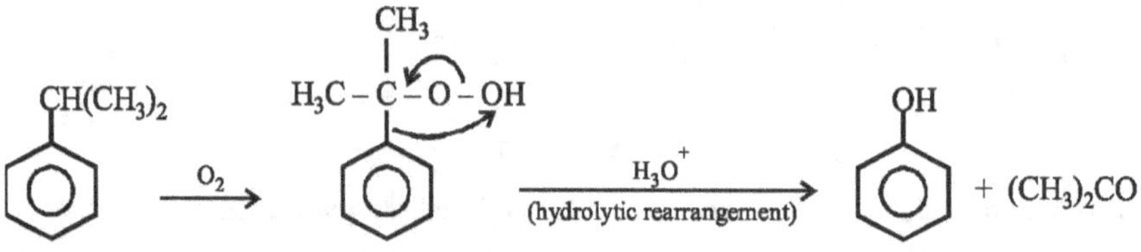

[reaction scheme: Cumene (with CH(CH$_3$)$_2$) $\xrightarrow{O_2}$ Cumene hydroperoxide (H$_3$C–C(CH$_3$)–O–OH) $\xrightarrow[\text{(hydrolytic rearrangement)}]{H_3O^+}$ phenol (OH) + (CH$_3$)$_2$CO]

This step involves migration of phenyl group to electron-deficient oxygen.

18. (c)

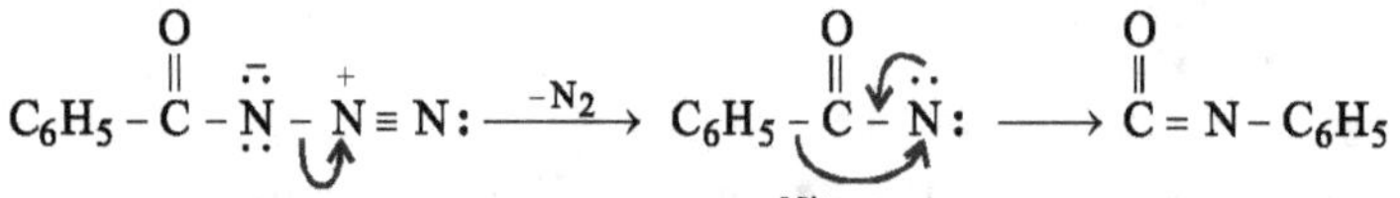

$$C_6H_5 - \overset{\overset{O}{\|}}{C} - \overset{..}{\underset{..}{N}} - \overset{+}{N} \equiv N : \xrightarrow{-N_2} C_6H_5 - \overset{\overset{O}{\|}}{C} - \overset{..}{N} : \longrightarrow \overset{\overset{O}{\|}}{C} = N - C_6H_5$$

Nitrene
(electron–deficient N)

19. A-q, r; B-p, s; C-p, r; D-p, r

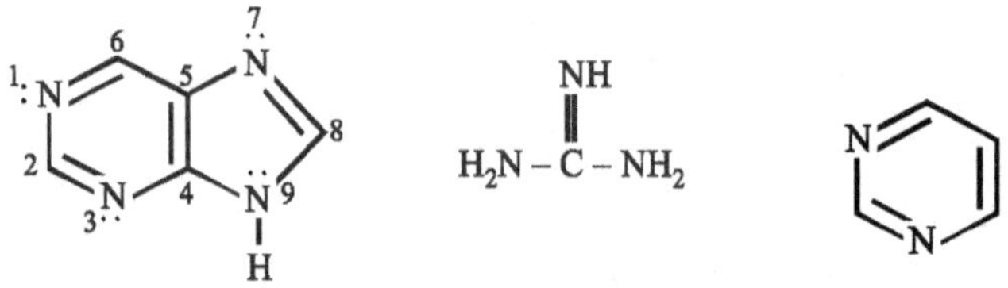

[structures: (A) purine-type fused bicyclic ring with numbered positions 1–9 and N–H; (B) guanidine H$_2$N–C(=NH)–NH$_2$; (C) pyrimidine ring]

    (A)   (B)   (C)

(A) A is aromatic due to 10 π electrons, N$_1$, N$_3$ and N$_7$ are sp^2 hybridised their ℓp present in sp^2 orbital are localised hence undergo protonation. The N$_9$ is also sp^2 hybridised but its ℓp is in p-orbital hence involved in delocalisation, and thus not basic.

(B) Due to resonance, all the three nitrogens of guanidine are identical. It is not cyclic, hence non-aromatic.

(C-D) As mentioned above in (A), here the two nitrogens are identical, and the compound is aromatic due to the presence of aromatic sextet.

20. (A)→ p, q, s, t; (B) → s, t; (C) → p; (D) → r

(A) $CH_3CH_2CH_2CN \xrightarrow[\substack{SnCl_2/HCl \text{ or} \\ DIBAL-H}]{Pd-C/H_2 \text{ or}} CH_3CH_2CH_2CH_2NH_2$

$CH_3CH_2CH_2CN \xrightarrow[H_2O]{OH^-} CH_3CH_2CH_2COO^-$

(B) $CH_3CH_2OCOCH_3 \xrightarrow{DIBAL-H} CH_3CH_2OH$

$CH_3CH_2OCOCH_3 \xrightarrow[H_2O]{OH^-} CH_3CH_2OH + CH_3COO^-$

(C) $CH_3CH = CHCH_2OH \xrightarrow{Pd-C/H_2} CH_3CH_2CH_2CH_2OH$

(D) $CH_3CH_2CH_2CH_2NH_2 \xrightarrow[KOH]{CHCl_3} CH_3CH_2CH_2CH_2NC$

$CH_3CH_2CH_2CH_2NC$
Isonitrile (foul smelling)

1. **(b)** In DNA and RNA, heterocyclic base and phosphate ester linkages are at C_1' and C_5' respectively of the sugar molecule.

2. **(b)** Cyclization of the open chain structure of D-(+)-glucose has created a new stereocenter at C_1 which explains the existence of two cyclic forms of D-(+)-glucose, namely α– and β–. These two cyclic forms are diasteromers, such diastereomers which differ only in the configuration of chiral carbon developed on hemiacetal formation (it is C_1 in glucose and C_2 in fructose) are called **anomers** and the hemiacetal carbon (C_1 or C_2) is called the **anomeric carbon.**

α–D-(+)-Glucopyranose
m.p. 146°C ; $[\alpha]_D = + 112.2°$
(36% at equilibrium)

Open chain form
of D-(+)-glucose
(negligible % at equilibrium)

β–D-(+)-Glucopyranose
m.p. 150°C ; $[\alpha]_D = + 18.7°$
(64% at equilibrium)

3. **(b)** **Molisch's Test :** This is a general test for carbohydrates. One or two drops of alcoholic solution of α-naphthol is added to 2 mL glucose solution. 1 mL of conc. H_2SO_4 solution is added carefully along the sides of the test-tube. The formation of a violet ring at the junction of two liquids confirms the presence of a carbohydrate or sugar.

4. **(a)** $6CO_2 + 12NADPH + 18ATP \rightarrow C_6H_{12}O_6 + 12NADP + 18ADP$

5. **(d)** The correct structure of thymine is

Thymine (T)

6. **(c)** Butyric acid also known as butanoic acid is found in milk, and butter and is a product of anaerobic fermentation. It has an unpleasant smell and acrid taste.

7. **(b, c)** We know that carbohydrates having acetal linkage are non-reducing while that with hemiacetal linkage are reducing. In the give structure,
X has acetal linkage, hence non-reducing.
Y has hemiacetal linkage, hence reducing.
Further **X** is α-anomer, while **Y** is β-anomer of D-(+)-glucose.

8. **(a, c)** Epimers are those carbohydrates which differ in the configuration around only one asymmetric carbon atom (of course other than C_1). I and II are C-2 epimers, while I and III are C-4 epimers.

9. **(b, c, d)** Fruit mainly contains fructose, hence the latter is commonly known as fruit sugar.

10. **(a, b, c)** Glucose, fructose and mannose differ only in configuration at C_1 and C_2 and hence give same osazone.

11. **(10)**

D-sorbose

4-Chiral centres, terminal groups same
Total stereoisomers $2^{4-1} + 2^{(4/2)-1} = 10$

12. **(3)** 3-moles of phenylhydrazine reacts with one mole of glucose to form osazone.

13. **(3)**

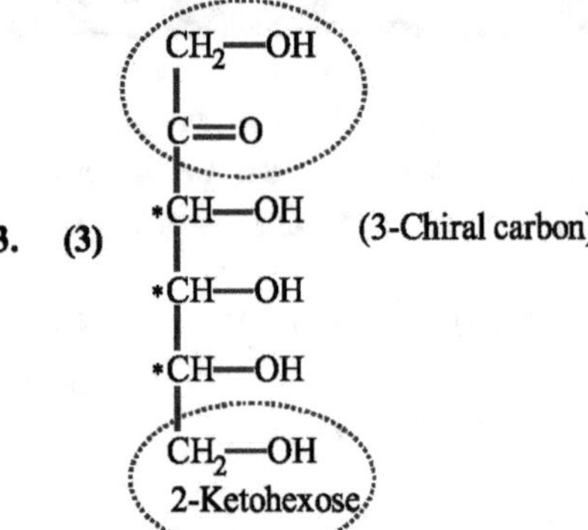

(3-Chiral carbon)

14. **(8)** Each mole of the compound consume 5 moles of HIO_4.

∴ No. of moles of $HIO_4 = 16 \times 5 = 80$

$$X = \frac{80}{10} = 8$$

15. **(b)** The (ii) series of reactions points out for the presence of a ketonic group in A, hence A must be D-fructose. The series D- is indicated as we get D-fructose in (i) series of reactions.

16. **(a)** C on oxidation gives an optically inactive glycaric acid, which is indicative of following structure for C.

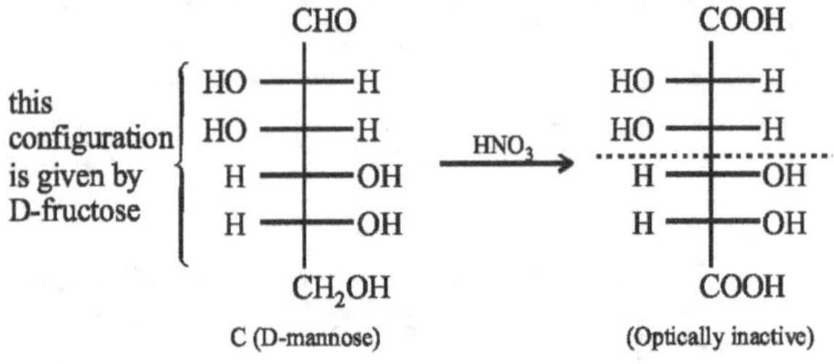

this configuration is given by D-fructose

C (D-mannose)

(Optically inactive)

Thus B should have following structure.

B (D-glucose)

Optically active

17. (d) & 18. (b)

Adipic acid

(i) SOCl$_2$
(ii) NH$_3$

Br$_2$/KOH
(Hoffmann bromamide reaction)

Br$_2$/P
(HVZ reaction)

Intramolecular S$_N$2

Proline

19. A-p, s; B-p, q, r; C-p, s; D-p, r

20. A-p, r, s; B-q, r; C-p, r, s; D-p, r, s

1. (b)

$$-CH_2\diagdown \overset{CH_3}{\underset{}{C}}=C\overset{H}{\underset{CH_2}{}} \quad \overset{CH_2}{\underset{CH_3}{}}C=C\overset{CH_2}{\underset{H}{}} \quad \overset{CH_3}{\underset{CH_2}{}}C=C\overset{H}{\underset{CH_2-}{}}$$

Natural rubber
(All cis configuration)

All statements except (b) are correct

2. (c)
$$H_2N-(CH_2-)_6\,NH_2 + Cl-\overset{O}{\overset{\|}{C}}-(CH_2)_8-\overset{O}{\overset{\|}{C}}-Cl$$
Hexamethylene diamine $\qquad$ Sebacoyl chloride

$$\overset{\Delta}{\longrightarrow} -HN-(CH_2)_6-(NH-\overset{O}{\overset{\|}{C}}-(CH_2)_8-\overset{O}{\overset{\|}{C}}-)_n$$
Nylon 6, 10

3. (d) Polyhydroxybutyrate-co-β-hydroxyvalerate or PHBV is a biodegradable polymer and thus it can be used as biomaterials in orthopaedic devices and in controlled drug release.

$$CH_3-CHCH_2COOH + CH_3CH_2-CH-CH_2COOH$$
$$\underset{OH}{\qquad\quad |\qquad\qquad\qquad\qquad\qquad |}$$
$$\qquad\quad OH \qquad\qquad\qquad\qquad\qquad\quad OH$$

$$\left[O-\overset{CH_3}{\overset{|}{HC}}-CH_2-\overset{O}{\overset{\|}{C}}-O-\overset{C_2H_5}{\overset{|}{CH}}-CH_2-\overset{O}{\overset{\|}{C}}\right]_n$$

PHBV

4. (a) Terylene is prepared by condensing dimethylterephthalate and ethylene glycol in presence of a weak base, (calcium acetate). Methanol is eliminated during condensation.

$$nH_3COOC-\langle\bigcirc\rangle-COOCH_3 + nHOCH_2-CH_2OH$$
Dimethylterephthalate $\qquad\qquad$ Ethylene glycol

$$\xrightarrow[300°C]{-CH_3OH} \left[-\overset{}{\underset{O}{\overset{\|}{C}}}-\langle\bigcirc\rangle-\overset{}{\underset{O}{\overset{\|}{C}}}-OCH_2-OCH_2-\right]_n$$
$$\qquad\qquad\qquad\qquad\qquad Terylene$$

5. (d) In polymerisation of 1,3-butadiene either 1,4-polymerisation or 1,2-polymerisation occurs. In case of 1,4-polymerisation, the double bond shifts at C_2 and C_4 carbon, while the chain propagates from C_1 and C_4 end. In this either trans or cis polymeric chain is formed. Option (a) and (b) represent 'trans' and 'cis' 1,4 polymerisation respectively.
Option (c) resembles 1,2 polymerisation, where as option (d) most unlikely to happen.

6. (c) Ebonite is a hard highly vulcanized rubber, containing 20-30% sulphur.

7. (b)
$$nCH_2=CH-CH=CH_2 + n\,\langle\bigcirc\rangle\overset{CH=CH_2}{}\xrightarrow[Polymerisation]{Na, Heat}$$
1, 3-Butadiene $\qquad\qquad\qquad\qquad$ Styrene

$$(-CH_2-CH=CH-CH_2-CH-CH_2-)_n$$
Butadiene - Styrene copolymer (SBR or BUNA - S)

8. (a) Vulcanization is a process in which natural rubber is treated with sulphur and certain organic compounds which accelerate the reaction between the rubber and sulphur. Thus about 5% S is used for making tyre rubber, 20-25% S for making ebonite and 30% S for making battery case rubber.

9. (d) Neoprene is an addition polymer of isoprene.

$$nCH_2=CH-\overset{Cl}{\overset{|}{C}}=CH_2\xrightarrow{O_2\text{ or peroxides}}$$
Chloroprene

$$\left(-CH_2-\overset{Cl}{\overset{|}{C}}=CH-CH_2-\right)_n$$
Neoprene

10. (b) Nylon is a condensation polymer

11. (b) Biodegradable polymer is Nylon-2-Nylon-6 which is copolymer of glycine (H_2N-CH_2-COOH) and amino caproic acid ($H_2N-(CH_2)_5-COOH$).
$$nH_2N-CH_2-COOH +$$
$$\text{glycine} \quad nH_2N-(CH_2)_5-COOH$$
$$\qquad\qquad\qquad\text{amino caproic acid}$$
$$\downarrow$$
$$\left(HN-CH_2-\overset{O}{\overset{\|}{C}}-HN-(CH_2)_5-\overset{O}{\overset{\|}{C}}\right)_n$$
$$nylon-2-nylon-6$$

12. (a) It is present in the cell wall of plant cell.

13. (b) Nylon is a polyamide fibre. It is prepared by the condensation polymerisation of adipic acid ($HOOC.(CH_2)_4COOH$) and hexamethylene diamine ($H_2N.(CH_2)_6.NH_2$).

14. **(c)** Polythene is a linear polymer

15. **(a, b, c)**
These do not contain EDG or EWG, so they can be prepared by free radical addition polymerisation.

16. **(a, b, c)**
Polyester and polyamide undergo condensation polymerisation.

17. **(a)** Nylon-5, 10 refers to 5-C-atom diamine and 10-C-atom dibasic acid (first numeral refers to diamine and second numeral refers to dicaboxylic acid).

18. **(a, c)**

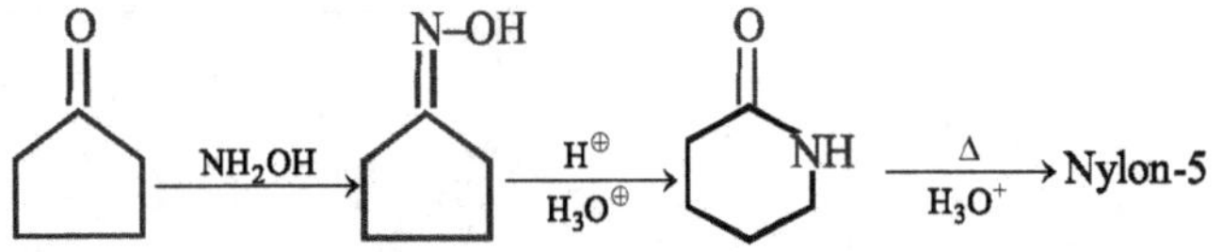

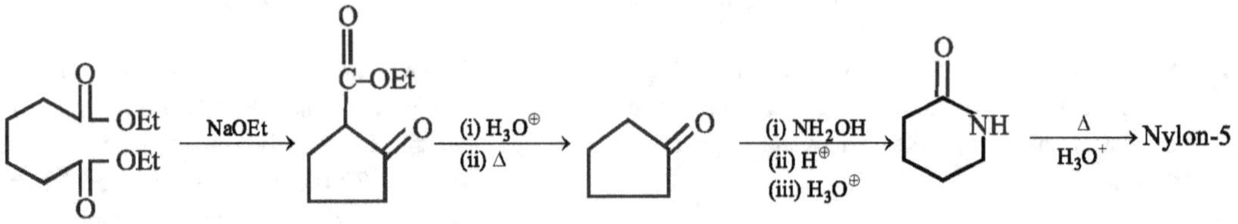

19. **(a, b, d)** Rayon is made of cellulose.

20. **(a, b, c, d)**
(a) Butyl rubber also refers to butadiene.
(b) Nitrile rubber refers to Buna-N.
(c) ABS (refers to acrylonitrile butadiene styrene).
(d) SBR refers to styrene butadiene rubber)

21. **(a, c, d)**

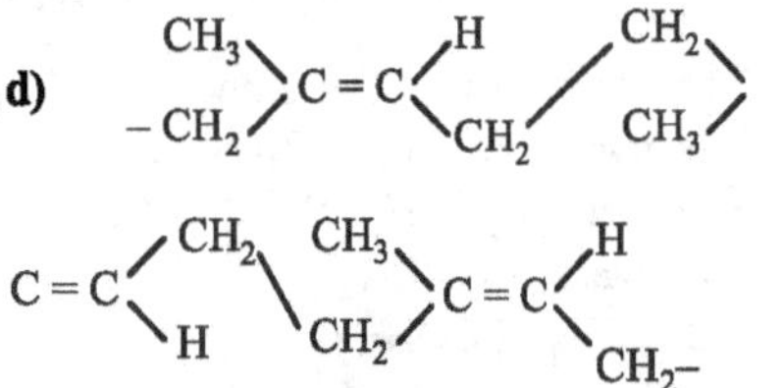

Natural rubber
(All cis configuration)

22. **(b, c, d)** Neoprene is a polymer of chloroprene.

Mock Test Full Syllabus Chemistry

Paper - 1

SECTION – I – Multiple Correct Choice Type

This section contains 7 multiple choice quesitons. Each question has 4 choices (a), (b), (c) and (d) for its answer, out of which ONE OR MORE is/are correct.

1. Which of the following is wrong

(a) 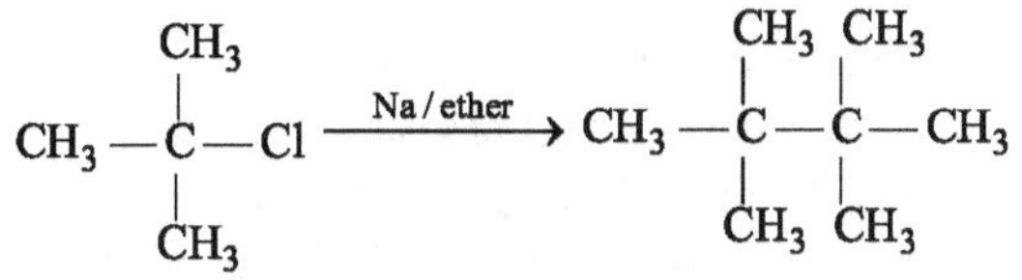 $CH_3-\underset{\underset{CH_3}{|}}{\overset{\overset{CH_3}{|}}{C}}-Cl \xrightarrow{Na\,/\,ether} CH_3-\underset{\underset{CH_3}{|}}{\overset{\overset{CH_3}{|}}{C}}-\underset{\underset{CH_3}{|}}{\overset{\overset{CH_3}{|}}{C}}-CH_3$

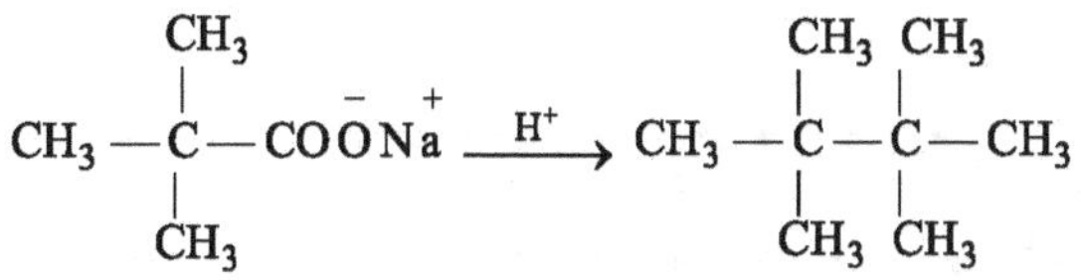

(b)

$CH_3-\underset{\underset{CH_3}{|}}{\overset{\overset{CH_3}{|}}{C}}-\overset{-}{C}\overset{+}{OONa} \xrightarrow{H^+} CH_3-\underset{\underset{CH_3}{|}}{\overset{\overset{CH_3}{|}}{C}}-\underset{\underset{CH_3}{|}}{\overset{\overset{CH_3}{|}}{C}}-CH_3$

(c) $\underset{\underset{CH_3}{}}{\overset{\overset{C_2H_5}{}}{C}}=\underset{\underset{CH_3}{}}{\overset{\overset{C_2H_5}{}}{C}} \xrightarrow{H_2\,/\,Ni}$

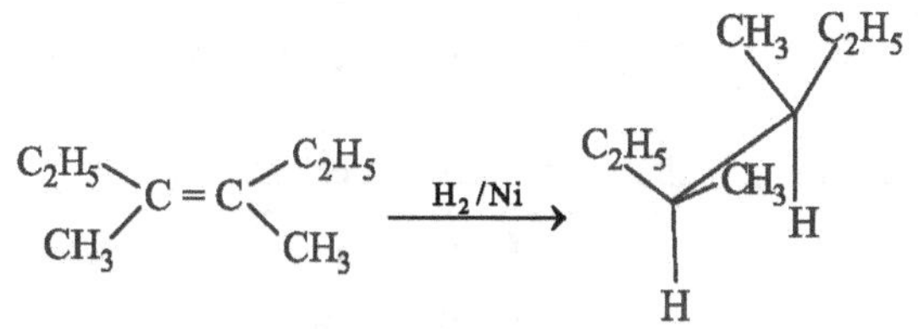

(d) 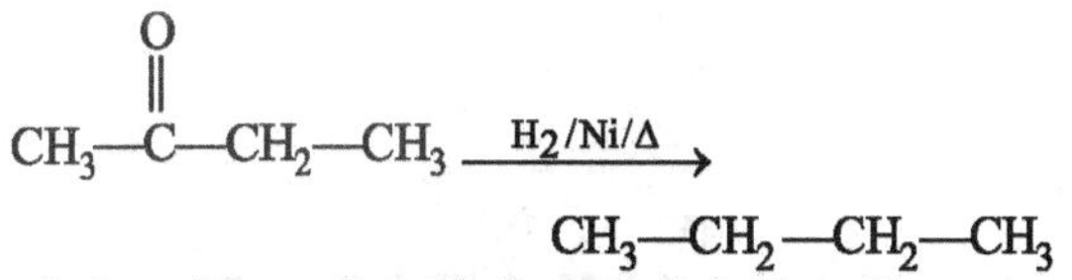 $CH_3-\overset{\overset{O}{\|}}{C}-CH_2-CH_3 \xrightarrow{H_2/Ni/\Delta}$
$CH_3-CH_2-CH_2-CH_3$

2. The enthalpy of formation of ethane, ethylene and benzene from the gaseous atoms are -2839.2, -2275.2 and -5536 kJ mol^{-1} respectively. The bond enthalpy of C–H bond is given as equal to 410.87 kJ mol^{-1}.
Correct options are
(a) Bond enthalpy of C–C bond = 373.98 kJ mol^{-1}
(b) Bond enthalpy of C=C bond = 631.72 kJ mol^{-1}
(c) resonance energy compared to Kekule structure $=-53.68$ kJ mol^{-1}
(d) Bond enthalpy of C–C bond = 631.72 kJ mol^{-1}

3. Choose the correct statement.
(a) The nodal surface of 2s-orbital exists at a distance 1.058 Å from the nucleus.
(b) in the plots of radial probability versus distances from the nucleus, the number of peaks equal to $n-\ell$.
(c) The opposite lobes of p-orbital and d-orbital have the same sign.
(d) Orbitals of a particular type will have different angular wave function, depending upon the value of n.

4. In a reaction between A and B, the initial rate of reaction was measured for different initial concentrations of A and B as given below : [Given log 1.5 = 0.17609, log 2 = 0.3010]

A/M	0.20	0.20	0.40
B/M	0.30	0.10	0.05
R_0/M s^{-1}	5.07×10^{-5}	5.07×10^{-5}	7.6×10^{-5}

(a) The order of reaction with respect to A is 0.5
(b) The order of reaction with respect to B is 0.5
(c) The order of reaction with respect to B is 0
(d) The order of reaction with respect to A is 1.5

5. The following conversion reaction can be carried out by using reaction sequence/s.

(a) $\xrightarrow{Zn/Hg/HCl,\Delta} \xrightarrow{Br_2/hv} \xrightarrow{KCN} \xrightarrow{H_3O^+,\Delta}$

(b) $\xrightarrow{NaBH_4} \xrightarrow{Al_2O_3,\Delta} \xrightarrow{O_3/H_2O(oxidative)}$

(c) $\xrightarrow{Heat} \xrightarrow{I_2/NaOH,\Delta} \xrightarrow{H^+}$

(d) $KMnO_4/OH^-/$ heat

6. Which of the following statement(s) is/are true?
(a) $[PtCl_2(NH_3)_4]Br_2$ will exhibit ionization isomerism
(b) $[Co(NO_2)(NH_3)_5]^{2+}$ will display linkage isomerism
(c) $[Co(NH_3)_6][Cr(CN)_6]$ will exhibit coordination isomerism
(d) The oxidation number of Pt in the coordination compound $Na[Pt(C_2H_4)Cl_3]$ is +3.

7. Which of the following statement(s) is/are correct?
(a) $TeCl_4$ has trigonal bipyramidal structure with one position occupied by a lone pair
(b) $TeCl_4$ reacts with HCl to form $[TeCl_6]^{2-}$ complex ion
(c) $[TeCl_6]^{2-}$ is isomorphous with $[SiF_6]^{2-}$ and $[SbCl_6]^{2-}$
(d) None is correct

SECTION – II – Integer Answer Type

This section contains 5 questions. The answer to each of the questions is a single-digit integer, ranging from 0 to 9. The appropriate bubbles below the respective question numbers in the ORS have to be darkened. For example, if the correct answers to question numbers X, Y, Z and W (say) are 6, 0, 9 and 2, respectively, then the correct darkening of bubbles will look like the following:

X	Y	Z	W
⓪	⓪	⓪	⓪
①	①	①	①
②	②	②	②
③	③	③	③
④	④	④	④
⑤	⑤	⑤	⑤
⑥	⑥	⑥	⑥
⑦	⑦	⑦	⑦
⑧	⑧	⑧	⑧
⑨	⑨	⑨	⑨

8. One molal solution of a carboxylic acid in benzene shows the elevation of boiling point of 1.518 K. If the degree of association of the acid in benzene in percent is expressed as 40A then find the value of 'A'. (K_b for benzene = 2.53 K kg mol^{-1}) :

9. A compound of metal ion M^{x+} ($Z = 24$) has a spin only magnetic moment of $\sqrt{15}$ B.M. Find the number of unpaired electrons in the compound.

10. Sulfuryl chloride (SO_2Cl_2) reacts with water to give a mixture of H_2SO_4 and HCl. How many moles of baryta would be required to neutralize the solution formed by adding 1 mol of SO_2Cl_2 to excess of water?

11. H_2 and D_2 gases at a pressure of 1 atm each at 25°C are in equilibrium with a solution containing H^+ and D^+ ions. If $E^\circ_{D^+/D_2} = -0.296\,V$, calculate log $[D^+]/[H^+]$.

12. The density of solid water (ie. ice) at 25°C is 0.98 g cm^{-2} while that of liquid mercury at the same temperature is 13.60 g cm^{-3}. If the percentage of height of the ice above the surface of a container filled with mercury is expressed as $100 - A$ then find the value of 'A'.

SECTION – III - Matching Type

This section contains 6 questions of Matching Type, contains two tables each having 3 columns and 4 rows. Based on each table, there are three questions. Each question has four options (a), (b), (c) and (d) ONLY ONE of these four options is correct.

(Qs. 13-15): By appropriately matching the information given in the three columns of the following table, give the answer of the question that follows.

Column I contains compound and Column II & III contains their CFSE value and dipule moment respectively.

Column I		Column II		Column III	
		CFSE (Δ°)		μ spin (B.M)	
(I)	d^3 (high spin)	(i)	−1.6	(P)	1.73
(II)	d^4 (low spin)	(ii)	−1.8	(Q)	4.90
(III)	d^6 (high spin)	(iii)	−1.2	(R)	2.83
(IV)	d^7 (low spin)	(iv)	−0.4	(S)	3.87

13. Find suitable combination which has highest dipole moment

(a) (I)(ii)(Q)   (b) (IV)(iii)(S)   (c) (III)(iv)(Q)   (d) (II)(i)(Q)

14. e_g^0 configuration is shown by which combination

(a) (III)(i)(P)   (b) (III)(iii)(R)   (c) (IV)(i)(P)   (d) (I)(iii)(S)

15. Correct combination is

(a) (I)(ii)(S)   (b) (I)(iii)(Q)   (c) (IV)(ii)(P)   (d) (IV)(iv)(R)

(Qs. 16-18): By appropriately matching the information given in the three columns of the following table, give the answer of the question that follows.

Column I, II & III contains starting material, factors responsible for reaction & type of products / intermediate respectively.

Column I		Column II		Column III	
(I)	$CH_3CH_2CH=CHCH_3 + HCl$	(i)	Rearrangement	(P)	1, 2 and 1, 4 addition product
(II)	$CH_2=CH-CH=CH_2 + HCl$	(ii)	Inductive effect	(Q)	Stable carbocation
(III)	$C_6H_5CH=CH\,CH_3 + HBr$	(iii)	Hyper conjugation	(R)	1, 2-hydride shift
(IV)	$C_6H_5CH_2CH=CH_2 + HBr$	(iv)	Resonance	(S)	Position isomers

16. For the reaction given in column I, the only correct combination is

(a) (I) (ii) (P)   (b) (I) (iv) (S)   (c) (I) (ii) (S)   (d) (I) (iii) (P)

17. For the reaction given in column I, the only correct combination is

(a) (II) (i) (P)   (b) (II) (iv) (P)   (c) (II) (iv) (R)   (d) (II) (iii) (S)

18. For the reaction given in column I, the only correct combination is

(a) (IV) (i) (R)   (b) (IV) (ii) (Q)   (c) (IV) (i) (P)   (d) (IV) (iv) (R)

Paper -2

SECTION – I - Single Correct Choice Type

This section contains 7 multiple choice questions. Each question has 4 choices (a), (b), (c) and (d) for its answer, out of which ONLY ONE is correct.

1. One gram of commercial $AgNO_3$ is dissolved in 50 mL of water. It is treated with 50 mL of a KI solution. The silver iodide thus precipitated is filtered off. Excess of KI in the filtrate is titrated with $M/10\ KIO_3$ solution in presence of 6 M HCl till all I^- ions are converted into ICl. It requires 50 mL of $M/10\ KIO_3$ solution. Twenty millilitres of the same stock solution of KI requires 30 mL of $M/10\ KIO_3$ under similar conditions. Calculate the percentage of $AgNO_3$ in the sample.

(Reaction : $KIO_3 + 2KI + 6HCl \rightarrow 3ICl + 3KCl + 3H_2O$.)

(a) 85   (b) 80

(c) 75   (d) 90

2. An ideal gas undergoes a single-stage expansion against a constant opposing pressure P_2 from P_1, V_1, T to P_2, V_2, T. What is the largest mass m which can be lifted through a height h in this expansion ?

(a) $\dfrac{nRT}{gh}\left(1+\dfrac{P_2}{P_1}\right)$ (b) $\dfrac{nRT}{gh}\left(1+\dfrac{P_1}{P_2}\right)$

(c) $\dfrac{nRT}{gh}\left(1-\dfrac{P_2}{P_1}\right)$ (d) $\dfrac{nRT}{gh}\left(1-\dfrac{P_1}{P_2}\right)$

3. Which of the following is correct set of physical properties of the geometrical isomers –

$$CH_3\!\!\diagdown C = C \diagup\!\!H \qquad CH_3\!\!\diagdown C = C \diagup\!\!Cl$$
$$H\diagup \qquad \diagdown Cl \qquad H\diagup \qquad \diagdown H$$
$$\text{I} \qquad\qquad \text{II}$$

	Dipole moment	Boiling point	Melting point	Stability
(a)	I > II	I > II	II > I	I > II
(b)	II > I	II > I	II > I	II > I
(c)	I > II	I > II	I > II	I > II
(d)	II > I	II > I	I > II	I > II

4. The percentage void space per unit volume of unit cell in zinc fluoride structure is

(a) 15.03%   (b) 22.18%

(c) 18.23%   (d) 25.07%

5. Electrolysis is carried out in three cells : (a) – $1.0\ M$ $CuSO_4$, Pt electrodes; (b) – $1.0\ M$ $CuSO_4$, Copper electrodes; (c) – $1.0\ M$ KCl, Pt electrodes. If volume of electrolytic solution is maintained constant in each of the cells, which is correct set of pH changes in (a), (b) and (c) cells respectively?

(a) increase in all the three

(b) decrease in all the three

(c) increase, constant, increase

(d) decrease, constant, increase

6. The value of $\Delta_f G°$ for formation of Cr_2O_3 is $-540\ kJ\ mol^{-1}$ and that of Al_2O_3 is $-827\ kJ\ mol^{-1}$. Is the reduction of Cr_2O_3 possible with Al ?

(a) Yes   (b) No

(c) data insufficient   (d) None of these

7. Which of the following statements is/are correct?

(1) OF_2, Cl_2O and Br_2O are tetrahedral with two positions occupied by two lone pairs of electrons

(2) In OF_2, the bond angle is less than 109°28'

(3) In Cl_2O, the bond angle is greater than 109°28'

(4) In Br_2O the bond angle is greater than 111°

(a) 1, 2, 3, 4   (b) 1, 3, 4

(c) 1, 2, 4   (d) 1, 3

SECTION – II - Multiple Correct Choice Type

This section contains 7 multiple choice questions. Each question has 4 choices (a), (b), (c) and (d) for its answer, out of which ONE OR MORE is/are correct.

8. Which of the following statement/s with regard to quantum number is/are correct?

(a) The azimuthal quantum number gives the contribution of energy due to angular momentum towards the total energy of the electron

(b) The azimuthal quantum number gives the relative of energies of subshells belonging to the same shell

   (c)   The orbital angular momentum is given by azimuthal quantum number which is equal to $\dfrac{h}{2\pi}\sqrt{\ell(\ell+1)}$

   (d)   The orbital angular momentum depends on the value of 'n'

9. PCl_5 dissociates into PCl_3 and Cl_2 thus

$$PCl_5(g) \rightleftharpoons PCl_3(g) + Cl_2(g)$$

If the total pressure of the system in equilibrium is P at a density ρ and temperature T. The vapour density of the gas mixture at equilibrium has the value of 62 when the temperature is 230°C.

Correct options are

   (a)   Degree of dissociation = 0.68

   (b)   Value of P/ρ = 0.3327

   (c)   Degree of dissociation = 0.3327

   (d)   Value of P/ρ = 0.68

10. Which of the following statements are not correct

   (a)   A meso compound has chiral centres but exhibits no optical activity

   (b)   A meso compound has no chiral centres and thus are optically inactive

   (c)   A meso compound has molecules which are superimposable on their mirror images even though they contain chiral centres

   (d)   A meso compound is optically inactive because the rotation caused by any molecule is cancelled by an equal and opposite rotation caused by another molecules that is the mirror image of the first.

11. Choose the correct statements.

   (a)   Vacancy defects lower the density of the substance

   (b)   Interstitial defects increase the density of the substance

   (c)   Schottky defects, preserve the electrical neutrality of the crystal.

   (d)   Frenkel defects do not affect the density of the crystal.

12. In which of the following pairs hybridisation of the central atom is same ?

   (a) ClF_3, ClF_3O (b) ClF_3O, ClF_3O_2

   (c) $(ClF_2O)^+, (ClF_4O)^-$ (d) $(ClF_4O)^- (XeOF_4)$

13. One mole of an ideal gas is subjected to a reversible process that involves two steps (and). The pressure at A and C is same. Consider the graph and choose correct statements.

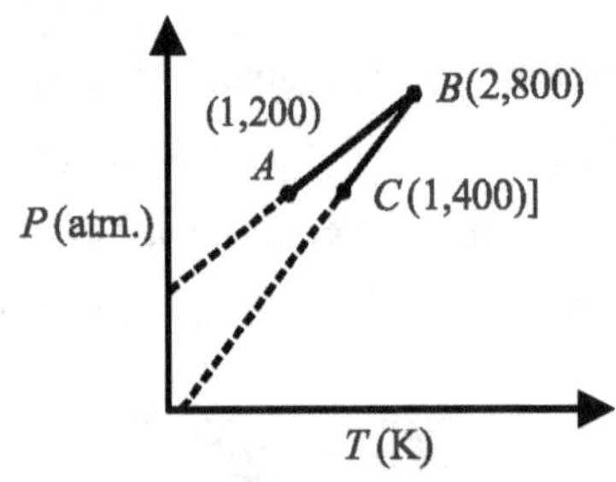

   (a)   Work done is zero

   (b)   In path, work will be done on the gas by the surroundings

   (c)   Volume of gas at $C = 2 \times$ Volume of gas at A

   (d)   Volume of gas at B is 32.8

14. Among the following compounds, which will react with acetone to give a product containing $> C = N -$bond ?

   (a) $C_6H_5NH_2$ (b) $(CH_3)_3N$

   (c) $C_6H_5NHC_6H_5$ (d) $C_6H_5NHNH_2$.

SECTION – III - Comprehension Type

This section contains 2 paragraphs. Each paragraph has 2 multiple choice questions based on a paragraph. Each question has 4 choices (a), (b), (c) and (d) for its answer, out of which ONLY ONE is correct.

PARAGRAPH - 1

When anions and cation approach each other, the valence shell of anions are pulled towards a cation, is known as polarisation and ability of the cation to polarize the anion is called as polarising power of cation. Due to polarisation, sharing of electrons occurs between two ions to some extent and bond shows some covalent character. Fajan's suggested following factors on which polarisation depend.

(i)   As the charge on cation or anion increases polarisation increases.

(ii)   Size of cation decreases or size of anion increases, polarisation increases.

(iii)   Cation with pseudo noble gas configuration shows highest polarisation power.

15. Which is most covalent in nature

   (a) NaCl   (b) $MgCl_2$

   (c) $AlCl_3$ (d) $CaCl_2$

16. Which is having highest melting point?

   (a) LiF   (b) LiCl

   (c) LiBr   (d) LiI

PARAGRAPH - 2

A hydrocarbon (A) of molecular weight 54 reacts with excess of Br_2 in CCl_4 to give a compound (B) whose molecular weight is 593% more than that of (A) However, on catalytic hydrogenation with excess of hydrogen, (A) forms (C) whose molecular weight is only 7.4% more than that of (A) (A) reacts with CH_3CH_2Br in the presence of $NaNH_2$ to give another hydrocarbon (D), which on ozonolysis yields diketone (E),(E) on oxidation gives propanoic acid.

17. Structure of C is

   (a) $CH_3{-}CH_2{-}C{\equiv}CH$ (b) $CH_3{-}CH_2{-}CH_2{-}CH_3$

   (c) $CH_3{-}CH_2{-}C{\equiv}C{-}C_2H_5$ (d) CH_3CH_2COOH

18. Structure of D is

   (a) $CH_3{-}CH_2{-}C{\equiv}CH$ (b) $CH_3{-}CH_2{-}CH_2{-}CH_3$

   (c) $CH_3{-}CH_2{-}C{\equiv}C{-}C_2H_5$ (d) CH_3CH_2COOH

SOLUTIONS

ANSWER KEY - PAPER 1							
1	(a, c)	6	(a, b, c)	11	5	16	(c)
2	(a, b, c)	7	(a, b, c)	12	7	17	(b)
3	(c, d)	8	2	13	(c)	18	(d)
4	(a, c)	9	3	14	(d)		
5	(b, c, d)	10	2	15	(c)		

ANSWER KEY - PAPER 2							
1	(c)	6	(d)	11	(a,c,d)	16	(a)
2	(a)	7	(b)	12	(a,c)	17	(b)
3	(b)	8	(a,b)	13	(b, c)	18	(a)
4	(c)	9	(a,c,d)	14	(a, c)		
5	(a)	10	(a,b,c)	15	(d)		

EXPLANATORY NOTES

Paper 1

1. (a, c)

(a) is wrong because Wurtz's reaction is not applicable for 3° alkane.

(c) is wrong because the addition on cis form gives meso product in suitable condition.

2. (a, b, c)

Bond enthalpy of C – C bond

= Enthalpy required to break C_2H_6 into gaseous atoms

$\qquad$ – 6 × bond enthalpy of C – H bond

= 2839.2 KJ mol^{-1} – 6 × 410.87 kJ mol^{-1} = 373.98 kJ mol^{-1}

Bond enthalpy of C = C bond = Enthalpy required to break C_2H_4 into gaseous atoms – 4 × bond enthalpy of C – H bond = 2275.2 kJ mol^{-1} – 4 × 410.87 kJ mol^{-1}

$\qquad$ = 631.72 kJ mol^{-1}

For the formation of benzene having Kekule structure, we have to form 3C – C bonds, 3C = C bonds and 6C – H bonds for which enthalpy released is

[3 (–373.98) + 3 (–631.72) + 6(–410.87)] = –5482.32 kJ mol^{-1}

But the given value of $\Delta_f H$ is $\Delta_f H$ (actual) = – 5536 kJ mol^{-1}

Hence resonance energy compared to Kekule structure
= $\Delta_f H$ (actual) – $\Delta_f H$ (Kekule structure)

= (–5536 + 5482.32) = – 53.68 kJ mol^{-1}

3. (c, d)

The opposite lobes of p-orbital have different sign but opposite lobes of d-orbitals have the same sign (two lobes have +ve sign while other two lobes have -ve sign). Orbitals of a particular type will have the same angular wave function irrespective of the value, n.

4. (a, c)

Let the rate equation be

Rate, $R_0 = k [A]^n [B]^m$

Using the given data, one can write

$\qquad 5.07 \times 10^{-5} = k (0.2)^n (0.3)^m \qquad$ .... (1)

$\qquad 5.07 \times 10^{-5} = k (0.2)^n (0.1)^m \qquad$ .... (2)

$\qquad 7.6 \times 10^{-5} = k (0.4)^n (0.05)^m \qquad$ .... (3)

From equation (1) and (2)

$$\frac{5.07 \times 10^{-5}}{5.07 \times 10^{-5}} = \frac{k(0.2)^n (0.3)^m}{k(0.2)^n (0.1)^m} = \left(\frac{0.3}{0.1}\right)^m = 3^m$$

$1 = 3^m$; This gives, m = 0

From eqs. (2) and (3),

$$\frac{7.6 \times 10^{-5}}{5.07 \times 10^{-5}} = \frac{k(0.4)^n (0.05)^m}{k(0.2)^n (0.1)^m} = \left(\frac{0.4}{0.2}\right)^n \left(\frac{0.05}{0.10}\right)^m$$

$$= 2^n \times 2^{-m} = 2^{n-m} = 2^n$$

$1.5 = 2^n$

$n \log 2 = \log 1.5$

$n = \log 1.5 / \log 2 = 0.17609 / 0.3010 = 0.58 \simeq 0.5$

Thus the order of reaction with respect to A is 0.5, and with respect to B is 0.

5. (b, c, d)

(b) 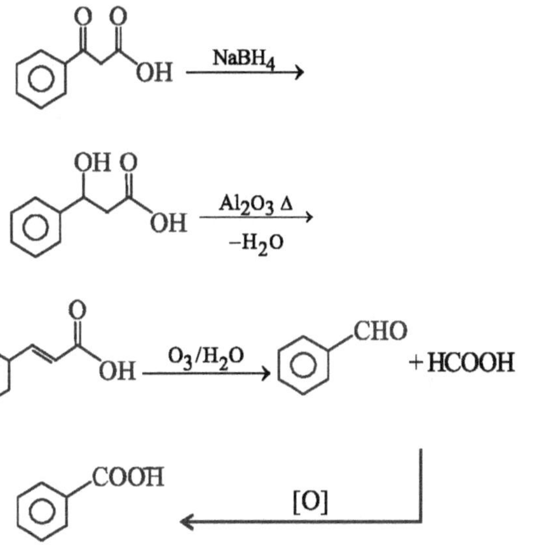 [Structure: 1-phenyl-1,3-dioxo butanoic acid] $\xrightarrow{NaBH_4}$

[Structure: 3-hydroxy-3-phenyl propanoic acid] $\xrightarrow[-H_2O]{Al_2O_3\ \Delta}$

[Structure: cinnamic acid] $\xrightarrow{O_3/H_2O}$ [PhCHO] $+ HCOOH$

[Structure: benzoic acid, COOH] $\xleftarrow{[O]}$

(c) 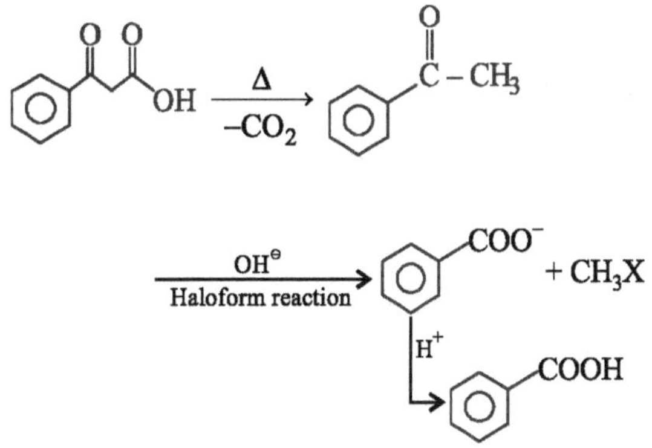 [Structure: 1-phenyl-1,3-dioxobutanoic acid] $\xrightarrow[-CO_2]{\Delta}$ [Structure: $\overset{O}{\overset{\|}{C}}-CH_3$ acetophenone]

$\xrightarrow[\text{Haloform reaction}]{OH^{\ominus}}$ [Structure: benzoate, COO^-] $+ CH_3X$

$\xrightarrow{H^+}$ [Structure: benzoic acid, COOH]

(d) 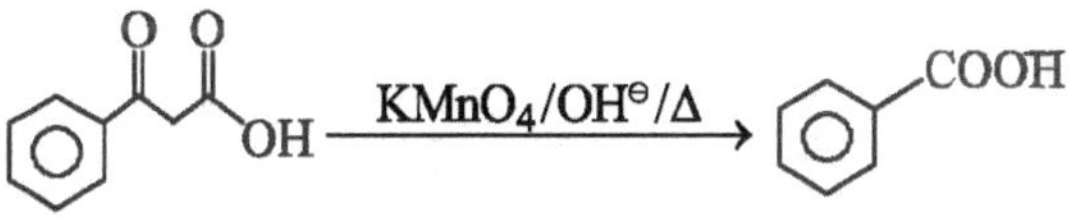 [Structure: 1-phenyl-1,3-dioxobutanoic acid] $\xrightarrow{KMnO_4/OH^{\ominus}/\Delta}$ [Structure: benzoic acid, COOH]

6. (a, b, c)

(a) $[PtCl_2(NH_3)_4]Br_2$ is isomeric with $[PtBr_2(NH_3)_4]Cl_2$

(b) $[Co(NO_2)(NH_3)_5]^{2+}$ is isomeric with $[Pt(ONO)(NH_3)_5]^{2+}$

(c) $[Co(NH_3)_6][Cr(CN)_6]$ is isomeric with $[Cr(NH_3)_6][Co(CN)_6]$

(d) O.N. of Pt in the complex is +2.

7. (a, b, c)

(a) Four unpaired electrons can form bonds with four Cl atoms giving rise to sp^3d hybridisation.

(b) $TeCl_4 + 2HCl \rightarrow H_2[TeCl_6]$

8. Ans : 2

$\Delta T_b(\text{normal}) = K_b m = 2.53 \times 1 = 2.53\ K;$

$$i = \frac{\Delta T_{b(obs)}}{\Delta T_{b(nor)}} = \frac{1.518}{2.53} = 0.6$$

$$i = 0.6 = 1 - \left(1 - \frac{1}{n}\right)\alpha = 1 - \left(1 - \frac{1}{2}\right)\alpha\ ;\ \alpha = 0.8 = 80\%$$

Given $80 = 40A$

$\therefore\ \mathbf{A = 2}$

9. Ans : 3

Magnetic moment $= \sqrt{n(n+2)} = \sqrt{15}$ B.M. (given)

$\Rightarrow n = 3$

10. Ans : 2

$SO_2Cl_2 + 2H_2O \rightarrow H_2SO_4 + 2HCl$

$\underset{\text{Baryta}}{H_2SO_4 + Ba(OH)_2} \rightarrow BaSO_4 + 2H_2O$

$2HCl + Ba(OH)_2 \rightarrow BaCl_2 + 2H_2O$

11. Ans : 5

$2H^+_{(aq)} + 2e^- \longrightarrow H_{2(g)}, E^\circ = 0.0V$ ......(i)

$2D^+_{(aq)} + 2e^- \longrightarrow D_{2(g)}, E^\circ = -0.296V$ ......(ii)

(i) $-$ (ii), $2H^+_{(aq)} + D_{2(g)} \longrightarrow H_{2(g)} + 2D^+_{(aq)}$,

$E^\circ_{cell} = 0.296V$

$$E_{cell} = 0 = E^\circ_{cell} - \frac{0.0592}{2}\log\frac{P_{H_2} \times [D^+_{(aq)}]^2}{P_{D_2}[H^+_{(aq)}]^2};$$

$$\log\frac{[D^+_{(aq)}]}{[H^+_{(aq)}]} = \frac{E^\circ_{cell}}{0.0592} = \frac{0.296}{0.0592} = 5$$

12. Ans : 7

Suppose $x\%$ of height of ice immerses in mercury.

For floating condition, weight of ice

　　　　　　　　= weight of displaced Hg

or　　$100 \times d_{ice} \times g = x \times d_{Hg} \times g$

or　　$100 \times 0.98 \times g = x \times 13.60 \times g \Rightarrow x = 7.3$

Hence, % height remaining above the surface of Hg

　　　　$= 100 - 7.3 = 92.3 \approx 93$

Given :　　$93 = 100 - A$

$\therefore\ \ A = 7$

13. (c)　d^6 (high spin)

$\underline{\ 1\ 1\ }\ e_g^2$　CFSE $= -0.4 \times 4 + 0.6 \times 2$

$\underline{1\ 1\ 1}\ t_{2g}^4$　　　　　$= 0.4$

(n = 4)

$$\mu\ \text{spin} = \sqrt{n(n+2)}\ \text{B.M}$$
$$= \sqrt{4(4+2)} = \sqrt{24} = 4.90\ \text{B.M}$$

14. (d) $d^3 =$ high spin μ spin $= \sqrt{n(n+2)}$ B.M

$$\underline{\uparrow\,\uparrow\,\uparrow}\ \ ^{--e_g^0}_{t_{2g}^3}$$

$(n = 3)$ $\sqrt{3(3+2)}$

$\sqrt{15}$

CFSE $= -0.4 \times 3$ $= 3.87$ B.M
$= -1.2$

15. (c) d^7 (low spin) $\underline{\uparrow}\ -e_g^1$ CFSE $= -0.4 \times 6 + 0.6 \times 1$
$= -1.8$

$$\underline{\uparrow\downarrow\,\uparrow\downarrow\,\uparrow\downarrow}\ t_{2g}^6$$

$n = 1$

μ spin $= \sqrt{n(n+2)}$ B.M

$= \sqrt{1(1+2)}$

$= \sqrt{3}$

$= 1.73$ B.M

16. (c) $CH_3CH_2CH_2\overset{+}{C}HCH_3 \xleftarrow{\ H^+\ } CH_3CH_2CH = CHCH_3 \xrightarrow{\ H^+\ } CH_3CH_2\overset{+}{C}HCH_2CH_3$

(Five hyperconjugative structures)   Highly favoured due to inductive of ethyl group (4 hyperconjugative structures)

$\Big\downarrow Cl^-$ $\Big\downarrow Cl^-$

$$CH_3CH_2CH_2\underset{\underset{Cl}{|}}{C}HCH_3 \qquad\qquad CH_3CH_2\underset{\underset{Cl}{|}}{C}HCH_2CH_3$$

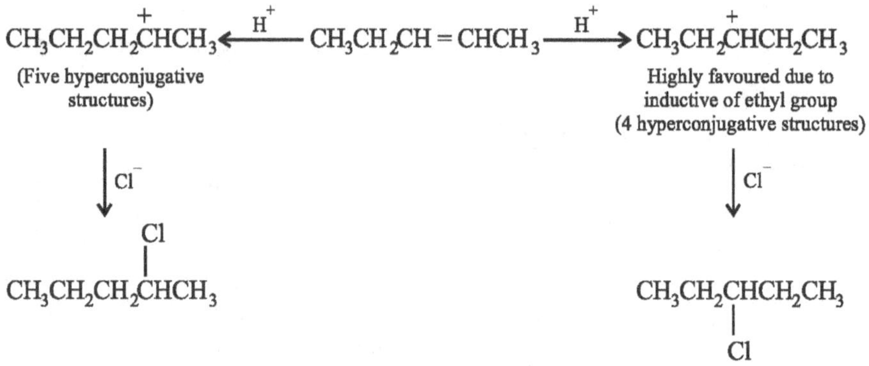

17. (b) $CH_2 = CH - CH = CH_2 \xrightarrow{\ H^+\ } \left[CH_3\overset{+}{C}HCH = CH_2 \longleftrightarrow CH_3CH = CH\overset{+}{C}H_2 \right]$

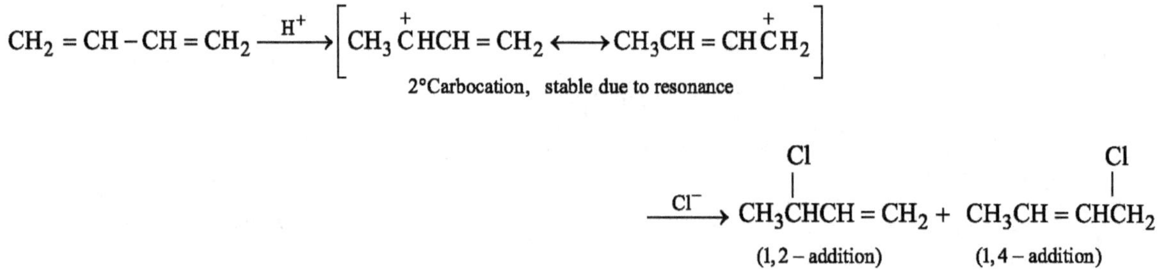

2°Carbocation, stable due to resonance

$$\xrightarrow{\ Cl^-\ } CH_3\underset{\underset{Cl}{|}}{C}HCH = CH_2 + CH_3CH = CH\underset{\underset{Cl}{|}}{C}H_2$$

(1, 2 – addition)   (1, 4 – addition)

18. (d)   (C$_6$H$_5$)$- CH_2CH = CH_2 + H^+ \longrightarrow$ (C$_6$H$_5$)$- CH_2\overset{+}{C}HCH_3 \xrightarrow[\text{hydride shift}]{1, 2-}$

2° carbocation

$$\text{(C}_6\text{H}_5)-\overset{+}{C}HCH_2CH_3 \xrightarrow{\ Br^-\ } \text{(C}_6\text{H}_5)-\underset{\underset{Br}{|}}{C}HCH_2CH_3$$

More stable benzyl carbocation

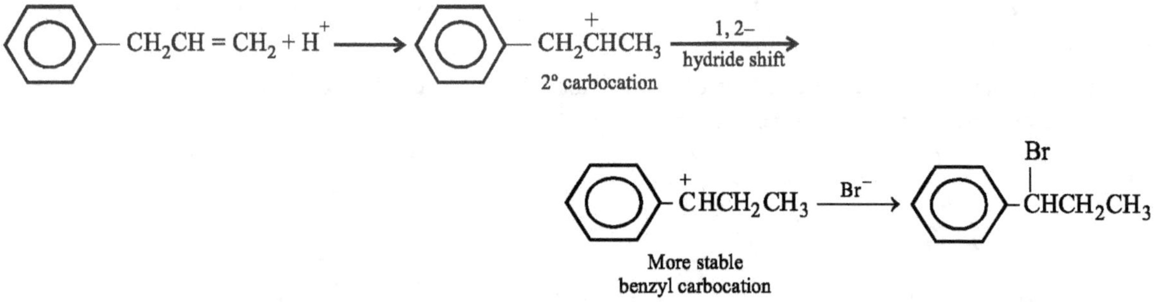

Paper 2

1. (a) It is given that 20 mL of stock solution of KI requires 30 mL of M/10 KIO_3 solution to convert I^- ions into ICl according to the reaction

$$KIO_3 + 2KI + 6HCl \rightarrow 3ICl + 3KCl + 3H_2O$$

For 50 mL of KI solution, the required volume of KIO_3 solution would be

$$\frac{30 \text{ mL of } KIO_3 \text{ solution}}{20 \text{ mL of KI solution}} \times 50 \text{ mL of KI}$$

solution = 75 mL of KIO_3 solution

After treating 50 mL of KI solution with 1 g $AgNO_3$ sample, the volume of KIO_3 solution used is 50 mL. This means KI equivalent to 25 mL of KIO_3 solution is used in precipitating out Ag^+ ions from 50 mL of KI solution.

Amount of KIO_3 in 25 mL of M/10 KIO_3 solution (25 mL)

$$\left(\frac{1}{10} M\right) = \left(\frac{25}{100} L\right)\left(\frac{1}{10} \text{ mol L}^{-1}\right) = 0.0025 \text{ mol}$$

Amount of KI equivalent to this amount

$= 2 \times 0.0025$ mol

Mass of $AgNO_3$ precipitated out

$= 2 \times 0.0025 \times 170 \text{ g} = 0.85 \text{ g}$

Percent of $AgNO_3$ in the sample $= \dfrac{0.85g}{1.0 \text{ g}} \times 100 = 85.$

2. (c) The maximum work done by the system $= P_2(V_2 - V_1)$

$$\therefore P_2(V_2 - V_1) = mgh \text{ or } P_2\left(\frac{nRT}{P_2} - \frac{nRT}{P_1}\right) = mgh$$

$$\text{or } mgh = nRT\left(1 - \frac{P_2}{P_1}\right) \text{ or } m = \frac{nRT}{gh}\left(1 - \frac{P_2}{P_1}\right)$$

3. (c) In compounds

$$\underset{I}{\overset{CH_3}{\underset{H}{\diagdown}}C=C\overset{H}{\underset{Cl}{\diagup}}} \quad \underset{II}{\overset{CH_3}{\underset{H}{\diagdown}}C=C\overset{Cl}{\underset{H}{\diagup}}} \quad \text{first has}$$

more dipole moment than second.

Therefore its boiling point will be higher. Melting point depends on symmetry therefore I has higher melting point than II. Steric crowding in II is more than I therefore I is more stable than II.

4. (d) Anions occupy fcc positions and half of the tetrahedral holes are occupied by cations. Since there are four anions and 8 tetrahedral holes per unit cell, the fraction of volume occupied by spheres per unit volume of the unit cell is

$$= \frac{4\times\left(\frac{4}{3}\pi r_a^3\right) + \frac{1}{2}\times 8\times\left(\frac{4}{3}\pi r_c^3\right)}{16\sqrt{2}r_a^3} = \frac{\pi}{3\sqrt{2}}\left\{1+\left(\frac{r_c}{r_a}\right)^3\right\}$$

$\because$ for tetrahedral holes,

$$\frac{r_c}{r_a} = 0.225$$

$$= \frac{\pi}{3\sqrt{2}}\{1+(0.225)^3\} = 0.7493$$

$\therefore$ Void volume $= 1 - 0.7493$

$$= 0.2507/\text{unit volume of unit cell.}$$

% void space = 25.07%

5. (d)

(a) Cathode : $Cu^{2+}_{(aq)} + 2e^- \longrightarrow Cu_{(s)}$

Anode : $H_2O \longrightarrow 2H^+ + \dfrac{1}{2}O_2 + 2e^-$

pH decreases.

(b) Cathode : $Cu^{2+}_{(aq)} + 2e^- \longrightarrow Cu_{(s)}$

Anode : $Cu_{(s)} \longrightarrow Cu^{2+}_{(aq)} + 2e^-$

pH remains unchanged.

(c) Cathode : $2H_2O + 2e^- \longrightarrow H_2 + 2OH^-_{(aq)}$

Anode : $2Cl^- \longrightarrow Cl_{2\,(aq)} + 2e^-$

pH increases.

6. (a) Reduction of Cr_2O_3 with Al can be described by the equation $Cr_2O_3(s) + 2Al(s) \xrightarrow{\text{heat}} 2Cr(s) + Al_2O_3(s)$

Then, $\Delta_r G° = \Sigma\Delta_f G° \text{ (products)} - \Sigma\Delta_f G° \text{ (reactants)}$

$\Delta_r G° = (\Delta_f G°(Al_2O_3) + 2\,\Delta_f G°(Cr) - (\Delta_f G°(Cr_2O_3)$
$+ 2\Delta_f G°(Al))$

$\Delta_r G° = (-827 \text{ kJ mol}^{-1} + 0) - (-540 \text{ kJ mol}^{-1} + 0) = -287 \text{ kJ mol}^{-1}$

Since $\Delta_r G°$ for the reduction of Cr_2O_3 with aluminium is negative, hence the reduction of Cr_2O_3 with aluminium is possible.

7. (a)

(1) Due to sp^3 hybridisation

(2) Bond angles are distorted due to lone pairs. In OF_2, the bonding electrons are nearer the F atom due to its greater electronegativity. Thus repulsion between lone pairs is greater than that between bond pairs. Hence bond angle is less than 109°28'.

(3) In Cl_2O, the bonding electrons are nearer the oxygen atom, because it is more electronegative than chlorine. Repulsion between bond pairs now exceeds that between lone pairs. Hence the bond angle is greater (111°) than 109°28'.

(4) The difference between electronegativities of Br and O is greater than that between Cl and O, so bonding electrons are even closer to O in Br_2O. Thus repulsion between bond pairs should be even greater, and a bond angle greater than $111°$ is expected.

8. (a, b, c)

The orbital angular momentum depends on the value of ℓ and not n.

9. (a, b)

$$PCl_5(g) \rightleftharpoons PCl_3(g) + Cl_2(g)$$

Since $PV = nRT = \dfrac{w}{M} RT$

$$M = \dfrac{w\,RT}{PV} = \dfrac{\rho RT}{P}$$

$$\therefore V.D.(d) = \dfrac{\rho RT}{2P}$$

$$\begin{array}{llll} & PCl_5(g) \rightleftharpoons & PCl_3(g) & + & Cl_2(g) \\ \text{Initial} & C & 0 & & 0 \\ \text{At eq.m.} & C(1-\alpha) & C\alpha & & C\alpha \end{array}$$

$$\dfrac{\text{Total moles at equilibrium}}{\text{Total initial moles}} = \dfrac{\text{Initial vapour density}}{\text{Vapour density at equilibrium}}$$

$$\dfrac{C(1+\alpha)}{C} = \dfrac{D}{d}$$

$$\Rightarrow 1+\alpha = \dfrac{M/2}{\rho RT/2P} = \dfrac{PM}{\rho RT} \qquad \left[\therefore \alpha = \dfrac{PM}{\rho RT} - 1 \right]$$

If, $d = 62$, $\dfrac{M}{2} = \dfrac{208.5}{2} = 104.25$

$$\alpha = \dfrac{104.25 - 62}{62} = 0.68$$

$$\therefore \dfrac{P}{\rho} = \dfrac{(1+\alpha)\,RT}{M} = 0.3327\,\text{atm}/(\text{gm/L})$$

10. (b, c)

A meso compound has minimum two chiral centres and it has a plane of symmetry and it is optically inactive.

11. (a, b, c, d)

(a) Vacancy defects lower the density of the substance

(b) Interstitial defects increase the density of the substance

(c) Schottky defects, preserve the electrical neutrality of the crystal.

(d) Frenkel defects do not affect the density of the crystal.

Hence all statements are correct.

12. (a, b, d) Steric number of $ClF_3 = 3 + 2 = 5$

Steric number of $ClF_3O = 4 + 1 = 5$

Steric number of $ClF_3O_2 = 5 + 0 = 5$

Steric number of $(ClF_2O)^+ = 3 + 1 = 4$

Steric number of $(ClF_4O)^- = 5 + 1 = 6$

Steric number of $XeOF_4 = 5 + 1 = 6$

So answer are (abd) as steric no. are same for these molecules and hybridisation is same in each pair.

13. (c, d) Volume of A,

$$V_A = \dfrac{1 \times R \times 200}{1} = 200R \quad [\because PV = nRT]$$

$$= 200 \times 0.082 = 16.4\,\text{L}$$

gives work in isothermal and reversible expansion of an ideal gas

$$V_B = \dfrac{0.082 \times 800}{2} = 32.8\text{L}$$

$$V_C = \dfrac{6.082 \times 400}{1} = 32.8\text{L}$$

Since $V_B > V_A$, expansion of gas occurs along A and B and work is done by the gas.

14. (a, d) $C_6H_5NH_2 + O = C(CH_3)_2 \xrightarrow{-H_2O} C_6H_5N = C(CH_3)_2$

$$C_6H_5NHNH_2 + O = C(CH_3)_2 \xrightarrow{-H_2O}$$

$$C_6H_5NHN = C(CH_3)_2$$

15. (c) Higher charge density on Al leads to higher polarising power of Al^{3+} cation. So $AlCl_3$ is most covalent in nature.

16. (a) LiF is most ionic (F^- is small in size therefore it has least polarisability). Therefore, it has higher melting point.

17. (b) 18. (c)

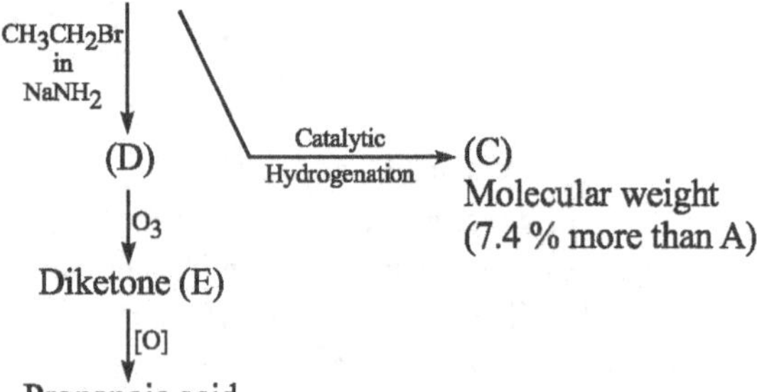

To 100 gm of (A), add Br_2 and the new weight is 593 gm

$\therefore$ To 54 gm of (A), add Br_2 and the new weight is

$$\dfrac{593 \times 54}{100} = 320.2\,\text{gm}$$

$$\therefore \text{No of moles of } Br_2 = \frac{\text{Weight}}{\text{Molecular weight}} = \frac{320.2}{160}$$

$= 2 \text{ moles}$

(i) As two moles of Br_2 were added, compound has two π bond hence general formula of A should be :

(C_nH_{2n-2})

$C_nH_{2n-2} = 54$

$12n + 2n - 2 = 54$

$n = 4 \therefore$ molecular formula $= C_4H_6$

(ii) (A) reacts with CH_3CH_2Br in presence of $NaNH_2$ thus, compound (A) should be terminal alkyne,

i.e. 1-butyne

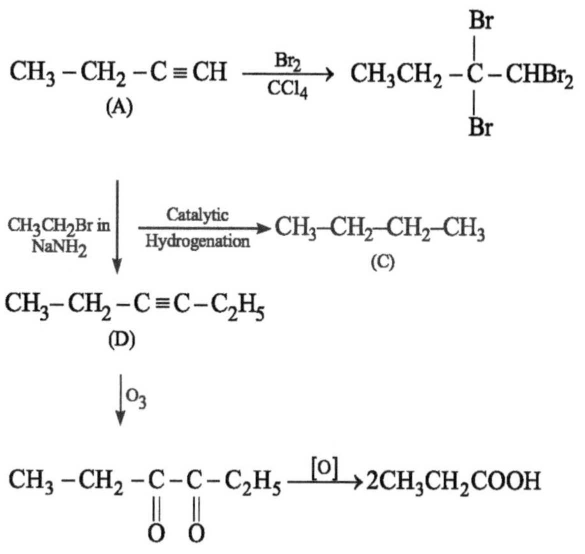

$$CH_3 - CH_2 - C \equiv CH \xrightarrow[CCl_4]{Br_2} CH_3CH_2 - \underset{\underset{Br}{|}}{\overset{\overset{Br}{|}}{C}} - CHBr_2$$

(A)

$$CH_3CH_2Br \text{ in } NaNH_2 \downarrow$$

$$CH_3 - CH_2 - C \equiv C - C_2H_5$$

(D)

$$\xrightarrow[\text{Hydrogenation}]{\text{Catalytic}} CH_3-CH_2-CH_2-CH_3$$

(C)

$$\downarrow O_3$$

$$CH_3 - CH_2 - \underset{\underset{O}{\|}}{C} - \underset{\underset{O}{\|}}{C} - C_2H_5 \xrightarrow{[O]} 2CH_3CH_2COOH$$